Birdwatching guide to Oman
2nd edition

by Dave E. Sargeant
and Hanne & Jens Eriksen

Sponsored by

Al Roya Publishing

ISBN 978-9948-03-643-2

Birdwatching
guide to
Oman

AL ROYA PUBLISHING

2008

P. O. Pox 343, P. C. Code 118, Al Harthy Complex
Muscat, Sultanate of Oman
Tel.: +968 2456 2138. Fax: +968 2456 2194
Email: alroya@alroya.net
website: www.alroya.com

Publisher
Hatim Al Taie

Text
© Dave E. Sargeant
© Hanne & Jens Eriksen

Photographs
© Hanne & Jens Eriksen

Maps
© Dave E. Sargeant

Layout
Hanne & Jens Eriksen

Printed by: Al Anan Printing Press
Registration No.: 71/2008
ISBN: 978-9948-03-643-2

Acknowledge
The authors wish
staff at Al Roya Publ
their help and encourag
during this project. We a
thank the members of the O
Bird Records Committee and
hundreds of birdwatchers who,
over the years, have sent in their
bird observations, and without
whose help this book could not
have been written. We also thank
the Ministry of Tourism for their
support and Oman Wastewater
Services Company for their gen-
erous sponsorship of this book.

February 2008
Dave E. Sargeant
Hanne & Jens Eriksen

Black-winged Stilt

This publication is available in all leading bookstores in Oman. For additional marketing related information, please contact Al Roya Publishing.

Al-dhais

Responsibilities. Results.
This is where they meet.

"The manmade lagoons at Al Ansab are fed by surplus water pumped into the ponds from our sewage treatment plant. OWSC is delighted to have played a role in creating this little birdwatcher's paradise, home to over 200 species of birds.

Many of them have been caught on camera by the photographer duo, Hanne & Jens Eriksen, in their latest book, 'Birdwatching guide to Oman', which we are proud to sponsor.

We invite you to read the book, enjoy the Al Ansab experience and share our commitment towards keeping Oman clean, green and beautiful."

Omar Al Wahaibi
CEO
Oman Wastewater Services Company

Muscat Wastewater Project
Protecting the Environment, Serving Society.

Oman Wastewater Services Company is a government owned entity engaged in building and operating world-class wastewater systems in Muscat. The large scale projects consist of building and operating wastewater networks, pumping stations and sewage treatment plants. The projects have significant health, environment, social and economic benefits.

الشركة العمانية
لخدمات الصرف الصحي ش.م.ع.م

OMAN WASTEWATER
SERVICES COMPANY S.A.O.C

Oman Wastewater Services Company SAOC. PO Box 1047, PC 133, Al Khuwair, Sultanate of Oman.
Toll-free 800 77 111 www.omanwsc.com

DDB

TABLE OF CONTENTS

Tristram's Grackles on Arabian Camel

INTRODUCTION

Following the success of our *Birdwatching guide to Oman*, published in 2001, *Birdwatching guide to Oman, 2nd edition* is the completely revised and updated edition, reflecting our most recent knowledge of Oman's birds, and the large scale changes to Oman's infrastructure and tourism facilities. Owing to extensive paving of roads throughout the country all maps have been redrawn, and incorporate GPS coordinates, based on WGS84 datum. Additionally these data can be downloaded from the BirdsOman website at www.birdsoman.com in Garmin mps format that can be read into most GPS utilities, including Google Earth.

Although some of the bird watching sites previously covered have disappeared, others are new, and so the number of sites covered in this edition is unchanged. All tourist information has been rewritten and expanded to include some of the growing number of hotels, tour operators, car rental companies and tourist infrastructure. With the important upgrade of the telecommunications systems in 2004 all telephone numbers in Oman were changed to eight digits. Species statuses and site lists have been updated to reflect all reported bird observations up till the end of December 2007.

Birdwatching guide to Oman is intended as a stepping stone into the fascinating world of birds in the Sultanate of Oman. We hope to guide the keen world-travelling birders to their most wanted species, other birdwatchers to various birding hot spots, and general naturalists to many happy hours in nature with the added spice of birds.

Recent years have witnessed a rapidly growing demand for information related to where, when, how and what to do during a visit to Oman. Eco-tourists are knocking on the door in increasing numbers. Together this prompted us to rewrite this book to address this increasing demand. It is our hope that *Birdwatching guide to Oman* will continue to encourage many more birders and naturalists alike to come and enjoy the country, its wildlife and its warm and hospitable people. Everyone will welcome you and wish you a most pleasant stay - *Ahlan wa Sahlan*.

Why is Oman attractive on the global circuit of travelling birders? Its position, on the edge of the Western Palearctic, together with its location between Europe, Africa and Asia, means the avifauna of three zoo-geographical areas are represented in Oman. Most of the 495 (as of 1 January 2008) species on the Oman Bird List are also found on the Western Palearctic bird list. The north, with its close proximity to the Indian subcontinent, adds many eastern species to the list, whereas the south is home to numerous African ones. Consequently Oman offers birds from three continents in one country.

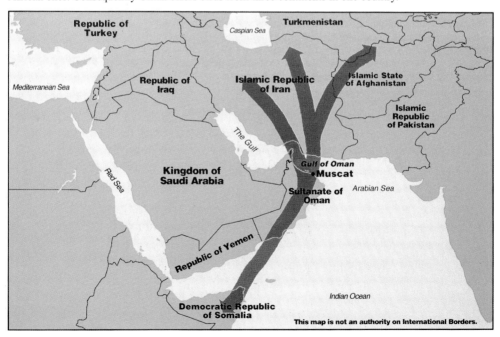

This map is not an authority on International Borders.

The scenery is varied with 1,700 km of coastline, comprising sandy beaches, lagoons, mudflats and fjords. Inland one finds large mountain ranges reaching 3,000m, agricultural land, majestic sand dunes, and a large stony desert plain dividing the north from the south. For even more variation, the southern mountain ranges are hit by monsoon rain from June to September, turning the whole area into a lush, green and mist-covered landscape.

Greater Spotted Eagle

Bird recording in Oman

All bird records in Oman are stored in a computer database belonging to the Oman Bird Records Committee that also acts as the country's rarity committee. The Recorder is responsible for the day to day running and updating of the database, which now holds more than 370,000 records starting with a record of 'black birds' - undoubtedly Socotra Cormorants - from Hasikiyah Island by the Arabian seafarer Ibn Battuta in 1329.

As Oman has relatively few resident birdwatchers, the Recorder relies to a large extent on visiting birdwatchers sending reports of their visits. These need not be a fancy, official tour report, but could in some cases simply be a photocopy of a field notebook from which the necessary information can be extracted. However, the following information is greatly appreciated for each observation:

Common (or scientific) name of bird seen (or heard)
Counts of birds seen (an exact number or an approximation). 'Common', '+' or 'a few' is not
        very useful for database entry and processing.
Date of observation
Place of observation
Anything else that might be interesting (breeding data, migration, feeding data, age, sex etc.)

Ideally, reports should be submitted on the official recording forms, which is easy to use for the observer, and make data entry into the database much quicker. A copy of the report form is available from the Recorder upon request or can be downloaded from the internet: at www.birdsoman.com.

Birds with ten or fewer accepted records are considered vagrants and require a detailed description and/or photograph(s) before they can be accepted. So does any sighting of birds not listed on the *Oman Bird List, Edition 6*, (Eriksen, Victor and Sargeant, 2003). A Rare Bird Report form can similarly be downloaded as above. Please feel free to make as many copies of these forms as needed.

All bird reports should be sent to: The Recorder, Oman Bird Records Committee, P O Box 246, Muscat 113, Sultanate of Oman, email: akalat@gmail.com or hjoman@gmail.com.

Visiting birdwatchers looking for seabirds at Ras Al Khabbah (site 3.5)

THE PRACTICAL GUIDE

Flights and getting here

Muscat, the capital of Oman, is built around old Muscat that today is only a tiny part of the huge, extended Capital area. The airport of Muscat is As Seeb International Airport (international designation MCT), connected by daily flights from Europe, North America, Africa, and both the Near and Far East - the choice is manifold. Muscat is less than an hour's flight from either Dubai or Abu Dhabi in the United Arab Emirates and several flights arrive in Muscat via these cities. Oman Air and Jazeera Airways have direct flights between Dubai and Salalah.

Visas

To enter Oman a valid passport and a visa are required. The government encourages tourism as a means of diversifying the oil based economy, such that holders of passports from a long list of countries can obtain a tourist visa on arrival. These visas are valid for one month and can be renewed twice for additional months. Visa regulations can change frequently, so the Royal Oman Police website www.rop. gov.om should be consulted for up to date information. Visitors unable to obtain a visa on arrival can arrange one through a tour operator, a hotel in Oman, or any Omani embassy around the world. Additional information on all aspects of tourism to Oman is available at www.destinationoman.com.

Money

The currency is the Rial Omani (RO) with RO 1 divided into 1000 baisas. The Rial is tied to the US dollar at a fixed rate of RO 1 = $ 2.60.

US dollars in cash or traveller's checks are easily exchanged in banks and money exchange offices, as are major international currencies. Banks will change other currencies as well, but experience has shown that the US$ is the easiest currency for travel to Oman. Euros € cash are also readily exchanged. Most visitors buy Rials immediately upon arrival at As Seeb International Airport, in the arrival hall, but exchange rates on larger amounts can be negotiated with money exchange offices in towns.

On departure, surplus Rials can be readily exchanged in the airport departure hall or transit lounge. Airport tax is included in the ticket price. Credit cards are widely accepted in larger shops, restaurants, hotels and petrol stations. ATM machines are widely available throughout the country in all sizeable towns.

Language

The official language in Oman is Arabic. English is used alongside Arabic in many official events, publications, road signs, car registration plates etc. Daily newspapers are published in both Arabic and English. In the larger shops both languages are spoken as well. Due to the historic ties between Oman and Eastern Africa, Swahili is sometimes spoken, particularly in Al Batinah region.

Useful Arabic Phrases

As-salaam alaykum	peace be upon you (the most common greeting)
Wa'alaykum assalam	(reply)
Kayf halik (m)	how are you?
Kayf halish (f)	how are you?
Bikhayr shukran	fine, thanks
Bikhair, Al Hamdulilah	well, thank God

Marhaba	hello, welcome
Ma'asalama	goodbye
Sabah alkhair	good morning
Sabah inoor	(the reply)
Massa alkhair	good evening
Massa inoor	the reply
Ahlan Wa Sahlan	welcome
Shukran	thank you
Afwan	(reply) you are welcome
Min fadlikh	please
Mumkin sura min fadlikh?	may I take your photograph, please?
Mataam	restaurant
Mustashfa	hospital
Kahwa	coffee
Shai	tea
Sukkar	sugar
Halib	milk
Ma'a	water
Na'am	yes
La	no
Eish	what
Min	who
Laish	why
Wain	where
Matta	when
Zain	good
Yallah	hurry up
Bass	enough
Eish Al muskelah	what's the problem?
Mafeeh muskelah	no problem
Eish ismak	what is your name
Ismi Hannah	my name is Hannah
Bait	house
Yimkin	perhaps
Kam	how many?
Bikam	how much?
Fulous	money
Shuway shuway	slowly
Shouf	look
Dishdasha	long sleeved garment worn by Omani men
Khanjah	a traditional knife, the official symbol of Oman
Souq	Arabic market usually in the centre of town
Wilayat	region of Oman ruled by a Wali (governor)
Madina	city
Mina	port
Jabal	mountain
Bahar	sea
Bandar	port or city
Funduk	hotel
Sayarah	car
Karib	boat
Shati	beach

Ramlah	sand
Sabkha	salt flat
Sayh	plain, plateau
Wadi	dry river bed which floods with water from the surrounding mountains after rain
Khawr	inlet, lagoon or fjord
Ayn	spring
Tawi	water well
Dhow	traditional wooden boat
Falaj	channel carrying water from spring to village
Khareef	the monsoon season in Dhofar
Tayer, Tuyour	bird, birds

Sifr	0		
Wahid	1		
Ithneen	2	Sabt	Saturday
Thalatha	3	Ahad	Sunday
Arba'a	4	Athneen	Monday
Khamsa	5	Thulatha	Tuesday
Sitta	6	Arba'a	Wednesday
Sab'a	7	Khamis	Thursday
Thamanya	8	Juma	Friday
Tis'a	9		
Ashra	10		

Time and telephone

The time zone for Oman is GMT + 4 hours. Clocks are not adjusted for summer time. Fixed-line telephone numbers throughout Oman are eight digit numbers, and have no area codes; simply dial the number from any phone. Likewise for mobile (GSM) numbers which are also eight digit. The International dialling code for Oman is +968. To dial out internationally from Oman, the international access number is 00 followed by the country code; thus, to call UK, dial 0044 and then the number.

Travel and getting around

Internal flights

Flights from Muscat to Salalah in the south are scheduled several times daily, whilst to Khasab, on the Musandam Peninsula in the north, a few times a week. Flights to other cities are of little interest to a visiting birder as everything is within reasonable reach by vehicle from Muscat, Salalah or Khasab. All domestic flights are operated by Oman Air. For details and schedules refer to their website: www.omanair. aero/wy/

Buses and taxis

Bus services operate between major towns and Muscat's main bus terminal which is located in Ruwi. Taxis, reasonably priced, and readily available along most roads in the city, are simply caught by flagging them down. Generally they are shared, so check that a taxi is going towards your destination if you are joining one with other passengers already seated. For those wishing a taxi on their own, after flagging down an empty one it is recommended to negotiate the price prior to starting off on the journey. Taxis are always waiting at the airport and at major hotels. All taxis are licensed, and can be readily identified by their distinctive orange and white design. Few are metered, so some bargaining on the price is expected. Recently, a couple of companies have introduced metered taxis, which are coloured differently (red and yellow, or blue and white), and charge only the metered rate.

Driving and petrol

Driving is on the right. Petrol is cheap by European standards and served by three companies across Oman: Al Maha, Oman Oil and Shell. In the capital area, prices are fixed at 120 baisa/litre for Super (leaded), 114 baisa/litre for Regular (unleaded) and 114.6 baisa/litre for diesel. Elsewhere prices can be slightly higher depending on transportation costs. Fuel is now widely available throughout Oman. For all sites covered in this guide, no special arrangements need be considered to carry additional fuel. However, it is prudent to keep the fuel tank topped-up in more remote areas, as occasionally there can be more than 100 kilometres between stations.

Great care should be taken when driving after rains, especially in city areas. Long hot periods of relentless sun without rain allow the accumulation of a thin film of tyre rubber and engine oil to build up on highways. When rain falls, this film becomes treacherous; much like black ice in Europe.

Car rental

Car rental is the easiest way of visiting the various birding locations. Saloon cars, four-wheel drives (4WD), minibuses and buses can all be rented. Car rental offices abound in the larger towns, but the easiest choice is to pre-arrange collection at the airport on arrival. Below are given, in alphabetic order, the contact details for companies represented at As Seeb International Airport in Muscat.

Al Abaqira Luxury limousine Service, Rent a Car Tour, tel: 2451 0294 (airport), tel/fax: 2469 4699, email: abqlimos@hotmail.com

Avis, tel: 2460 1224, 2460 7235, email: avisoman@omantel.net.om, info: www.avisoman.com/

Budget Car Rental, tel: 2479 4721, fax: 2479 8144, email: budgetom@omantel.net.om, info: www.budget-middle-east.com/

Europcar, tel: 2451 9014, fax: 2452 1369, email: europcar@ajitkhimjigroup.com

Hertz, tel: 2452 1187 (airport), 2456 6208 (main office), fax: 2456 6125, info: www.nttoman.com/hertz/index.html

Mark Rent a Car, tel: 2451 0033 (airport), 2478 6775/229 (main office), fax: 2478 6885, email: mark@omantel.net.om, info: www.markrentacar.com

Sixt Car Rental, tel: 2451 0224, fax: 2451 0933, email: tracbest@omantel.net.om, info: www.e-sixt.com/main/car-rental/Oman/

Thrifty Car Rental, tel: 2452 1189 (airport), 2448 9648 (main office), fax: 2448 2512, email: haditha@omantel.net.om

Value Plus Rent a Car, tel: 2451 0292 (airport), 2459 7264 (main office), fax: 2451 0876, email: vicseeb@otegroup.com, info: www.valueoman.com

Prices vary according to car size, length of rental and season etc. As a guideline, though, the basic rate for the smallest car starts around RO 15 per day and for a 4WD drive about RO 40 per day. Contact the companies for further details and specific rates. One way rental is possible but does entail a heavy fee.

Boat rental

Groups and/or individuals may want to hire a boat to do some seabird watching that at times can be extremely rewarding. Below are some possible contacts. Alternatively, try contacting one of the tour operators listed below.

Al Inshirah Restaurant on Muttrah corniche that, besides providing an international cuisine, specialises in dhow cruises, cruise and buffet tours and have 25/60 persons dhows for hire, tel: 2471 1292, fax: 2471 2642.

Arabian Sea Safaris, tel: 2493 223, fax: 2469 3224, email: arabseas@omantel.net.om, info: www.arabianseasafaris.com

As Sawadi Beach Resort, tel: 2689 5545, fax 2689 5535, email: sales@alsawadibeach.com, info: www.alsawadibeach.com

Bluzone Watersports, tel/fax: 2473 7293, email: bluzone@omantel.net.om, info: www.bluzonediving.com

Muscat Diving and Adventure Centre, tel: 2448 5663, email: mdacoman@omantel.net.om

Fishermen all along the coast or at the pier at Muttrah fish market may be willing to take visitors out for a birdwatching trip. Negotiate a fair price.

Tour operators

Many tour operators provide service to visiting tourists. Details of a few catering for birdwatchers are given below. See the section on **Books and maps**, p 18, for additional information.

Al Nahdha Tourism, Tel: 2479 5206 Fax: 2479 9928, email: touroman@shanfari.com

Bahwan Tours, tel: 2470 6798, fax: 2479 4189, email: gm@bahwantravels.com, btatours@omantel.net.om, info: www.bahwantravelgroup.com. General tour operator.

Ian Harrison, former Secretary of the Oman Bird Records Committee, has been the leader of a number of bird tours throughout Oman where he lived for over twenty years, email: ianbirds@gmail.com

Mezoon Travel, tel: 2479 6680–85, fax: 2478 4710, email: info@mezoontravel.co.om, info: www.mezoontravel.com/. General tour operator.

Muscat Diving and Adventure Centre, tel: 2448 5663, fax: 2448 5774, email: mdacoman@omantel.net.om, info: www.omandiving.com. This company caters for birdwatchers and runs a Bed & Breakfast. Camping equipment can be rented.

Vision International LLC, tel: 2448 8770, fax: 2448 8771, email: siwoman@omantel.net.om. Siw Rantapää-Buring of Vision International LLC has proven a great help for many visiting birdwatchers and their families. Siw is experienced in accommodating birders and their special requests and provides professional birding logistics at all levels. Services include visa and airport pickup, Bed & Breakfast, car and boat hire, securing of various permits, arranging an itinerary or an evening of Omani entertainment. Siw will advice on 'birding only' tours and on mixed activity tours as well, where the Omani culture will be a part of the visit.

Zubair Tours, tel: 2469 2940, fax: 2469 2950, email: inbound@zaharatours.com, info: www.zaharatours.com. General tour and bird tour operator.

Hotels and accommodation

Tourist accommodation in Oman ranges from extremely luxurious hotels to very simple guest-houses. The intention here is to provide contact details for hotels that for one reason or another have been frequented by visiting birdwatchers. For convenience, the information has been divided into the ten bird-watching regions covered in this book. The number of bird symbols are price indicators only; it will be for the individual to obtain a specific price. Prices change, vary according to season, and may be negotiable. A 17% tax is applicable and may or may not be included in the price quoted by the hotel. Equally, break-fast may or may not be included. Check websites where possible or inquire about special offers currently available for the intended time of visit.

For additional hotel information, contact a tour operator or consult publications listed in the **Maps and books** section, p 18.

🐦🐦🐦🐦🐦 Expect room rates to start around or above RO 100 per night
🐦🐦🐦🐦 Expect room rates to start between RO 60 and RO 80
🐦🐦🐦 Expect room rates to start between RO 40 and RO 60
🐦🐦 Expect room rates to start between RO 20 and RO 40
🐦 Expect room rates to start around or below RO 20

1 The Capital Area

🐦🐦🐦🐦🐦 **Al Bustan Palace Hotel** (on isolated beach and amongst spectacular mountains away from the city, has extensive gardens, site 1.5), tel: 2479 9666, fax: 2470 6300, email: albustan@albustanpalace.com, info: www.albustanpalace.com

🐦🐦🐦🐦🐦 **Shangri-La's Barr Al Jissah Resort and Spa** (on a headland southeast of Muscat), tel: 2477 6666, email: slmu@shangri-la.com, info: www.shangri-la.com

🐦🐦🐦🐦🐦 **Grand Hyatt Muscat** (on the beach), tel: 2464 1234, fax: 2460 5282, email: hyattmct@omantel.net.om

🐦🐦🐦🐦🐦 **Hotel InterContinental Muscat** (on the beach, close-by Al Qurm Natural Park, site 1.2), tel: 2460 0500, fax: 2460 0012, email: muscat@interconti.com, www.ichotelsgroup.com

🐦🐦🐦🐦🐦 **Sheraton Hotel**, tel: 2477 2772, fax : 2479 5791, email: reservations.muscat.oman@sheraton.com, info: www.sheraton.com/oman

🐦🐦🐦🐦🐦 **Crowne Plaza Muscat** (well established garden overlooking bay and sea, and close to Al Qurm Natural Park, site 1.2), tel: 2466 0660, fax: 2466 0600, email: cpmuscat@cpmuscat.com, info: www.cpmuscat.com

🐦🐦🐦🐦🐦 **Radisson SAS Hotel**, tel: 2448 7777, fax: 2448 7774/8, email: muscat.reservations@radissonsas.com, info: www.radisson.com

🐦🐦🐦🐦🐦 **Golden Tulip Seeb** (near As Seeb International Airport), tel: 2451 0300, fax: 2451 0055, email: admin@goldentulipseeb.com, info: www.goldentulipseeb.com

🐦🐦🐦🐦 **Muscat Holiday Hotel**, tel: 2459 6400, fax: 2450 2191, email: amhi33@omantel.net.om

🐦🐦🐦 **Majan Continental Hotel**, tel: 2459 2900, fax 2459 2979, email: info@majanhotel.com, info: www.majanhotel.com

Vision International LLC, Siw Rantapää-Buring runs a Bed and Breakfast facility (see section on **Tour operators**, p 13, for further information), tel: 2448 8770, fax: 2448 8771, email: siwoman@omantel.net.om

Qurm Beach Hotel (close to beach and Al Qurm Natural Park, site 1.2), tel: 2456 4070, fax: 2456 0761, email: qbhotel@omantel.net.om

Marina Hotel (near Muttrah corniche and old souq), tel: 2471 1711, fax: 2471 1313, email: marina1@omantel.net.om

Al Sanar Hotel, (near Muttrah corniche and old souq), 2471 4196, fax: 2471 4994, email: alsanar@omantel.net.om

Corniche Hotel, (near Muttrah corniche and old souq), tel: 2471 4707, fax: 2471 4770, email: corniche_hotel@mjsoman.com

Naseem Hotel, (near Muttrah corniche and old souq), tel: 2471 2418, fax: 2471 1728

Al-Moosa Beach Rest House, Yiti (on the beach, 30 minutes from the city, see site 1.4), tel: 2458 6119, 9932 3762, email: anosh@omantel.net.om

2 Al Batinah

As Sawadi Beach Resort (at Ras As Sawadi, site 2.1), tel: 2679 5545, fax: 2489 5535, email: reservations@alsawadibeach.com, info: www.alsawadibeach.com

Sohar Beach Hotel, tel: 2684 1111, fax: 2684 3766, email: soharhtl@omantel.net.om, info: www.soharbeach.com

Al Wadi Hotel (in Sohar, near Sun Farms, site 2.2), tel: 2684 0058, fax: 2684 1997, email: gmalwadi@omanhotels.com, info: www.omanhotels.com

Green Oasis Hotel (5 km inland), tel: 2684 6440/077, 9905 3009, fax: 2684 6441, email: alwahah@omantel.net.om

3 The Northeast Coast

Sur Mercure Hotel (in Sur, site 3.2), tel: 2554 3777, fax: 2554 2626, email : reservationssur@omanhotels.com, info: www.omanhotels.com

Sur Beach Hotel (in Sur, site 3.2), tel: 2554 2227, fax: 2544 2228, email: surbhtl@omantel.net.om, info: www.surhotel.com

Ras Al Hadd Beach Hotel (situated on the northern side of Khawr Al Hajar at Ras Al Hadd), tel: 9937 6989, fax: 9931 4002, email: surbhtl@omantel.net.om, or contact the main office at Sur Beach Hotel.

Turtle Beach Resort (situated on the southern side of Khawr Al Hajar at Ras Al Hadd), tel: 9900 7709, reservations: 2554 3400, email: surtour@omantel.net.om

4 Al Hajar Mountains

Nizwa Hotel (between Nizwa and Birkat Al Mawz, gateway to Jabal Shams, site 4.2), tel: 2543 1616, fax: 2543 1619, email: nizhotel@omantel.net.om, info: www.goldentulipnizwa.com

Al Jabal Al Akhdar Hotel (at Sayq, site 4.3), tel: 2542 9009, fax: 2542 9119, email: jakhotel@omantel.net.om

Falaj Daris Hotel (in Nizwa, gateway to Jabal Shams, site 4.2), tel: 2541 0500, fax: 2541 0537, email: fdhnizwa@omantel.net.om, info: www.falajdarishotel.com

Nizwa Guest House (in Nizwa, gateway to Jabal Shams, site 4.2), tel: 2541 2402, fax: 2541 2405, email: nghnizwa@hotmail.com

Jabal Shams Camping and Travelling Centre (at Jabal Shams, site 4.2), tel: 2542 3651, 9938 2639. Rooms and camp sites. Rooms include breakfast and dinner

Jabal Shams Resthouse (at Jabal Shams, site 4.2). Under construction. Rates likely to be similar to Jabal Shams Camping and Travelling Centre

Majan Guest House (in Nizwa, gateway to Jabal Shams, site 4.2), tel: 2543 1910, fax: 2543 1911, info: www.majangh.com

5 Musandam

Golden Tulip Resort (on a headland a few km outside Khasab), tel: 2673 0777, 2673 1356, fax: 2673 0888, email: info@goldentulipkhasab.com, info: www.goldentulipkhasab.com

Khasab Hotel (in Khasab), tel: 2673 0267, 2673 0271, fax: 2673 0989, email: khoman@omantel.net.om

Esra Hotel Apartments (in Khasab), tel: 2673 0562, email: esrahotl@omantel.net.om

The Lake Hotel (in Khasab), tel: 2673 1667, fax: 2673 1676, email: info@khasablakehotel.com, info: www.khasablakehotel.com

6 Al Buraymi Area

Al Buraymi Hotel, tel: 2565 2010, 2565 2011, email: buraimihotel@yahoo.com; please note that to go to Al Buraymi from Muscat, Sohar or Nizwa requires crossing the Oman/UAE border, which will entail an additional visa upon return

7 The Central Desert

Qatbit Motel and Resthouse (site 7.4), tel: 9908 5686 or 9215 4378, email: qitbit_motel@rediffmail.com

🐦🐦 **Al Ghaftayn Resthouse** (site 7.2), tel: 9948 5881, fax: 2329 7103

🐦🐦 **Al Ghabah Resthouse**, (site 7.2), tel: 9935 8639

🐦🐦 **Thumrayt Turist Motel** (along main highway), tel: 2327 9371, 9967 9380, fax: 2327 9373, email: thumotel@omantel.net.om

🐦🐦 **Thumrayt Suites** (situated behind the Shell petrol station in Thumrayt), tel: 9925 4238

🐦 **Hayma Rest House** (in Hayma), tel: 2343 6061

🐦 **Al Wusta Tourism Motel** (in Hayma), tel: 2343 6016, 9904 1513

8 Barr Al Hikman and Masirah

🐦🐦🐦🐦🐦 **Golden Tulip Resort** (on the east coast of Masirah). This hotel is under construction.

🐦🐦 **Mahawt Motel** (in Al Hijj, site 8.1), tel: 9937 7839

🐦🐦 **Al Jazeera Guesthouse** (west of Al Hijj), tel/fax: 9982 0882

🐦🐦 **Masirah Hotel** (in Hilf, site 8.2), tel: 2550 4401, 2550 4477, fax: 2550 4411

🐦🐦 **Shannah Tourism Rest House** (situated near the ferry terminal at Shannah, site 8.1). Was closed for renovation in 2007. May reopen in 2008.

9 The Southeast Coast

🐦 **Shati Ash Shuwayamiyyah Resthouse** (situated adjacent to the petrol station in Shuwayamiyyah, site 9.4), tel: 9938 2202

10 Dhofar

🐦🐦🐦🐦🐦 **Hilton Hotel Salalah** (on the beach near Salalah Port), tel: 2321 1234, fax: 2321 0084, reservations: www.hilton.com, email: sllbc@omantel.net.om

🐦🐦🐦🐦🐦 **Crowne Plaza Salalah** (on the beach, with nice garden), tel: 2323 5333, fax: 2323 5137, email: cpsalalah@cpsalalah.com, info: www.ichotelsgroup.com/h/d/cp/1/en/home

🐦🐦🐦 **Hamilton Plaza Hotel** (all rooms with kitchen, in northern part of Salalah), tel: 2321 1025, fax: 2321 1187

🐦🐦 **Salalah Beach Villas and Spa** (birdwatcher friendly, on the beach and very close to East Khawr, site 10.2), tel: 2323 5999, fax: 2323 5599, email: beachspa@omantel.net.om

🐦🐦 **Dhofar Hotel** (in Salalah town), tel: 2329 2272, fax: 2329 4358, email: dhfhotel@omantel.net.om

🐦 **Al Nile Hotel Suites** (Al Sa'ada Area situated on the eastern side of Salalah city), tel: 2322 5804, fax: 2322 5805. Room rates reduced between September and June.

Camping

Camping is popular amongst expatriates in Oman and may be an option for visiting birdwatchers at certain locations. Few official campsites exist, however, so simply choose a suitable, undisturbed location for a night camp. If the camp is near the sea, be aware of the incoming tide (check the tide line). Pitch a tent or put up camp beds and sleep under the stars. Even though days are warm to hot, nights in the desert can be cool and sometimes wet from dew fall, so make sure to bring a sleeping bag or some other form of cover. Naturally, it is necessary to leave the area as clean and beautiful as it was found; carry all litter away and dispose of it properly. Also bring a shovel and toilet paper. Avoid camping in *wadis* (dry riverbeds) if there is any sign of rain - *wadis* may suddenly turn into roaring rivers when rainwater is rushing down from the mountains. Camping equipment may be bought in Oman.

One popular campsite is at the turtle-watching beach at Ras Al Jinz (site 3.4). Permits to camp and to go with a ranger in the evening to see egg-laying Green Turtles can be obtained from the Director General of Nature Conservation at the Ministry of Environment and Climatic Affairs in Muscat at tel: 2460 2285 fax: 2469 2462. In the application, state all names, nationalities, number of children, date of visit, telephone, if any and car registration number, if known. The cost is RO 3/adult/night and RO 1/child/night. If space is available at the campground, it is possible to obtain and pay for the permit at the entrance to the reserve, but weekends in October and November may be busy.

Food

Restaurants are widespread, and there is always a place to buy a meal in the cities. A whole spectrum of choice is available in Muscat; one can dine as royalty in some of the best hotels in the world, or choose to enjoy the sound of the sea together with good food at one of the many seafront restaurants. Several fast-food outlets operate in major towns across the country. Simple, local fare found in more rural areas is inexpensive and easy to find. Many of the larger restaurants are licensed to serve alcohol.

A range of supermarkets and grocery stores are found throughout, as well as local markets, and convenience stores at petrol stations. Even in small villages at least one shop selling basic food items can usually be found.

Books and maps

Maps and books are available from bookshops in the Capital area and Salalah. Many larger hotels also have bookshops. For information on books on Oman and other items, consult the website: www.soukofoman.com under Books On Oman.

Of the following, the first two books are a must for successful birdwatching in Oman.

Oman Bird List, edition 6 (2003), by J. Eriksen, D. E. Sargeant and R. Victor, Centre for Environmental Studies and Research, Sultan Qaboos University, Muscat. Gives the status of every species recorded in Oman with breeding maps for all breeding birds and histograms for all migrating species. Available from the Family Bookshop

Field Guide to the Birds of the Middle East (1996), by R. F. Porter, S. Christensen and P. Schiermacher-Hansen, Poyser, London. The standard field guide for the area. In Europe can be obtained from good bookshops or Natural History Book Service at www.nhbs.com

Common Birds in Oman: an identification guide (2006), by H. and J. Eriksen, Al Roya Publishing, Muscat. Available from leading bookshops in Oman and from NHBS

Oman 2day, a monthly magazine published by Apex Publishing, with articles on Oman and tourist information on time out, sports, contacts and information on hotels, restaurants, car hire, tour operators, diving, shops and miscellaneous.

Oman, A comprehensive Guide to the Sultanate of Oman (1999), Al Roya Publishing

Muscat, The Jewel of Arabia, Al Roya Publishing, 1998

Maps

National Survey Authority, Oman 1 : 1,300,000

Al Roya Publishing, Tourist Map, Oman 1 : 1,300,000

Apex Publishing, Tourist Map, Oman 1 : 1,300,000 with details of Capital Area and Salalah.

Health

The warm weather necessitates drinking lots of fluid, preferably water. Ensure a good intake of fluids throughout the day. Bottled water is readily available and tap water is safe to drink as it is chlorinated. For protection against the strong sun, wear a hat, sun screen and sunglasses.

Officially Oman is no longer considered a malaria risk. However, cases do occur, as travellers enter from other infected areas nearby. Most resident birders choose not to take medication against malaria. Should someone be unfortunate enough to become sick or injured, hospitals and clinics can be found throughout the country, with excellent facilities in the cities. Visitors should consider health insurance when travelling to Oman.

Miscellaneous

Dress code. The recommended dress code for women is a pair of loose trousers or a skirt at least to the knee, together with a short or long-sleeved blouse. On the beach a one-piece swimsuit or shorts and a sleeveless blouse may be worn. Men are recommended to wear long trousers except when on the beach.

Weekends in Oman are Thursday/Friday.

Ramadan. Oman follows the Islamic calendar which is 11-12 days shorter than the Gregorian calendar. One month of the year, Ramadan, is the holy month when Muslims fast during the day but take meals at night and before sunrise. During this month visitors are requested to abstain from eating, drinking and smoking in public during daylight hours and to dress more conservatively than normally. Note that alcohol is not served during this period, and most restaurants are closed throughout the day, opening only at sunset. Also, working hours are reduced for many people and the streets seem quiet during daylight hours. However, the streets become very much alive during the evening and night when it is popular to visit friends and family to celebrate the holy month. In 2008 Ramadan is expected to be around 31st August to 29th September. It is not possible to give exact dates as it depends on the sighting of the new moon. In 2009, Ramadan will start 11-12 days earlier and so on.

Customs regulations. Standard international regulations apply and visitors are allowed to bring one bottle of alcohol into Oman when arriving at As Seeb International Airport.

Business hours. Government: Saturday to Wednesday 07h30 - 14h30. Banks: Saturday to Wednesday 08h00 - 13h00 and Thursday 08h00 - 12h00. Shops: Saturday to Thursday 09h00 - 13h00 and 16h30 - 20h00. Friday: 16h30 - 20h00. Shop hours vary; some may open earlier/later and many stay open till late at night. Larger supermarkets are often open throughout the day, but not 24 hours. Currently the only 24 hour opening for basic provisions are petrol stations with their associated convenience stores.

Electricity. 220/240 volts, 50 Hz. with three-pin British style plugs. Adapters can be bought locally.

Telephone cards are available in shops, petrol stations and supermarkets.

Internet Cafes are readily found in larger towns.

Climate and when to go

Both birds and birders feel their best during the cooler half of the year from October to March. Of this period, the middle four months usually provide the best weather one could wish for, with clear blue skies and temperatures between 20 °C and 30 °C over most of the country. Temperatures during October and March fluctuate between hot and warm. Outside of the southern monsoon, rain is a rare possibility anywhere, but most likely from late December through March, although many places receive no rain at all some years. Precipitation is most likely in the mountains where it usually falls as heavy showers which quickly dissipate. September and April/May are hot with maximum daily temperatures around 40 °C, but do give the opportunity to witness migration and some of the Salalah specialities.

Salalah, in the south, has its own distinctive climate, greatly influenced by the Indian Ocean monsoon from June to September. The affect is not heavy rain, but rather a constant drizzle, especially in the mountains, where visibility is greatly reduced. The humidity on the coast is high, and the sea extremely rough. Summer breeders arrive from Africa to Salalah in late April/early May and even though it is hot, it is the peak time to seek out these species. Most leave between September and November. Seabird watching from the shore can be good in September, though is sometimes not possible due to fog and mist. As the month passes the visibility improves.

November is the most popular month for visiting birders; the weather is likely to be brilliant, wintering birds are settling in, and it is peak time for raptors. Additionally some late migrants linger well into October and early November. December, January and February are the coolest and most pleasant months and wintering birds are plentiful and can be found all over the country. With the warmer weather in March, migratory movements start.

Call 2451 9113 to get the latest weather report anywhere in Oman.

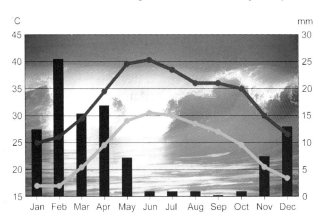

Average monthly maximum (red dots) and minimum (green dots) temperature, and rainfall (blue columns) in Muscat.

Average monthly maximum (red dots) and minimum (green dots) temperature, and rainfall (blue columns) in Salalah.

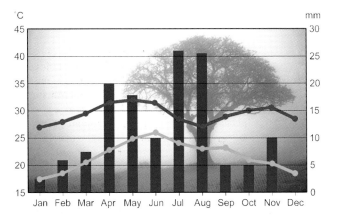

THE BIRD CALENDAR

January

Being the middle of winter, this is one of the coolest and most pleasant months to visit Oman. Higher water levels in *khawrs* attract the full set of wintering **wildfowl**, including **Pintail**, **Wigeon**, **Gadwall**, **Mallard**, and **Teal** as well as the scarcer **Ferruginous Duck** and the occasional rarity such as **Greylag Goose** or **Red-crested Pochard**. Huge concentrations of gulls - including **Great Black-headed Gull** - are found along all coasts, especially in the east and south where they find rich feeding. Added to this, massive **wader** concentrations occur at Barr Al Hikman, Arabia's most important wetland site, where possibly more than a million individuals overwinter. **Socotra Cormorant**, which disperse from their Arabian Gulf breeding colonies, can be found along the Musandam coast.

January is a good time to find the scarcer, settled winter visitors like **Eastern Pied Wheatear** and **Plain Leaf-Warbler** in the north, as well as **Eversmann's Redstart** in Musandam. Despite being the 'middle of winter', some early movements of returning migrants is evident, as large numbers of **Pallid Swift** stream northward along eastern coasts, and breeding of some starts in the north. Many early breeders such as **Striated Scops Owl** and **Southern Grey Shrike** are already setting up territories, and display activity indicates nesting of common garden species like **Laughing Dove** and **Yellow-vented Bulbul**.

Eversmann's Redstart, male

February

In some years, when winter rain falls, formerly barren areas suddenly spring to life and butterflies are much in evidence. The resulting increase in insect life prompts increased breeding activity among resident species such as **Indian Roller**, **Little Owl** and early breeding **Grey Francolin**. The return northward migration becomes more visible with **Sand Martin** and **Barn Swallow** numbers augmented by arrivals from farther south, as well as small numbers of early migrants such as **Yellow Wagtail**.

Garganey, the males in full breeding plumage, appear and **wildfowl** numbers fluctuate as the passage northward gathers momentum towards the month end. A fall off in the number of certain wintering species occurs toward the end of the month, with the first departures of wintering **Steppe** and **Greater Spotted Eagles**. Similarly, small numbers of **Black Redstart**, **Stonechat**, **Tawny Pipit**, **Desert Wheatear** and others start to leave.

Many of the interior desert species such as **Southern Grey Shrike**, **Hoopoe Lark**, and **Brown-necked Raven**, breed at this time in order to avoid the intense summer heat.

March

As the hours of daylight increase, the feeling that winter is over begins to have a marked effect on wintering visitors, the bulk of which have left by the end of the month. The number, both of individuals and species that have wintered in Africa, increases with a marked movement of warblers such as **White-throat**, **Chiffchaff**, and **Ménétries's Warbler** as well as **Common Redstart**. By the month end, the first of the summer breeders arrive, with small numbers of **Blue-cheeked Bee-eater** and **Yellow-throated Sparrow** appearing. On beaches of the north and east coast, **Great Black-headed Gulls** moult into their immaculate breeding plumage before disappearing northward to central Asia by the month end.

In the *wadis* of south Oman, the breeding of the residents such as **Rüppell's Weaver**, **African Rock Bunting** and **Tristram's Grackle** is well underway. Offshore, **Masked Boobies** concentrate at their breeding grounds on Al Hallaniyyat Islands. With breeding starting, or well underway, March is an optimal time for finding certain species best located by voice, particularly the mangrove specialist **Sykes's Warbler** which is only found in the north.

With the increasing temperatures, mountain species like **Wood Pigeon**, **Long-billed Pipit** and **Scrub Warbler** ascend to higher levels. **Hume's Wheatear** will be breeding at lower elevations, and, the much scarcer, **Hooded Wheatear** higher in the mountains.

April

The rapidly increasing temperatures throughout this month give added urgency to the northerly passage of migrants that now rarely stay longer than the few days required to refuel for their long desert crossings. April is a month of great change, with an almost total clear out of winter visitors and a settling-in of the summer breeders.

Many rarer migrants are best found at this time including **White-throated Robin** as well as **Steppe Grey**, **Lesser Grey**, **Woodchat** and **Masked Shrikes**. The potential for spring vagrants peaks in mid-month, and this is a good time for **Ortolan**, **Black-headed** and **Cinereous Buntings**, particularly in Musandam. Occasionally, large numbers of **Lesser Kestrel**, **Rock Thrush**, and **Common Redstart** pass through the mountains, and **European Nightjars** appear in the *wadis* of the south in good numbers. Many migrants are in full breeding plumage including several identifiable forms of **Yellow Wagtail** such as *beama, thunbergi, flava, feldegg, lutea, flavissima, taivana,* and *cinereocapilla.*

Breeding **Blue-cheeked Bee-eaters** are joined by the much scarcer **European Bee-eater**. Late in the month sees the arrival of the first **Persian Shearwater**, **Red-billed Tropicbird** and **Jouanin's Petrel** off southern coasts. **Singing Bush Larks** arrive in force and take up residence in farmlands around Salalah.

May

Although the last of the spring migration tapers off, numbers of a few species, such as **Rufous Bush Robin**, **Upcher's Warbler** and **Spotted Flycatcher**, peak at this time. During mid-month a massive passage of **Marsh Warblers** occurs, when they sometimes seem to be falling out of every bush in the country.

In the *wadis* of Dhofar, the summer breeders, **Grey-headed Kingfisher**, **Bruce's Green Pigeon** and **Didric Cuckoo** arrive ahead of the monsoon to establish territories. In the north, the first of the **Sooty Falcons** arrive.

Some of the later breeders are active at this time, including **Grey Francolin** and **Yellow-vented Bulbul**. Despite the heat, some of the arid *wadis* of the north hold breeding **Yellow-throated Sparrow** in small numbers.

Activity increases offshore with **Bridled Terns** on their breeding colonies, and good numbers of **White-cheeked Tern** appear along all coasts. A number of non-breeding **waders**, and a few wintering gulls not having returned north to breed, now settle in for a long hot summer. The more common species include **Grey Plover**, **Oystercatcher**, **Lesser Sand Plover**, **Bar-tailed Godwit**, and **Caspian** and **Siberian Gulls**.

June

Although this is the hottest month in the north and interior, the arrival of the southwest monsoon in Dhofar enshrouds the southern coast in mist and rain, and starts to turn the *wadis* and mountain slopes green. The abundance of food prompts breeding activity for resident and visiting species alike. This is also the time that African oddities such as **Allen's Gallinule** can turn up in Dhofar.

In the north, birdwatchers often take to the highest mountains to escape the coastal heat and humidity, where camping is excellent. Most of the mountain species breed at this time including **Scrub Warbler** and **Long-billed Pipit**. In the interior, **sandgrouse**, **Golden Eagle** and **Long-legged Buzzard** are most easily found due to the availability of water only at permanent oases.

July

Visiting seabirds from Antarctica and the southern oceans such as **Wilson's Storm-petrel** and **Pale-footed Shearwater** are now common off southern and eastern headlands. The brief lull in migration activity experienced in June is broken toward the end of July when the first of the **waders** commence their return journey, with small numbers of **Curlew Sandpiper**, **Little Stint**, **Redshank** and **Common Sandpiper** appearing. These are soon joined on beaches and *khawrs* by **Grey Heron** and **Little Egret** arriving for the winter.

Although uncommon, **Roseate Tern** can be found in small numbers along the east coast, as well as small numbers of **Sooty Gull** from post-breeding dispersal. Despite the heat some opportunist residents of Al Batinah including **Grey Francolin**, **Laughing Dove**, and **House Sparrow** are still raising young.

August

Wader migration is now very much in evidence, and a good variety can be found at all lagoons and *khawrs*, including interior ponds and oases. These will include the first of the **Broad-billed Sandpiper**, **Common Snipe**, **Black-tailed Godwit**, **Marsh Sandpiper** and **Pacific Golden Plover**. **Red-necked Phalarope** frequently occur well inland. **Crab Plover**, which will have been largely absent, now disperse from their breeding grounds on Masirah and appear along the east coast.

Along the coast, **tern** numbers build up strongly, and **Caspian** and **Siberian Gull** start to arrive in increasing numbers. **Garganey** usually appear toward the end of the month passing through on their way farther south. Of the passerines, **Barn Swallow** and **Sand Martin** are in evidence and the first **Yellow** and **Citrine Wagtails** appear. Occasionally large flocks of **White Stork** have been noted.
Although this is still a month when few of the true winter visitors arrive, **Common Kingfisher** and **Grey Wagtail** are an exception when they start to move in toward month end.

September

The number and variety of the passerine migrants increase, with good numbers of **European Roller**, **Tawny Pipit**, **Spotted Flycatcher** and **Olivaceous Warbler** to be found. Some rarer **waders**, including **Caspian Plover**, might appear on farmland and small numbers of **White-tailed Plover** and **Cream-coloured Courser** are regular. Grassy fields can attract large numbers of **Short-toed Lark**, **pipits** and **wagtails**. **Yellow-throated Sparrow** are often seen in sizeable flocks and all three species of *Porzana* crakes can be found together at *khawrs* in Dhofar. The peak passerine migration coincides with the fledging of the majority of the **Sooty Falcon**, and small numbers are seen most evenings over Muscat.

With the clearing of the southwest monsoon, sea-watching is at its best with the greatest number of seabird species present, as both summer breeders and visitors from southern oceans are still present. Off Dhofar, **Jouanin's Petrel**, **Wilson's Storm-petrel**, **Pale-footed Shearwater**, and **Persian Shearwater** are all likely to be encountered on the same sea-watch.

Many more winter visitors start to arrive with numbers of **Short-toed Eagle**, **Pallid Harrier**, and **Montagu's Harrier** increasing. Among the passerines, **Isabelline**, **Desert**, **Red-tailed** and **Eastern Pied Wheatears** all start to move in, as well as small numbers of **Bluethroat** and **Blue Rock Thrush**. Al Hajar Mountains are often alive with migrants in vegetated *wadis*, with **Barred Warbler** a regular occurrence.

October

For visiting birdwatchers, October provides the best opportunity to observe the greatest selection of species in Oman. Not only are small numbers of lingering summer visitors present, but toward the end of the month wintering **eagles** start to arrive.

The continuing migration provides a wide selection of migrants, and the chances of interesting vagrants are high, especially in such outposts as Masirah and Musandam. Additionally, as migration moves through the country on a broad front, the central desert oases and small farms, act as a magnet for rare migrants and vagrants that over the years have produced many spectacular finds.

Duck numbers increase, although most are in eclipse plumage. The start of winter is heralded by the arrival of **Steppe**, **Greater Spotted** and **Imperial Eagles** from central Asia which begin to appear in the vicinity of waste disposal sites.

In the far south a few **Grey-headed Kingfisher** and **Bruce's Green Pigeon** can still be found. Small numbers of **Pheasant-tailed Jacana** start to arrive from the Indian sub-continent. **Persian Shearwaters** are still common off coasts, and now appear farther north as they disperse from their breeding sites.

The last of the late breeding **Sooty Falcon** can still be found until the end of the month, as well as the last of the breeding **Red-billed Tropicbird**.

November

Winter is approaching, and all summer visitors and breeders have departed. Numbers of seabirds, other than **gulls** and **terns**, start to dwindle, and are almost completely absent by month end. Despite the slowdown in passage, this month has great potential for vagrants.

Eagles reach their peak numbers, as many are still moving through to wintering sites farther south. **Caspian** and **Siberian Gulls** are present in massive numbers along all coasts and are joined by **Slender-billed** and **Black-headed Gulls** in increasing numbers. Rare **waders** such as **Sociable Plover** may turn up on farmlands in north and south Oman.

As temperatures in the mountains drop, higher altitude species such as **Scrub Warbler** and **Long-billed Pipit** descend, and often appear at the coast in suitable habitat. Masirah continues to act as a migrant trap and **Red-breasted Flycatchers** are regular and, occasionally, a few **Forest Wagtails** turn up as well. Muntasar has in recent years attracted small, but regular numbers of **Grey Hypocolius** some of which may stay till March.

December

Winter is now well set in with **duck**, **eagle**, and **wader** numbers largely stable. The last of the winter visitors arrive including **Great Black-headed Gull**.

Other species including **Eastern Pied Wheatear** and **Plain Leaf Warbler** move into the more southerly parts of their wintering range of northern Oman, and a few late, irregular stragglers such as **Short-eared Owl** and **Black-throated Thrush** sometimes turn up.

Some of the most common winter visitors like **Desert Wheatear** and **Isabelline Wheatear** are widespread and common throughout the interior, and **Red-tailed Wheatear** can be found along the rocky coastal plains of the northern half of the country.

SUGGESTED ITINERARIES

With so many interesting sites in Oman, birdwatchers are almost spoilt for choice. To aid the initial planning of an itinerary some suggestions are given here to provide a starting point for more detailed research.

Evidently, the time of year and the intended length of stay in Oman will dictate, to some extent, the sites best visited. Although most visitors will plan to spend two or three weeks in Oman, suggestions are also provided for the business visitor with a spare weekend, or an even shorter stop-over in Muscat.

The majority of visitors will choose to visit during the cooler half of the year between October and March. A two week trip during this period could be split with a week each in the north and south. In the north, a day or two can be spent in the Capital Area, concentrating on Qurayyat, Al Qurm Natural Park, and Al Amrat Waste Disposal Site, followed by three to four days along Al Batinah taking in sites between Ras As Sawadi and Khatmat Milahah. In the south all the main coastal sites can be covered in four to five days. Time-permitting, a short trip to the desert locations such as Al Balid Farm, Muntasar and Qatbit can be included.

For those with three weeks, the extra time offers some flexibility which might provide for a more leisurely pace of the above, plus driving between Muscat and Salalah, and possibly including time in Al Hajar Mountains. Other alternatives would be to include a trip to Musandam, a trip down the east coast via Qurayyat, Sur, Ras Al Hadd and Ras Al Khabbah, or Barr Al Hikman, Masirah and the southeast coast as far as Khawr Dhurf and Ash Shuwaymiyyah.

Even with only a week it is possible to sample a cross-section of both north and south Oman by spending two to three days based in the Capital area and the rest in Salalah. Visitors with only a long weekend need to choose between the north and south. The south is recommended as the species diversity is greatest and includes the attraction of some Arabian specialities like **Yemen Serin** and **Golden-winged Grosbeak**. For the casual visitor with only a single day to spare, a short visit to Al Qurm Natural Park, Al Ansab Lagoons, Al Amrat Waste Disposal Site or Qurayyat is recommended.

For visitors during the summer months from May to August the focus shifts toward the seabirds. In the north, sites such as Ras As Sawadi and Qurayyat become relatively more interesting with summering **terns**. Sea-watching from eastern headlands can be productive. This is also an interesting time for observing resident species in the central desert, although the fierce heat will deter most visitors, and is not recommended for those inexperienced to extreme conditions. The arrival of the southern monsoon makes Salalah cool, and although visibility can be a problem in the mountains, all the coastal sites are still excellent.

Jouanin's Petrel

The Sultanate of Oman

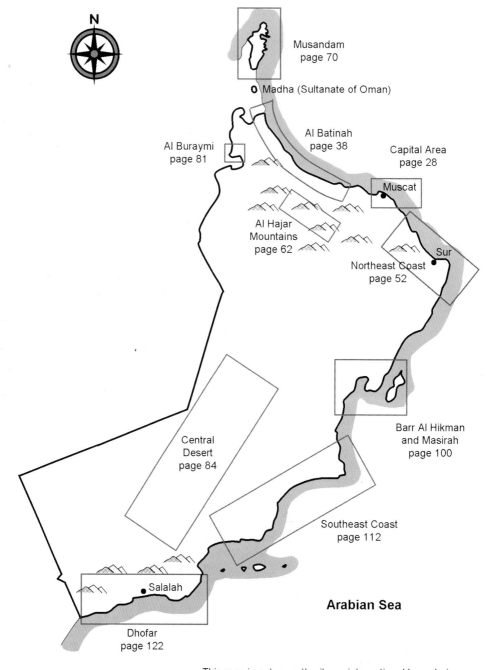

Musandam
page 70

O Madha (Sultanate of Oman)

Al Batinah
page 38

Capital Area
page 28

Al Buraymi
page 81

Muscat

Al Hajar
Mountains
page 62

Sur

Northeast Coast
page 52

Central
Desert
page 84

Barr Al Hikman
and Masirah
page 100

Southeast Coast
page 112

Arabian Sea

Salalah

Dhofar
page 122

This map is not an authority on international boundaries

THE SITE GUIDE

The Site Guide section presents over 60 of Oman's top birdwatching sites, grouped into ten distinct regions, as shown on the map opposite. Each region is given an introduction providing a general overview of access, habitats and the more interesting species that occur. Both common resident and migratory species are listed.

More detailed descriptions then follow for the sites within each region. The country's top birdwatching sites have been given three stars (***) and are not to be missed. Two stars (**) indicate excellent sites, while a single star (*) is applied to sites that can be visited, time permitting. These are followed by a 2WD/4WD symbol, indicating whether the area can be accessed in an ordinary saloon car or requires a four wheel drive, plus a summary of key species. A schematic map, with key GPS coordinates, accompanies all site descriptions and should help greatly in the field. All GPS coordinates are also available on the www.birdsoman.com for download. When constructing maps, emphasis has been placed on user-friendliness and the diagrams do not necessarily include every single road or track, nor are they drawn to scale. However, all important distances are shown in kilometres to assist finding the place. For quick reference, the legends used in the diagrams are shown at the back of this book. Distances measured by different vehicles may differ slightly and are consequently given to the nearest 0.1 km for distances less than 10 km, or often to the nearest kilometre if over 10 km.

A massive program of paving graded roads in rural areas is underway and some roads may have been paved or realigned when a birdwatcher arrives at the scene. A few sites require a permit for visiting and details are provided on how to obtain such a permit. Information given is correct at the time of publication. The site maps should be used in connection with a tourist map of Oman which is readily obtained (see **Books and maps**, p 18).

A word on place names is relevant here. Arabic names are not easily transcribed into English and thus several spellings may be used. As an example, a lagoon is a *khawr* or a *khor*, and the coastal town southeast of Muscat could be spelled Quriyat or Qurayyat. We have used the official English place names as required by the National Survey Authority in Oman, and which in most cases are the same as shown on the tourist maps. Road signs in the field may differ considerably from these spellings, though, and some flexibility should be allowed for.

Details of the more interesting birds and when they can be expected are given under each site. Where space allows, a photograph of the site or a particularly relevant bird is shown.

A complete list of birds, including their relative abundance, for each site is included in the summarised tables in the **Site Species Lists** (p156).

Common bird names and taxonomy generally follow that proposed by Porter *et al.* (1996), the standard field guide for the Middle East. Exceptions include the large white-headed gulls where we have used **Baltic Gull** for *Larus fuscus fuscus*, **Siberian Gull** for *L. heuglini*, and **Caspian Gull** for *L. cachinnans* including *barabensis*. The **Great Grey Shrike** complex has been divided into resident **Southern Grey Shrike** *Lanius (excubitor) meridionalis* including *aucheri* and visiting **Steppe Grey Shrike** *L. (excubitor/meridionalis) pallidirostris*. The eagle owl in Oman is assumed to be **Desert Eagle Owl** *Bubo (bubo) ascalaphus*. The form of **Booted Warbler** in mangroves of northern Oman is **Sykes's Warbler** *Hippolais (caligata) rama*. For more details on these and other birds, see the **Bird Finder** section (p182).

Desert Eagle Owl

1   Capital Area

Most birdwatchers, residents and visitors alike, will initially base themselves within the Capital Area. The surrounding habitats, consisting of rocky hills, vegetated *wadis*, sandy coastlines, gardens and parkland offer several interesting birdwatching sites. Although the more important sites are covered individually, almost any area with water, scrub or trees attracts birds. Simply driving out of the city and stopping at likely looking habitat will produce migrants during the appropriate seasons, and many of the specialised resident species such as **Hume's Wheatear** are widespread and found readily. A number of non-native species, such as **Ring-necked Parakeet**, **Common Mynah** and **House Crow**, are well established and spreading from the Capital Area.

Listed below are common, widespread species easily seen within, or around, the Capital Area. These are generally not discussed in the individual site accounts.

Common resident species:

Striated Heron	Swift Tern	Arabian Babbler
Western Reef Heron	Laughing Dove	Purple Sunbird
Egyptian Vulture	Ring-necked Parakeet	House Crow
Osprey	Little Green Bee-eater	Brown-necked Raven
Grey Francolin	Indian Roller	Common Mynah
Black-winged Stilt	Crested Lark	House Sparrow
Kentish Plover	African Rock Martin	Indian Silverbill
Red-wattled Plover	Yellow-vented Bulbul	
Sooty Gull	Graceful Prinia	

Common migrant and seasonal species:

Cormorant	Curlew Sandpiper	Pallid Swift
Cattle Egret	Dunlin	Barn Swallow
Little Egret	Ruff	Yellow Wagtail
Great White Egret	Common Snipe	White Wagtail
Grey Heron	Bar-tailed Godwit	Rufous Bush Robin
Greater Flamingo	Whimbrel	Spotted Flycatcher
Teal	Curlew	
Garganey	Redshank	
Marsh Harrier	Greenshank	
Ringed Plover	Wood Sandpiper	
Lesser Sand Plover	Common Sandpiper	
Greater Sand Plover	Slender-billed Gull	
Grey Plover	Caspian Gull	
Sanderling	Sandwich Tern	
Little Stint	Collared Dove	

Hume's Wheatear

Waypoints and Coordinates			
A	A01	N23 35.168	E58 17.463
B	B59	N23 35.278	E58 22.999
C	B58	N23 35.366	E58 24.462
D	B57	N23 35.916	E58 26.619
E	A80	N23 37.037	E58 29.680
F	A81	N23 36.733	E58 29.572
G	A83	N23 35.486	E58 31.551
H	D01	N23 35.139	E58 32.301
J	D02	N23 34.938	E58 32.708
K	D09	N23 32.165	E58 40.484
N	B89	N23 36.900	E58 32.680
P	D22	N23 37.389	E58 33.709
R	D14	N23 35.224	E58 33.600
S	D19	N23 34.021	E58 36.457
T	A89	N23 28.058	E58 29.586
V	N01	N23 34.693	E58 17.695
X	D45	N23 34.939	E58 21.572
Y	D39	N23 33.768	E58 20.300

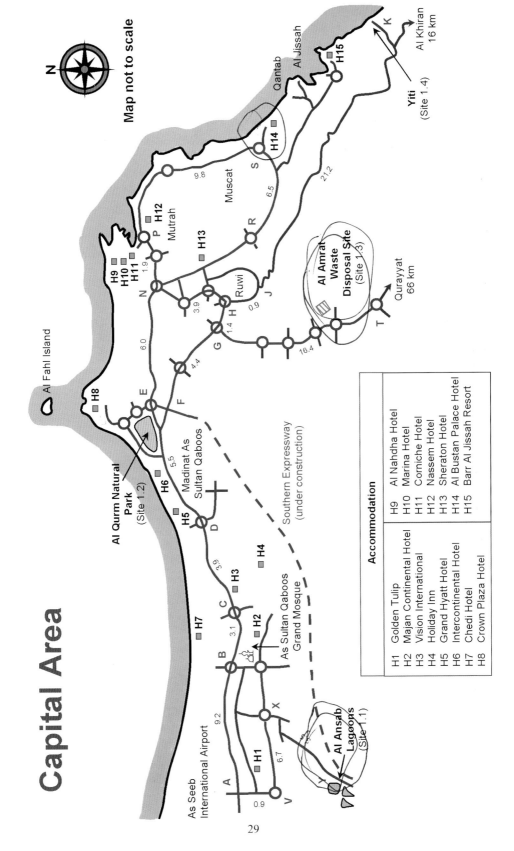

Capital Area

Map not to scale

N

Al Fahl Island

As Seeb
International Airport

Al Qurm Natural
Park
(Site 1.2)

Al Ansab
Lagoons
(Site 1.1)

As Sultan Qaboos
Grand Mosque

Madinat As
Sultan Qaboos

Southern Expressway
(under construction)

Mutrah

Muscat

Ruwi

Qantab

Al Jissah

Yiti
(Site 1.4)

Al Khiran
16 km

Al Amrat
Waste
Disposal Site
(Site 1.3)

Qurayyat
66 km

9.2
6.7
0.9
3.1
3.9
5.5
4.4
6.0
3.9
1.9
9.8
1.4
0.9
6.5
21.2
16.4

A
V
B
X
C
D
F
E
G
H
J
N
R
S
K
T

H1
H2
H3
H4
H5
H6
H7
H8
H9
H10
H11
H12
H13
H14
H15

P

Accommodation			
H1	Golden Tulip	H9	Al Nahdha Hotel
H2	Majan Continental Hotel	H10	Marina Hotel
H3	Vision International	H11	Corniche Hotel
H4	Holiday Inn	H12	Nassem Hotel
H5	Grand Hyatt Hotel	H13	Sheraton Hotel
H6	Intercontinental Hotel	H14	Al Bustan Palace Hotel
H7	Chedi Hotel	H15	Barr Al Jissah Resort
H8	Crown Plaza Hotel		

1.1 Al Ansab Lagoons *** 2WD

Key species: Little Grebe, Black-necked Grebe, ducks including Ferruginous Duck, Greater Spotted Eagle, Steppe Eagle, White-tailed Plover, Black-winged stilts and other waders, Lichtenstein's Sandgrouse, Egyptian Nightjar, wagtails, House Bunting, migrants.

The man-made lagoons at Al Ansab Sewage Treatment Plant, formerly the top birding spot of the Capital Area, are fed by surplus water pumped into the settling ponds from the adjacent treatment plant. During 2006 and 2007 a massive construction project has been ongoing here, related to waste water management of the Muscat area. Over the next 2-3 years the lagoons are to expanded to create new and significantly enhanced habitats, with the formation of a nature reserve for bird conservation and environmental education. The new site will also include a visitor centre, associated facilities and open, landscape planting with native species. The new lagoons will be managed to create open margins and reedbeds for breeding and migrant species. At present the area is fenced, so access is limited, but once the developments have been completed public access will be available..

Access is straightforward, though likely to change in the near term with the construction of the southern expressway which will pass very close by. Each pond should be thoroughly explored and the *wadi* on the far side can be productive for migrants.

From early autumn the lagoons are teeming with **herons** including **Night Heron**, **Indian Pond Heron** and **Purple Heron** together with small numbers of a variety of **waders** such as **White-tailed Plover**, **Spotted Redshank**, **Marsh**, **Green** and **Wood Sandpiper** together with **Little** and **Temminck's Stint**. **Whiskered** and **White-winged Black Tern** are both present and can cause confusion in non-breeding plumage. **Cormorants** join the many **herons** fishing at ponds with over 200 by mid winter. **Marsh Harrier** patrols the reed beds, and from mid-October **Greater Spotted** (including the *fulvescens* type), and **Steppe Eagle** make an appearance. At dusk a few dozen **Lichtenstein's Sandgrouse** come to drink from shallow edges. **Little Grebe** is resident while **Black-necked Grebe** occurs in small numbers from October to February. A variety of ducks including **Ferruginous Duck** and **Pochard** can be seen in mid-winter. **Egyptian Nightjar** has been regular on the dikes in January and February, and may return once disturbance reduces. In autumn, any reed edges might produce **Spotted**, **Baillon's** or **Little Crake**. **Wagtails** and **swallows** are common from October to April as are **Water Pipit** and **Bluethroat** during mid-winter. **Clamorous Reed Warbler** can be heard from the reed beds and **House Bunting** and **Desert Lark** frequent the surrounding hills. In recent years **Little Bittern** are thought to have started breeding in the spring. **Black-winged Stilt** and **Red-wattled Plover** are resident and breed during the hottest time of the year, though numbers fluctuate from year to year.

As Al Ansab Lagoons have been covered extensively by resident birdwatchers over the past 20 years, the total species list is over 270, including many vagrants.

Accommodation: hotel in Muscat.

Al Ansab Lagoons

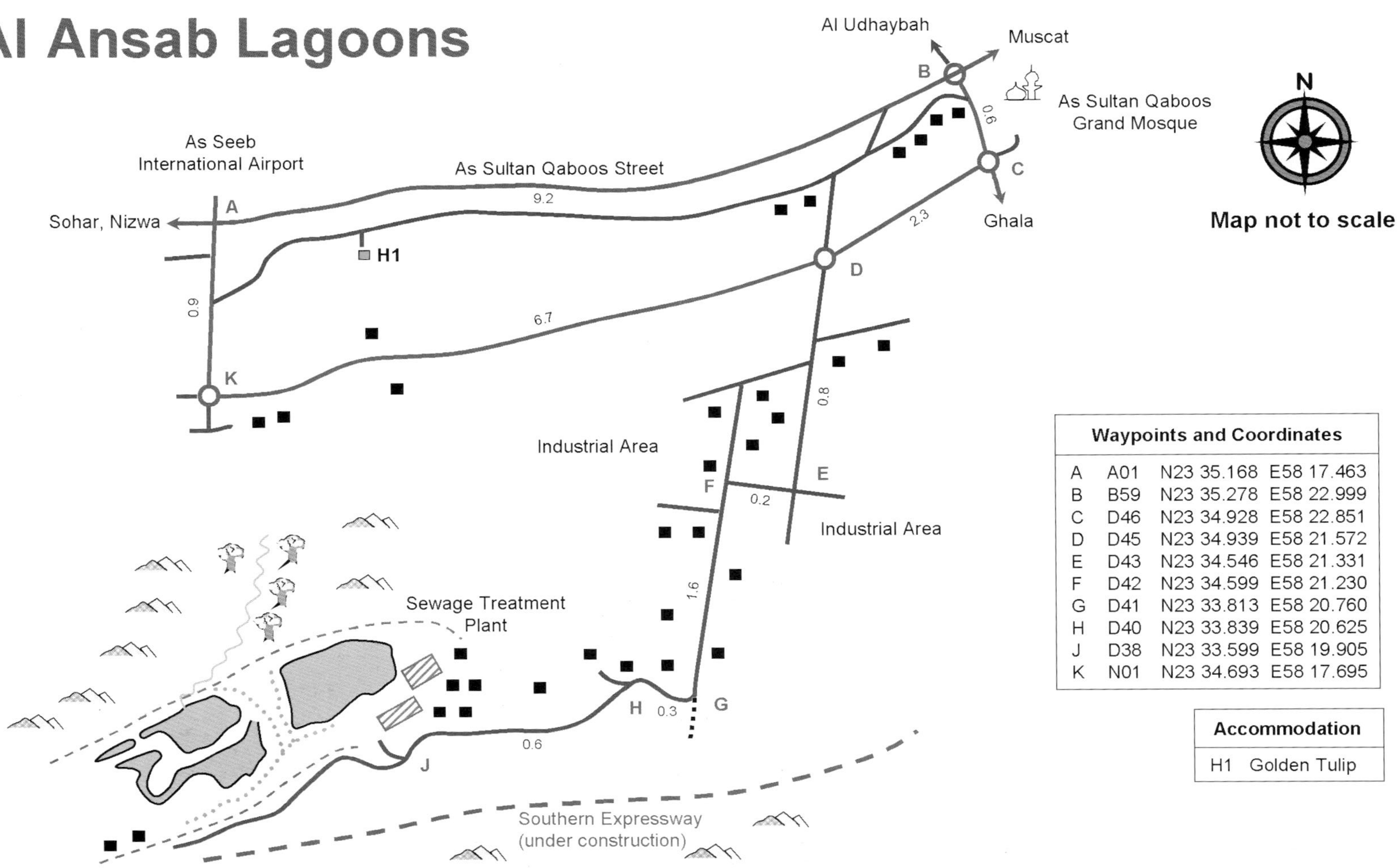

Al Udhaybah
Muscat
As Sultan Qaboos
Grand Mosque
As Seeb
International Airport
As Sultan Qaboos Street
Sohar, Nizwa
Ghala
H1
Industrial Area
Industrial Area
Sewage Treatment
Plant
Southern Expressway
(under construction)
A
B
C
D
E
F
G
H
J
K
9.2
6.7
0.9
0.6
2.3
0.8
0.2
1.6
0.3
0.6
N
Map not to scale

Waypoints and Coordinates			
A	A01	N23 35.168	E58 17.463
B	B59	N23 35.278	E58 22.999
C	D46	N23 34.928	E58 22.851
D	D45	N23 34.939	E58 21.572
E	D43	N23 34.546	E58 21.331
F	D42	N23 34.599	E58 21.230
G	D41	N23 33.813	E58 20.760
H	D40	N23 33.839	E58 20.625
J	D38	N23 33.599	E58 19.905
K	N01	N23 34.693	E58 17.695

Accommodation	
H1	Golden Tulip

Key species: Indian Pond Heron, Sooty Falcon, Terek Sandpiper, Pacific Golden Plover, White-cheeked Bulbul, Hoopoe, Bluethroat, migrants.

Although surrounded by urban development, a popular recreational site, a venue for important festivals and under increasing habitat encroachment, Al Qurm Natural Park still offers interesting bird-watching and an easy introduction to the birds of Oman. An astonishing total of 283 species, 57% of the total on the *Oman Bird List*, has been recorded from the park, mainly on account of the mixture of open water, scrub, mangrove and beach habitats.

Situated 8 km west of old Muscat, the park is well signposted off the main highway. The large artificial waterfall within is readily noticed en route to the airport, especially at night when attractively lit.

The park proper is open only from 16h00, so on shorter winter days only an hour or so of daylight remains. Fortunately, the best birdwatching areas are viewable near the rear entrance behind the waterfall, where a stroll along the fence provides views into the scrub and temporary pools behind the mangroves. This rear entrance provides the easiest and quickest access for birdwatchers. To drive from the main entrance, return to the highway and head toward the airport, turning right after 2.3 km, straight across the next roundabout, and follow the road to the parking area.

Pacific Golden Plover

In winter the small, but permanent, pools usually hold **Pacific Golden Plover**, **Temminck's Stint**, and a scattering of other **waders** and water birds. Regular **raptors** include **Greater Spotted Eagle** and **Marsh Harrier**. In the taller grass and reeds look for **Bluethroat** and *maura* '**Siberian' Stonechat**. For those seeking an identification challenge, **Indian Pond Heron** and **Squacco Heron** both occur.

During migration almost anything can turn up, and many rarities have been recorded. Regular migrants include **Hobby**, **Spotted** and **Baillon's Crake** and **Ménétries's**, **Olivaceous** and **Upcher's Warbler**. The scrub here is the best place in the Capital Area to find **White-cheeked Bulbul**, an increasing, but still uncommon, recent invader. On summer evenings **Sooty Falcons** hunt over the park, and large numbers of **Ring-necked Parakeets** pass overhead to their roost in the InterContinental Hotel gardens (1.5). Observers should note that unusual species are frequent at Al Qurm Natural Park, which is a hot-spot for escapees from the local pet shop. **Waxbills**, **munias**, **bishops** and various **weavers** are all regularly recorded. Inside the park, the large artificial lake occasionally attracts **Black-necked Grebe**, **Ferruginous Duck** and **terns**, whilst among the trees, resident species include **Hoopoe**, **Arabian Babbler**, and **Red-vented Bulbul**.

To view the mangroves and beach, drive to the bridge over the inlet at the northwest corner of the park. In winter small numbers of **waders**, **gulls** and **terns** are present at the outflow. Scanning the mangrove edge usually produces **Striated Heron** and **Common Kingfisher**. Odd species occur with some regularity - recent observations have included **Intermediate Egret**, **Greylag Goose**, **Great Knot**, **Pied Stonechat** and **Rustic Bunting**. A few **terns** can usually be seen at sea, including **Bridled** and **White-cheeked Tern** in summer.

The large, rocky Al Fahl Island, clearly visible offshore, holds good numbers of **Sooty Falcon** and a few **Red-billed Tropicbird**. To visit, negotiate with one of the local fishermen from the harbours of Muscat or Sidab or join one of the dolphin watching safaris and ask them to make a loop around Fahl. Alternatively, with sufficient people, arrange a dhow trip through a local travel agent. This would also provide the opportunity to travel farther out in search of **seabirds** such as **Persian**, **Pale-footed** and **Wedge-tailed Shearwater**, **Jouanin's Petrel**, **Wilson's Storm-petrel** and **Red-necked Phalarope**.

Accommodation: hotel in Muscat.

Al Qurm Natural Park

Map not to scale

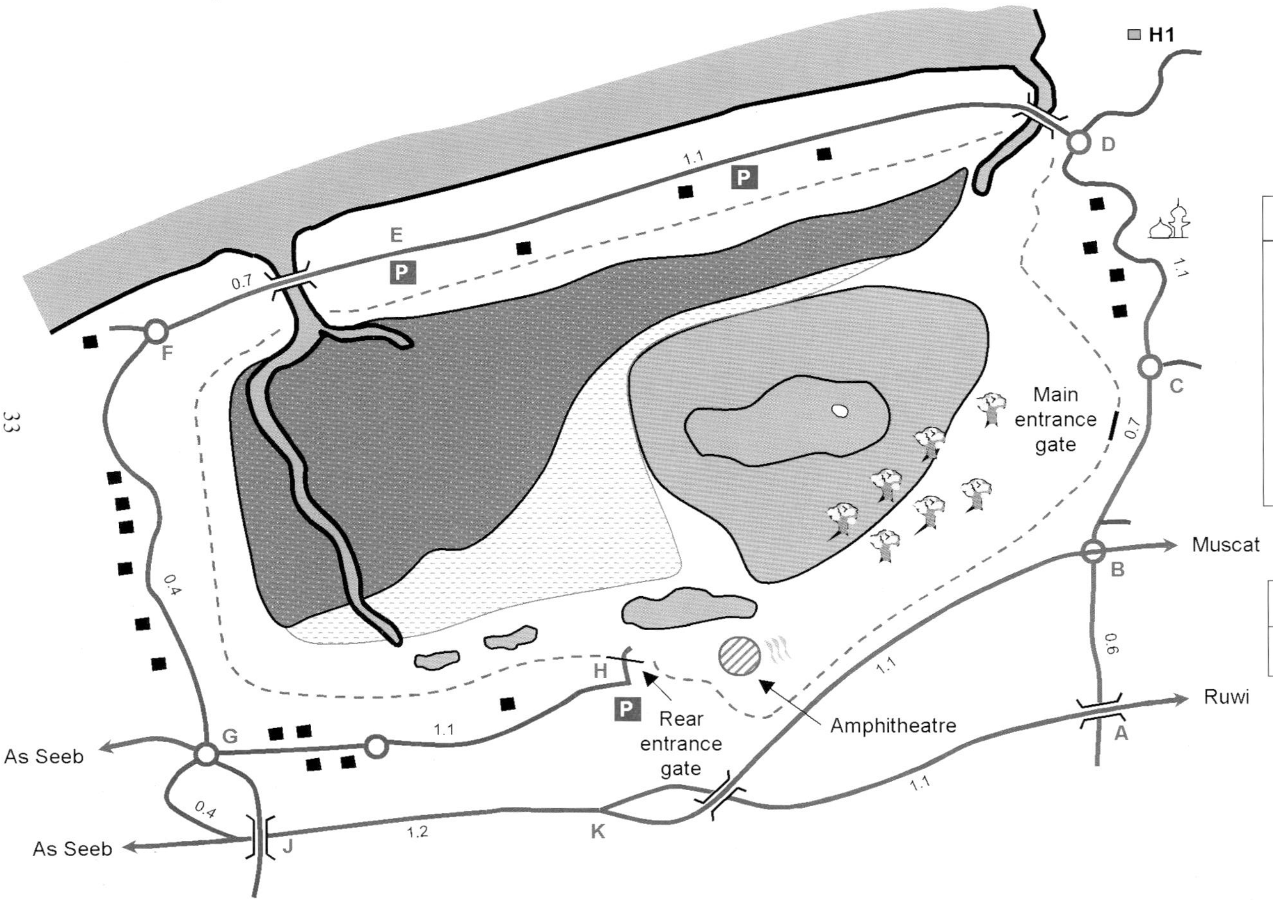

Waypoints and Coordinates

A	A84	N23 32.124	E58 30.716
B	T02	N23 37.043	E58 29.686
C	T01	N23 37.371	E58 29.508
D	T10	N23 37.561	E58 28.943
E	T09	N23 37.324	E58 28.425
F	T08	N23 37.115	E58 28.119
G	T05	N23 36.884	E58 28.262
H	T06	N23 36.975	E58 28.908
J	T04	N23 36.812	E58 28.361
K	T03	N23 36.867	E58 29.056

Accommodation

H1	Crowne Plaza

H1

Muscat

Ruwi

Main entrance gate

Amphitheatre

Rear entrance gate

As Seeb

As Seeb

1.1

0.7

0.6

1.1

1.4

1.1

1.1

1.2

1.1

0.4

0.4

0.7

33

1.3 Al Amrat Waste Disposal Site **   2WD

Key species: vultures, Greater Spotted Eagle, Steppe Eagle, Imperial Eagle, Hume's Wheatear, Red-tailed Wheatear, House Bunting, warblers, migrants.

With the closure of the old Sunub waste disposal site, Al Amrat has become the best place in the Capital Area to watch **eagles**. Dumping of offal from slaughterhouses is now, unfortunately, greatly reduced, which has resulted in falling numbers of **eagles**. However, from mid-October eagles commence arriving from Central Asia, peaking in the first half of November, with many over-wintering. **Egyptian Vulture** is always present in good numbers, with the occasional **Lappet-faced Vulture** as well.

Al Amrat Waste Disposal Site is not open to the public, though individual birdwatchers can ask politely at the gate, stating they simply wish to watch birds. Under no circumstance should the daily work at the site be interfered with. To avoid disappointment, however, a permit should be obtained in advance, especially by bird tour operators arriving in several cars or a minibus. Applications for a permit should be made at the nearby municipality office stating who is visiting and when. The office is located on the eastern side of the main road between Al Hajir roundabout and the turning to the waste disposal site, and can be recognized as the official-looking building with the Omani flag flying over it. Office hours are from 07h30 to 14h30, Saturday to Wednesday. A permit would normally take 24 hours to process. Local travel agents would not be expected to help in this with the exception of Siw Rantapää-Buring of Vision International (see **Tour operators**, p 13) who has assisted many bird tour groups and individuals.

The majority of **eagles** present will be **Steppe Eagles** of any age group which will be a challenge to sort out. Several **Greater Spotted** and a few **Imperial Eagles** can be found as well. Al Amrat is a good place to find the resident **Hume's Wheatear** and wintering **Red-tailed Wheatear**. These are best looked for shortly after the entrance where the access road crosses a shallow *wadi* with scattered trees on the rocky slopes. **Brown-necked Raven**, **House Bunting** and **Desert Lark** are common year-round. **Scrub Warbler** descending from the surrounding mountains has been seen in mid-winter.

Accommodation: hotel in Muscat.

Imperial Eagle, immature

Al Amrat Waste Disposal Site

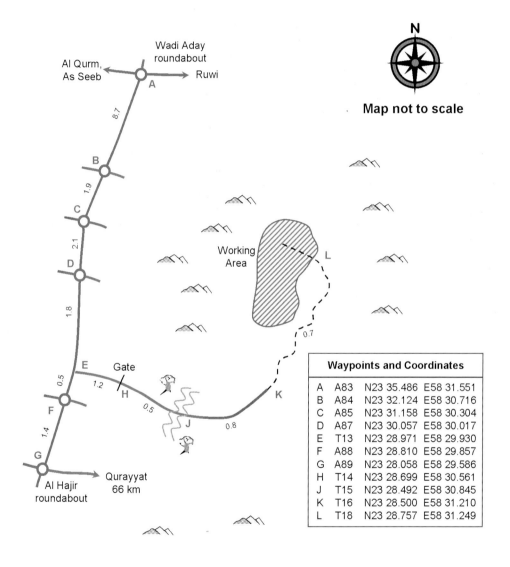

Wadi Aday roundabout

Al Qurm, As Seeb

Ruwi

A

8.7

B

1.9

C

2.1

D

1.8

E

0.5

Gate

1.2

H

0.5

F

1.4

J

0.8

G

Al Hajir roundabout

Qurayyat 66 km

Working Area

L

0.7

K

N

Map not to scale

Waypoints and Coordinates		
A	A83	N23 35.486 E58 31.551
B	A84	N23 32.124 E58 30.716
C	A85	N23 31.158 E58 30.304
D	A87	N23 30.057 E58 30.017
E	T13	N23 28.971 E58 29.930
F	A88	N23 28.810 E58 29.857
G	A89	N23 28.058 E58 29.586
H	T14	N23 28.699 E58 30.561
J	T15	N23 28.492 E58 30.845
K	T16	N23 28.500 E58 31.210
L	T18	N23 28.757 E58 31.249

1.4 Yiti *   2WD

Key species: herons, waders, Great Black-headed Gull, gulls, terns, Hume's Wheatear.

Yiti is a coastal village located about 20 km southeast of Muscat. The coastal lagoon is a convenient place to look for more common species of **herons**, **waders**, **gulls** and **terns** while the sandy beaches may hold additional species.

Yiti is reached from the capital area by turning off at Al Hamriyyah roundabout near Ruwi. Continue along the street, which would eventually become the one-way Ruwi High Street, but make a right turn after 0.9 km. This turn was formerly signed to Yiti, but currently no indication exists. Continue for a further kilometre along the narrow, winding street through the old town of Al Hamriyyah. After the last house the road climbs abruptly and after another 500 metres one might for all purposes be 500 km away from the city. This road is now paved all the way to Yiti, as well as farther down the coast toward As Sifah. The later half of this road runs though Wadi AlMayh, where migrants can be searched for in the many small farms, palms,
and other vegetation.

The lagoon should be scanned for **herons** and **waders** as sometimes unusual species turn up. Any of the rocky slopes with thin tree cover can hold **Hume's Wheatear**. The biggest attraction at Yiti, however, is undoubtedly the presence, sometimes in the hundreds, of **Great Black-headed Gull** from late-December to March. Several other species of **gulls** and **terns** may be present as well.

Note that this area is earmarked for future hotel and residental development, which might affect the attraction of the *khawr* to migrants and **waders**.

Accommodation: hotel in Muscat or Al-Moosa Beach Rest House in Yiti, right on the beach.

1.5 Hotel Gardens and Parkland *   2WD

Key species: White-cheeked Bulbul, Red-vented Bulbul, Hume's Wheatear, Blue Rock Thrush, migrants.

With the "greening" of Muscat over the past twenty five years many formerly barren areas, transformed into parks and gardens, now offer important havens for birds - residents and visitors alike. Some of the best are the gardens of the larger hotels at which many visitors will stay.

Close to Al Qurm Natural Park, the InterContinental Hotel garden has some larger trees, which are a major roost for **Ring-necked Parakeet**. Undoubtedly, the premier gardens for birdwatchers are those of Al Bustan Palace Hotel, 6 km south of Muscat, itself worth visiting simply to admire its grandeur and magnificent location. The gardens and adjacent scrub are most interesting during migration when **warblers**, **pipits** and **wheatears** occur. Rarer migrants appear with regularity, and have included **Koel**, **Wryneck** and **Spanish Sparrow**. In winter, **Hooded Wheatear**, **Long-billed Pipit**, and **Blue Rock Thrush** are possible. Likely resident species include **Hoopoe** and **White-cheeked** and **Red-vented Bulbul**. **Little Owl** has been heard from the surrounding hills. **Hume's Wheatear** can be found along the road to Qantab. A good spot to find it is around the viewpoint about one km from the beginning of the Qantab road. A right hand turn, 3.1 km farther leads down a *wadi* to Bandar Jissah, which has a good swimming beach. This *wadi* is relatively vegetated, attracts migrants, and holds **Sand Partridge**, **Little Owl**, **Lichtenstein's Sandgrouse**, and **Hume's Wheatear** in small numbers. **Desert Lesser Whitethroat** and **Blue Rock Thrush** are likely in winter.

From all beach-side hotels it is worth scanning the sea for passing **waders**, **gulls** and **terns**. Visitors staying near the harbour at Muttrah can visit Riyam Park at the eastern end of the Corniche, where the trees and lawns attract migrants during spring and autumn.

The Golden Tulip, across from As Seeb International Airport, has a number of trees, lawns and a variety of shrubs worthy of a quick look. In recent years **Red-vented Bulbul** has bred here.

Accommodation: hotel in Muscat.

Yiti

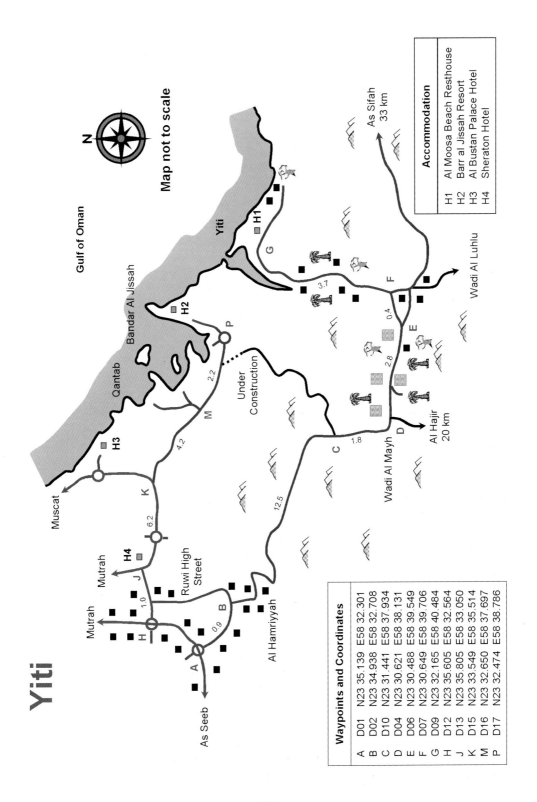

Gulf of Oman

Map not to scale

N

Muscat

Mutrah

Mutrah

As Seeb

Al Hamriyyah

Ruwi High Street

Qantab

Bandar Al Jissah

Yiti

Under Construction

Wadi Al Mayh

Wadi Al Luhlu

Al Hajir 20 km

As Sifah 33 km

H1
H2
H3
H4

Accommodation

H1	Al Moosa Beach Resthouse
H2	Barr al Jissah Resort
H3	Al Bustan Palace Hotel
H4	Sheraton Hotel

Waypoints and Coordinates

A	D01	N23 35.139	E58 32.301
B	D02	N23 34.938	E58 32.708
C	D10	N23 31.441	E58 37.934
D	D04	N23 30.621	E58 38.131
E	D06	N23 30.488	E58 39.549
F	D07	N23 30.649	E58 39.706
G	D09	N23 32.165	E58 40.484
H	D12	N23 35.605	E58 32.564
J	D13	N23 35.805	E58 33.050
K	D15	N23 33.549	E58 35.514
M	D16	N23 32.650	E58 37.697
P	D17	N23 32.474	E58 38.786

2 Al Batinah

Al Batinah, the coastal plain of northern Oman bordered to the west by Al Hajar Mountains, stretches from the Oman-UAE border southward as far as Naseem Park near Barka. Much of the natural habitat has been urbanised or converted into farmland and date plantations that attract large numbers of both resident and migratory birds. Common resident species include **Red-wattled Plover**, **Little Green Bee-eater**, **Crested Lark** and **Purple Sunbird**, as well as exotic introductions such as **Ring-necked Parakeet**, **Common Mynah** and **House Crow**.

Having a lengthy coastline, **ducks**, **herons**, **waders**, **gulls** and **terns** are a prominent part of the avifauna, especially during winter when huge numbers of **gulls** are present at the many small *khawrs* and inlets. Larger species such as **Egyptian Vulture**, **Spoonbill**, **Greater Flamingo** and **Osprey** are fairly numerous and conspicuous by their nature. In winter, several **eagle** species can be found all along Al Batinah, where they congregate at farmlands and waste disposal sites.

Importantly, a few areas of mangrove still remain, principally at Shinas and Liwa where the critically endangered local form of **White-collared Kingfisher** may be found. A small mangrove reforestation project recently started at Ras As Sawadi, has been doing well, though its future is unsure as this area is earmarked for tourist development.

The six sites described below are considered the best representative samples of shore, waterside, woodland and farmland habitats along Al Batinah, but are by no means exhaustive. Any well-wooded *wadi*, small *khawr* or well-watered field will attract resident and migrant species.

Listed below are common, widespread species easily found along Al Batinah. They are generally not discussed in the individual site accounts.

Common resident species:

Striated Heron	Swift Tern	Arabian Babbler
Western Reef Heron	Laughing Dove	Purple Sunbird
Egyptian Vulture	Ring-necked Parakeet	House Crow
Osprey	Little Green Bee-eater	Brown-necked Raven
Grey Francolin	Indian Roller	Common Mynah
Black-winged Stilt	Crested Lark	House Sparrow
Kentish Plover	African Rock Martin	Indian Silverbill
Red-wattled Plover	Yellow-vented Bulbul	
Sooty Gull	Graceful Prinia	

Common migrant and seasonal species:

Cormorant	Common Snipe
Cattle Egret	Bar-tailed Godwit
Little Egret	Whimbrel
Great White Egret	Curlew
Grey Heron	Spotted Redshank
Greater Flamingo	Redshank
Teal	Greenshank
Garganey	Wood Sandpiper
Marsh Harrier	Common Sandpiper
Ringed Plover	Slender-billed Gull
Lesser Sand Plover	Caspian Gull
Greater Sand Plover	Sandwich Tern
Grey Plover	Collared Dove
Sanderling	Pallid Swift
Little Stint	Barn Swallow
Curlew Sandpiper	Yellow Wagtail
Dunlin	White Wagtail
Ruff	Desert Wheatear

Osprey

Al Batinah

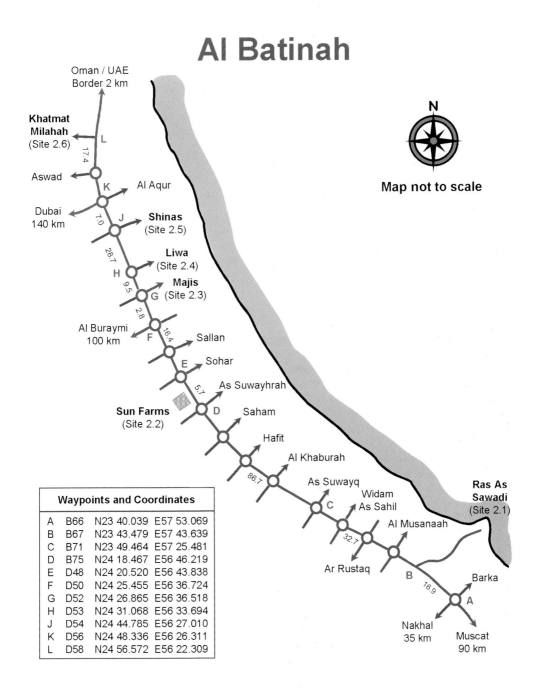

Oman / UAE
Border 2 km

**Khatmat
Milahah**
(Site 2.6)

L

17.4

Aswad

K

Al Aqur

Dubai
140 km

7.0

J

Shinas
(Site 2.5)

28.7

Liwa
(Site 2.4)

H

9.5

Majis
G (Site 2.3)

2.8

Al Buraymi
100 km

F

16.4

Sallan

E

Sohar

5.7

As Suwayhrah

Sun Farms
(Site 2.2)

D

Saham

Hafit

Al Khaburah

86.7

As Suwayq

Widam
As Sahil

C

Al Musanaah

32.7

Ar Rustaq

B

16.9

Barka

A

**Ras As
Sawadi**
(Site 2.1)

Nakhal
35 km

Muscat
90 km

N

Map not to scale

Waypoints and Coordinates			
A	B66	N23 40.039	E57 53.069
B	B67	N23 43.479	E57 43.639
C	B71	N23 49.464	E57 25.481
D	B75	N24 18.467	E56 46.219
E	D48	N24 20.520	E56 43.838
F	D50	N24 25.455	E56 36.724
G	D52	N24 26.865	E56 36.518
H	D53	N24 31.068	E56 33.694
J	D54	N24 44.785	E56 27.010
K	D56	N24 48.336	E56 26.311
L	D58	N24 56.572	E56 22.309

2.1 Ras As Sawadi *

Key species: Sooty Falcon, Great Black-headed Gull, Caspian Tern, Hoopoe Lark, Upcher's Warbler, Desert Warbler, Yellow-throated Sparrow, waders, terns.

Ras As Sawadi is a low-lying sandy headland, easily reached within an hour's drive, 90 km northwest of Muscat. The area is a favourite weekend destination with a safe swimming beach, small picnic area and As Sawadi Beach Resort offering recreational facilities and handy accommodation. Birdwatchers will find the hotel gardens of interest, especially during migration, as they are the only well-vegetated spot at the end of the spit. They are also one of the few sites in Oman where **Red-vented Bulbul** can be found reliably.

A series of rocky islands just offshore can be visited by asking one of the boatmen to take you across. Expect to pay about RO 6 for a return trip. The largest and closest island is the most interesting, and holds a few **Sooty Falcons** from late-April to early-November, and frequently a few migrants. A climb to the fortification at the top provides excellent views across the surrounding area as well as a good sea-watching vantage point from which **Persian Shearwater** and **Red-billed Tropicbird** are occasionally seen.

If undisturbed, the beaches, and especially the mouth of the small *khawr* 0.9 km to the south, hold a variety of **waders**, and frequently large numbers of **gulls** and **terns**. **Great Black-headed Gull** is present from December to March, and **Caspian**, **Gull-billed**, and **White-cheeked Tern** are regular. The dunes behind the *khawr* are one of the few sites on Al Batinah coast where **Hoopoe Lark** is found regularly. A few tracks, to the south of the village, crossing the low dunes can be explored with 4WD.

The road from the main highway to Ras As Sawadi, runs through a series of small settlements,

As Sawadi Island

behind which the habitat, to the west of the road, is well-wooded. The best spot is the large area of **Ghaf** *Prosopis cineraria* trees on the left having turned off the highway. Anywhere here is worth exploring for migrants, such as **Upcher's Warbler** that can be expected in early May. Winter visitors include **Peregrine** and **Barbary Falcon**, various **eagles** and both **Ménétries's** and **Desert Warbler**. From late-April to July, **Yellow-throated Sparrow** breeds.

As Sawadi Beach Resort arranges regular dive trips out to the Daymaniyat Islands, 25 km offshore. In summer, these provide an opportunity to see **Red-billed Tropicbird**, **Wilson's Storm-petrel**, **Sooty Falcon** and the large numbers of breeding **Bridled Tern**, as well as do some snorkelling. Note that the islands contain strictly protected seabird colonies and turtle nesting beaches, so boat landings are not permitted.

The whole Sawadi area is earmarked for a massive tourist development in the near future with hotels, marina and a golf course all planned.

Accommodation: As Sawadi Beach Resort or a hotel in Muscat or Sohar.

Ras As Sawadi

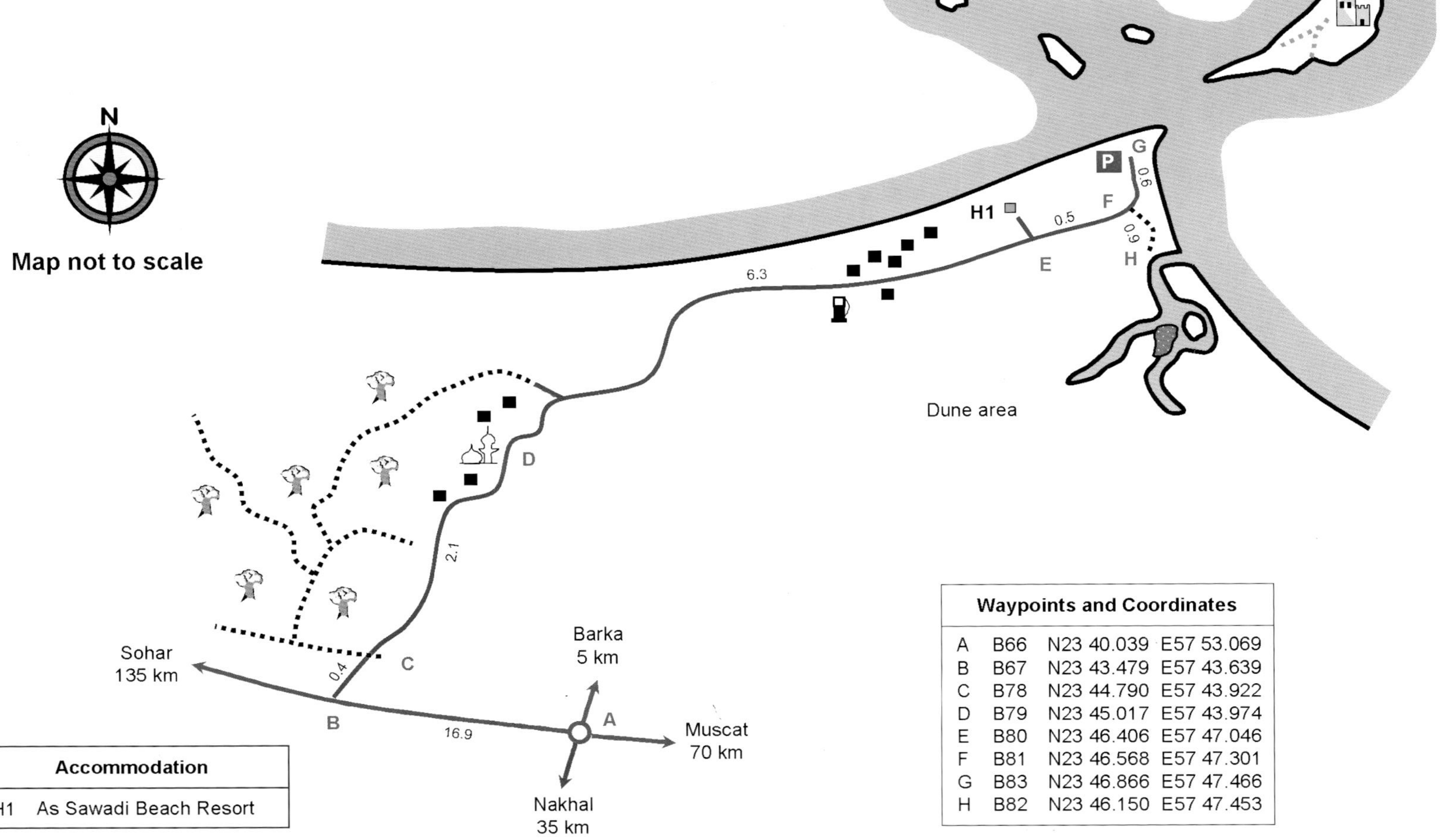

N
Map not to scale
P
G
0.6
F
0.5
H1
E
0.9
H
6.3
Dune area
D
2.1
C
0.4
B
16.9
A
Sohar
135 km
Barka
5 km
Muscat
70 km
Nakhal
35 km

Accommodation	
H1	As Sawadi Beach Resort

Waypoints and Coordinates

A	B66	N23 40.039	E57 53.069
B	B67	N23 43.479	E57 43.639
C	B78	N23 44.790	E57 43.922
D	B79	N23 45.017	E57 43.974
E	B80	N23 46.406	E57 47.046
F	B81	N23 46.568	E57 47.301
G	B83	N23 46.866	E57 47.466
H	B82	N23 46.150	E57 47.453

2.2 Sun Farms, Sohar ***

Key species: Cattle Egret, eagles, Lesser Kestrel, Cream-coloured Courser, Collared Pratincole, Sociable Plover, White-tailed Plover, other waders, terns, doves, bee-eaters, rollers, Bimaculated Lark, other larks, swallows, pipits, wagtails, wheatears, shrikes, starlings, Corn Bunting.

The extensive grasslands at Sun Farms attract a multitude of both resident and migratory birds and comprise easily the most important birdwatching site on Al Batinah. During migration and winter a full day here should produce 70-80 species some of which are difficult to find elsewhere in the country. **Small Skylark** and **Blyth's Pipit** are probably overlooked elsewhere, but are both reported regularly from here. A full day is needed to give justice to this excellent area.

Sun Farms is privately owned and thus not open to the public. A visit requires a permit which must be applied for well in advance, especially if a larger birdwatching group hopes to visit. The written application should be addressed to the Farm Manager, Sun Farm, P. O. Box 66, Sohar 311, fax 2584 2363, email: oadc@omzest.com, and should include names of visitors and date and time of the proposed visit. Local travel agent and tour operator Siw Rantapää-Buring (see **Tour operators**, p 13) has been able to obtain permits for birdwatching groups in the past. The farm has welcomed birdwatchers provided the normal work on the farm is not obstructed. Individuals or small groups of birdwatchers may be able to enter the farm by just turning up at the gate. As a courtesy a letter of thanks should be sent to the farm after the visit, perhaps with a list of the birds seen.

The huge farm has a number of fields irrigated either by central pivots or piped irrigation. A paved road gives access to all fields and it is possible to drive around each field on tracks, though some can be rough or dusty. Do not drive on the fields themselves. Recently-cut grassy fields are the most interesting from a birdwatching point of view, but other crops attract birds as well. The settling ponds at the cow sheds near the entrance to the farm always hold interesting species.

White Wagtail *personata*

The grassy fields are excellent for **Pacific Golden**, **Sociable** and **White-tailed Plover** during migration and in winter with **Caspian Plover** a possibility in autumn. **Lapwing** has been seen on a number of occasions in winter and **Cream-coloured Courser** is always a possibility. Large numbers of **larks**, **pipits** and **wagtails** can be present as well, including **Bimaculated Lark**, **Skylark**, **Small Skylark**, **Richard's**, **Blyth's** and **Red-throated Pipit** and **Citrine Wagtail**, in addition to the ubiquitous **Crested Lark**, **Black-crowned Finch Lark** and **Tawny Pipit**. The distinctive *personata* race of **White Wagtail** and several races of **Yellow Wagtail** should be looked for, especially in the cow pens. **Starling**, **Rose-coloured Starling** and **Corn Bunting** are found regularly. **Raptors** such as **Greater Spotted** and **Imperial Eagle** as well as **Saker** and **Peregrine Falcon** often put in an appearance. Large numbers of **Marsh** and **Montagu's Harriers** may be present as well as a few **Pallid Harriers**. **Cattle Egret** is found in increasing numbers near the cow sheds and the settling ponds where both **Whiskered** and **White-winged Black Terns** occur as well. **Wheatears** of several species can be found with **Isabelline** and **Desert Wheatear** being the most common.

In early spring **Quail** is heard and sometimes seen. **Blue-cheeked** and **European Bee-eaters** arrive in mid to late-March and sometimes nest side by side in the waste disposal area reached on the track across from the big barn in the middle of the farm. **Lesser Kestrel** may be seen hovering over the fields in April when up to 150 have been seen. Good numbers of **European Roller** in addition to the abundant, resident **Indian Roller** can be seen in April and May when also **Turtle Dove** mix with the thousands of **Collared Doves**.

Accommodation: hotel in Sohar.

Sun Farms, Sohar

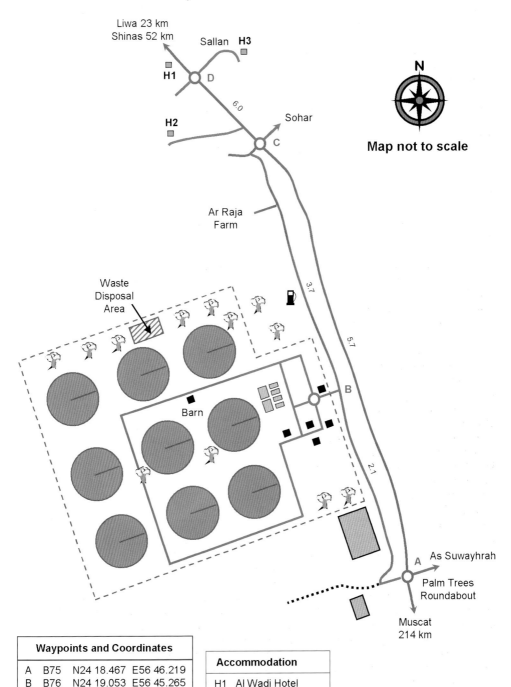

Liwa 23 km
Shinas 52 km

Sallan **H3**

H1 D

H2

6.0

Sohar

N

Map not to scale

Ar Raja
Farm

3.7

Waste
Disposal
Area

5.7

Barn

B

2.1

As Suwayhrah

A

Palm Trees
Roundabout

Muscat
214 km

Waypoints and Coordinates			
A	B75	N24 18.467	E56 46.219
B	B76	N24 19.053	E56 45.265
C	D48	N24 20.520	E56 43.838
D	D49	N24 23.065	E56 42.081

Accommodation	
H1	Al Wadi Hotel
H2	Green Oasis Hotel
H3	Sohar Beach Hotel

Key species: gulls, terns, Blue-cheeked Bee-eater, migrants.

Majis is typical of many of the small towns and villages along Al Batinah, in having a fair amount of fishing activity along the beach, accompanied inland by a selection of small farming plots, scrub and fields. Large areas of similar habitat have been lost to large scale developments such as the Sohar Port to the north, but those remaining are worth investigating, time permitting.

Majis can be visited as a short detour when travelling between Muscat and sites around Sohar and further north. Turning off at the Sohar Port, the paved road skirts the port with a series of open fields, farms and larger trees immediately adjacent to the road that can be explored on foot. Once at the beach a track runs for more than two kilometres, past numerous fishing boats, and at the right time of day, when fisherman are returning, is a magnet for scavenging **gulls**. Good numbers of **gulls** and **terns**, including **White-cheeked** and **Bridled Tern** in summer, are usually present offshore. After 2.5 km, a rough track can be followed through a variety of scrub and fields, looping back to the main highway. **Blue-cheeked Bee-eater** breed in the area, and can readily be found between late April and September. Any trees, scrub and fields should be checked for migrant **warblers**, **shrikes**, **flycatchers**, **pipits**, **larks** and **buntings**. This area has not been well explored, as most visitors pass by to better-known sites farther north.

Accommodation: camping or a hotel in Sohar.

Blue-cheeked Bee-eater

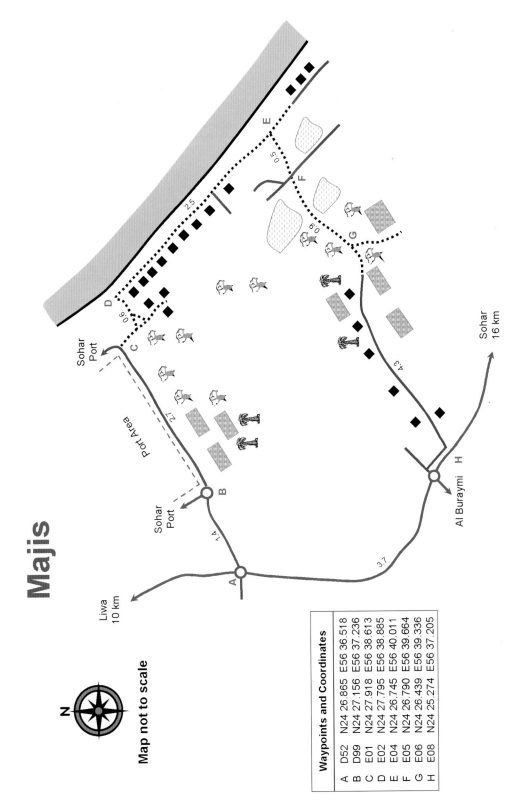

Majis

Map not to scale

N

Liwa
10 km

Sohar
Port

Sohar
Port

Port Area

Sohar
Port

Sohar
16 km

Al Buraymi

A

B

C

D

E

F

G

H

1.4

2.7

0.6

2.5

0.5

0.9

4.3

3.7

Waypoints and Coordinates		
A	D52	N24 26.865 E56 36.518
B	D99	N24 27.156 E56 37.236
C	E01	N24 27.918 E56 38.613
D	E02	N24 27.795 E56 38.885
E	E04	N24 26.745 E56 40.011
F	E05	N24 26.790 E56 39.664
G	E06	N24 26.439 E56 39.336
H	E08	N24 25.274 E56 37.205

Key species: Indian Pond Heron, White-collared Kingfisher, Sykes's Warbler.

The mangroves just north of the village of Liwa, 30 km north of Sohar, are important as one of the few remaining places for the critically endangered *kalbaensis* race of the **White-collared Kingfisher**. In recent years sightings here have increased, while those at Shinas have decreased, and the bird might now breed here, although in very small numbers as the mangroves are not extensive.

White-collared Kingfisher

Access is via the paved road to the north, just before Liwa village. An early morning visit is advisable to minimise possible disturbance from the adjacent picnic site. The most likely area for the kingfisher is the beach side of the mangrove, northward from the picnic area. The inlet reached after 1.1 km should have a fair collection of **gulls** and **terns** present.

The other speciality of the Liwa mangroves is **Sykes's Warbler** which breeds in small numbers but is often located only by song. Look out also for **Indian Pond Heron**, especially in winter. Other, unexpected species have been observed including **Water Rail**.

The track branching off northwest just before the picnic site curves around the opposite side of the mangroves, but does not provide close approach and the mangroves are rather small and have recently been fenced. Species in this open area will include **Greater Spotted Eagle**, **Black-crowned Finch Lark**, and **Desert Wheatear**. A large northbound migration of **terns** can be witnessed in late April including **Little Tern**.

The beach at Liwa fishing village should be checked in winter for **gulls**, **terns** and **waders**. Accommodation: camping or a hotel in Sohar.

Liwa

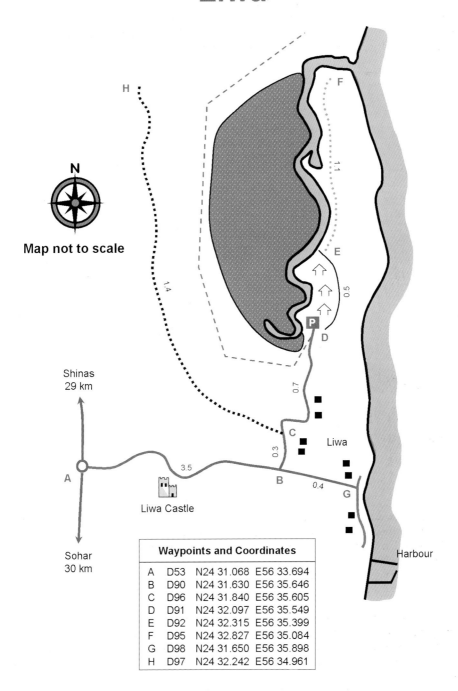

Map not to scale

Shinas
29 km

Sohar
30 km

Liwa Castle

Liwa

Harbour

Waypoints and Coordinates			
A	D53	N24 31.068	E56 33.694
B	D90	N24 31.630	E56 35.646
C	D96	N24 31.840	E56 35.605
D	D91	N24 32.097	E56 35.549
E	D92	N24 32.315	E56 35.399
F	D95	N24 32.827	E56 35.084
G	D98	N24 31.650	E56 35.898
H	D97	N24 32.242	E56 34.961

2.5 Shinas ** 2WD/4WD

Key species: Indian Pond Heron, Great Stone Plover, Great Black-headed Gull, Namaqua Dove, White-collared Kingfisher, Sykes's Warbler.

The small, but rapidly expanding, fishing town of Shinas, 60 km north of Sohar, supports a variety of **terns**, **gulls**, and **waders** attracted to the surrounding series of inlets and mudflats. The small area of mangrove is the only site in northern Oman, other than Liwa, for the two mangrove specialities: **White-collared Kingfisher** and **Sykes's Warbler**.

To find the kingfisher, plan to start early morning at the mangrove, when the bird is most likely to be vocal. Low tide is preferred, as the mud exposed at the base of the mangrove entices the bird into the open to feed. The best views of the mangrove edge are obtained from the picnic site. In recent years sightings of this species have become less frequent, and the new development adjacent is likely to have an even greater impact on the status of this species in Oman.

The easiest access is the paved road 5.5 km south of Shinas. Beware of the surrounding *sabkha*

Great Stone Plover

flats, which after rain are impassible even to 4WD. The flats are good for **Chestnut-bellied Sandgrouse, Black-crowned Finch Lark** and the occasional **Desert Warbler**.

The outlet here is usually packed with **gulls** and **terns**, that should include **Lesser Crested Tern**, and in late winter, good numbers of **Great Black-headed Gull**. Scan the drier sand banks, just above the high tide line for **Great Stone Plover**, one or more of which have wintered in this spot most years. The scattered **waders** are likely to include both **Greater** and **Lesser Sand Plovers**, as well as **Terek Sandpiper**.

At low tide the exposed mud around the mangrove is a good place to find **Indian Pond Heron**, though **Squacco Heron** also occurs to add confusion. Look also inside the mangroves for the uncommon and highly localised **Sykes's Warbler**, most easily located by song between February and May.

Back toward Shinas, explore any areas of scrub and fields. **Namaqua Dove** is regular in this area and probably breeds. Various **wheatears**, including **Pied Wheatear** occur on migration.

The harbour at Shinas, as with all harbours along Al Batinah coast, will have large flocks of wintering **gulls**, and the series of tidal lagoons both sides of the town hold numerous **waders**, with **Crab Plover** a regular visitor.

North of the town toward Khatmat Milahah, the road crosses a *wadi* that can be accessed by a dirt track beside the petrol station. Depending on the water level, the *khawr* holds a variety of **ducks**, **herons**, **waders** and **terns**. The dense area of trees just to the south of the *khawr* is good for migrant **warblers**, and probably holds resident **Striated Scops Owl**. Unless there has been recent rain, the whole area can be driven on the numerous tracks, even with 2WD.

Accommodation: camping or a hotel in Sohar.

Shinas

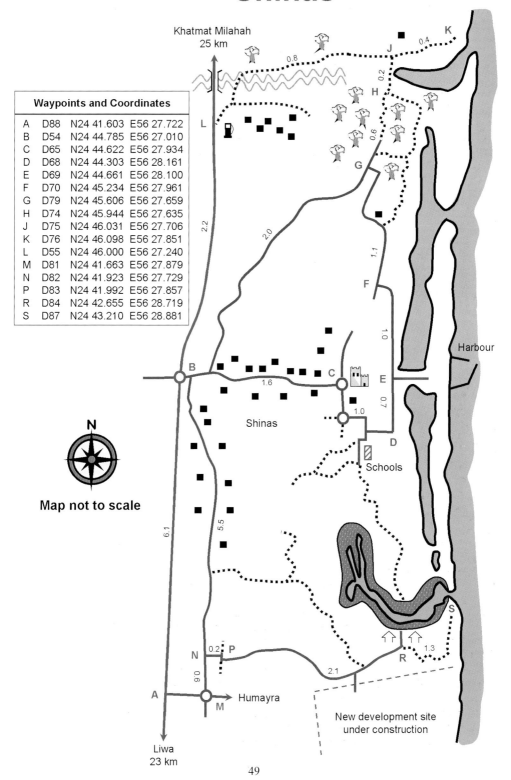

Khatmat Milahah
25 km

Waypoints and Coordinates			
A	D88	N24 41.603	E56 27.722
B	D54	N24 44.785	E56 27.010
C	D65	N24 44.622	E56 27.934
D	D68	N24 44.303	E56 28.161
E	D69	N24 44.661	E56 28.100
F	D70	N24 45.234	E56 27.961
G	D79	N24 45.606	E56 27.659
H	D74	N24 45.944	E56 27.635
J	D75	N24 46.031	E56 27.706
K	D76	N24 46.098	E56 27.851
L	D55	N24 46.000	E56 27.240
M	D81	N24 41.663	E56 27.879
N	D82	N24 41.923	E56 27.729
P	D83	N24 41.992	E56 27.857
R	D84	N24 42.655	E56 28.719
S	D87	N24 43.210	E56 28.881

N

Map not to scale

Harbour

Shinas

Schools

Humayra

New development site
under construction

Liwa
23 km

49

Key species: Striated Scops Owl, Plain Leaf Warbler, Desert Lesser Whitethroat, Ménétries's Warbler, Orphean Warbler, Eastern Pied Wheatear, Yellow-throated Sparrow.

The tree-studded plain at Khatmat Milahah is important for two key species - **Eastern Pied Wheatear** and **Plain Leaf Warbler** - as it forms the most southerly site where both winter regularly. Although very arid, underground water, fed from the mountains, supports a sizeable area of larger trees as well as small arable patches important to the local population, human, goat and camel alike.

Being just a couple of km south of the Oman - UAE border and 300 km from Muscat, this is the most northerly point that visitors are likely to visit, unless venturing to Musandam. A rough track, 200 metres north of the paved road into the village, drivable by 2WD, gives access to the area, which is best explored on foot. The first kilometre of this track, with the larger **Ghaf** *Prosopis cineraria* trees is the best. This site is best visited early in the day before it gets too hot and activity slows.

If camping, Khatmat Milahah is one of the prime sites in Oman for **Striated Scops Owl**, although getting to grips with it can be frustrating, as the area is large. Unless calling they are almost impossible to find, but when they do so, it is usually possible to walk right up to them. The call, a soft "hoo" spaced at about one-second intervals, carries far, but has a quality that makes the bird appear much farther away than it is. The main calling season is from late-January to April, with birds mostly vocal from 21h00 to 22h00 and 02h00 to 04h00.

Timing of a visit to Khatmat Milahah can be crucial. Both **Eastern Pied Wheatear** and **Plain Leaf Warbler** rarely arrive before November or stay beyond early-March. Other regular winter visitors to be expected are **Ménétries's**, **Orphean** and **Desert Warbler**, **Desert Lesser Whitethroat** and **Black Redstart**. Keep an eye out for **Stone Curlew** that sometimes winter in the area. **Raptors** recorded with regularity include **Lappet-faced Vulture**, **Bonelli's** and **Short-toed Eagle** and **Sparrowhawk**. During migration, **pipits**, **warblers**, **shrikes** and **wheatears** occur - the latter comprising **Northern**, **Isabelline**, **Desert**, **Pied** and **Red-tailed Wheatear**. **Barn Owl** is probably resident in the area, as is **Lichtenstein's Sandgrouse** on the stony plains farther along the track together with **Black-crowned Finch Lark**. For those visiting during the hotter months, **Yellow-throated Sparrow** breeds from April to July.

Accommodation: camping or a hotel in Sohar.

Khatmat Milahah

Khatmat Milahah

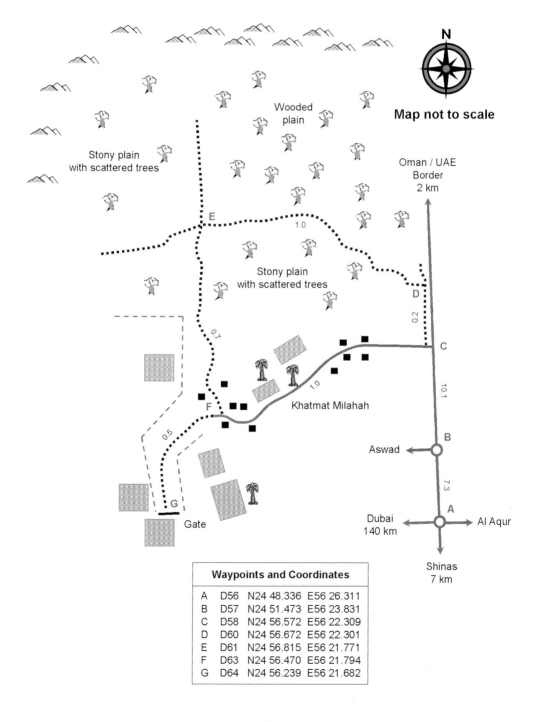

Waypoints and Coordinates			
A	D56	N24 48.336	E56 26.311
B	D57	N24 51.473	E56 23.831
C	D58	N24 56.572	E56 22.309
D	D60	N24 56.672	E56 22.301
E	D61	N24 56.815	E56 21.771
F	D63	N24 56.470	E56 21.794
G	D64	N24 56.239	E56 21.682

3 The Northeast Coast

Due to a mixture of rocky coasts, sandy beaches and tidal lagoons, the northeast coast, from Qurayyat via Wadi Ash Shab, Tiwi, Sur, Ras Al Hadd and south toward Al Ashkharah, holds some interesting places for the birdwatcher. Ras Al Hadd and nearby Ras Al Jinz are famous for their turtle beaches where 20,000 **Green Turtles** *Chelonia mydas* come ashore each year to lay their eggs, principally between August and December. Nearby Khawr Jirama is the most reliable place in Oman, outside the Barr Al Hikman - Masirah area, to find **Crab Plover**. The cliffs at Ras Al Khabbah are an excellent place to watch the autumn and spring migrations of **waders**, **gulls** and **terns**, as well as good for observing pelagic **seabirds**.

Although Qurayyat is easily covered on a one-day trip from the Capital area, Ras Al Hadd and nearby sites require more time. A two day round trip taking the inland route through Ibra and Al Kamil and returning via Sur and Tiwi makes for an exciting journey through magnificent scenery. **Lappet-faced Vulture** is regularly seen near Ibra and a waste disposal site at Al Mintirib often holds **Greater Spotted**, **Steppe** and **Imperial Eagle** in winter. **Whales** and **dolphins** have regularly been observed from land at Ras Al Hadd and Ras Al Khabbah, though a telescope will be needed to identify the species. **Indian Roller** and **House Crow**, while abundant along Al Batinah coast find their eastern and southernmost distribution near Sur.

Listed below are common, widespread species easily found along the northeast coast. These are generally not discussed in the individual site accounts.

Common resident species:

Western Reef Heron	Indian Roller	Purple Sunbird
Sooty Gull	Crested Lark	House Crow
Swift Tern	African Rock Martin	Brown-necked Raven
Laughing Dove	Yellow-vented Bulbul	House Sparrow
Little Green Bee-eater	Graceful Prinia	Indian Silverbill

Common migrant and seasonal species:

Little Egret	Collared Dove	White Wagtail
Great White Egret	Barn Swallow	Desert Wheatear
Grey Heron	Yellow Wagtail	Spotted Flycatcher
Greater Flamingo		
Osprey		
Ringed Plover		
Lesser Sand Plover		
Greater Sand Plover		
Grey Plover		
Sanderling		
Little Stint		
Curlew Sandpiper		
Dunlin		
Bar-tailed Godwit		
Whimbrel		
Curlew		
Redshank		
Greenshank		
Whimbrel		
Curlew		
Common Sandpiper		
Slender-billed Gull		
Caspian Gull		
Sandwich Tern		

Great Black-headed Gull

52

Northeast Coast

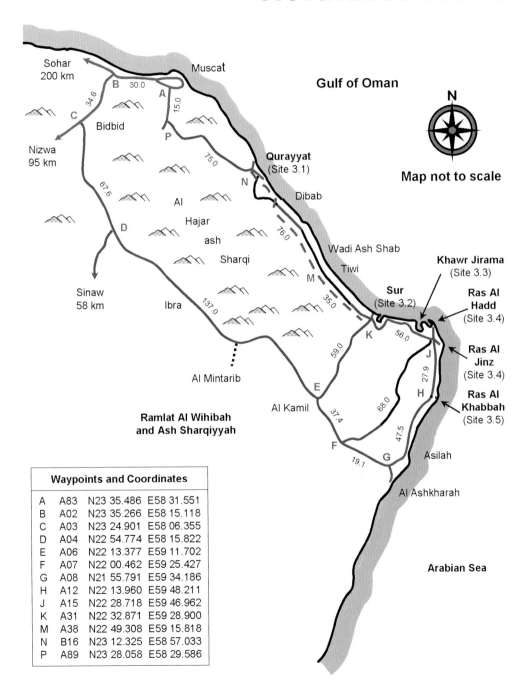

Sohar
200 km

Muscat

Gulf of Oman

N

Map not to scale

B 30.0

A

34.6

C

15.0

Bidbid

P

Nizwa
95 km

75.0

Qurayyat
(Site 3.1)

N

Dibab

67.6

Al

Hajar

D

ash

76.0

Wadi Ash Shab

Sharqi

Tiwi

M

Khawr Jirama
(Site 3.3)

Sinaw
58 km

Ibra

137.0

35.0

Sur
(Site 3.2)

**Ras Al
Hadd**
(Site 3.4)

K

56.0

59.0

J

**Ras Al
Jinz**
(Site 3.4)

Al Mintarib

E

27.9

H

**Ras Al
Khabbah**
(Site 3.5)

Al Kamil

37.4

68.0

**Ramlat Al Wihibah
and Ash Sharqiyyah**

F

47.5

G

Asilah

19.1

Al Ashkharah

Arabian Sea

Waypoints and Coordinates			
A	A83	N23 35.486	E58 31.551
B	A02	N23 35.266	E58 15.118
C	A03	N23 24.901	E58 06.355
D	A04	N22 54.774	E58 15.822
E	A06	N22 13.377	E59 11.702
F	A07	N22 00.462	E59 25.427
G	A08	N21 55.791	E59 34.186
H	A12	N22 13.960	E59 48.211
J	A15	N22 28.718	E59 46.962
K	A31	N22 32.871	E59 28.900
M	A38	N22 49.308	E59 15.818
N	B16	N23 12.325	E58 57.033
P	A89	N23 28.058	E58 29.586

Key species: Persian Shearwater, Indian Pond Heron, Sand Partridge, Avocet, Great Black-headed Gull, Caspian Tern, Gull-billed Tern, Roseate Tern, Black-crowned Finch Lark, House Bunting.

Qurayyat, a rapidly-expanding fishing town on the northeast coast, can be visited either as a day trip from Muscat or as part of a longer trip down the coastal road to Ras Al Hadd (3.4) and Khawr Jirama (3.3), via Tiwi and Sur. From Muscat it is an easy one-hour drive through the scenic foothills of the eastern Al Hajar Mountains. This road crosses many *wadis*, offering interesting stops en route. One attractive spot is the extensive, tree-covered Wadi Hayfadh, around the 40 km marker from Qurayyat, where regular visitors such as **Desert Lesser Whitethroat, Olivaceous Warbler, Rufous Bush Chat** and **shrikes** can be expected. **Striated Scops Owl** and **Lichtenstein's Sandgrouse** are resident here and might be worth searching for around dusk. At Sawaqm, 20 km from Qurayyat, those with a 4WD can choose the cross-country route through Wadi Mijlas, the entrance to which is the huge canyon, clearly visible, to the north of the road. Simply follow the *wadi* to Qurayyat, along which **Hume's Wheatear** and **House Bunting** are relatively common, as well as **Red-tailed Wheatear** in winter.

The varied habitats around Qurayyat often produce a sizable daily species tally. A series of small *khawrs* is interspersed with woodland, scrub and farmland, plus a waste disposal site for added variety.

Starting in Qurayyat town itself, the beach and harbour are usually packed with gulls - **Caspian, Siberian**, and **Slender-billed Gull** in winter, **Sooty Gull** in summer. The few sand bars in the harbour should have roosting **terns** and **waders**. The mangroves at the northern end of town are rather degraded, but the beach and small inlet, north of the harbour, will have **waders** and **herons**.

Retrace your steps through town, turn left at the park 1.3 km from the fort, and head back toward the harbour. After 0.8 km take the wide dirt track to the beach. The beach at point **E** is the favoured spot for roosting **gulls** and **terns**. From December to March **Great Black-headed Gull** is common. In summer most **gulls**, other than **Sooty**, will have departed, although stragglers sometimes remain. **Terns** are usually present in good numbers, mostly **Sandwich, Swift**, and **Lesser Crested** with the occasional **Caspian Tern**. **White-cheeked Tern** is common in summer. **Skuas**, attracted to the large gull and tern concentrations can often be seen offshore.

Khawr Al Milh attracts a selection of **waders**, and is the most regular site for **Avocet** in north Oman. It also attracts roosting **terns** that, from June to August, include small numbers of **Roseate Tern**. The dunes on the south side of the *khawr* are good for **Black-crowned Finch Lark**.

Khawr Al Khubar is quite disturbed, with usually few birds, but is worth a scan in passing, with **Indian Pond Heron** regular in winter. In contrast, Khawr Al Mahadin and its adjacent trees are well worth checking. This *khawr* is a regular wintering spot for **Striated Heron** and the trees inevitably attract a host of migrant **warblers** and others such as **Hoopoe** and **Wryneck**. The dunes behind, with their low scrub, are a good place to find **Desert Warbler** in winter.

Khawr Sallan has the largest areas of mud and attracts **waders**, including **Crab Plover**. The *khawr* next to the small fishing village at Daghmar is usually barren, though sea-watching from the beach in summer can produce **Wilson's Storm-petrel, Persian Shearwater, Bridled Tern**, sometimes **Roseate Tern** and rarely **Jouanin's Petrel, Pale-footed Shearwater** or **Lesser Noddy**.

In winter, the rubbish tip is not to be missed. **Steppe Eagle** and **Greater Spotted Eagle** are fairly common, and **Imperial Eagle** usually present.

Another area worthy of investigation is the *wadi* west of the rubbish tip. The *wadi* has only low scrub, but is good for **Desert Lark, Sand Partridge, Red-tailed Wheatear** and **House Bunting**.

Lastly, the trees and fields around the very distinctive conical hill, **U** on the map, are well worth checking. In winter, the larger trees have **Orphean Warbler** and **Isabelline Shrike**. The fields can be good for **pipits** and **wagtails**. In winter **raptors** such as **Bonelli's, Greater Spotted** and **Short-toed Eagle** plus **Peregrine** and **Barbary Falcon** are occasionally recorded.

Those with additional time and a 4WD can follow the scenic coast road toward Sur. Allow at least three hours for the drive excluding stops. Any of the *wadis* or small fields en route is worth exploring, and **Red-tailed Wheatear** is common in winter, as is **Hume's Wheatear** and **Desert Lark**. The twenty or so km stretch of stony plains after Dibab, 35 km from Qurayyat, is good for **Mountain Gazelle, Desert**

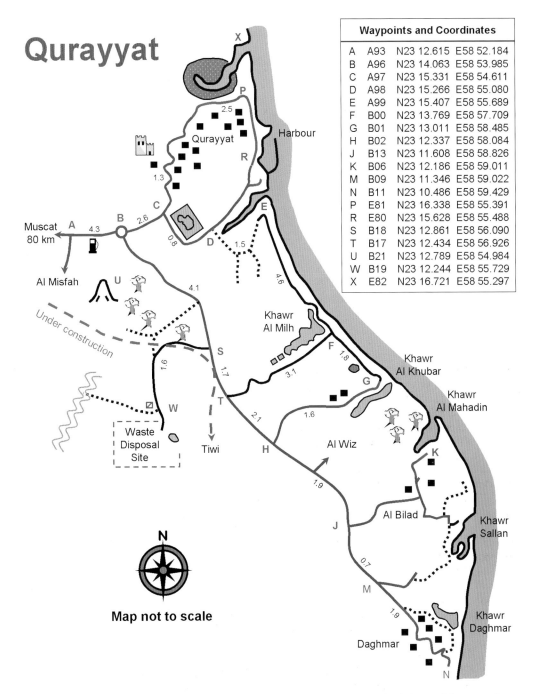

Qurayyat

Muscat
80 km

Al Misfah

Qurayyat

Harbour

Khawr
Al Milh

Khawr
Al Khubar

Khawr
Al Mahadin

Al Wiz

Khawr
Sallan

Waste
Disposal
Site

Tiwi

Al Bilad

Under construction

Khawr
Daghmar

Daghmar

Map not to scale

N

Warbler and **Lichtenstein's Sandgrouse**. The magnificent gorge at Wadi Ash Shab, two kilometres from Tiwi, can be hiked in less than an hour and holds **Bonelli's Eagle**.

The construction of a dual carriageway between Muscat and Sur, via Qurayyat, is well advanced, and will result in a massive increase of traffic along this coastal route. The actual route across the Qurayyat map is unknown at the time of writing, but will likely be across the plain between points **U** and **S** on the map, joining with the new Tiwi road.

Accommodation: camping or a hotel in Muscat.

3.2 Sur Lagoon and Sewage Treatment Plant *   2WD

Key species: ducks, seabirds, waders, gulls, terns, migrants.

Sur is the main town of northeastern Oman. It has a proud history of construction of traditional boats (*dhows*) that can still be seen today near the landing site of the passenger ferry to Al Ayjah. The main attraction for birdwatchers, however, is the beach between the boat factory and the harbour as well as the tidal mudflats and exposed sand banks in Sur lagoon.

The lagoon always holds a variety of **herons**, **waders**, **gulls** and **terns** including **Terek Sandpiper** and **Caspian Tern**. It is also a good locality for observing **Striated Heron**, a common species that can be difficult to locate at times. Excellent views of the lagoon can be obtained from the Corniche road in Sur or along the ten kilometre paved road to Al Ayjah.

In autumn fishermen can be seen hauling hundreds of huge tuna onto the beach just east of the new harbour. The tuna hunt sardines offshore, which are in turn followed by **seabirds**. Here, as at Ras Al Hadd, taking a boat offshore will likely produce some interesting pelagic species at the right time of year. Boats can be negotiated with the local fishermen.

The small sewage treatment plant, a few kilometres west of Sur, can be interesting, especially following rains, when temporary pools attract **grebes**, **ducks** and **waders**. The surrounding scrub usually holds migrants and other winter visitors including **warblers**, **wagtails** and **pipits**. The settling ponds themselves are concrete, so tend not to be particularly productive. However, several of these are congested with reeds, which consequently attract **Clamorous Reed Warbler**, and hold breeding **Moorhen**. The sewage

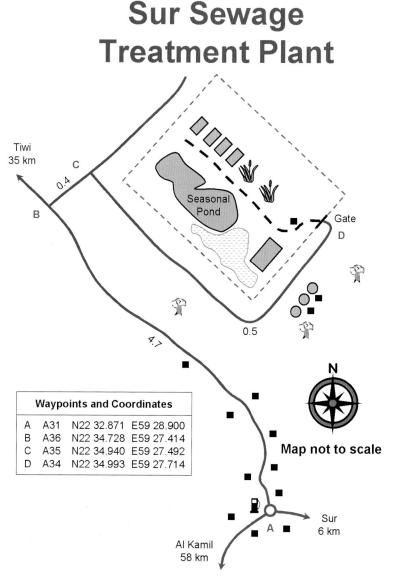

Waypoints and Coordinates

A	A31	N22 32.871	E59 28.900
B	A36	N22 34.728	E59 27.414
C	A35	N22 34.940	E59 27.492
D	A34	N22 34.993	E59 27.714

Tiwi 35 km

Seasonal Pond

Gate

Map not to scale

Sur 6 km

Al Kamil 58 km

Sur

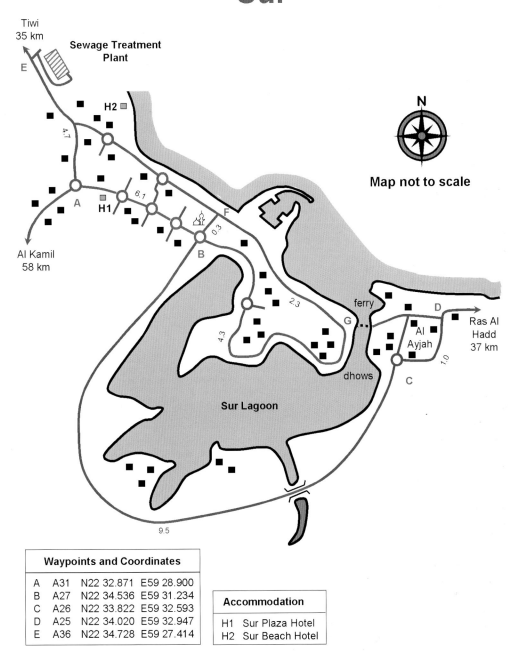

Tiwi
35 km

**Sewage Treatment
Plant**

E

H2

N

Map not to scale

4.7

H1

A

6.1

F

0.3

Al Kamil
58 km

B

2.3

ferry

D

G

Al
Ayjah

Ras Al
Hadd
37 km

4.3

1.0

dhows

C

Sur Lagoon

9.5

Waypoints and Coordinates			
A	A31	N22 32.871	E59 28.900
B	A27	N22 34.536	E59 31.234
C	A26	N22 33.822	E59 32.593
D	A25	N22 34.020	E59 32.947
E	A36	N22 34.728	E59 27.414

Accommodation	
H1	Sur Plaza Hotel
H2	Sur Beach Hotel

treatment plant lies just off the Sur to Qalhat road, and although can be viewed from outside the fence, access can be gained by asking the supervisor at the small building just inside the entrance.

The coast from Sur towards the Capital area passes through spectacular scenery and a few interesting sites for birds. For details, see under Qurayyat (3.1).

Accommodation: camping or a hotel in Sur.

3.3 Khawr Jirama ** 2WD/4WD

Key species: Crab Plover, other waders, Gull-billed Tern.

Khawr Jirama is a shallow tidal lagoon southwest of Ras Al Hadd. From August to May the mudflats support a large variety of **flamingos**, **herons** and **waders**. The most sought-after species is undoubtedly **Crab Plover** - often seen in numbers of 50 or more. This makes Khawr Jirama the most reliable site in Oman for this species, outside the Barr Al Hikman - Masirah area that can be difficult to access.

To reach Khawr Jirama, take the road from Ras Al Hadd towards Sur, as far as the village at the western end. At the first house in the village take a track on the right that heads across the *sabkha* towards the rocky island surrounded by mangrove. When passable, the track ends at a sand spit next to the mangrove; otherwise leave the vehicle and walk the last few hundred metres. **Crab Plover** is usually scattered with a few to the left of the island, but many more to the right. To obtain good views it may be necessary to wade out into the soft mud, so make sure to bring water for cleaning the feet afterwards.

Several other interesting waders, including **Broad-billed** and **Terek Sandpiper**, should be present and **Gull-billed Tern** is relatively common. A number of **Greater Flamingo** is present year-round.

Accommodation: camping or a hotel in Sur or Ras Al Hadd.

3.4 Ras Al Hadd and Ras Al Jinz * 2WD/4WD

Key species: Persian Shearwater, Jouanin's Petrel, seabirds, waders, Great Black-headed Gull, terns, Red-tailed Wheatear, migrants.

Ras Al Hadd and Ras Al Jinz form the easternmost point of Oman and the Arabian Peninsula. The recent paving of the road from Asilah to Ras Al Hadd has opened the area to tourism, with much development destined to take place along this coastline over the next few years. However, parts of these coastal beaches are protected as a turtle sanctuary, where **Green Turtle** *Chelonia mydas* come ashore each year to lay their eggs, especially from July to November. While both places have free access during the day, a permit is needed to stay overnight at the campground at Ras Al Jinz or join a ranger to watch the turtles laying. During the day the whole area is freely open and one of the best ways to see the turtles is to go to the beach at sunrise and hopefully witness the last few females heading for the sea.

For the birdwatcher there is interesting wildlife beside turtles. **Desert**, **Red-tailed** and sometimes **Hooded Wheatear** may be found around the campground. The best sites for birds, however, are near the village of Ras Al Hadd. The newly paved road passes the fort and follows the coastline along Khawr Al Hajar. **Herons** and **waders** should be present and, with luck, a few **Crab Plover**. The road passes several *dhows* (traditional fishing boats) and terminates at the desalination plant. The low rocks here are a regular site in winter for **Red-tailed Wheatear**. A hundred metres farther is a dilapidated picnic site that is a good spot for sea-watching. **Jouanin's Petrel, Pale-footed, Wedge-tailed** and **Persian Shearwaters, Wilson's Storm-petrel** and **Masked Booby** have all been seen in autumn. Huge flocks of **Red-necked Phalaropes** may be seen in rafts offshore and **Humpback Whale** may add to the attractions. A better option for sea-watching is to negotiate with one of the local fishermen to take a boat offshore, where **petrels, shearwaters, terns** and **skuas** can be observed at closer range. The sandy northeastern point can be good for migrant **gulls** and **terns**. From mid September to early October, numerous **White Stork** can sometimes be found on the beach, stopping off on their long migration, where they are attracted to the emerging young turtles.

From early January hundreds of **Great Black-headed Gull** gather at Ras Al Hadd along with other gull species. By mid-February they are in their gorgeous breeding plumage, and then start to move north in late-February.

Accommodation: camping or one of the hotels at Ras Al Hadd or in Sur. A permit for camping at Ras Al Jinz and seeing the turtles lay eggs can be obtained beforehand at the Ministry of Environment and Climatic Affairs in Al Khuwair in the Capital area. The application giving names of all persons in the party can be faxed to 2469 2462, but the permits must be picked up at the Ministry. Most travel agents

Khawr Jirama, Ras Al Hadd and Ras Al Jinz

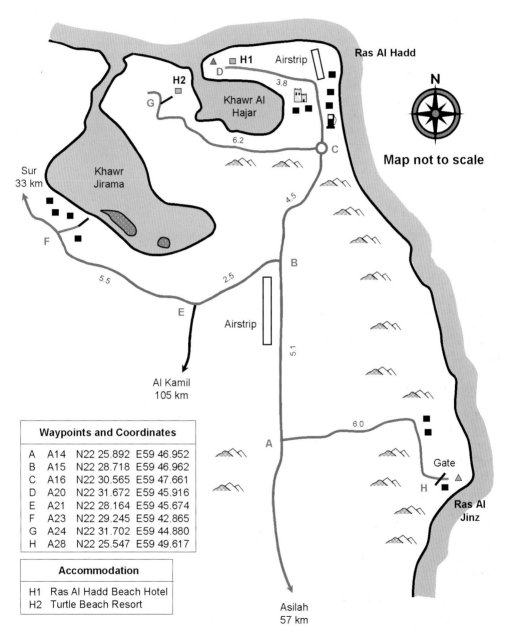

Ras Al Hadd

Airstrip

H1

H2

D

G

Khawr Al Hajar

3.8

6.2

Sur 33 km

Khawr Jirama

C

N

Map not to scale

4.5

F

5.5

2.5

B

Airstrip

E

5.1

Al Kamil 105 km

6.0

A

Gate

H

Ras Al Jinz

Waypoints and Coordinates			
A	A14	N22 25.892	E59 46.952
B	A15	N22 28.718	E59 46.962
C	A16	N22 30.565	E59 47.661
D	A20	N22 31.672	E59 45.916
E	A21	N22 28.164	E59 45.674
F	A23	N22 29.245	E59 42.865
G	A24	N22 31.702	E59 44.880
H	A28	N22 25.547	E59 49.617

Accommodation	
H1	Ras Al Hadd Beach Hotel
H2	Turtle Beach Resort

Asilah 57 km

can organize the permits. Permits cost RO 3 per person for camping and turtle watching, or RO 1 to solely join the ranger and watch the turtles laying. It is also possible to obtain the permits just by turning up at the gate at Ras Al Jinz, but weekends in October and November can be busy and the campground could be full; mid week or other times of year should be easy.

3.5 Ras Al Khabbah and Ar Ruways **   2WD

Key species: seabirds, waders, gulls, terns.

The high cliffs at Ras Al Khabbah offer a sweeping view of the Arabian Sea. From September **waders**, **gulls** and **terns** heading south along the coast pass very close to the headland. Standing on the top, most birds are seen from above though some **gulls** make a shortcut overhead. **Seabirds** are very much in evidence and Ras Al Khabbah is one of the best sea-watching sites in Oman, with **Persian Shearwater**, **Jouanin's Petrel**, **Wilson's Storm-petrel** and **Flesh-footed Shearwater** all regular.

The headland is located 23 km south of the turning to Ras Al Jinz, and, although not signposted, is obvious on approach. From the south, the main road follows the beaches then, seven kilometres past Ar Ruways, rises onto the headland. A rough track leads out to the tip. Although a few picnic shelters are found, none are positioned suitably for sea-watching. With no shade on the barren rock, protection from the sun is advisable if a long watch is planned.

Ras Al Khabbah

Red-billed Tropicbird and **Masked Booby** are quite regular and **Peregrine**, **Saker** and **Barbary Falcon** have offered superb views. Vagrants should be looked for as **Lesser Frigatebird**, **Cory's Shearwater**, **White-faced Storm-petrel**, **Swinhoe's Storm-petrel**, an **albatross** species and **South Polar Skua** have been seen over the years.

When passing the fishing village of Ar Ruways, the abundance of **gulls** and **terns** around the boats and resting along the beach attracts attention. Amongst the hoards of **Sooty Gulls** and a variety of **terns**, **Lesser Crested Tern** is usually present, and **Great Black-headed Gull** should be present from December to March. Those interested in a boat trip to sea should be able to negotiate with one of the local fishermen.

Accommodation: camping or a hotel at Ras Al Hadd.

Ras Al Khabbah and Ar Ruways

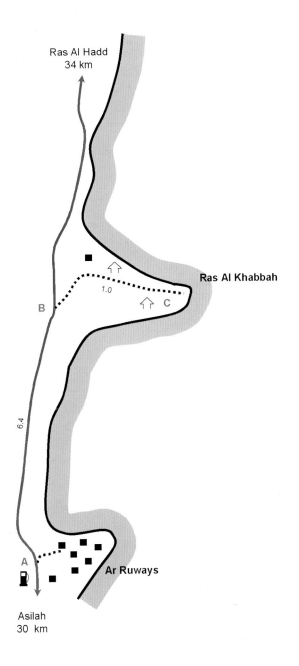

Ras Al Hadd
34 km

Ras Al Khabbah

1.0

B

C

6.4

A

Ar Ruways

Asilah
30 km

Waypoints and Coordinates			
A	A11	N22 11.294	E59 45.961
B	A12	N22 13.960	E59 48.211
C	A13	N22 13.580	E59 48.564

N

Map not to scale

4 Al Hajar Mountains

The Jabal Al Hajar is a long mountain range extending from north of Sohar to the southeast as far as Sur. These high mountains back Al Batinah plain and provide a valuable source of water. Even in summer heavy thunder showers are not unusual. The highest, central area called Al Jabal Al Akhdar is bound loosely by the circular route from Nakhal to Ar Rustaq, Bahla and Nizwa, along which are many impressive views. Oman's highest point, Jabal Shams at 3,009 m, is located here.

Due to the extremely rough terrain, few roads cross the mountains. However, many graded roads and rough tracks penetrate the northern and southern sides, providing access to numerous beautiful *wadis*, mountains and their birds. Formerly, only lower altitudes were generally accessible by 2WD, but with the recent paving of roads up Jabal Shams and to the Sayq Plateau, higher altitudes are now accessible. However, to really explore these mountains a 4WD is essential and mandatory for the Sayq Plateau.

Although birds in these mountains are generally not numerous, nor species diversity high, many of the mountain species of north Oman such as **Hume's Wheatear**, **Striated Scops Owl**, **Long-billed Pipit** and **Scrub Warbler** can be found over a relatively large altitudinal range. Others, including **Arabian Partridge**, **Wood Pigeon** and **Hooded Wheatear**, are scarce and difficult to locate. During spring and autumn, many of the high passes and *wadis* attract migrants in good numbers and variety, and unexpected oddities frequently occur. In the last few years new suspected breeding species for Oman, such as **Isabelline Shrike** and **Isabelline Wheatear** have been found here.

Summer is an especially attractive time to visit the high mountains in order to escape the oppressive heat in the lowlands, and camping is extremely pleasant. Conversely, in winter the nights can approach freezing point, so come prepared. Snowfall is a rare occurrence at Jabal Shams.

Listed below are common, widespread species easily seen in the central Al Hajar Mountains. These are not discussed specifically in the individual site accounts.

Common resident species:

Egyptian Vulture	Desert Lark	Purple Sunbird
Kestrel	African Rock Martin	Brown-necked Raven
Rock Dove	Yellow-vented Bulbul	House Bunting
Laughing Dove	Arabian Babbler	

Al Hajar Mountains

Al Hajar Mountains

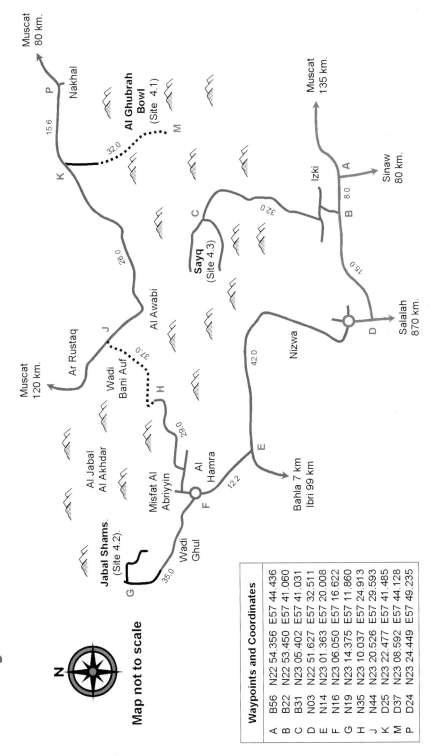

Map not to scale

Muscat 80 km.

Nakhal

P

15.6

K

32.0

Al Ghubrah Bowl
(Site 4.1)

M

26.0

Ar Rustaq

Muscat 120 km.

J

Wadi Bani Auf

37.0

Al Awabi

H

29.0

Sayq
(Site 4.3)

C

32.0

Izki

Muscat 135 km.

A

B

8.0

Sinaw 80 km.

15.0

D

Salalah 870 km.

Nizwa

42.0

Al Jabal Al Akhdar

Misfat Al Abriyyin

Al Hamra

F

12.2

E

Bahla 7 km
Ibri 99 km

Jabal Shams.
(Site 4.2).

G

35.0

Wadi Ghul

Waypoints and Coordinates			
A	B56	N22 54.356	E57 44.436
B	B22	N22 53.450	E57 41.060
C	B31	N23 05.402	E57 41.031
D	N03	N22 51.627	E57 32.511
E	N14	N23 01.363	E57 20.008
F	N16	N23 06.050	E57 16.622
G	N19	N23 14.375	E57 11.860
H	N35	N23 10.037	E57 24.913
J	N44	N23 20.526	E57 29.593
K	D25	N23 22.477	E57 41.485
M	D37	N23 08.592	E57 44.128
P	D24	N23 24.449	E57 49.235

63

4.1 Al Ghubrah Bowl *

4WD

Key species: Sand Partridge, Wood Pigeon, Striated Scops Owl, Long-billed Pipit, Red-tailed Wheatear, Hume's Wheatear, Blue Rock Thrush, House Bunting, migrants.

Being within 100 km of Muscat, Al Ghubrah Bowl, offering both spectacular scenery and fine birdwatching, makes an excellent and easy one-day excursion. This trip requires 4WD and should not be attempted if rainfall is expected in Al Hajar Mountains, as the only access into, and out of, the bowl is through the impressive gorges of Wadi Sabt, which floods during heavy rains. The *wadi* is very good for **Sand Partridge**, **Hume's Wheatear** and **House Bunting**, and holds **Blue Rock Thrush** in winter.

Once through Wadi Sabt, the scenery widens into a vast stony plain, 20 km across, surrounded by the imposing cliffs of Al Jabal Al Akhdar. The plains, dotted with trees, especially on the western side, support **Lichtenstein's Sandgrouse** and **Red-tailed Wheatear** in winter. For those camping, **Striated Scops Owl** occurs and should be calling from January to April.

Several tracks that branch out from the main track across the centre of the bowl offer possibilities to explore all 'corners.' Many of the *wadis* have large trees that hold migrants and winter visitors. Near the southern end, the track forks and ascends steeply to the villages of Wukan and Hadash. The slopes above these villages are wooded and from February to March hold the rare and elusive **Wood Pigeon**, before the birds ascend to breed. Check the scrub for **Long-billed Pipit** and **Scrub Warbler** in winter, and watch overhead for **Lappet-faced Vulture** soaring above the cliff faces.

Wukan village in Al Ghubrah Bowl

The village of Wukan is a favourite weekend destination during early spring when the flowering pomegranate and apricot trees add colour to the scenic beauty. A footpath follows the *falaj* up the side of the mountain and offers spectacular views across the bowl.

Accommodation: camping, a hotel in Muscat or As Sawadi Beach Resort (2.1).

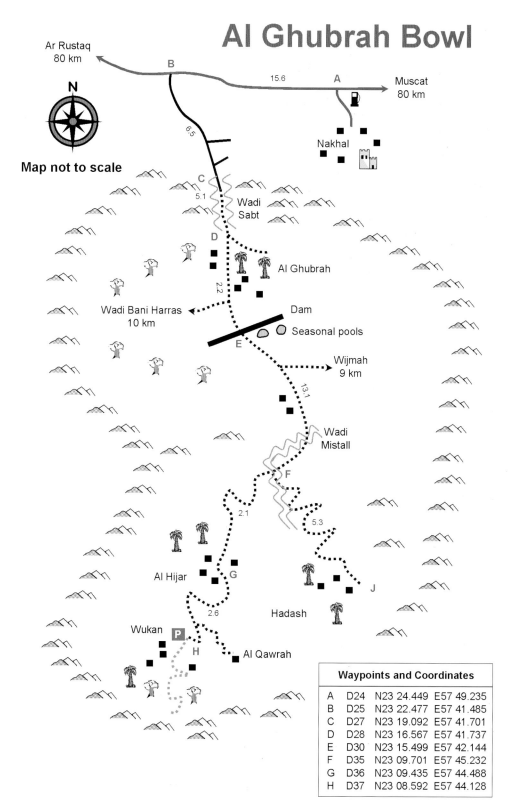

Al Ghubrah Bowl

Ar Rustaq
80 km

B

N

Map not to scale

15.6

A

Muscat
80 km

Nakhal

6.5

C

5.1

Wadi
Sabt

D

Al Ghubrah

2.2

Wadi Bani Harras
10 km

Dam

E

Seasonal pools

Wijmah
9 km

13.1

Wadi
Mistall

F

2.1

5.3

Al Hijar

G

J

Hadash

2.6

Wukan

P

H

Al Qawrah

Waypoints and Coordinates			
A	D24	N23 24.449	E57 49.235
B	D25	N23 22.477	E57 41.485
C	D27	N23 19.092	E57 41.701
D	D28	N23 16.567	E57 41.737
E	D30	N23 15.499	E57 42.144
F	D35	N23 09.701	E57 45.232
G	D36	N23 09.435	E57 44.488
H	D37	N23 08.592	E57 44.128

4.2 Jabal Shams *

4WD

Key species: Lappet-faced Vulture, Hooded Wheatear, Hume's Wheatear, Scrub Warbler.

At 3,009 m, Jabal Shams ("the Sun Mountain") is the highest mountain in Oman. In summer when the coastal plain and the inland desert are sweltering in heat, Jabal Shams is delightfully pleasant. In winter it can be decidedly cold, though, and snowfalls have occurred.

The last portion of the road, to the summit of Jabal Shams, is closed to the public. With a 4WD drive it is possible to reach about 2,200 m. From the Nizwa - Bahla road take the paved road towards Al Hamra and turn left after 12.2 km. This passes some interesting hillside ruins at Wadi Ghul before ascending steeply towards Jabal Shams. At several spots along this route local villagers may be waiting to sell rugs and other colourful handcrafts made from goat hair. *Wadis* with trees in this area should be explored for migrants and **Hume's Wheatear** is common. Just before the closed gate, some 46.9 km from Al Hamra road, is a rough track signposted toward Al Khitaym (Al Khateen). The track dips at first then skirts a hillside before leveling out on a plateau beyond. The track continues for several kilometres along the spectacular canyon which has been called the "Little Grand Canyon." The track ends in Al Khitaym village from where it is possible to start the popular "canyon walk" - a footpath along the face of the canyon offering great views and photography.

Birds here are not numerous, but interesting species such as **Long-billed Pipit**, **Hooded Wheatear** and **Scrub Warbler** may be seen. Both **Sand Partridge** and **Arabian Partridge** are possible while the skies should be scanned for **Lappet-faced Vulture**. For more detail, see Eriksen (2008).

With the paving of the road most of the way up Jabal Shams, tourist infrastructure has developed and one resthouse has opened at the top, with a second one due to open shortly.

Other mountain roads in this area include the easy drive from Al Hamra to Misfat Al Abriyyin. This delightful village hangs precariously on a hillside and its relatively lush gardens may hold interesting species during migration. Al Hutah cave, a few kilometres to the east of Al Hamra, and recently been opened to the public, is well worth the detour. Five kilometres before the cave the newly paved road up the escarpment has few birds but interesting scenery. The track from the top of the escarpment toward Ar Rustaq and Nakhal is very steep, rough and has excellent scenery, but should not be attempted by inexperienced 4WD drivers.

Accommodation: Jabal Shams Camping and Traveling Centre, Jabal Shams Resthouse, camping or a hotel in Nizwa.

Jabal Shams

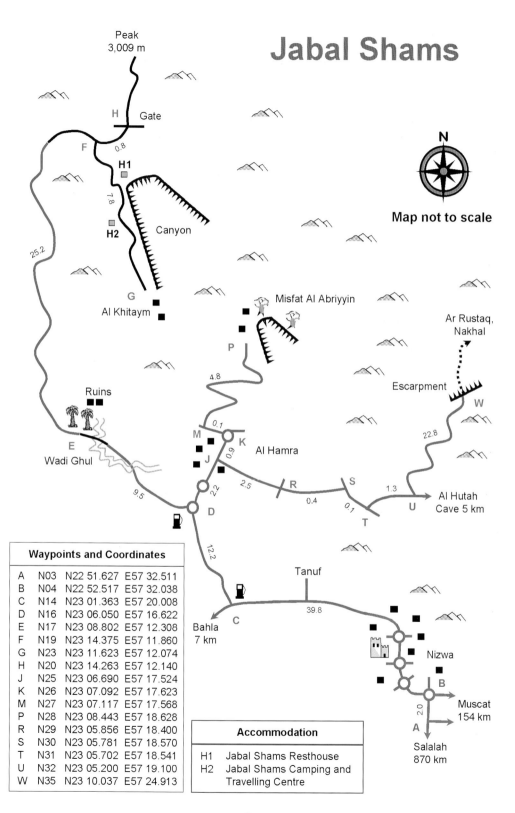

Jabal Shams

Map not to scale

Peak
3,009 m

H — Gate
F — 0.8
H1 — Jabal Shams Resthouse
7.8
H2
Canyon
25.2
G
Al Khitaym
Ruins
E
Wadi Ghul
9.5

Misfat Al Abriyyin

Ar Rustaq,
Nakhal

Escarpment
W
22.8

P
4.8

M — 0.1 — K
J — 0.9 — Al Hamra
D — 2.2 — 2.5 — R — S — 1.3 — U — Al Hutah
0.4 — 0.1 — T — Cave 5 km

12.2

Tanuf

39.8

Bahla
7 km
C

Nizwa

Muscat
154 km
2.0
A
B
Salalah
870 km

Waypoints and Coordinates

A	N03	N22 51.627	E57 32.511
B	N04	N22 52.517	E57 32.038
C	N14	N23 01.363	E57 20.008
D	N16	N23 06.050	E57 16.622
E	N17	N23 08.802	E57 12.308
F	N19	N23 14.375	E57 11.860
G	N23	N23 11.623	E57 12.074
H	N20	N23 14.263	E57 12.140
J	N25	N23 06.690	E57 17.524
K	N26	N23 07.092	E57 17.623
M	N27	N23 07.117	E57 17.568
P	N28	N23 08.443	E57 18.628
R	N29	N23 05.856	E57 18.400
S	N30	N23 05.781	E57 18.570
T	N31	N23 05.702	E57 18.541
U	N32	N23 05.200	E57 19.100
W	N35	N23 10.037	E57 24.913

Accommodation

H1	Jabal Shams Resthouse
H2	Jabal Shams Camping and Travelling Centre

4.3 Sayq Plateau *

Key species: Lappet-faced Vulture, Arabian Partridge, Sand Partridge, Wood Pigeon, Striated Scops Owl, Long-billed Pipit, Scrub Warbler, Plain Leaf Warbler, Red-tailed Wheatear, Hume's Wheatear, Blue Rock Thrush, House Bunting, migrants.

Cool climate and magnificent scenery combined with the majestic beauty of the old juniper and wild olive trees make the Sayq Plateau a unique experience in Oman. The upper elevations, above 2,300 m, are a great escape from the heat in the lowlands, especially in summer when camping is ideal. Most of the mountain specialities of the north are readily found, especially **Wood Pigeon** which is more common here than anywhere else in Oman. Migrants passing over the high mountains are attracted to the more densely vegetated *wadis*. For a detailed description of the hole area, see Eriksen (2008).

Access, via the village of Birkat Al Mawz, is signposted as Al Jabal Al Akhdar off the main Muscat to Nizwa road, and follows the newly paved road through the military checkpoint and up to the plateau. Note that although the road is immaculately conditioned, only 4WD vehicles are permitted to pass the military checkpoint.

Just before the checkpoint, Wadi Al Muaydin holds species typical of Al Hajar Mountains such as **Hume's Wheatear** and **Striated Scops Owl**, and the larger trees attract migrants.

Climbing the mountain, species such as **Sand Partridge**, **Long-billed Pipit**, **Hume's Wheatear**, **Blue Rock Thrush** and **House Bunting** should be encountered. The first well-wooded *wadi*, at **F** on the map, just before Al Manakhir turnoff is a prime spot for migrants and should be checked for **warblers** during migration periods. Just beyond, the fields and orchard around Hayl Al Yaman are worth a look.

In winter, one of the most interesting areas is Wadi Bani Habib, where the large trees, orchards and small terraces along the *wadi* are a haunt for **Plain Leaf Warbler**. **Thrushes** and other oddities such as **Siskin** have also been recorded. The abandoned village is a major tourist attraction in summer, with the parking area sometimes overflowing. Although steps lead down from the north side of the parking area, birders are better served by taking the steps down to the south side, walking along the *wadi* bottom and returning up the northern steps. This is due to the southern steps being more difficult to find from the bottom of the *wadi*.

For further spectacular views the villages of Ash Shirayjah and Sayq, on the edge of the plateau, should be visited. Orchards and scrub around the villages are worth checking. The roads down to these villages are very steep, requiring 4WD low ratio. Production of rose water is an important local commodity in several villages. The rose petals are harvested in April when **European Bee-eaters** are regular migrants. The official, and well-marked, walking trail between Aqor and Sayq, wanders through orchards and terraces, and is well worth a couple of hours in any season.

Higher elevations are accessed by taking the right hand turning after Al Jabal Al Akhdar Hotel. Turning right again at **N** on the map, old juniper and olive trees are common, and small groups of **Wood Pigeon** can be encountered. Check any of the surrounding vegetation for migrants. **Scrub Warbler** and **Long-billed Pipit** are commonest at these altitudes, as is **Striated Scops Owl** though finding them is never easy. **Arabian Partridge** is known, but rare.

The road to the north, opposite an old quarry at **P** on the map and signposted "A'Roos", is the start of a scenic drive with several impressive lookouts toward Jabal Shams. The high cliffs are good places to search for **Lappet-faced Vulture**. Another *wadi*, at **R** on the map, that can be good for migrants, is crossed 10 km out along this road. At the right time of year this hold an impressive assortment of **warblers**, **chats** and **flycatchers**.

Accommodation: camping or Al Jabal Al Akhdar Hotel.

Waypoints and Coordinates		
A	B22	N22 53.450 E57 41.060
B	B23	N22 55.027 E57 40.345
C	B24	N22 55.251 E57 39.756
D	B25	N22 55.381 E57 40.025
E	B26	N22 56.959 E57 40.269
F	B28	N23 04.422 E57 42.793
G	B29	N23 04.364 E57 42.530
H	B31	N23 05.402 E57 41.031
J	B39	N23 04.682 E57 40.238
K	B35	N23 04.125 E57 38.748
L	B36	N23 04.276 E57 36.261
M	B37	N23 04.148 E57 38.317
N	B38	N23 04.304 E57 40.041
P	B46	N23 07.131 E57 36.216
R	B53	N23 08.847 E57 32.514
S	B54	N23 08.976 E57 32.841
T	B55	N23 09.425 E57 32.514
U	B49	N23 07.483 E57 34.073

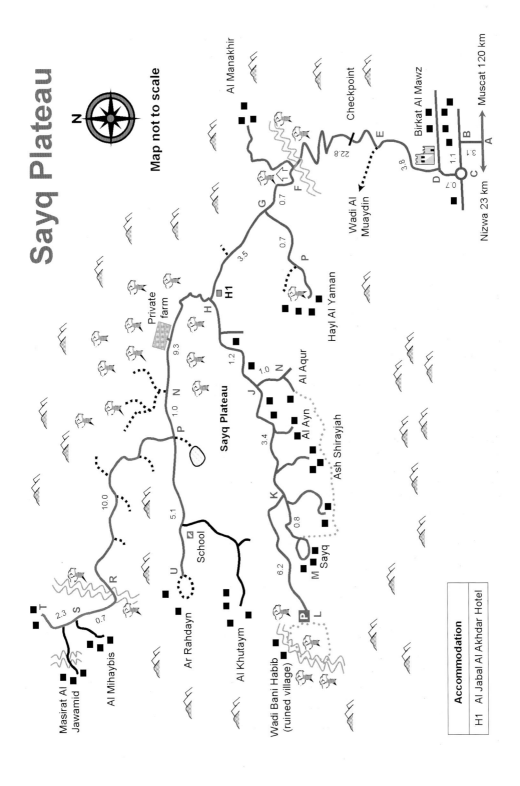

Sayq Plateau

Map not to scale

N

Al Manakhir

Checkpoint

Birkat Al Mawz

Muscat 120 km

Wadi Al Muaydin

22.8

E

3.8

D

1.1

B

A

3.1

C

0.7

Nizwa 23 km

G

0.7

F

0.7

T

3.5

P

Private farm

H1

H

9.3

N

1.2

Hayl Al Yaman

P

1.0

N

1.0

Al Aqur

Sayq Plateau

J

3.4

Al Ayn

Ash Shirayjah

10.0

5.1

K

0.8

School

U

Ar Rahdayn

M

Sayq

6.2

Al Khutaym

R

2.3

S

0.7

T

P

L

Masirat Al Jawamid

Al Mihaybis

Wadi Bani Habib
(ruined village)

Accommodation

H1	Al Jabal Al Akhdar Hotel

69

5 Musandam

Musandam is like no other region in Oman or Arabia. The spectacular coastal cliffs plunging straight into the sea create fjords that are more reminiscent of western Norway than the desert landscapes most people associate with Arabia. A quick look at a map of Arabia will show Musandam as forming part of a land bridge between Arabia and central Asia and indeed, parts of mainland Musandam is less than 60 km from the Republic of Iran. On rare, clear days the mountains of Iran are clearly visible. This topography attracts migrant birds, especially in spring, and some exciting discoveries have been made in recent years.

Access from Muscat, is not straightforward, even for resident birdwatchers from Oman. As Musandam is separated from the rest of Oman by a strip of the United Arab Emirates, a drive from Muscat will require leaving Oman, entering UAE, leaving UAE and entering Oman again, thus passing four border posts and the same number on the return journey. Car insurance coverage for the trip through UAE will be required, as well as a multi-entry road pass for resident birdwatchers. For visiting, foreign birdwatchers it is important when entering Oman, to do so on a **single** entry visa, rather than a multiple entry visa. This is because multiple entry visas require that the visa holder remains outside Oman for a minimum of three weeks between visits. So in order to visit Musandam, the visitor must purchase single entry visas at each border crossing.

Birdwatchers traveling from UAE have easier access, by crossing the border post at Tibat along the western coast, but should ensure that insurance on the vehicle covers Oman. Alternatively, one can fly to Musandam on scheduled flights by Oman Air from As Seeb International Airport to the main town of Khasab. Cars can be rented at Khasab Airport or through hotels in town, but a 4WD will usually come with a driver. This may be a more practical option for many visiting birdwatchers. A current drawback is that flights only operate on Thursdays and Fridays, although the situation could well change as tourism to the area opens up. Flights to Musandam should be checked as cancellations may take place during public holidays.

Most birders driving to Musandam will enter at Tibat and follow the beautiful, paved coastal road to Khasab, and by graded road beyond. Alternatively, the mountain road from Daba on the east coast of UAE, which requires 4WD, passes through spectacular Wadi Khabb Shamsi which at its narrowest place allows just one car through at a time. **Hume's Wheatear** is abundant here as well as **Chukar**, found in Musandam and nowhere else in Oman. The Omani border post is not reached till Wadi Al Bih so this part of Musandam can be freely explored by UAE birders. Unfortunately, it is not possible to drive north from the border post in Wadi Al Bih towards Khasab.

Since Musandam is not as easy to reach as other parts of the country, the whole region is grossly under-watched as far as birds are concerned. Yet Musandam holds some interesting sites that are well worth the effort to visit, especially during the spring migration in April. The autumn migration has hardly been studied, and discoveries in winter suggest that the rare **Eversmann's Redstart** winters in small numbers.

Listed below are common, widespread species easily seen in the Musandam region. These are generally not discussed in the individual site accounts.

Common resident species:

Western Reef Heron	Indian Roller	Hume's Wheatear
Grey Heron	Desert Lark	Graceful Prinia
Sooty Gull	Crested Lark	Purple Sunbird
Rock Dove	African Rock Martin	House Sparrow
Laughing Dove	Yellow-vented Bulbul	House Bunting

Common migrant and seasonal species:

Kestrel	Common Sandpiper	Barn Swallow
Curlew	Slender-billed Gull	Desert Wheatear
Redshank	Swift Tern	Isabelline Wheatear
Greenshank	Sandwich Tern	Desert Lesser Whitethroat

Musandam

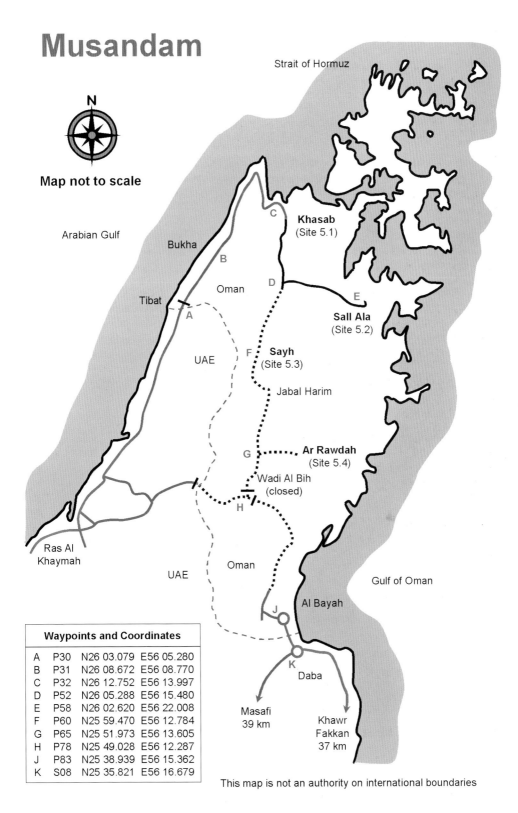

Strait of Hormuz

Map not to scale

Arabian Gulf

Bukha

Khasab
(Site 5.1)

C

B

D

Oman

Tibat

E

A

Sall Ala
(Site 5.2)

UAE

F **Sayh**
(Site 5.3)

Jabal Harim

G ••••••• **Ar Rawdah**
(Site 5.4)

Wadi Al Bih
(closed)

H

Ras Al
Khaymah

Oman

UAE

Gulf of Oman

J
Al Bayah

K
Daba

Masafi
39 km

Khawr
Fakkan
37 km

Waypoints and Coordinates			
A	P30	N26 03.079	E56 05.280
B	P31	N26 08.672	E56 08.770
C	P32	N26 12.752	E56 13.997
D	P52	N26 05.288	E56 15.480
E	P58	N26 02.620	E56 22.008
F	P60	N25 59.470	E56 12.784
G	P65	N25 51.973	E56 13.605
H	P78	N25 49.028	E56 12.287
J	P83	N25 38.939	E56 15.362
K	S08	N25 35.821	E56 16.679

This map is not an authority on international boundaries

5.1 Khasab *

Key species: seabirds, herons, waders, gulls, terns, migrants.

Khasab is the main town in Musandam and the destination for the twice weekly flights by Oman Air from As Seeb International Airport (Muscat). The town can be reached by 2WD on the spectacular road from Tibat and the UAE border on the west coast. However, to fully explore the area, and the best birdwatching sites beyond Khasab, a 4WD is necessary.

Unfortunately the construction of the new port at Khasab destroyed the extensive tidal mudflats in Khasab bay, so only a few **gulls** and **waders** can now be found around the harbour. The lush gardens and plantations in Khasab attract migrants. The series of well vegetated fields just east of the town centre, at Al Waym, are well worth checking during migration; **Red-throated Pipit**, **Ortolan** and **Black-headed Bunting** are very regular in spring.

South of Khasab the road crosses Khasab dam, below which a few ponds may hold **Red-wattled Plover** and, in winter, a small number of **ducks**. The nearby waste disposal site can also be explored.

A small sewage treatment site just west of the airport has a few settling ponds and an area of reeds which could potentially attract **crakes** on migration, none of which has as yet been recorded from Musandam.

From Khasab it is possible to join one of the *dhow* trips into the fjord country which should provide some **seabirds**, and **Sooty Tern** breeds in small numbers on isolated islets. Ask at a travel agency or at the hotels for a boat trip schedule. They last from a few hours to all day trips to Kumzar on the north coast of the Musandam Peninsula.

Socotra Cormorants

The paved road west of Khasab passes several bays before crossing over the mountains and descending onto the west coast. Roosting flocks of **gulls** and **terns** may be seen all along this road and **Socotra Cormorant** can be abundant in winter. In one or two places it is possible to seawatch from headlands along this road with **Persian Shearwater** recorded in good numbers in early spring, along with good migrations of **gulls** and **terns**.

Accommodation: camping or a hotel in Khasab.

Khasab

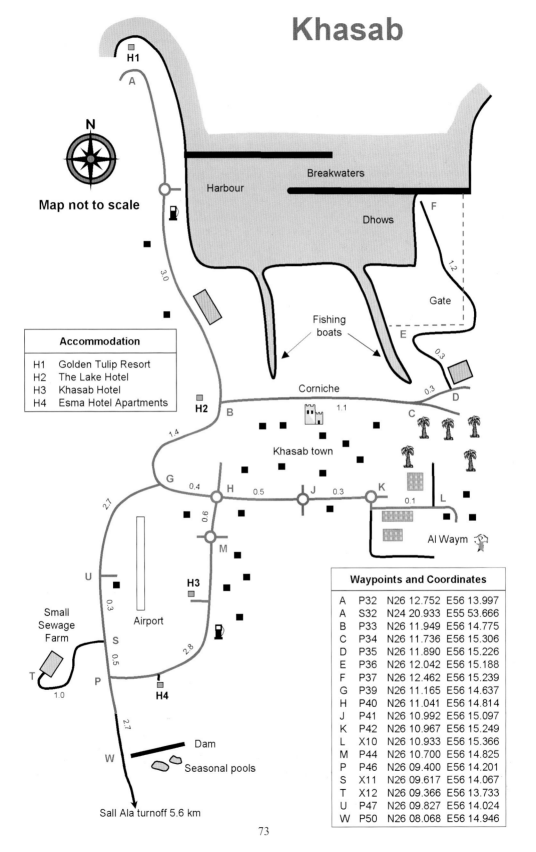

Map not to scale

N

H1

A

Harbour

Breakwaters

Dhows

Gate

F

1.2

E

3.0

Fishing
boats

0.3

0.3

D

Accommodation

H1	Golden Tulip Resort
H2	The Lake Hotel
H3	Khasab Hotel
H4	Esma Hotel Apartments

Corniche

H2

B

1.4

Khasab town

1.1

C

G

0.4

H

0.5

J

0.3

K

0.1

L

Al Waym

2.7

0.6

U

M

Small
Sewage
Farm

0.3

Airport

H3

Dam

Seasonal pools

S

0.5

T

1.0

P

H4

2.8

2.7

W

Sall Ala turnoff 5.6 km

Waypoints and Coordinates			
A	P32	N26 12.752	E56 13.997
A	S32	N24 20.933	E55 53.666
B	P33	N26 11.949	E56 14.775
C	P34	N26 11.736	E56 15.306
D	P35	N26 11.890	E56 15.226
E	P36	N26 12.042	E56 15.188
F	P37	N26 12.462	E56 15.239
G	P39	N26 11.165	E56 14.637
H	P40	N26 11.041	E56 14.814
J	P41	N26 10.992	E56 15.097
K	P42	N26 10.967	E56 15.249
L	X10	N26 10.933	E56 15.366
M	P44	N26 10.700	E56 14.825
P	P46	N26 09.400	E56 14.201
S	X11	N26 09.617	E56 14.067
T	X12	N26 09.366	E56 13.733
U	P47	N26 09.827	E56 14.024
W	P50	N26 08.068	E56 14.946

5.2 Sall Ala **   4WD

Key species: Chukar, White-throated Robin, Common Redstart, Eastern Pied Wheatear, Plain Leaf Warbler, other warblers, buntings, migrants.

The graded road southeast of Khasab runs through a wide, open *wadi* known as Wadi Sall Al Ala. After 12 km from the turnoff, a relatively well-wooded plain called Al Khalidiyyah comes into view on the right. This plain can be flooded after rain, but is usually barren of any undergrowth due to overgrazing by goats. A picnic site with a children's playground is found at the centre of the woodland. Nevertheless, the trees attract many migrants and winter visitors. **Eastern Pied Wheatear** is regular, together with **Plain Leaf Warbler**, which can be common from November to March, with up to 30 birds present. **Southern Grey Shrike** breeds during the winter months.

Spring migration in April is an exciting time and the woods may hold **White-throated Robin** and various **buntings** though **Common Redstart** will probably be the most numerous. The nearby grassy plains attract hovering **Lesser Kestrel** at this time as well. The autumn migration has not been well studied, but a **Grey Hypocolius** was once seen in late November. **Chukar**, **Sand Partridge**, **Striated Scops Owl** and **Little Owl** are resident in the surrounding hills.

About half way to Sall Ala a road leads northward up the hillside towards Khawr An Najd. The view from the top is awesome, with the road descending through several hairpins to the coast and several shaded picnic spots.

Accommodation: camping or a hotel in Khasab.

Al Khalidiyyah after winter rains

Chukar

Sall Ala

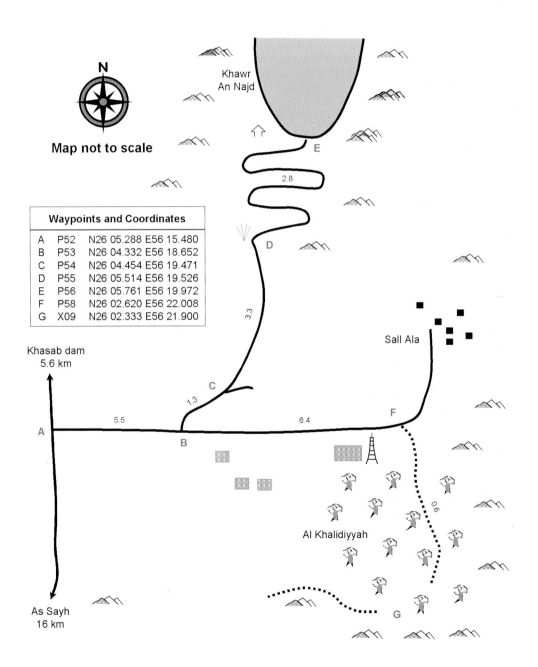

N

Map not to scale

Khawr
An Najd

Waypoints and Coordinates		
A	P52	N26 05.288 E56 15.480
B	P53	N26 04.332 E56 18.652
C	P54	N26 04.454 E56 19.471
D	P55	N26 05.514 E56 19.526
E	P56	N26 05.761 E56 19.972
F	P58	N26 02.620 E56 22.008
G	X09	N26 02.333 E56 21.900

E

2.8

D

3.3

Sall Ala

Khasab dam
5.6 km

C

1.3

5.5

A

B

6.4

F

Al Khalidiyyah

0.6

As Sayh
16 km

G

5.3 As Sayh Plateau ***   4WD

Key species: Lesser Kestrel, Chukar, Sand Partridge, Common Cuckoo, Little Owl, White-throated Robin, Eversmann's Redstart, Common Redstart, Pied Wheatear, Hooded Wheatear, Eastern Pied Wheatear, Rock Thrush, Blue Rock Thrush, Song Thrush, warblers, Semi-collared Flycatcher, Lesser Grey Shrike, Woodchat Shrike, Cinereous Bunting, Ortolan Bunting, Black-headed Bunting, other migrants.

As Sayh Plateau at 1,200 m in the Musandam mountains is probably the most exciting bird-watching site in the region. The plateau is a flat, grassy plain surrounded by steep hillsides. Access is by 4WD along the steep, twisting road from Khasab passing right by the plateau 16 km after the Sall Ala turnoff. Do not drive on the plateau itself as it may destroy the fragile vegetation and is not appreciated by the locals. On foot the whole plain and surrounding hillsides can be explored freely. The small, fenced-in plots of agriculture are particularly interesting places to look for birds and just about anything may turn up during migration.

Resident species include **Chukar** and **Sand Partridge** on the surrounding hillsides and there is usually a pair of **Little Owls** near the north end of the plateau. The most exciting time is during spring migration and mid-April has proven particularly good. **Common Cuckoo** is calling from the hills and may breed. The following species, regularly recorded in spring, give an idea of the potential of this site: **Lesser Kestrel**, **Kestrel**, **Saker Falcon**, **Pallid Swift**, **Tree Pipit**, **Rufous Bush Robin**, **White-throated Robin**, **Black Redstart**, **Common Redstart**, **Whinchat**, **Northern Wheatear**, **Pied Wheatear**, **Red-tailed Wheatear**, **Rock Thrush**, **Blue Rock Thrush**, **Isabelline**, **Woodchat** and **Lesser Grey Shrike**, and **Cinereous**, **Grey-necked**, **Black-headed** and **Ortolan Bunting**, in addition to common resident species. Other regular spring migrants have included various species of **warblers**, **Semi-collared Flycatcher** and **Masked Shrike**. Even a **Grey Hypocolius** has turned up.

Though spring migration peaks in April, earlier and later dates should also prove interesting, but little is known at present. In winter **Eversmann's Redstart** is a regular visitor in small numbers as are **Blue Rock Thrush** and **Song Thrush**. Clearly, the area is worthy of further exploration and exciting discoveries will surely be made.

Farther up the road a small plateau is reached after 5 km before the road peaks at 1,700 metres at the radar station. Small plots and bushy *wadis* are also found in this area, and regularly hold migrants. **Hooded Wheatear** is uncommon but regularly recorded anywhere in this region. These areas warrant further exploration and make for good camping sites.

Accommodation: camping or a hotel in Khasab.

As Sayh

As Sayh (Plateau)

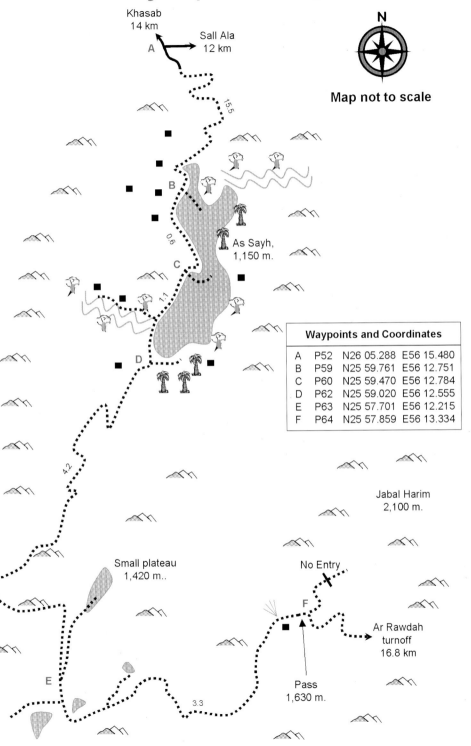

Khasab
14 km

Sall Ala
12 km

A

15.5

Map not to scale

N

B

0.6

As Sayh,
1,150 m.

C

1.1

D

4.2

Jabal Harim
2,100 m.

Small plateau
1,420 m..

No Entry

F

Ar Rawdah
turnoff
16.8 km

E

Pass
1,630 m.

3.3

Waypoints and Coordinates		
A	P52	N26 05.288 E56 15.480
B	P59	N25 59.761 E56 12.751
C	P60	N25 59.470 E56 12.784
D	P62	N25 59.020 E56 12.555
E	P63	N25 57.701 E56 12.215
F	P64	N25 57.859 E56 13.334

5.4 Ar Rawdah Bowl *

Key species: Short-toed Eagle, Lesser Kestrel, European Roller, White-throated Robin, Blue Rock Thrush, Scrub Warbler, Orphean Warbler, Woodchat Shrike, migrants.

Ar Rawdah bowl is located in the southern part of Musandam and is a flat plain surrounded by steep mountains. From Khasab it is reached via the mountain road past As Sayh Plateau (5.3) and Jabal Harim. About 56 km from Khasab a road on the left, just after the descent from the mountains and signposted "Rawdah", leads into the bowl. The well-wooded plain can be explored by 4WD or on foot. In many ways Ar Rawdah is similar to Al Khalidiyyah in Sall Ala (5.2) and probably holds similar species. However, Ar Rawdah has been visited much less frequently by birdwatchers and is in need of further study. Most visits have been during spring migration in April when species such as **Short-toed Eagle**, **Lesser Kestrel**, **European Roller**, **White-throated Robin** and **Woodchat Shrike** have been noted. In winter **Blue Rock Thrush** is regular and resident species include **Chukar**, **Sand Partridge**, **Scrub Warbler** and **Trumpeter Finch**. Farther south the mountain road approaches the border post at Wadi Al Bih; along the way a few isolated fields and trees are passed which can be inspected for migrants. It is not possible to get through the border post.

Accommodation: camping or a hotel in Khasab.

Ar Rawdah Bowl after winter rains

Ar Rawdah Bowl

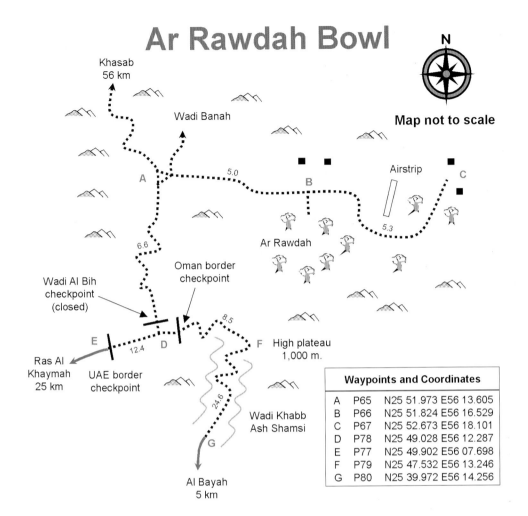

Khasab
56 km

Wadi Banah

N

Map not to scale

Airstrip

A   5.0   B   C

Ar Rawdah   5.3

6.6

Oman border
checkpoint

Wadi Al Bih
checkpoint
(closed)

8.5

E   D   F   High plateau
1,000 m.

12.4

Ras Al
Khaymah
25 km

UAE border
checkpoint

24.6

Wadi Khabb
Ash Shamsi

G

Al Bayah
5 km

Waypoints and Coordinates		
A	P65	N25 51.973 E56 13.605
B	P66	N25 51.824 E56 16.529
C	P67	N25 52.673 E56 18.101
D	P78	N25 49.028 E56 12.287
E	P77	N25 49.902 E56 07.698
F	P79	N25 47.532 E56 13.246
G	P80	N25 39.972 E56 14.256

5.5 Strait of Hormuz *   4WD

Key species: seabirds.

The Strait of Hormuz separates the Sultanate of Oman (Musandam region) from the Republic of Iran. It is quite narrow (less than 60 km at the narrowest point). Not surprisingly, the currents are fierce as all water in and out of the Arabian Gulf must pass through here with the rising and falling tides.

No regular study has been carried out on the birds in the strait and most records are from ships passing to and from the Gulf. There are several offshore islands with the Quoin Islands forming the northernmost point in Oman. **Red-billed Tropicbird**, **Osprey**, **Bridled Tern** and **Pallid Swift** nest on some of these islands.

To get out into the Strait of Hormuz one should contact a travel agency or a hotel in Khasab. Regular *dhow* trips take visitors out, and a trip to Kumzar on the north coast of the Musandam Peninsula goes at least some way into the strait. It may also be possible to negotiate a trip with a local fisherman in Khasab or one of the other villages along the coast.

Additional species that have been seen regularly in the Strait of Hormuz include **Wedge-tailed** and **Persian Shearwaters**, **Wilson's Storm-petrel**, **Socotra Cormorant**, **Sooty Falcon** and **Sooty Tern**. Further exploration might prove quite productive and would be highly welcome.

Accommodation: camping, hotel in Khasab or an overnight *dhow* trip.

Indian Roller

6 Al Buraymi Area

Due to the position of the Oman-UAE border post, well inside Oman, all sites covered in this area are more easily accessed, without restriction, from UAE. Foreign nationals resident in Oman need to obtain a road pass to cross the border and re-enter Oman on the return journey. Visiting birdwatchers of certain nationalities should be able to cross the border, but will require another entry visa on return to Oman.

Being within the interior desert the climate differs markedly from the coast, 100 km to the east, with temperature extremes more marked. Birdwatching in the winter is very pleasant, rapidly becoming very hot after sunrise during spring and autumn. Campers in winter should be prepared for cold evenings.

The immediate environs of Al Buraymi with its gardens and parks host a similar collection of species to that of Al Batinah, including the usual exotic introductions. Outside the city, desert species predominate, with only the real desert specialists remaining throughout the year, augmented by wintering and opportunist seasonal migrants.

Trumpeter Finch

Listed below are common, widespread species easily seen in Al Buraymi area. These are generally not discussed in the individual site accounts.

Common resident species:

Grey Francolin	Indian Roller	Arabian Babbler
Red-wattled Plover	Desert Lark	Purple Sunbird
Rock Dove	Crested Lark	Southern Grey Shrike
Laughing Dove	African Rock Martin	Brown-necked Raven
Ring-necked Parakeet	Yellow-vented Bulbul	Common Mynah
Little Green Bee-eater	Graceful Prinia	House Sparrow

Common migrant and seasonal species:

Collared Dove	Barn Swallow	Desert Wheatear
Pallid Swift	Citrine Wagtail	Desert Lesser Whitethroat
Blue-cheeked Bee-eater	White Wagtail	Isabelline Shrike

6.1 Fossil Valley *   2WD

Key species: Black-crowned Finch Lark, Pied Wheatear, Red-tailed Wheatear, Hume's Wheatear, Upcher's Warbler, Ménétries's Warbler, Desert Warbler, Desert Lesser Whitethroat.

The name Fossil Valley derives from the proliferation of small marine fossils contained in the rocks of the surrounding hills, making this a great site for fossil hunters. The valley itself is a wide, open sandy plain with scrub and a few scattered trees.

Fossil Valley is 10 km northeast of Al Buraymi on the Mahdah road. Access is via any of a series of tracks criss-crossing the plain, starting about 500 metres before the "Welcome to the Wilayat of Mahdah" sign. Unless it has rained these tracks are passable by 2WD.

The most interesting time to visit is during migration when the plain attracts **pipits** and **wheatears**, including **Isabelline**, **Northern**, and **Pied Wheatear** as well as **shrikes** such as **Isabelline**, **Steppe Grey** and **Woodchat Shrike**. In winter this is a regular site for **Short-toed Eagle**, **Black-crowned Finch Lark**, **Desert Lark**, **Desert Warbler**, **Desert Lesser Whitethroat** and **Red-tailed Wheatear**. In spring **Upcher's Warbler**, **Pale Rock Sparrow** and **Yellow-throated Sparrow** are uncommon but regular. **Little Owl** is fairly numerous on the surrounding hills.

6.2 Jabal Qatar (Hanging Gardens) **   4WD/2WD

Key species: Bonelli's Eagle, Barbary Falcon, Sand Partridge, Lichtenstein's Sandgrouse, Desert Lark, Hume's Wheatear, Red-tailed Wheatear, Upcher's Warbler, Plain Leaf Warbler, Trumpeter Finch.

The Jabal Qatar escarpment, 18 km northeast of Buraymi, dominating the surrounding plains, is often referred to as "Hanging Gardens", on account of the noticeably green vines hanging on its face.

Access is via a rough track, 4.5 km north of Al Buraymi Sewage Plant (6.3). Initially the track crosses stony plains with scattered trees, before descending into a *wadi* at the base of the escarpment, the last few hundred metres of which is drivable only by 4WD. Although uncommon, this *wadi* is the most consistent place in Oman to find **Trumpeter Finch**, due in part to the presence of a permanent spring found by climbing a few hundred metres up the *wadi*. Other interesting species include **Bonelli's Eagle**, **Barbary Falcon**, **Sand Partridge**, **Scrub Warbler**, **Hume's Wheatear**, **House Bunting**, and possibly **Lappet-faced Vulture**. **Lichtenstein's Sandgrouse** come to drink at the spring some evenings. **Desert Eagle Owl** has been recorded.

Species to look for on the surrounding plains include **Lichtenstein's Sandgrouse**, **Desert Lark**, **Red-tailed Wheatear**, **Plain Leaf Warbler** and **Desert Lesser Whitethroat**. During migration, **wheatears** and **warblers** can be numerous.

6.3 Al Buraymi Sewage Plant *   2WD

Key species: Egyptian Goose, waders, Southern Grey Shrike, migrants.

Situated 13 km northeast of Al Buraymi on the Mahdah road, these sewage ponds, although small, are a potential magnet for migrants and winter visitors alike. The ponds are fairly recent, and the species list is still growing, but with a habitat mixture of open water, reeds and marshy grass they boast great potential. Direct access to the ponds is via the paved road to the right 2.9 km north of Fossil Valley (6.1), from where it is possible to walk between the various ponds.

Being so close to UAE, where **Egyptian Goose** has a well-established population, this site will probably become the first place for this species to be recorded with regularity in Oman. The adjacent rubbish tip attracts large numbers of **Egyptian Vulture** and **Brown-necked Raven**.

Accommodation: camping or a hotel in Al Buraymi.

Jabal Qatar, Fossil Valley and Al Buraymi Sewage Plant

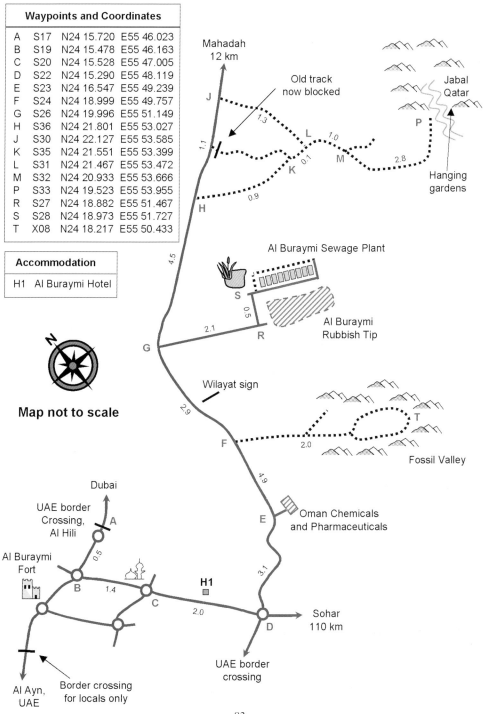

Waypoints and Coordinates

A	S17	N24 15.720	E55 46.023
B	S19	N24 15.478	E55 46.163
C	S20	N24 15.528	E55 47.005
D	S22	N24 15.290	E55 48.119
E	S23	N24 16.547	E55 49.239
F	S24	N24 18.999	E55 49.757
G	S26	N24 19.996	E55 51.149
H	S36	N24 21.801	E55 53.027
J	S30	N24 22.127	E55 53.585
K	S35	N24 21.551	E55 53.399
L	S31	N24 21.467	E55 53.472
M	S32	N24 20.933	E55 53.666
P	S33	N24 19.523	E55 53.955
R	S27	N24 18.882	E55 51.467
S	S28	N24 18.973	E55 51.727
T	X08	N24 18.217	E55 50.433

Accommodation

H1	Al Buraymi Hotel

Map not to scale

Mahadah 12 km

Old track now blocked

Jabal Qatar

Hanging gardens

Al Buraymi Sewage Plant

Al Buraymi Rubbish Tip

Wilayat sign

Fossil Valley

Dubai

UAE border Crossing, Al Hili

Al Buraymi Fort

Oman Chemicals and Pharmaceuticals

H1

Sohar 110 km

UAE border crossing

Al Ayn, UAE

Border crossing for locals only

7 The Central Desert

Surrounded by Al Hajar Mountains in the north, the Dhofar Mountains in the south, Ar Rub Al Khali (The Empty Quarter) in the west and the Arabian Sea coast in the east lies a vast open area of gravel plains and sand dunes. Stretching some 800 km from north to south and 200 km east to west it covers about three quarters of Oman's land mass.

Although the area is thinly populated by both man and beast, there are several interesting places for the birdwatcher. Most good sites are close to the paved Muscat - Salalah highway, making access relatively straightforward, except for Jaluni, home of the Arabian Oryx Sanctuary, which is located some distance away from the highway and requires prior arrangement to visit.

The 1,040 km drive from Muscat to Salalah takes 10-12 hours not counting rest stops. Birds are not numerous along the road. Every hour or so, a Hoopoe Lark will fly up next to the road revealing its black and white wing pattern or a pair of Brown-necked Ravens pass by. To find the interesting birds requires a more thorough search. An overnight break, camping or staying at one of several resthouses en route, allows visiting several of the sites mentioned below. Birdwatchers flying to Salalah will miss these sites and with them some interesting birding. Some southern locations, though, can be reached on a one or two day trip into the desert from Salalah.

Sand dunes, Ar Rub Al Khali

Listed below are common, widespread species easily seen in the central desert. These are not generally discussed in the individual site accounts.

Common resident species:

Laughing Dove	Hoopoe Lark	Brown-necked Raven
Black-crowned Finch Lark	Southern Grey Shrike	

Common migrant or seasonal species:

Barn Swallow	Desert Wheatear	Isabelline Shrike
Isabelline Wheatear		

Central Desert

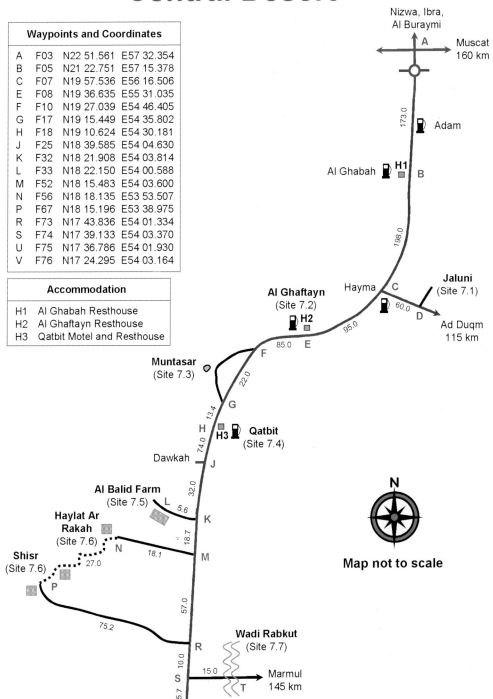

Waypoints and Coordinates

A	F03	N22 51.561	E57 32.354
B	F05	N21 22.751	E57 15.378
C	F07	N19 57.536	E56 16.506
E	F08	N19 36.635	E55 31.035
F	F10	N19 27.039	E54 46.405
G	F17	N19 15.449	E54 35.802
H	F18	N19 10.624	E54 30.181
J	F25	N18 39.585	E54 04.630
K	F32	N18 21.908	E54 03.814
L	F33	N18 22.150	E54 00.588
M	F52	N18 15.483	E54 03.600
N	F56	N18 18.135	E53 53.507
P	F67	N18 15.196	E53 38.975
R	F73	N17 43.836	E54 01.334
S	F74	N17 39.133	E54 03.370
U	F75	N17 36.786	E54 01.930
V	F76	N17 24.295	E54 03.164

Accommodation

H1	Al Ghabah Resthouse
H2	Al Ghaftayn Resthouse
H3	Qatbit Motel and Resthouse

Nizwa, Ibra, Al Buraymi

Muscat 160 km

173.0

Adam

Al Ghabah H1 B

198.0

Jaluni (Site 7.1)

Hayma C

60.0 D

Ad Duqm 115 km

Al Ghaftayn (Site 7.2) H2

95.0

85.0 E

F

Muntasar (Site 7.3)

22.0

13.4

G

74.0

H H3 Qatbit (Site 7.4)

Dawkah J

32.0

Al Balid Farm (Site 7.5) L

5.6

K

Haylat Ar Rakah (Site 7.6) N

18.7

Shisr (Site 7.6)

27.0 18.1

M

P

57.0

75.2

R Wadi Rabkut (Site 7.7)

S 10.0

15.0 Marmul 145 km

T

U Thumrayt

5.7

23.6 Thumrayt waste disposal site (Site 7.8)

V

Salalah 50 km

N

Map not to scale

85

Key species: Houbara Bustard, Stone Curlew, Spotted Thick-knee, Cream-coloured Courser, Lichtenstein's Sandgrouse, Crowned Sandgrouse, Chestnut-bellied Sandgrouse, Little Owl, Bar-tailed Desert Lark, migrants, rarities.

Jaluni is the field station of the Arabian Oryx Project located on the flat desert plain of the Jiddat Al Harasis. The area is east of the Muscat - Salalah road and north of the Hayma - Ad Duqm road. No map is provided as visitors should not attempt to find the area on their own. Birdwatchers wanting to visit must seek prior permission from the project head office in Muscat. Write to: Arabian Oryx Project, P O Box 246, Muscat 113, Sultanate of Oman, fax 2469 3884, email: acedrc@omantel.net.om stating the desired date. If a visit is granted, the staff from the field station may pick up the visitors in Hayma or other agreed location and lead the way to Jaluni. Travel agents in the Capital area may also secure a permit. For resident birdwatchers the easiest way to visit may be to join the Historical Association of Oman on one of their yearly or twice yearly visits to Jaluni.

The Arabian Oryx Project was set up to reintroduce the **Arabian Oryx** *Oryx leucoryx* into the wild and monitor their progress. The field station is manned by a manager and a biologist as well as support staff and a number of Omani rangers. Due to poaching, few oryx remain in the wild; the population is now confined to a large enclosure at the headquarters. For over two decades the project has carried out studies on the oryx as well as other wildlife including birds and records have been collected throughout this period making Jaluni one of the best studied sites in central Oman.

Houbara Bustard

For birdwatchers the key species is probably the **Houbara Bustard** of the subspecies *macqueenii* ('**Macqueen's Bustard**') which is resident and breeds on the Jiddat. Although the rangers make almost daily sightings of Houbara, the area covered is vast and a visitor will be lucky to see one. Other possible birds include wintering **Stone Curlew** and breeding **Spotted Thick-knee** and **Cream-coloured Courser**. Two artificial pools at the field station attract hundreds of **Crowned** and **Chestnut-bellied Sandgrouse** each morning with a few **Spotted Sandgrouse** sometimes seen as well. After dusk **Lichtenstein's Sandgrouse** come to drink.

The well-wooded Wadi Jaluni holds resident **Little Owl** and is a draw for migrants such as **European Nightjar**, **Blue-cheeked** and **European Bee-eater**, **European Roller**, and various **pipits**, **wheatears**, **thrushes**, **warblers**, **shrikes** and **buntings** at the appropriate times. Rarities that have turned up at Jaluni include **Abdim's Stork**, **Koel**, **Ring Ouzel**, **Yellow-browed Warbler**, **Brambling** and **Yellow-breasted Bunting**. An astounding selection of **herons**, **waders**, **gulls** and **terns** have been recorded this far away from the coast.

The surrounding plains can be productive as well. In April the drawn-out whistle of the **Bar-tailed Desert Lark** from the top of a bush makes the area one of the best places to find this otherwise elusive species in Oman.

Other wildlife also command attention. **Mountain** (or **Arabian**) **Gazelle** *Gazella gazella* is common and the attractive **Rüppell's Sand Fox** *Vulpes ruepellii* is occasionally seen. **Yellow-spotted Agamas** *Agama flavimaculata* advertise their presence in the top of an **Acacia** tree in spring by their vivid blue colour and orange tail, but they will lose their colour immediately one approaches.

Accommodation: camping or a hotel in Hayma.

7.2 Al Ghaftayn Hotel *

Key species: migrants.

Those driving the Muscat – Salalah road have the possibility for a stop at Al Ghaftayn Hotel or Resthouse, about 635 km south of Muscat and 95 km west of Hayma. Although past its former glory, due to the diminishing number of watered trees, a short stop is always worthwhile. The walled garden attracts birds, especially during migration. Spring passage from early-March to mid-May is the most interesting season. Regular migrants include **European Roller**, **Rufous Bush Robin**, **Olivaceous**, **Upcher's** and **Ménétries's Warbler**, **Whitethroat** and **Spotted Flycatcher**. Unusual species that have turned up at Al Ghaftayn include **Short-toed Eagle**, **Red-necked Phalarope**, **Wryneck**, **Rock Thrush**, **Wood Warbler**, **Golden Oriole**, **Rose-coloured Starling**, **Common Rosefinch** and **Ortolan Bunting** to mention a few. **Red-breasted Flycatcher** is regular in autumn.

European Roller

Al Ghabah Hotel, 293 km farther north, should be similar, but in recent years care of the garden has been abandoned totally. It will be worth a stop if the garden should ever be re-established.

Accommodation: camping or Al Ghaftayn Hotel.

Key species: Pallid Harrier, Long-legged Buzzard, Golden Eagle, Crowned, Spotted and Chestnut-bellied Sandgrouse, Turtle Dove, European Roller, larks, pipits, warblers, wheatears, shrikes, Rose-coloured Starling, buntings, other migrants, rarities.

Muntasar is a desert oasis with a permanent water supply from an underground spring. Part of the water is stored in two cement troughs, but surplus water flows into standing pools lined with sedges. Small farming operations have been attempted at the site over the years, but all have failed, perhaps due to the high sulphur content of the water. Date palms and other trees are established. From the north, Muntasar is reached by taking the turnoff 85 km southwest of Al Ghaftayn Hotel or, if coming from the south, 13.4 km north of Qatbit Motel. Both turnoffs are well signposted. The last few km to the oasis is via rough and sandy tracks though 2WDs can pass with care. Care should be taken in remembering the route driven as once away from the main road, the area is open and featureless; a GPS is recommended.

Year-round Muntasar is an excellent birdwatching site, though spring, summer and autumn are most productive. The pools attract a variety of **herons**, **ducks** and **waders** on migration which seem unusual so far from the coast. The biggest attraction, however, is the daily arrival of hundreds or even thousands of **sandgrouse** that come to drink. Most will be **Spotted Sandgrouse**, and Muntasar is by far the best place in Oman to see this species; **Crowned** and **Chestnut-bellied Sandgrouse** are common as well. The birds start to arrive around 09h00 in winter, somewhat earlier in summer. By 11h00 they may all have departed.

Long-legged Buzzard and Golden Eagle are other star attractions. During the warmer seasons several of the former and a few of the latter may come to drink. Noon is the peak time for these species. **Turtle Dove** stays throughout the summer and probably breeds. **Pallid Harrier**, including adult males, as well as **Red-breasted Flycatcher**, is regularly seen during autumn and winter. Migration seasons are particularly interesting with **bee-eaters**, **rollers**, **larks**, **pipits**, **wheatears**, **thrushes**, **warblers**, **shrikes**, **starlings**, **sparrows** and **buntings** all being possible. In recent years **Grey Hypocolius** has been recorded with regularity between November and March, and it seems likely that a small wintering population has established itself. Vagrants have included **Black-winged Pratincole**, **Koel**, **Eye-browed Thrush**, **Brahminy** and **Wattled Starling**, and **Siskin**.

Accommodation: camping, Al Ghaftayn Hotel, Qatbit Motel or a hotel in Salalah.

Grey Hypocolius

Muntasar

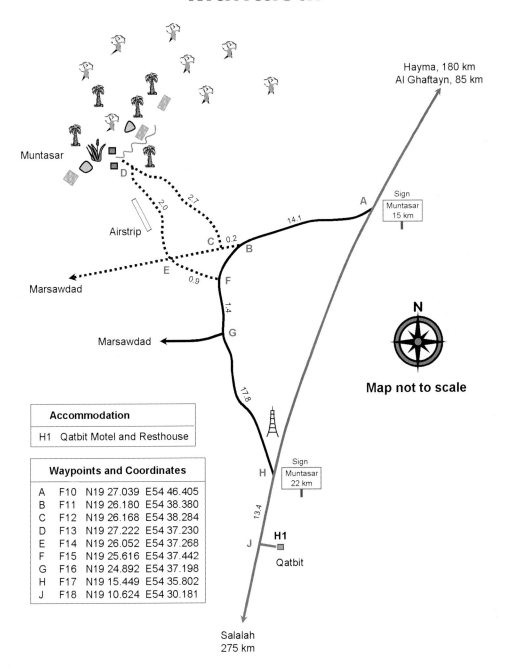

Hayma, 180 km
Al Ghaftayn, 85 km

Muntasar

Airstrip

Marsawdad

Marsawdad

D

A

Sign
Muntasar
15 km

14.1

2.7

2.0

C 0.2

B

E

0.9

F

1.4

G

17.8

H

Sign
Muntasar
22 km

13.4

J H1

Qatbit

Salalah
275 km

N

Map not to scale

Accommodation	
H1	Qatbit Motel and Resthouse

Waypoints and Coordinates			
A	F10	N19 27.039	E54 46.405
B	F11	N19 26.180	E54 38.380
C	F12	N19 26.168	E54 38.284
D	F13	N19 27.222	E54 37.230
E	F14	N19 26.052	E54 37.268
F	F15	N19 25.616	E54 37.442
G	F16	N19 24.892	E54 37.198
H	F17	N19 15.449	E54 35.802
J	F18	N19 10.624	E54 30.181

7.4 Qatbit ***   2WD

Key species: warblers, wheatears, shrikes, buntings, other migrants, rarities.

     Located 13.4 km south of the southerly turning to Muntasar is the Qatbit Motel, one of the primary migration hotspots of the central desert. The ground layout is identical to the other two hotels on the Nizwa - Salalah road at Al Ghabah and Al Ghaftayn (site 7.2), but Qatbit is far superior to either as irrigation of the garden has been maintained over the years. Helpfully, the vegetation includes a mix of trees and shrubs in addition to the ubiquitous **Mesquite** *Prosopis juliflora* found at the others. The management at the hotel is keen to attract both birds and birders and the motel is conveniently placed to stay for a thorough exploration of several other sites, though Al Ghaftayn Hotel is better priced, cleaner and serves proper meals. A birders logbook can be found at the reception desk at Qatbit, in which we would encourage visitors to record their observations. During migration anything can turn up and vagrants have included a string of notables such as **Indian Hawk Cuckoo, White-throated Bee-eater, Cyprus Pied Wheatear, Robin, Grasshopper Warbler, Black Drongo** and **Cretzschmar's Bunting**. The odd and bizarre have similarly been recorded, with records of **Cormorant, Striated Heron, Osprey**, and **gulls**. In recent winters sightings of **Grey Hypocolius** have increased, which are likely to refer to individuals commuting between here and Muntasar. In good years, **Nile Valley Sunbird**, can be found in taller trees around the hotel building. Even **Dunn's Lark** and **Houbara Bustard** have been seen in the vicinity, though sightings of the latter would be considered immense luck.

Spotted and Crowned Sandgrouse

     Having explored the hotel grounds, birders should check the permanent spring, small pool and few trees and reeds located just east of the hotel. Both **Spotted** and **Crowned Sandgrouse** come to drink though in much smaller numbers than at Muntasar. Tired migrants sometimes rest in the thick cover, and have included half a dozen **European Scops Owl** in October.

     Finally, time-permitting, a small, now abandoned, farm 19.3 km toward Salalah, at Qatbit South can be checked. Small numbers of migrants, **warblers, flycatchers** and **shrikes** are likely to be present during peak migration. Previously this was a regular wintering area for **Red-breasted Flycatcher**, but the lack of irrigation now means the dying trees are less attractive.

     Accommodation: camping, Al Ghaftayn Hotel, Qatbit Motel or a hotel in Salalah.

Qatbit

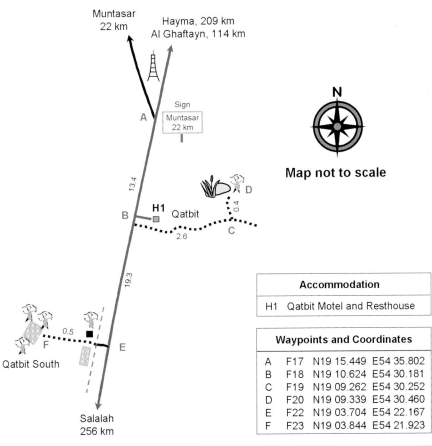

Muntasar
22 km

Hayma, 209 km
Al Ghaftayn, 114 km

Sign
Muntasar
22 km

N

Map not to scale

13.4

A

H1   Qatbit
B

D

0.4

C

2.6

19.3

0.5

F

E

Qatbit South

Salalah
256 km

Accommodation	
H1	Qatbit Motel and Resthouse

Waypoints and Coordinates			
A	F17	N19 15.449	E54 35.802
B	F18	N19 10.624	E54 30.181
C	F19	N19 09.262	E54 30.252
D	F20	N19 09.339	E54 30.460
E	F22	N19 03.704	E54 22.167
F	F23	N19 03.844	E54 21.923

Masked Shrike at Qatbit oasis

7.5 Al Balid Farm *

2WD/4WD

Key species: White Stork, larks, pipits, migrants.

In recent years a number of farming projects have sprung up in the area between Qatbit and Thumrayt. With their green fields set in a barren desert landscape they act as magnets to migrant and resident birds alike. One of the biggest farms is Al Balid Farm located 32 km south of Dawkah and 6 km west of the main highway. This, and other farms in the area, is infrequently visited by birdwatchers and the species list would undoubtedly increase with better coverage. The road sign may say 'Al Beed Farm.'

In autumn as many as 250 **White Storks** have made a stopover. **Kestrel** and **Long-legged Buzzard** are regular and various **larks**, including both **Dunn's** and **Bar-tailed Desert Lark**, have been seen, with **Hoopoe Lark** a virtual certainty. **Pipits**, **wagtails** and **wheatears** are much in evidence and trees and bushes should be checked for **warblers** and other migrants.

There are several other farms in this neighbourhood, all of which can be explored. The fields are large and will take some time and effort to go through. The effort could be well rewarded.

The old farming community at Dawkah has unfortunately been abandoned for some years, and most trees have died from lack of water. However a permanent spring still supports an area of sedge, and attracts **larks**, migrants and the occasional **Spotted** or **Crowned Sandgrouse**. **European Scops Owl** and **Pallid Harrier** including adult males have been regular in autumn and **European Nightjar** in spring. An area of date palms still persists, which is always worth checking for **warblers**, and **Common Rosefinch** is frequently observed. **Grey Hypocolius** has been seen in the palms in winter. If farming starts up again, Dawkah would undoubtedly resume its status as a major birdwatching site.

Accommodation: camping or a hotel in Salalah or Thumrayt.

Long-legged Buzzard

Al Balid Farm

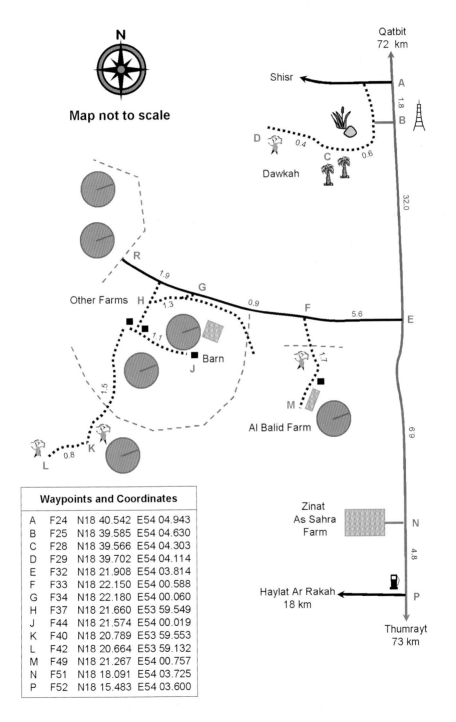

N

Map not to scale

Qatbit
72 km

Shisr

A

1.8

B

D
0.4

C
0.6

Dawkah

32.0

R

1.9

G

Other Farms H

1.3

0.9

F

5.6

E

1.1

Barn

J

1.7

1.5

M

Al Balid Farm

6.9

K

0.8

L

Zinat
As Sahra
Farm

N

4.8

Haylat Ar Rakah
18 km

P

Thumrayt
73 km

Waypoints and Coordinates			
A	F24	N18 40.542	E54 04.943
B	F25	N18 39.585	E54 04.630
C	F28	N18 39.566	E54 04.303
D	F29	N18 39.702	E54 04.114
E	F32	N18 21.908	E54 03.814
F	F33	N18 22.150	E54 00.588
G	F34	N18 22.180	E54 00.060
H	F37	N18 21.660	E53 59.549
J	F44	N18 21.574	E54 00.019
K	F40	N18 20.789	E53 59.553
L	F42	N18 20.664	E53 59.132
M	F49	N18 21.267	E54 00.757
N	F51	N18 18.091	E54 03.725
P	F52	N18 15.483	E54 03.600

7.6 Haylat Ar Rakah and Shisr **

Key species: sandgrouse, Hoopoe Lark, Dunn's Lark, migrants, rarities

Both these new sites are accessed on unpaved roads west of the Muscat – Salalah highway. The closer site, at Haylat Ar Rakah, has the better road, but neither may be passable by 2WD following rain. A 4WD is recommended for the wash-boarded longer drive to Shisr and, once there, reaching the irrigated pivot fields is only possible with 4WD. The 26 km sand track across the desert directly from Haylat Ar Rakah to Shisr can save driving the long way around, but requires a GPS and sand-driving experience,

Bar-tailed Desert Lark

as the going can be very soft in places. This track, starting from Haylat Ar Rakah, cannot be driven in a straight line, and loosely follows a set of power lines, which then divert southward, at which point Shisr can be seen in the distance slightly to the right. For birders interested in driving this track, the GPS route (waypoints F56 through F63) are given below. Note that this track could change over time with moving sand and rains.

Both sites have been rather neglected by visiting and resident birders alike, but with cultivation of grass on a larger scale having recently commenced in Shisr, this site looks set to become one of the premier migration points of the central desert. **Demoiselle Crane** has already been seen.

The combined species list for these sites is rather small at present, but likely to increase dramatically with better coverage. Birders in these areas are a novelty, so local people will be inquisitive of birders activities, and permission should be sought when wandering onto any fields.

Birding opportunities along the Haylat Ar Rakah road are limited to small farming lots, which appear to change from year to year, although one consistently better site, with some taller trees is found on the right 17 km from the main Salalah road. Any area of trees, date palms or cultivated fields are worth checking for migrants. Species to be expected during migration include **European Nightjar**, **Golden Oriole**, **Ménétries's Warbler**, **Desert Warbler**, and **Spotted Flycatcher**. Scarcer species that have been recorded to date have included **Green Warbler**, **Pale Rock Sparrow** and **Bar-tailed Desert Lark**.

At Shisr, other than the main grass pivots, a good area of trees and date palms, now unfortunately no longer irrigated, are found next to the important archeological ruins of Ubar. This area has produced **Grey Hypocolius**, **Masked Shrike**, and **Cretzschmar's Bunting**. Over the fields **eagles**, **herons**, **White Stork**, and **Long-legged Buzzard** can be found, while the surrounding desert might produce **Pallid Harrier**, **Crowned** and **Spotted Sandgrouse**, **Namaqua Dove**, **Hoopoe Lark** or the elusive **Bar-tailed Desert Lark** and **Dunn's Lark**.

Accommodation: camping or a hotel in Thumrayt or Salalah.

Haylat Ar Arakah - Shisr sand track			
C	F56	N18 18.135	E53 53.507
	F58	N18 18.156	E53 51.929
	F59	N18 17.589	E53 50.422
	F60	N18 16.904	E53 48.642
	F61	N18 16.038	E53 46.315
	F62	N18 15.510	E53 44.810
D	F63	N18 15.720	E53 41.987

Haylat Ar Rakah and Shisr

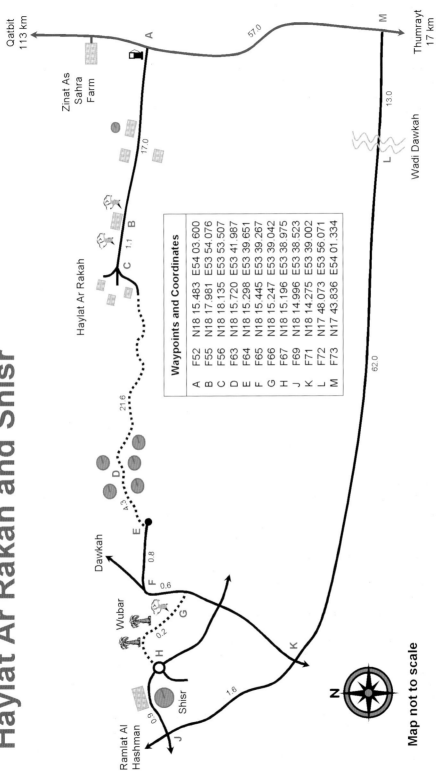

Waypoints and Coordinates

A	F52	N18 15.483	E54 03.600
B	F55	N18 17.981	E53 54.076
C	F56	N18 18.135	E53 53.507
D	F63	N18 15.720	E53 41.987
E	F64	N18 15.298	E53 39.651
F	F65	N18 15.445	E53 39.267
G	F66	N18 15.247	E53 39.042
H	F67	N18 15.196	E53 38.975
J	F69	N18 14.996	E53 38.523
K	F71	N18 14.275	E53 39.002
L	F72	N17 48.073	E53 56.071
M	F73	N17 43.836	E54 01.334

Qatbit
113 km

Zinat As
Sahra
Farm

Haylat Ar Rakah

Thumrayt
17 km

Wadi Dawkah

Dawkah

Wubar

Ramlat Al
Hashman

Shisr

Map not to scale

N

7.7 Wadi Rabkut *   4WD

Key species: Sand Partridge, Houbara Bustard, Dunn's Lark, Bar-tailed Desert Lark.

The paved road between Thumrayt and Marmul crosses a number of wide *wadis*, the first of which is Wadi Rabkut after 14 km. The *wadi* has a number of tall trees and low bushes and the area north of the road is open to exploration. Do not venture south of the road as this is part of a military bombing range.

A track leads north at the edge of the *wadi* for several km; following this track for one to two km and carefully scanning the *wadi* has proven a possible spot for **Houbara Bustard**, though sightings are by no means guaranteed. Other species seen with some regularity are the equally elusive **Sand Partridge**, **Dunn's Lark** and **Bar-tailed Desert Lark**.

With a 4WD it is possible to drive on the sandy tracks in the *wadi* itself, though this may not increase the chance of finding the **Houbara**. Probably the best strategy is to sit quietly at the edge in late afternoon overlooking a stretch of the *wadi*.

Accommodation: Camping or a hotel in Thumrayt or Salalah.

Young Arabian Camels in Wadi Rabkut

Wadi Rabkut

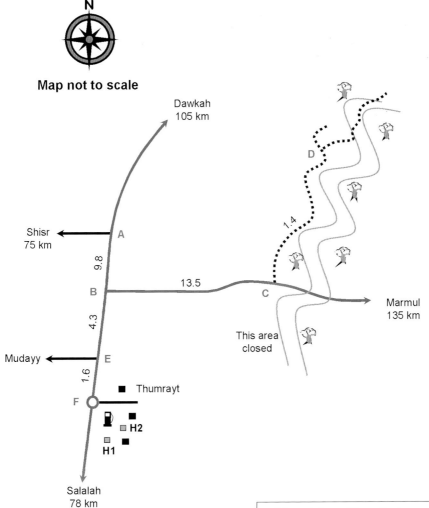

Map not to scale

Dawkah
105 km

Shisr
75 km

A

9.8

B

13.5

C

4.3

Marmul
135 km

This area
closed

Mudayy

E

1.6

F

■ Thumrayt

H2

H1

Salalah
78 km

1.4

D

Accommodation	
H1	Thumrayt Tourist Hotel
H2	Thumrayt Suites

Waypoints and Coordinates			
A	J09	N17 43.855	E54 01.329
B	J10	N17 39.119	E54 03.356
C	J11	N17 40.545	E54 09.754
D	J12	N17 41.309	E54 09.516
E	J13	N17 37.559	E54 01.702
F	J14	N17 36.741	E54 01.926

7.8 Thumrayt Waste Disposal Site *

2WD

Key species: Greater Spotted Eagle, Steppe Eagle, Imperial Eagle.

About 50 km north of Salalah and 1.5 km north of a graded road on the left signposted "Haluf 38 km", is the turnoff to the east for Thumrayt waste disposal site. The turning is marked only with a sign in Arabic, while the actual waste disposal site is situated three km further from the main road. The location is set among barren hills, that attract few species of birds, and the sole interest is the gathering of large **eagles** from mid-October to March. Most are **Steppe Eagles**, sometimes numbering a hundred or more, with fewer **Greater Spotted** and **Imperial Eagles** as well. The site is easy to reach and is worth a quick side trip on the way towards more interesting birdwatching sites. Access is unrestricted.

Accommodation: camping or a hotel in Salalah or Thumrayt.

Steppe Eagle

Thumrayt Waste Disposal Site

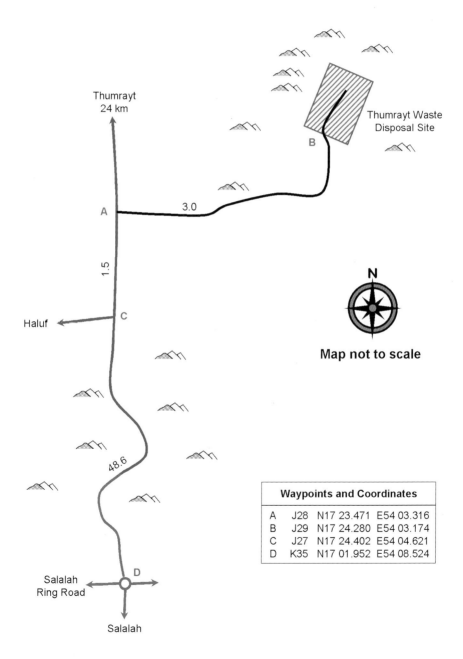

Thumrayt
24 km

Thumrayt Waste
Disposal Site

B

A   3.0

1.5

Haluf   C

N

Map not to scale

48.6

Salalah
Ring Road   D

Salalah

Waypoints and Coordinates		
A	J28	N17 23.471 E54 03.316
B	J29	N17 24.280 E54 03.174
C	J27	N17 24.402 E54 04.621
D	K35	N17 01.952 E54 08.524

8 Barr Al Hikman and Masirah

The mainland area of Barr Al Hikman and the island of Masirah are combined here, as together they form a special eco-system with birds moving freely across the dividing channel, Khawr Masirah. Formerly, the area was reached after a grueling drive for several hundred km on washboarded tracks and consequently, few birdwatchers visited. All this has now changed, with paved roads completed to Shannah, the ferry crossing point to Masirah. This has opened the area considerably, and weekend trips to Barr Al Hikman are now routinely made by resident birdwatchers from Muscat.

The island of Masirah can be reached by one of several car ferries that run between Shannah and Hilf, the small town at the northern end of Masirah. Ferries depart one to two hours before high tide, day and night. The crossing takes about 90 minutes and costs about RO 10 per vehicle each way. A tide table covering the whole country throughout the year is available from leading bookshops in the Capital area and costs RO 5. Crossings during daylight hours adds the possibility of **seabirds** with **shearwaters**, **Wilson's Storm-petrel** and **skuas** a possibility. Birdwatchers wishing to combine a visit to Masirah with Barr Al Hikman will require several days.

The number of species recorded at Barr Al Hikman is by no means near a high for Oman, but for sheer numbers of birds, Barr Al Hikman is unmatched in the country, or Arabia as a whole. Hundreds of thousands - if not millions - of birds pass through this areas each year and huge gatherings can be seen at any time between mid-August and May. When temperatures start to drop in northern climates, **flamingos**, **herons**, **waders**, **gulls** and **terns** start to move south, and for many Barr Al Hikman will be their destination. The extensive tidal mudflats are teeming with birds and great clouds of **plovers** and **sandpipers** can be seen. For birdwatchers the main attraction will surely be **Crab Plover** and **Great Knot**, both of which are quite easy to find.

Although the numbers of birds on Masirah are far lower than at Barr Al Hikman, it has proven a real hotspot for vagrants and the unusual. Several species of birds on the *Oman Bird List* have only been seen on Masirah; their discoveries due to dedicated resident birdwatchers in the past. A total of more than 330 species of birds has been recorded on Masirah including all 18 species of **terns** found in Arabia.

Despite the newly paved roads which make access to parts of Barr Al Hikman and to Masirah quite easy, other parts are still difficult to reach and requires careful preparation and local knowledge. A 4WD is absolutely necessary and one should not venture into remote areas with one vehicle alone.

A word of warning is appropriate here. Much of Barr Al Hikman is made up of *sabkha*, a mixture of sand, salt and mud. A well driven track on the *sabkha* can be as hard as tarmac, and even if the track is flooded it can be quite safe. But *sabkha* is treacherous. Do not attempt to drive on *sabkha* if there is no prior track, not even for a short distance. The surface may look dry, but the water level may just be a few cm below and one can sink in without warning. At best it will take hours to dig the car free and only if the trip has been well prepared. Experienced Barr Al Hikman travelers come with eight wooden planks and a good jack. If stuck, each wheel can be jacked-up and a plank placed underneath. By adding new planks under the tyres one can slowly back out of a troubled spot. Unless only easily accessible areas are visited, a birdwatching party should have at least two vehicles and carry long ropes, plenty of water, a GPS and good maps, though the latter are difficult to find. Also note that in this flat area a rise in seawater of just 10 cm will mean many km of flooded land. More than one birdwatching party have come late at night and set up camp on a small hill only to wake up with no land in sight in any direction! If this happens one has to wait for the next low tide. After rain, all *sabkha* may be impassable for weeks.

With careful preparations and common sense a visit to Barr Al Hikman can be a fantastic experience and would surely be a highlight of a bird trip to Oman for foreign birdwatchers.

Barr Al Hikman and Masirah

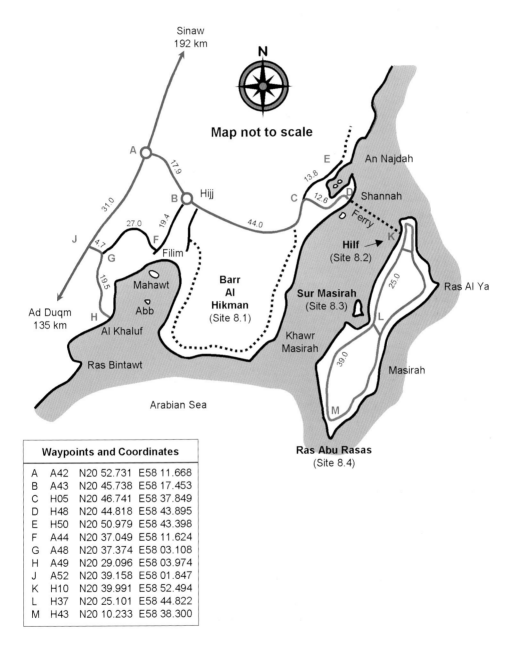

Sinaw
192 km

N

Map not to scale

A

Sinaw 192 km

17.9

31.0

B Hijj

27.0

19.4

44.0

J

4.7

F

Filim

G

19.5

Mahawt

Abb

H

Al Khaluf

Ras Bintawt

E

An Najdah

13.8

C

12.6

D

Shannah

Ferry

K

Hilf → (Site 8.2)

Barr
Al
Hikman
(Site 8.1)

Sur Masirah
(Site 8.3)

25.0

Ras Al Ya

L

Khawr
Masirah

39.0

Masirah

Arabian Sea

M

Ad Duqm
135 km

Ras Abu Rasas
(Site 8.4)

		Waypoints and Coordinates	
A	A42	N20 52.731	E58 11.668
B	A43	N20 45.738	E58 17.453
C	H05	N20 46.741	E58 37.849
D	H48	N20 44.818	E58 43.895
E	H50	N20 50.979	E58 43.398
F	A44	N20 37.049	E58 11.624
G	A48	N20 37.374	E58 03.108
H	A49	N20 29.096	E58 03.974
J	A52	N20 39.158	E58 01.847
K	H10	N20 39.991	E58 52.494
L	H37	N20 25.101	E58 44.822
M	H43	N20 10.233	E58 38.300

8.1 Barr Al Hikman ***   4WD

Key species: herons, Greater Flamingo, Avocet, Crab Plover, Great Knot, other waders, gulls, terns, Oriental White-eye.

For birdwatching on a grand scale, Barr Al Hikman is second to none in Oman or Arabia. The total number of birds runs easily into the hundreds of thousands. Whereas the number of species may not be so impressive, the total counts of some species are staggering.

Barr Al Hikman is a sandy peninsula approximately 30 by 30 km surrounded by extensive tidal mudflats. The area is now easily reached on paved roads from the Capital area via Sinaw. The turnoff for Al Hijj, the main village on Barr Al Hikman, is 192 km south of Sinaw. The road is now paved the whole stretch to Shannah, the ferry crossing point for Masirah. Though the paved roads give easy access to some parts of Barr Al Hikman, a 4WD is essential to fully explore the area.

Several good birdwatching spots are found around Barr Al Hikman and can be divided conveniently into the areas around Ghubbat Hashish bay and along the east coast, facing Masirah island.

Filim and Ghubbat Hashish

The village of Filim is reached by a graded road 19 km from the roundabout in Al Hijj. Good views can be had from the low rocky outcrops next to the desalination plant at the end of the road. At low tide the birds are very distant, but roosting flocks of **waders** can be studied at high tide. Flocks of up to 500 **Terek Sandpipers** have been seen from here in autumn and it will be a great challenge to sort out all the small **plovers**, **sandpipers** and **stints**.

An excellent observation point in the form of a long rock can sometimes, when the *sabkha* is dry, be reached 6 km west of Filim and is visible from the village. Take the graded road that runs west from the centre of the village for 0.7 km and turn left onto a track across the *sabkha.* Use common sense and attempt this only if the track is completely dry. The track ends at the rock, but may be too soft for the last few hundred metres. If so, walk the last bit and in any event, one will have to walk the last km or so to the southern tip of the rock. At high tide in the early morning there is a commanding view over the bay with the mangroves of Mahawt island in the back. **Greater Flamingos** number into the thousands and hundreds of **Western Reef Heron, Grey Heron, Great White Egret** and **Spoonbill** are easy to pick out. So too are **Oystercatcher, Avocet, Crab Plover, Whimbrel, Curlew** and **Bar-tailed Godwit** among the tens of thousands of roosting birds. **Slender-billed Gull** and **Caspian Tern** are common with **Gull-billed Tern** patrolling the still exposed mudflats and **Saunders's Tern** passing by. The smaller waders will be much harder to sort out, even with a telescope, and it may be necessary to walk out onto the mud. A good place is through a small clump of mangrove trees a few hundred metres back from the southern tip of the rock. In this area some 5,000 **Broad-billed Sandpipers**, which must represent a good percentage of the world's population, have been encountered and numbers of **Great Knot** have been seen, though this species is more easily found along the east coast of Barr Al Hikman. In addition there will be thousands upon thousands of **Lesser** and **Greater Sand Plover, Sanderling, Little Stint, Dunlin, Curlew Sandpiper, Redshank, Greenshank, Terek Sandpiper** and **Turnstone**.

Mahawt island with its extensive mangroves has recently gained ornithological importance with a newly discovered population of **Oriental White-eye** (Eriksen *et al.* 2001), the only place in Arabia where this bird has been found. Though it is possible to walk to the island at low tide, it would be difficult to get there, find the bird and return within one low tide period. A better choice is to hire a local fisherman in Filim and make a trip to the island at high tide. The best spot for the white-eye is the mangroves at the southern end, where one can enter a long channel and sit quietly in the boat. The white-eyes move through the mangrove canopy and should not be difficult to find. Another important recent find has been sightings of **White-collared Kingfisher**, a species under severe threat in northern Oman.

At the western end of Ghubbat Hashish lies the village of Khaluf. It can be reached via graded or paved roads or, at low tide, through a shortcut on the *sabkha* to Ras Az Zakhir and then along the beach to Khaluf. The rocky shore and sandy beaches hold a variety of **waders** and thousands of **gulls** in winter. Continuing up through the village away from the coast will lead around a headland and after about 5 km will end at a wide sandy beach. At low tide one can drive on the beach all the way to Ras Bintawt, though a detour around a *khawr* and a headland about midway is necessary. The beaches are roosting sites for tens

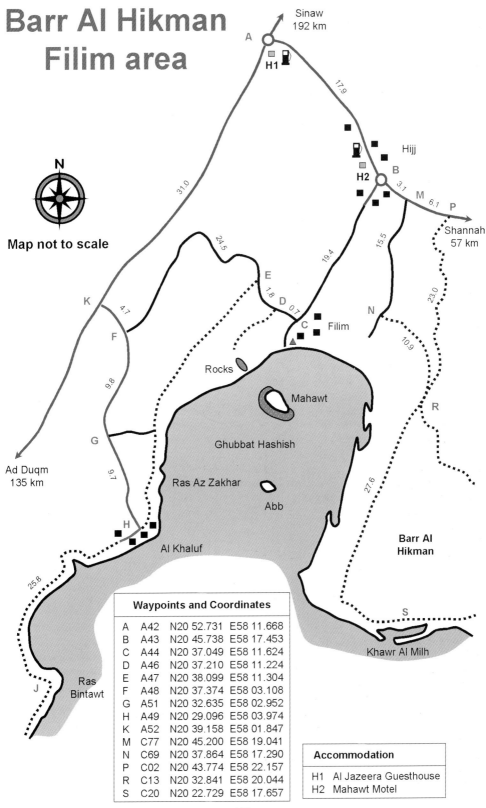

Barr Al Hikman
Filim area

Sinaw
192 km

A

H1

17.9

Hijj

H2

B

3.1

M

6.1

P

Shannah
57 km

N

Map not to scale

31.0

24.5

19.4

15.5

23.0

E

1.8

D

0.7

C

Filim

N

10.9

K

4.7

F

9.8

Rocks

Mahawt

R

G

9.7

Ghubbat Hashish

Ras Az Zakhar

Abb

Ad Duqm
135 km

H

**Barr Al
Hikman**

Al Khaluf

27.6

25.8

S

Khawr Al Milh

J

Ras
Bintawt

Waypoints and Coordinates			
A	A42	N20 52.731	E58 11.668
B	A43	N20 45.738	E58 17.453
C	A44	N20 37.049	E58 11.624
D	A46	N20 37.210	E58 11.224
E	A47	N20 38.099	E58 11.304
F	A48	N20 37.374	E58 03.108
G	A51	N20 32.635	E58 02.952
H	A49	N20 29.096	E58 03.974
K	A52	N20 39.158	E58 01.847
M	C77	N20 45.200	E58 19.041
N	C69	N20 37.864	E58 17.290
P	C02	N20 43.774	E58 22.157
R	C13	N20 32.841	E58 20.044
S	C20	N20 22.729	E58 17.657

Accommodation	
H1	Al Jazeera Guesthouse
H2	Mahawt Motel

103

of thousands of **gulls** and **terns** including hundreds of **Great Black-backed Gull** from January to March. The adjacent sand dunes are a favourite camping spot.

From Al Hijj it is possible, preferably with local knowledge and guidance, to get to the south shore of Barr Al Hikman. A graded track starts 3.1 km from the roundabout at Al Hijj. After about 16 km it is possible to branch off, and with a GPS navigate to a lagoon known as Khawr Al Milh which is a good birdwatching spot and a great camping area.

The East Coast and Khawr Barr Al Hikman

For even greater numbers of birds the east coast offers several good sites. Continue through the village of Al Hijj on the paved road for 44 km and turn right, which ends at the ferry terminal at Shannah after 12.6 km. At high tide the surrounding areas along the last several km will be flooded and many small **waders** may be seen. Before Shannah the area is drier and from the ferry point one can backtrack along the high tide mark for a few kilometres. At high tide there will be several roosting flocks of **waders**. Carefully scan the flocks of **Bar-tailed Godwit** for the odd **Great Knot** which can be surprisingly difficult to pick out, except from late-March when both species are in breeding plumage. Alternatively, go back a few kilometres and cross the narrow area of sabkha on any available track. The bay area is a major roosting site at high tide.

Jazirat Mawal is visible offshore and can be reached on foot at low tide, but be careful to return in time so as not to be trapped by the incoming tide.

Khawr Barr Al Hikman can be viewed from two sides. A track leads north just behind the Shannah Rest House and continues for about 4 km. From sand dunes at the end of this track there is a good view of the *khawr* in the early morning. Alternatively, one can go back to Al Hijj road and turn right towards An Najdah. Take one of the tracks leading closer to the *khawr* or walk out onto the mud.

The most reliable spot for **Great Knot** is the mudflats along the east coast. Go back towards Al Hijj for 8.8 km from the Shannah turnoff and take a track on the left just before a low gravel hill. The track goes over the hill and continues south through the *sabkha* for about 7 km. These tracks vary over the years, so accurate GPS readings are impossible to give. Sometimes it is possible to reach the coast near a small shelter, but often the last 0.5 km is flooded. If so, leave the vehicle and continue on foot. The little bay here is superb for birds. At high tide they are pushed up against the dry areas and the numbers and variety of birds are amazing. A careful scan through the thousands of **Bar-tailed Godwits** should produce several **Great Knots**.

If it is possible to reach the coast by vehicle, the tracks continue all the way along the east coast to the south shore of Barr Al Hikman. Make sure, though, to mark the exact turning point inland in some way for the return journey, as this flat and featureless area is very confusing.

Great Knots and Bar-tailed Godwits

With so many birds around it is quite difficult to pick out rarities, but a few have been noted over the years. Three records of **Slender-billed Curlew** exist and Oman's and Arabia's only record of **Far Eastern Curlew** is from Khawr Barr Al Hikman in October. In March 2001 an adult **Red-footed Booby** sat preening itself on the rocks at Khaluf. The whole area is difficult to assess properly, but with more coverage exciting discoveries will surely be made. For more details on the birds of Barr Al Hikman see Eriksen (1996).

Accommodation: camping, the Mahawt Motel in Al Hijj, the rest house at Shannah (if refurbished) or the Jazeera Guest House on the main road. Petrol is available at Al Hijj turnoff from the main Sinaw - Ad Duqm highway and in Al Hijj where shops and small restaurants are also found.

Barr Al Hikman
East Coast

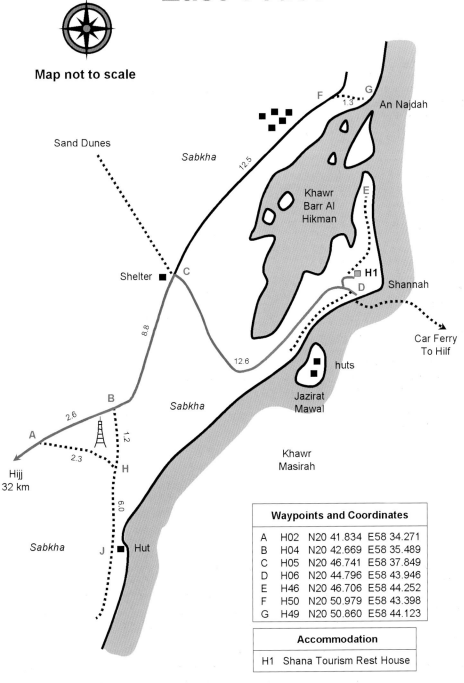

N

Map not to scale

Sand Dunes

Sabkha

F   G

1.3

An Najdah

12.5

Khawr
Barr Al
Hikman

E

Shelter ■ C

H1

D

Shannah

8.8

12.6

Car Ferry
To Hilf

B

Sabkha

huts

2.6

Jazirat
Mawal

A

1.2

Khawr
Masirah

2.3

H

Hijj
32 km

6.0

Sabkha

J ■ Hut

Waypoints and Coordinates			
A	H02	N20 41.834	E58 34.271
B	H04	N20 42.669	E58 35.489
C	H05	N20 46.741	E58 37.849
D	H06	N20 44.796	E58 43.946
E	H46	N20 46.706	E58 44.252
F	H50	N20 50.979	E58 43.398
G	H49	N20 50.860	E58 44.123

Accommodation	
H1	Shana Tourism Rest House

Key species: Rufous Turtle Dove, Pin-tailed Snipe, Koel, Olive-backed Pipit, migrants, vagrants.

With Masirah island being almost devoid of vegetation, the few wooded areas around Hilf, the principle town on Masirah, are a real migrant hotspot, offering one of the best opportunities in Oman for vagrants and the unexpected; a place where almost anything can, and has, turned up. The best time to visit is during the height of the spring or autumn migrations, from mid-April to mid-May and mid-September to mid-November, especially after rain, fog or poor weather, when spectacular falls can occur. Several rarer migrants turn up with some regularity, including **Pin-tailed Snipe**, **Great Snipe**, **Rufous Turtle Dove**, **Wryneck**, **Red-rumped Swallow**, **Forest Wagtail**, **Olive-backed Pipit**, **Black-throated Thrush**, **Green Warbler**, **Wood Warbler**, **Red-breasted** and **Semi-coloured Flycatcher**, **Common Rosefinch** and **Black-headed Bunting**. Small numbers of **Koel** have wintered consistently in the last few years. During winter months **waders** and **gulls** abound along the coast.

Olive-backed Pipit

Undoubtedly the best birding is at the orchard and sewage ponds four km south of town. The ponds themselves are surrounded by a locked gate, high walls and huge *Casuarina* trees that are visible from some distance. Staff work at the ponds from 07h00 to 12h00 daily, except Friday when no access is possible. The staff are accustomed to the few visiting birdwatchers, and after asking permission it is usually possible to walk inside to check the ponds, surrounding scrub, trees, and vegetable patches thoroughly. If access is denied a permit can be obtained in Hilf at the Municipality (*Baladiyah*) office near the ferry terminal. Over the last few years, development at the ponds have lead to a degradation of habitat, while the small orchard adjacent to the ponds, has matured and now usually holds more birds. With nowhere else to go, birds are sometimes 'falling out of every bush'. **Chestnut-bellied Sandgrouse** come regularly to drink during early morning. A small run-off to the beach can also be interesting. Check the beaches which usually hold an impressive assortment of roosting **gulls** and **terns**. It should be noted that at the time of writing some major expansion works were underway to expand the sewage works. This is likely to have a significant effect on access, habitat and birds.

Accommodation: camping or the Masirah Hotel located north of the ferry jetties. A new Golden Tulip Hotel is currently under construction on the east coast and may open in early 2008. Fuel and basic foodstuff are available in Hilf.

Hilf

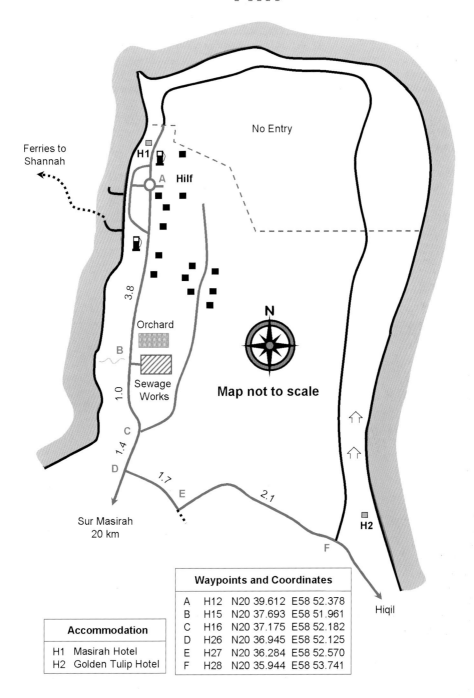

No Entry

Ferries to
Shannah

H1

Hilf
A

3.8

Orchard

B

Sewage
Works

1.0

C

1.4

D

1.7

E

2.1

N

Map not to scale

H2

F

Sur Masirah
20 km

Hiqil

Waypoints and Coordinates			
A	H12	N20 39.612	E58 52.378
B	H15	N20 37.693	E58 51.961
C	H16	N20 37.175	E58 52.182
D	H26	N20 36.945	E58 52.125
E	H27	N20 36.284	E58 52.570
F	H28	N20 35.944	E58 53.741

Accommodation	
H1	Masirah Hotel
H2	Golden Tulip Hotel

8.3 Sur Masirah **   4WD

Key species: herons, Crab Plover, waders, gulls, terns.

Sur Masirah, lying in a bay with extensive tidal mudflats, holds birds similar to those at Barr Al Hikman though in more moderate numbers. The area is reached by taking the paved road along the west coast of Masirah south from Hilf for about 34 km and turning right onto a rough track through a village 1.7 km south of the turnoff for Hiqil on the east coast. Once through the village the mudflats are obvious and several stops should be made before the track ends after 3.1 km at the sandy beach. From here one can walk north along a sand spit providing excellent views over the bay. Light is best in the afternoon.

Waders, **gulls** and **terns** are the most obvious birds of the mudflats with **Crab Plover** topping the wish list of birdwatchers. The wintering population of this species has been estimated at 2,000 for the whole bay area and with their conspicuous plumage and noisy behaviour they are difficult to miss. Other wintering populations with max. numbers given in parentheses include: **Oystercatcher** (3,000), **Kentish Plover** (300), **Lesser Sand Plover** (8,000), **Greater Sand Plover** (3,000), **Grey Plover** (1,600), **Sanderling** (1,500), **Little Stint** (500), **Curlew Sandpiper** (3,000), **Dunlin** (2,700), **Bar-tailed Godwit** (7,500), **Whimbrel** (700), **Curlew** (1,100), **Redshank** (2,000), **Greenshank** (100), **Terek Sandpiper** (40), **Turnstone** (1,900), **Sooty Gull** (2,500), **Great Black-headed Gull** (400), **Black-headed Gull** (400), **Slenderbilled Gull** (4,500), **Gull-billed Tern** (30), **Caspian Tern** (600), **Swift Tern** (1,000), **Lesser Crested Tern** (3,000), **Sandwich Tern** (1,000) and **Saunders's Tern** (500) with smaller number of several other species. In autumn 70,000 **White-cheeked Terns** have been recorded. Surprisingly, **Great Knot** has only been observed twice and in each case just a single bird.

During migration several other species may turn up and the trees around the village should be checked. In spring **Swift Terns** pair up before heading for a chosen breeding site, and courtship and aerial displays can be seen along the sand spit.

Accommodation: camping, the Masirah Hotel in Hilf or the Golden Tulip Hotel.

Great Black-headed Gull

Sur Masirah

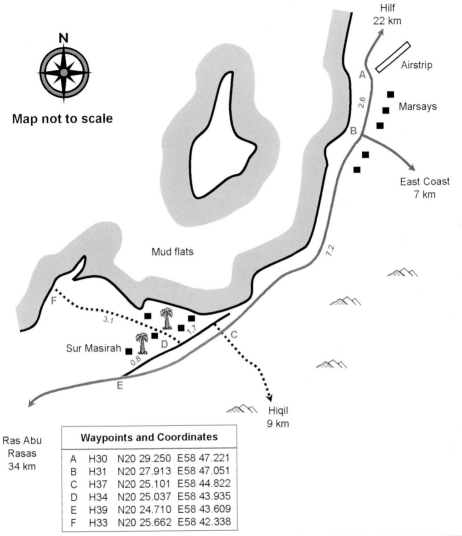

N

Map not to scale

Hilf
22 km

Airstrip

A

2.6

Marsays

B

East Coast
7 km

7.2

Mud flats

F

3.1

1.7

C

Sur Masirah

D

0.8

E

Hiqil
9 km

Ras Abu
Rasas
34 km

Waypoints and Coordinates			
A	H30	N20 29.250	E58 47.221
B	H31	N20 27.913	E58 47.051
C	H37	N20 25.101	E58 44.822
D	H34	N20 25.037	E58 43.935
E	H39	N20 24.710	E58 43.609
F	H33	N20 25.662	E58 42.338

Swift Terns

8.4 Ras Abu Rasas *   2WD

Key species: seabirds, gulls, Lesser Noddy, Common Noddy, other terns.

The southern tip of Masirah island, known as Ras Abu Rasas, is a rocky headland surrounded by sandy beaches. It is about 68 km south of Hilf along the west coast road. The headland can be surprisingly difficult to distinguish from other headlands with sand beaches, but the turnoff for Ras Abu Rasas is four km south of the paved turnoff to the eastern side of the island. A track leads to the tip of the headland.

Like other headlands, Ras Abu Rasas is a potential seabird watching point. **Jouanin's Petrel**, **Pale-footed** and **Persian Shearwaters**, **Wilson's Storm-petrel**, **Red-billed Tropicbird**, **Masked** and **Brown Booby**, and **Red-necked Phalarope** have been seen in addition to common **gulls** and **terns**. In summer the headland has proven a good spot for roosting **Lesser** and **Common Noddy** with about one hundred of each having been recorded in July. Massive flocks of **Swift Tern**, estimated at up to 5,000 birds, gather on the beaches in late spring with much courtship and aerial displays.

Masked Booby

The seas can be rough at Ras Abu Rasas and the wind strong. For some shelter for camping try the paved road mentioned above. After one km it crosses a *wadi* with a track leading south to potential picnic or camping spots.

Having arrived via the west coast road, one can return north along the east coast. A lagoon at Hiqil may hold **shorebirds** during migration and further north, at Ras Al Ya, is another potential sea-watching spot.

Accommodation: camping, the Masirah Hotel in Hilf or the Golden Tulip Hotel.

Ras Abu Rasas

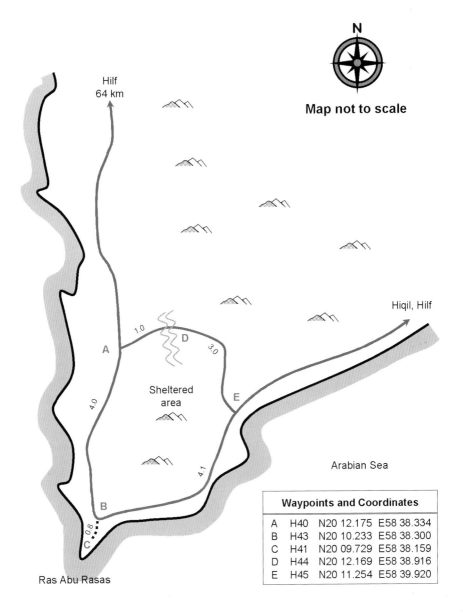

N

Map not to scale

Hilf
64 km

Hiqil, Hilf

1.0

A

D

3.0

Sheltered
area

E

4.0

4.1

B

0.8

C

Arabian Sea

Ras Abu Rasas

Waypoints and Coordinates			
A	H40	N20 12.175	E58 38.334
B	H43	N20 10.233	E58 38.300
C	H41	N20 09.729	E58 38.159
D	H44	N20 12.169	E58 38.916
E	H45	N20 11.254	E58 39.920

9 The Southeast Coast

The southeast of Oman is quite remote and will require several days from either Muscat or Salalah. However, the area is opening up rapidly with roads being paved at an astonishing rate. Over the last five years most roads to, and passing, these sites have been paved and work is in preparation to pave others. For the birdwatcher however, to explore this area a 4WD is still essential. Camping is the norm and most supplies should be brought along, although water and basic food items can be obtained in villages along the way. Shortages of fuel are a thing of the past as there are now several modern petrol stations scattered throughout.

The southeast is a beautiful, but thinly populated, area with long sandy beaches and rocky headlands. Several excellent birdwatching sites are found here, though distances between them are quite large. The keen birdwatcher will want to visit all. Ad Duqm is the main village near the east coast and from here a track leads to Ras Ad Duqm, a major birdwatching site. Further south Ras Madrakah can be explored for **seabirds**, but the main interest will be the small, but interesting Khawr Dhurf and the coastal lagoon called Khawr Ghawi near the village of Al Kahil. From here it is another few hours to Ash Shuwaymiyyah, where the beach and the hanging gardens in the nearby *wadi*, with their interesting birds, make the trip well worthwhile. Returning onto the escarpment north of Ash Shuwaymiyyah, the roads from Shalim lead north to Amal, Hayma and Muscat, or west through the vast oil fields of Marmul to Thumrayt and Salalah.

Few organized bird tours have included the southeast coast in their itinerary, but to get off the beaten track, this is a wonderful place to visit, especially in connection with Barr Al Hikman and Masirah to the north. With the rapidly improving infrastructure in this area, it is definitely worth considering.

Listed below are common, widespread species easily seen along the southeast coast. These are generally not discussed in the individual site accounts.

Western Reef Herons

Common resident species:

Laughing Dove	Southern Grey Shrike
Black-crowned Finch Lark	Brown-necked Raven
Hoopoe Lark	

Common migrant or seasonal species:

Western Reef Heron	Caspian Gull
Grey Heron	Sandwich Tern
Lesser Sand Plover	Barn Swallow
Greater Sand Plover	Isabelline Wheatear
Grey Plover	Desert Wheatear
Redshank	Isabelline Shrike
Sooty Gull	

	Waypoints and Coordinates		
A	F07	N19 57.536	E56 16.506
B	E14	N19 29.439	E57 34.955
C	E19	N19 09.585	E57 39.492
D	E70	N18 58.726	E57 48.033
E	E21	N18 57.018	E57 20.810
F	E33	N18 42.323	E56 40.312
G	E34	N18 35.178	E56 35.025
H	E42	N18 10.984	E56 32.671
J	E50	N18 07.057	E55 39.479
K	E55	N17 53.045	E55 36.157
L	X03	N18 10.100	E55 14.500
M	E65	N18 20.126	E55 38.830
N	E66	N18 32.656	E55 51.677
P	E67	N18 53.747	E56 16.484
R	X02	N19 50.050	E56 09.377
S	F08	N19 36.635	E55 31.035
T	F10	N19 27.039	E54 46.405
V	F18	N19 10.624	E54 30.181

Southeast Coast

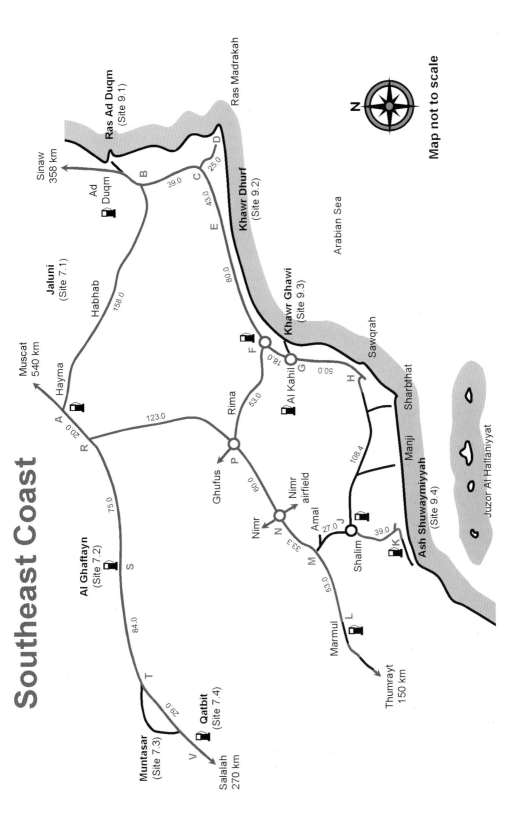

Map not to scale

N

9.1 Ad Duqm **   2WD/4WD

Key species: Socotra Cormorant, herons, Avocet, waders, Great Black-headed Gull, other gulls, terns.

Ad Duqm is the main village on the central east coast about 356 km south of Sinaw on the newly paved road. The village can also be reached from Hayma on the Muscat - Salalah highway. A new harbour is planned and may affect this site in the future. For birdwatchers the interesting area is near Ras Ad Duqm which, providing it has not rained, can be accessed by 2WD. The beaches around the fish factory attract thousands of **gulls** and **terns** and the extensive mudflats stretching northward are filled with **herons** and **waders** from early autumn to late spring.

By 4WD, from the petrol station in Al Duqm go north for 1.9 km and take the track on the right which after 5.3 km runs into the graded road from the south. This road ends at a fish factory. Backtrack for 0.7 km and take a track on the north leading along the shore to a rocky hill with a few huts. From the far side of this hill is a commanding view over the extensive mudflats. No roads lead into this area which is best explored on foot at low tide by walking along the sandy beach.

The massive gathering of **gulls** near the fish factory is worth a quick look, though most interest will be on the mudflats. A telescope is necessary and a single scan across the area has produced up to 37 **Ospreys** in winter. **Greater Flamingos** are conspicuous, and the small rocky outcrop in the middle is a favourite resting place for **Spoonbill** and various **herons**. The largest flock of **Avocet** in Oman numbering up to 175 is from here and a small flock of **Crab Plover** is usually present. The most numerous birds though will be the smaller **plovers** and **sandpipers**.

Sunset, Ras Ad Duqm

Ad Duqm

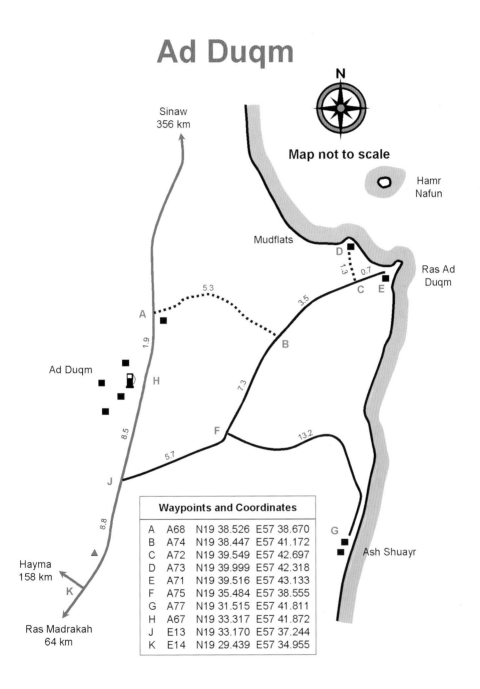

Map not to scale

Sinaw
356 km

Hamr
Nafun

Mudflats

Ras Ad
Duqm

Ad Duqm

Hayma
158 km

Ash Shuayr

Ras Madrakah
64 km

Waypoints and Coordinates			
A	A68	N19 38.526	E57 38.670
B	A74	N19 38.447	E57 41.172
C	A72	N19 39.549	E57 42.697
D	A73	N19 39.999	E57 42.318
E	A71	N19 39.516	E57 43.133
F	A75	N19 35.484	E57 38.555
G	A77	N19 31.515	E57 41.811
H	A67	N19 33.317	E57 41.872
J	E13	N19 33.170	E57 37.244
K	E14	N19 29.439	E57 34.955

Offshore, the flat-topped island of Hamr Nafun is clearly visible. It is a roosting site for a large flock of **Socotra Cormorant** numbering perhaps 10,000 birds. The flock is sometimes visible closer to shore, as the birds leap-frog each other in their characteristic feeding manner.

Accommodation: camping.

Key species: herons, Greater Flamingo, ducks, waders, gulls, terns.

The small fresh water lagoon of Khawr Dhurf is by far the most important wintering site for **ducks** anywhere between Muscat and Salalah. The lagoon is lined on the west side by tall sand dunes giving excellent views in the afternoon.

To reach Khawr Dhurf coming from Ad Duqm, head south towards Ras Madrakah and Sawqrah. Twenty km after the Ras Madrakah turn, the road crosses Wadi Gharm, which has a number of trees and is so far the southernmost site for **Grey Francolin** in Oman. **Spotted Thick-knees** also occur here and their Whimbrel-like call can be heard at night. After a further 23 km a few scattered palms can be seen on the left marking the site for Khawr Dhurf. Take the track leading off the main road to a small mosque and some water troughs and continue towards the sea.

Two species of **geese** and 13 species of **ducks** have been recorded at Khawr Dhurf, the most common being **Wigeon**, **Gadwall**, **Teal**, **Mallard**, **Pintail**, **Garganey**, **Shoveler** and **Pochard**. Often the total number exceeds 500. In addition, there are usually good numbers of **herons**, **Spoonbill**, **Greater Flamingo**, **Coot** and various species of **waders**, **gulls** and **terns**. **Avocet** is regular and there is even a record of **Slender-billed Curlew**: two birds seen February 1999. **Gull-billed** and **Caspian Tern** are common in winter and **Saunders's Terns** breed near the lagoon. **Crowned** and **Chestnut-bellied Sandgrouse** come to drink in the morning with **Spotted Sandgrouse** a possibility as well. On the surrounding plains, **Cream-coloured Courser** is as common as anywhere in Oman. A few migrants may be found and there always seems to be something unusual at this delightful spot.

Wigeon

Nearby Ras Madrakah is worth a visit if time allows. Situated where the coastline makes a sharp bend, the headland should be interesting for **seabirds**, but has not been fully studied. To reach Ras Madrakah go back on the Ad Duqm road and turn right. Continue for 25 km and take any of the multitude of tracks after the village, leading towards the sea.

Although all major roads in this area are now paved a 4WD is essential to go anywhere off road and fully explore the area.

Accommodation: camping.

Khawr Dhurf

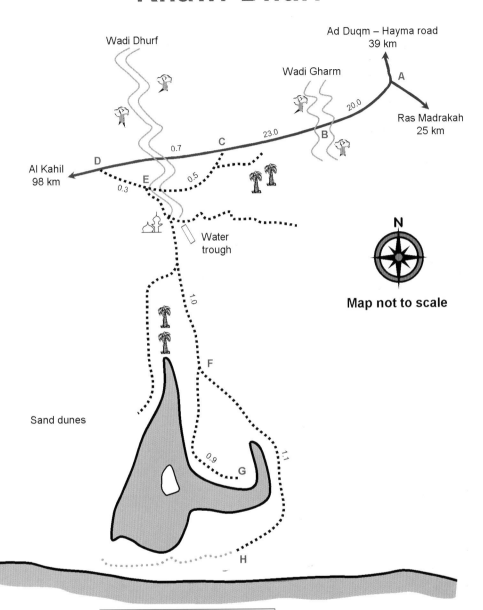

Ad Duqm – Hayma road
39 km

Wadi Dhurf

Wadi Gharm

A

Ras Madrakah
25 km

20.0

23.0

C

B

0.7

D

Al Kahil
98 km

E

0.5

0.3

Water
trough

1.0

N

Map not to scale

F

Sand dunes

0.9

G

1.1

H

Waypoints and Coordinates			
A	E19	N19 09.585	E57 39.492
B	E20	N19 01.846	E57 31.865
C	E21	N18 57.018	E57 20.810
D	E32	N18 56.959	E57 20.375
E	E31	N18 56.901	E57 20.538
F	E25	N18 56.369	E57 20.742
G	E24	N18 55.898	E57 20.814
H	E27	N18 55.806	E57 20.904

9.3 Khawr Ghawi **

4WD

Key species: herons, Greater Flamingo, Avocet, Crab Plover, Broad-billed Sandpiper, other waders, gulls terns.

Khawr Ghawi, also known as Khawr Shumayr, is a tidal lagoon about eight km long separated from the sea by a narrow sand spit, open at the northern end. It is the most important site south of Ad Duqm for **shorebirds** during migration and in winter.

From Khawr Dhurf (9.2) continue south for about 97 km and turn left at the new roundabout in the village of Al Kahil. From the south this turnoff is around 53 km north of Sawqrah. Drive through the village and turn right after 8.9 km onto a rough graded road that ends at the coast near a small pink lagoon, coloured by algae. From here a rough track leads south along the coast and soon the mouth of Khawr Ghawi will be evident. A number of tracks used by local fishermen give access to several good spots and at the bottom end a track leads at least some way up the sand spit, although the going is very soft. A particularly good area is at the middle of the *khawr* where an inlet is situated near a row of sand dunes.

Being open to the sea the water level fluctuates with the tides. At low tide much of the lagoon is dry and the birds disperse on the mudflats outside the sand spit. With the incoming tide the birds are pushed back into the lagoon and high tide roosts can be impressive. Hundreds of **Greater Flamingos** are the most obvious feature, but large numbers of **Spoonbill**, **Western Reef Heron**, **Great White Egret** and **Grey Heron** are present as well. Huge numbers of **waders** use the *khawr* for feeding and roosting. Most will be **sand plovers**, smaller **sandpipers**, **Redshank**, **Curlew** and **Turnstone**. About 100 each of **Avocet** and **Crab Plover** are usually found and several hundred **Broad-billed Sandpipers** have been recorded. Khawr Ghawi is a major wintering site for **gulls** and **terns**. Thousands of **Slender-billed Gull** and hundreds of **Caspian**, **Swift**, **Lesser Crested**, **Sandwich** and **Saunders's Tern** use the area along with smaller numbers of **Great Black-headed Gull** and **Gull-billed Tern**.

Farther north along the coast are smaller lagoons that can be explored. The birds will be similar to those at Khawr Ghawi, but numbers will be far more moderate.

Accommodation: camping.

Greater Flamingos

Khawr Ghawi

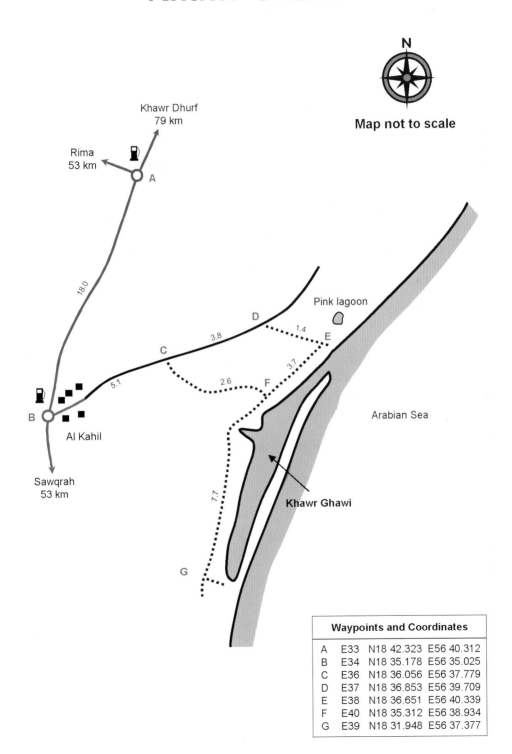

Map not to scale

Khawr Dhurf
79 km

Rima
53 km

A

18.0

Khawr Ghawi

Sawqrah
53 km

B

Al Kahil

5.1

C

3.8

D

1.4

E

3.7

F

2.6

7.7

G

Pink lagoon

Arabian Sea

Khawr Ghawi

Waypoints and Coordinates		
A	E33	N18 42.323 E56 40.312
B	E34	N18 35.178 E56 35.025
C	E36	N18 36.056 E56 37.779
D	E37	N18 36.853 E56 39.709
E	E38	N18 36.651 E56 40.339
F	E40	N18 35.312 E56 38.934
G	E39	N18 31.948 E56 37.377

9.4 Ash Shuwaymiyyah **   4WD

Key species: Masked Booby, Socotra Cormorant, Arabian Partridge, gulls, terns, Hume's Tawny Owl.

Ash Shuwaymiyyah is the name of a fishing village on the north shore of Al Hallaniyyat bay. For birdwatchers there are two important sites: the long, sandy beach stretching 20 km to the southwest, and the equally long Wadi Shuwaymiyyah that starts just at the western outskirts of the village.

To reach Ash Shuwaymiyyah, take the newly paved road south from Shalim which can be reached from the west, north or east on other graded roads. Due to its remoteness, this site is rarely visited by birdwatchers, but it is a delightful spot with some good birds.

A graded track leads west from the village just behind the low coastal dunes, and the occasional rough track can be taken down to the beach. Flocks of **Sanderlings** and a few **Curlews** will be present, but the main attraction is **Masked Booby** and **Socotra Cormorant**. Breeding year-round on the offshore islands, **Masked Boobies** use the bay as a fishing ground and often the birds can be seen diving right at the surf, giving excellent views.

Even more impressive is the flock of **Socotra Cormorant** normally present in the bay. The number of birds has been estimated at between 15,000 and 30,000 strong, and it is an impressive sight to see the whole flock fishing offshore. Sometimes they come ashore in one massive flock. The birds roost on the cliffs near the end of the track around Jinawt. In the morning, line after line of birds can be seen leaving the roosting site to feed. Jinawt is undoubtedly the most reliable site in Oman for this species.

The beaches hold a variety of **gulls** and **terns** in winter, especially at Jinawt where the fishermen haul in their catch. Look for **Hooded Wheatear** in this area a few kilometres back along the track.

Masked Boobies

Another site of major interest is the nearby *wadi*. A track heads north just after the last buildings at the western end of the village and then turns westward. The track is initially graded and easily drivable, but becomes rougher and more difficult after ten kilometres or so. The scenery in the *wadi* is impressive with cliffs towering 200 metres or more on either side with hanging gardens found in places where permanent springs seep from the rocks. Two such sites are clearly visible from the track and side tracks lead near them. The pools of water beneath the hanging gardens attract migrants and all four species of **sandgrouse** have been recorded. The track through the *wadi* ends, or rather becomes undrivable, after about 20 km from the village in an area with a number of date palms. This area is an excellent camping spot and a reliable site for **Hume's Tawny Owl**. It is also the northeastern limit of several Dhofar specialities such as **Blackstart**, **Palestine Sunbird**, **Tristram's Grackle** and **African Rock Bunting**. **Arabian Partridge** and **South Arabian Wheatear** are both resident and usually quite easy to find.

Accommodation: Shati Al Shuwaymiyyah Resthouse or camping.

Ash Shuwaymiyyah

Map not to scale

N

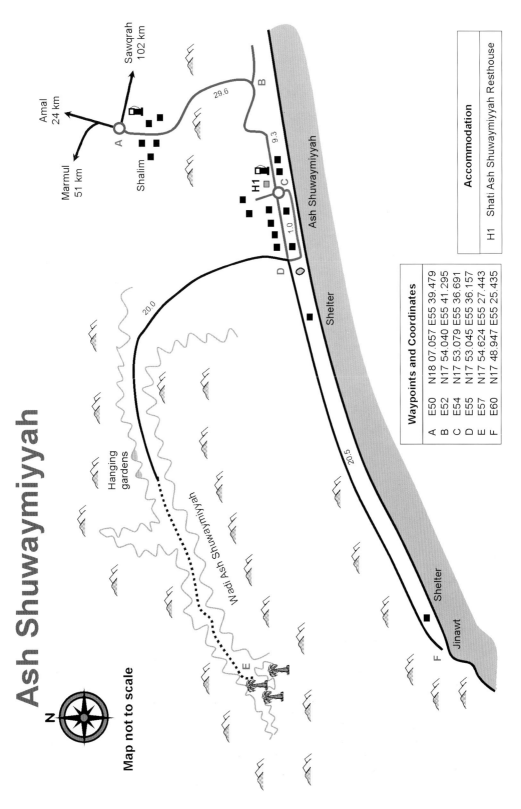

Amal 24 km

Marmul 51 km

Sawqrah 102 km

Shalim

A

29.6

B

9.3

H1

C

1.0

D

Ash Shuwaymiyyah

Shelter

20.0

Hanging gardens

Wadi Ash Shuwaymiyyah

E

20.5

Shelter

Jinawt

F

Waypoints and Coordinates		
A	E50	N18 07.057 E55 39.479
B	E52	N17 54.040 E55 41.295
C	E54	N17 53.079 E55 36.691
D	E55	N17 53.045 E55 36.157
E	E57	N17 54.624 E55 27.443
F	E60	N17 48.947 E55 25.435

Accommodation	
H1	Shati Ash Shuwaymiyyah Resthouse

10 Dhofar

Due to its sheer variety and diversity, the Dhofar region of the far south may be considered to offer the best birdwatching in Oman. The Dhofar mountains back a coastal plain containing numerous freshwater *khawrs* and seas that attract large numbers of **seabirds** in both summer and winter.

Biologically, the region is African, with over 600 km of barren desert to the north forming an effective isolating barrier from the predominantly Eurasian and Oriental avifaunas of the north. Many of the common species of the north, such as Purple Sunbird, Indian Roller, House Sparrow and Indian Silverbill are absent from the south.

One of the most striking climatic features is the summer monsoon between June and September, when the southern slope of the mountains is shrouded in fog and rain, temperatures drop, and the hillsides turn lush and green. This coincides with the arrival of several breeding visitors such as **Grey-headed Kingfisher**, **Bruce's Green Pigeon** and **Didric Cuckoo**, as well as **seabirds** from the southern oceans including **Pale-footed Shearwater** and **Wilson's Storm-petrel**.

Three principal habitats, each with its own specialities, will interest the birdwatcher: coastal lagoons, verdant *wadis*, and the offshore ocean.

The series of lagoons, stretching from Khawr Rawri in the east to Khawr Al Mughsayl in the west, holds **herons**, **flamingos**, **spoonbills**, **ibises** and **waders** throughout the year, as well as large numbers of wintering **wildfowl**. In addition, most of these *khawrs* have reeds, attracting migrant **crakes** and **warblers**.

The well-wooded *wadis* and permanent springs in the foothills contain most of the Dhofar specialities such as **Bruce's Green Pigeon**, **African Paradise Flycatcher**, **Arabian Warbler**, **Shining** and **Palestine Sunbird**, **White-breasted White-eye** and **Black-headed Tchagra**, with the hills immediately behind good for others like **Arabian Partridge**, **African Scops Owl** and **South Arabian Wheatear**.

Seabird enthusiasts will head for rocky promontories that provide exciting sea-watching almost throughout the year, offering good opportunities to observe **Persian Shearwater**, **Jouanin's Petrel**, **Wilson's Storm-petrel**, **Red-billed Tropicbird**, **Socotra Cormorant** and **Masked Booby** to name a few.

In several areas the Salalah plain contains rather dense woodlands which can attract migrants. However, these are not as good as they might first appear, having been infested with the invasive **Mesquite** *Prosopis juliflora*. An eradication campaign was conducted some years ago, and large areas were successfully cleared. However, the **Mesquite** is rapidly returning to clog the *wadis* of Dhofar once again.

Listed below are common, widespread species easily seen in Dhofar. These are generally not discussed in the individual site accounts.

Common resident species:

Western Reef Heron	Swift Tern	Tristram's Grackle
Little Egret	Sandwich Tern	Rüppell's Weaver
Grey Heron	Laughing Dove	African Silverbill
Glossy Ibis	Crested Lark	African Rock Bunting
Spoonbill	African Rock Martin	
Greater Flamingo	Yellow-vented Bulbul	
Kestrel	Graceful Prinia	
Moorhen	Clamorous Reed Warbler	
Coot	White-breasted White-eye	
Sooty Gull	Fan-tailed Raven	

Common migrant and seasonal species:

Teal	Slender-billed Gull
Pintail	Siberian Gull
Shoveler	Caspian Gull
Sanderling	Swift Tern
Little Stint	Barn Swallow
Common Sandpiper	White Wagtail
Sooty Gull	Desert Wheatear

Waypoints and Coordinates			
A	J21	N16 52.895	E53 46.549
B	K41	N16 56.935	E53 59.270
C	K39	N17 00.343	E54 02.457
D	K47	N17 01.519	E54 10.349
E	K35	N17 01.952	E54 08.524
F	K31	N17 07.115	E54 09.172
G	F81	N17 03.077	E54 13.100
H	F82	N17 07.491	E54 13.669
K	K06	N17 02.957	E54 23.956
M	G14	N17 06.380	E54 33.366
N	G22	N17 01.841	E54 36.778
P	K15	N16 59.294	E54 41.782
R	K19	N16 56.816	E54 47.869

Full day

East Khawr

Khawr Swli
Khawr Taqah
Khawr Rawri
~~Mir~~ Ras Mirbat @
Ras Janjari

↓

Mountani

1/2 day
Jarziz & Sahnawt Farms

East Khawr

Ayun Razet

Garbage tip ~~verification~~ plant
Water purification plant   Mr. Mahad issa

AROUND THE WORLD IN 7 DAYS

Embark on a gastronomic tour of the world with special Theme Nights at the Dolphin Beach restaurant. Relish different cuisines, unwind and live it up every day of the week. | 7 pm onwards.

SUNDAY - SEAFOOD NIGHT
Celebrate Sunday with a smoky seafood barbecue as the taste catches you hook, line and sinker.
OMR 15.0

MONDAY - THE WORLD OF KEBABS
Relish eclectic Persian, Turkish & Syrian Kebabs as you settle down with cold salads and divine desserts.
OMR 13.5

TUESDAY - ITALIAN NIGHT
Revel in the delights of Italian cuisine consisting of Antipasto buffet, live pasta counters, traditional grills and many more.
OMR 13.5

WEDNESDAY - INDIAN NIGHT
The flavour of India comes alive with traditional favourites like tandooris, tikkas, vegetarian grills and many more delectable surprises.
OMR 13.5

THURSDAY - LEBANESE NIGHT
Revel in the essence of Lebanon with an authentic barbecue, featuring the best of the country paired with a hot and cold buffet.
OMR 13.5

FRIDAY - OMANI NIGHT
Indulge in the true taste of tradition with Omani cuisine, served on the table with all dishes for sharing.
OMR 13.5

SATURDAY - STEAK HOUSE NIGHT
Enjoy a sizzling good time with exotic barbecues cooked international steakhouse style, accompanied by salads, soups, meats, desserts and many more delicacies.
OMR 13.5

All prices are subject to 17% tax and service charges.

For more information, please call +968 23238000 or email fb.cpsalalah@ihg.com

CROWNEPLAZA.COM/SALALAH   +968 23238000

Dhofar

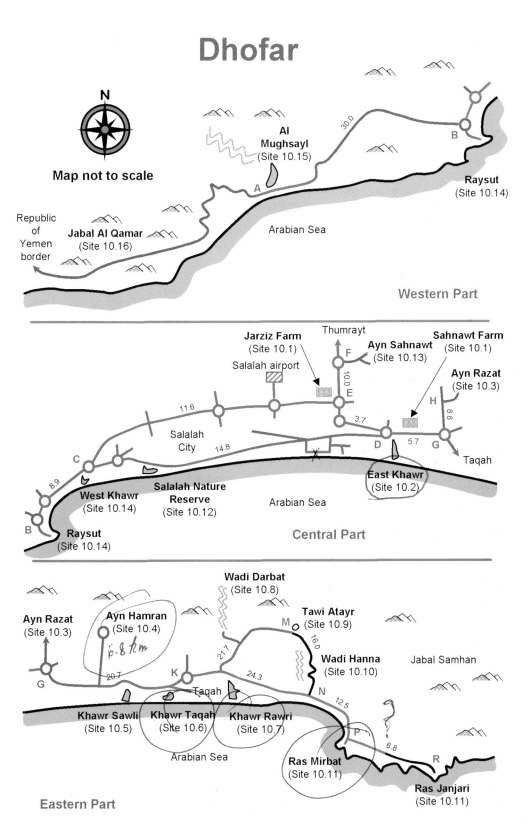

N

Map not to scale

Al Mughsayl (Site 10.15)

A

30.0

B

Raysut (Site 10.14)

Republic of Yemen border

Jabal Al Qamar (Site 10.16)

Arabian Sea

Western Part

Jarziz Farm (Site 10.1)

Thumrayt

Ayn Sahnawt (Site 10.13)

Sahnawt Farm (Site 10.1)

Salalah airport

F

Ayn Razat (Site 10.3)

E

10.0

H

8.6

11.6

Salalah City

3.7

D

5.7

G

14.8

X

Taqah

C

East Khawr (Site 10.2)

8.9

West Khawr (Site 10.14)

Salalah Nature Reserve (Site 10.12)

Arabian Sea

Central Part

B

Raysut (Site 10.14)

Wadi Darbat (Site 10.8)

Ayn Hamran (Site 10.4)

Tawi Atayr (Site 10.9)

M

Ayn Razat (Site 10.3)

6-8 km

16.0

Wadi Hanna (Site 10.10)

Jabal Samhan

21.7

G

20.7

K

24.3

Taqah

N

12.5

Khawr Sawli (Site 10.5)

Khawr Taqah (Site 10.6)

Khawr Rawri (Site 10.7)

P

6.8

R

Arabian Sea

Ras Mirbat (Site 10.11)

Ras Janjari (Site 10.11)

Eastern Part

10.1 Salalah Farms ***   2WD

Key species: Abdim's Stork, White Stork, harriers, eagles, Amur Falcon, Whiskered Tern, White-winged Black Tern, Namaqua Dove, Singing Bush Lark, Rose-coloured Starling, migrants, rarities.

Two huge farms known as Jarziz Farm along the Thumrayt road, and Sahnawt Farm along the Taqah road, are excellent birdwatching sites near the city of Salalah. Both are owned by the Dhofar Cattle Feed Co. and are thus private land. The farms are open from 07h00 to 19h00 Saturday to Thursday, but closed on Fridays and holidays. Both farms are administrated from Jarziz Farm so start here by asking permission at the office of the Public Relations Manager in the white building near the old entrance along the Thumrayt road. The gate is usually open; otherwise ask the gateman to gain entry. Birdwatchers are normally welcome, but access cannot be guaranteed and make sure only to drive on designated tracks and not on the fields themselves. Of course, the work on the farms should not be interfered with.

Each farm consists of huge grassy fields that attract numerous birds, especially during migration and in winter. Both farms should be investigated as they usually hold quite different birds. Dozens of **White Stork** overwinter and sometimes a number of **Abdim's Storks** are found as well. At dusk the number of **harriers** can be impressive and may include all four species, **Marsh**, **Hen**, **Montagu's** and **Pallid Harrier**. Eight species of **eagles** have been recorded with **Greater Spotted** and **Imperial Eagle** the most frequent. **Amur Falcon** is a regular passage migrant in late April and May. Though rare, both **Common** and **Demoiselle's Crane** have been found. An interesting variety of **waders** are usually present and may include **Cream-coloured Courser**, **Collared Pratincole**, **Pacific Golden Plover** and many more common species. **Whiskered** and **White-winged Black Tern** hunt for insects over the fields.

Namaqua Dove breeds on Sahnawt Farm and a good place to look for this species is near the farm buildings at the centre. **Grey-headed Kingfisher** is common in autumn after the breeding season. **Swifts** are numerous and have included **Alpine Swift** on several occasions.

Singing Bush Lark is abundant on each farm with perhaps more than 500 pairs. They start to arrive and sing from late January, and by April the air is vibrant with their song. A good variety and number of other **larks**, **swallows** and **pipits** may be found and the number of **Yellow** and **White Wagtails** can run into 1,000 or more. Other migrants and winter visitors include **wheatears**, **warblers** and **shrikes**. Over 100 **Rose-coloured Starlings** have been seen and a good place to look for them is the bushes near the telephone poles along the Thumrayt road at Jarziz Farm.

The birds at these farms have included a number of vagrants over the years, including **Harlequin Quail**, **Buff-breasted Sandpiper** and **Golden Pipit**.

Accommodation: camping or a hotel in Salalah.

White Storks at Jarziz Farm

Farmlands
(Jarziz & Sahnawt Farms)

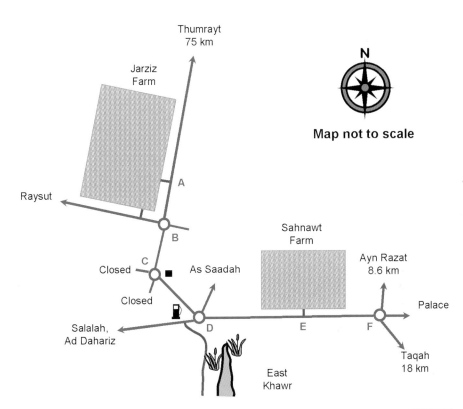

Thumrayt
75 km

Jarziz
Farm

N

Map not to scale

Raysut

A

B

C

Closed

As Saadah

Closed

Sahnawt
Farm

Ayn Razat
8.6 km

Palace

Salalah,
Ad Dahariz

D

E

F

Taqah
18 km

East
Khawr

African Silverbills

Waypoints and Coordinates			
A	K34	N17 02.387	E54 08.401
B	K49	N17 01.910	E54 08.564
C	K48	N17 01.573	E54 08.643
D	K47	N17 01.519	E54 10.349
E	F80	N17 02.166	E54 11.720
F	F81	N17 03.077	E54 13.100

10.2 East Khawr **   2WD

Key species: Little Bittern, Yellow Bittern, herons, ducks, crakes, waders, gulls, terns, migrants.

East Khawr, also called Khawr Dahariz, is located on the eastern outskirts of Salalah City. It is a coastal lagoon typical of the Dhofar region with extensive reed beds at the upper end, and a narrow sand bar at the beach end, that is sometimes breached after heavy rains, but soon reforms from wave action.

To reach East Khawr, head for the Dahariz roundabout with its Shell station. Right across from the southern entrance to the petrol station a track leads past a tall radio mast towards the sea where it joins another track running across the sand bar. Another track goes along the east side of the lagoon and eventually joins the main Salalah - Taqah highway.

As the *khawr* is so close to the city it receives quite a lot of disturbance, especially at the beach end. Yet it is always worth a visit and over 265 species of birds have been recorded. East Khawr is the easiest site in Oman to find **Yellow Bittern**. To find this bird, take the rough side track at the northeastern corner of the *khawr*, which ends at an opening in the reed beds. This track will need a 4WD, but one can simply walk the last couple of hundred metres. In early morning with the sun behind look for the bitterns which may be seen creeping through the reed beds on the other side, or flying up and down the narrow

Yellow Bittern

channel. Not much is known about the **Yellow Bittern** in Oman, but it has been seen from April to late-August, rarely to early-November and once in January. Beware of confusion with **Little Bittern** which is also found and breeds there.

Otherwise, East Khawr is a good place to find most of the waterbirds expected in Dhofar. A variety of **herons** is always present and in winter **ducks**, sometimes including **Ferruginous Duck**, are present. **Crakes** are regular near the reed beds and **Red-knobbed Coot** has been seen among the common **Coots**. Waders are much in evidence and the 47 species recorded include **Little Pratincole**, **Spur-winged Plover**, **Long-toed Stint** and **Wilson's Phalarope**. The number of **Kentish Plover** at the beach end can run into the hundreds. The beach always has an interesting selection of **gulls** and **terns** some of which frequent the lagoon for bathing. **Ospreys** are regularly seen in winter and up to six have been seen sitting on the wall on the east side. The upper end of the *khawr* can be good for migrants.

The track across the sand bar leads east along the coast for several km and passes a number of smaller lagoons. Each may hold similar species to East Khawr though usually in much smaller numbers.

Accommodation: camping or a hotel in Salalah.

East Khawr

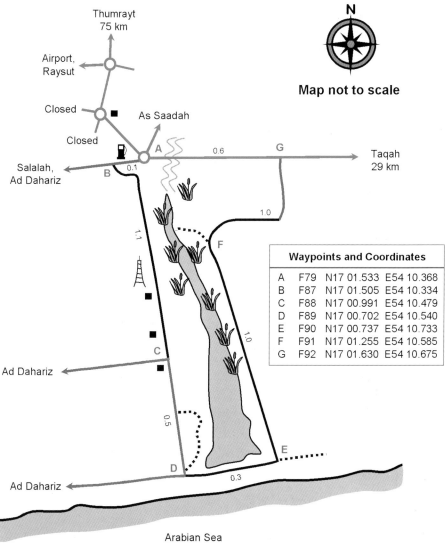

Thumrayt
75 km

Airport,
Raysut

Closed

Closed

As Saadah

Salalah,
Ad Dahariz

A

0.6

G

Taqah
29 km

B
0.1

1.0

1.1

F

1.0

C

Ad Dahariz

0.5

D

0.3

E

Ad Dahariz

Arabian Sea

Map not to scale

Waypoints and Coordinates

A	F79	N17 01.533	E54 10.368
B	F87	N17 01.505	E54 10.334
C	F88	N17 00.991	E54 10.479
D	F89	N17 00.702	E54 10.540
E	F90	N17 00.737	E54 10.733
F	F91	N17 01.255	E54 10.585
G	F92	N17 01.630	E54 10.675

Gulls and terns

10.3 Ayn Razat **   2WD

Key species: Bruce's Green Pigeon, Black-headed Tchagra, Palestine Sunbird, migrants.

Ayn Razat, a favourite picnic spot, 16 km northeast of Salalah, is best visited early morning whilst relatively quiet and undisturbed. Like most public parks in Oman the small, beautifully kept park at the centre may be closed until 16h00, but the surrounding trees and *wadi* are excellent for migrants and several local specialities. A natural spring gives rise to a small, permanent stream, the damp undergrowth of which supports residents such as **African Paradise Flycatcher**, **White-breasted White-eye** as well as migrant **Nightingale** and **Bluethroat**. When fruiting, the huge fig trees are one of the best places in Oman to find **Bruce's Green Pigeon**, a few of which are nearly always present, even in winter.

Bruce's Green Pigeon

The cultivated shrubs around the park, especially the flowering Hibiscus, attract good numbers of **Shining Sunbird**. This is also one of the more reliable spots for the somewhat nomadic **Palestine Sunbird** which, if not here, should be searched for in the **Sodom's Apple** *Calotropis procera* in the first part of the *wadi* to the north of the car park.

Check the rocky slopes and scrub around the spring for **Black-headed Tchagra** and **Arabian Warbler**, although the latter is not common. **Arabian Partridge** can sometimes be heard calling from the hills above. In summer both **Grey-headed Kingfisher** and **Didric Cuckoo** are common, occasionally lingering into October. The highly elusive **Golden-winged Grosbeak** is an irregular visitor from April to July. The cliffs above support **Short-toed** and **Bonelli's Eagle**, **Long-billed Pipit** in winter, and **Tristram's Grackle**. Both **African Scops Owl** and **Spotted Eagle Owl** occur, but are rare.

Before leaving, check the small enclosures of cultivated trees south of the park. These frequently hold migrant **warblers**, **chats**, **flycatchers** and **shrikes**.

Accommodation: camping or a hotel in Salalah.

Ayn Razat

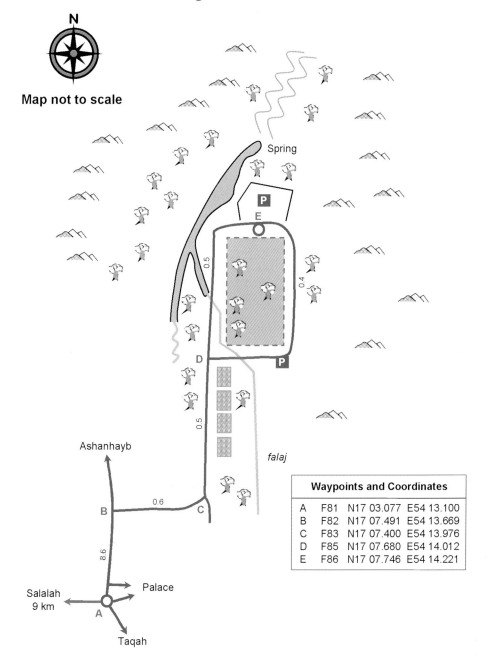

Map not to scale

Spring

P
E

0.5

0.4

D

P

0.5

Ashanhayb

falaj

0.6

B

C

9.6

Salalah
9 km

Palace

A

Taqah

Waypoints and Coordinates			
A	F81	N17 03.077	E54 13.100
B	F82	N17 07.491	E54 13.669
C	F83	N17 07.400	E54 13.976
D	F85	N17 07.680	E54 14.012
E	F86	N17 07.746	E54 14.221

10.4 Ayn Hamran ***   2WD

Key species: Verreaux's Eagle, Arabian Partridge, African Scops Owl, Spotted Eagle Owl, Grey-headed Kingfisher, Upcher's Warbler, Arabian Warbler, Palestine Sunbird, Black-crowned Tchagra, Golden-winged Grosbeak, African Rock Bunting, migrants.

For those with only limited time in south Oman, Ayn Hamran offers the best opportunity for finding most of the Dhofar specialities at one site. An early morning arrival is recommended, when the higher parts of the *wadi* are still in the shade of the mountains.

Ayn Hamran is a favourite picnic spot, especially in the summer when the *wadi* and surrounding hills are packed with campers from all over Arabia. During the summer rains the *wadi* is often in strong flow from the mountains, and even in the height of the dry season, in April/May, the natural spring provides a small permanent flow.

Access is via the paved road, signposted from the main Salalah - Mirbat highway. The surrounding desert plains are very arid and contrast starkly with the large verdant area of Ayn Hamran nestling below magnificent cliffs. Simply park by the traffic circle at the road terminus, and explore the surrounding *wadi*.

Arabian Partridge is most often seen on the floor of the *wadi*, especially beneath fruiting fig trees. A shy species, it prefers to run off undetected. Within the vicinity of the spring, **African Paradise Flycatcher**, **Blackstart**, **Shining Sunbird**, **White-breasted White-eye**, **Rüppell's Weaver**, **Tristram's Grackle** and **African Rock-Bunting** are common throughout the year, joined in summer by **Didric Cuckoo** and **Grey-headed Kingfisher**. **Black-crowned Tchagra** and **Arabian Warbler** are usually present up-slope from the spring - listen for their distinctive calls. **Bruce's Green Pigeon**, also best located by its whistling call, is most often found in the fruiting fig trees along the *wadi* bottom.

Scanning the cliffs above will reveal the usual flocks of **Fan-tailed Raven** and, in winter, any of a number of possible raptors including **Steppe**, **Imperial**, **Greater Spotted**, **Booted**, **Bonelli's** and **Short-toed Eagle**. This is also a reliable site for **Verreaux's Eagle**.

Of the more difficult species, **Golden-winged Grosbeak** is an uncommon but regular visitor during the rains from July to September, presumably from post-breeding dispersal, when immature birds are most often seen. **South Arabian Wheatear** occurs higher up the *wadi*, but is uncommon.

Ayn Hamran

A night visit is recommended for owls. At least one pair of **Spotted Eagle Owl** is resident in the *wadi* and can occasionally be found roosting by day. **African Scops Owl** is abundant by voice.

Ayn Hamran is an important feeding and resting point for migrants. At the appropriate time of year the *wadi* can be packed with an amazing collection of **warblers**, **flycatchers**, **wheatears**, **chats** and **shrikes**. Both **Nightingale** and **European Nightjar** pass through in large numbers. Interestingly, the **Nightingales** are singing in September. Almost anything can turn up - a highly recommended spot.

Accommodation: camping or a hotel in Salalah.

Ayn Hamran

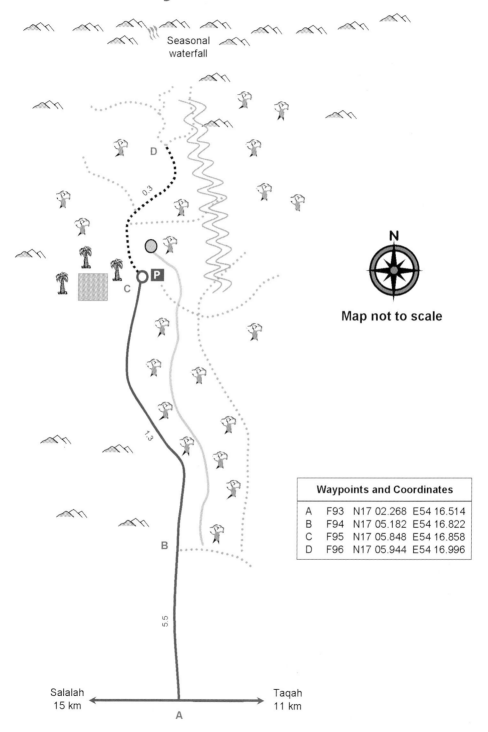

Seasonal waterfall

N

Map not to scale

Waypoints and Coordinates			
A	F93	N17 02.268	E54 16.514
B	F94	N17 05.182	E54 16.822
C	F95	N17 05.848	E54 16.858
D	F96	N17 05.944	E54 16.996

Salalah
15 km

Taqah
11 km

10.5 Khawr Sawli **   2WD/4WD

Key species: ducks, Baillon's Crake, Little Crake, waders.

Khawr Sawli is visible to the south of the highway, 16 km east of Salalah. Tracks leading through gates on the western side give access to the *khawr*, but - even if the gates are not locked - are only drivable by 4WD. Reed growth at the lagoon has intensified over recent years, and now open water is only visible from the beach end or from the hill inside the gate on the northeastern side. It is always interesting to walk along the reed edges. In the early morning and late afternoon, **Baillon's** and **Little Crake** come into the open to feed, and **herons** and **Little Bittern** are present. **Yellow Bittern** has been observed a few times, and almost certainly breeds.

Ducks are numerous in the winter, and careful scanning should pick out more interesting species with **Cotton Teal**, **Ferruginous Duck**, and **Red-crested Pochard** possible. **Waders** are common, both around the edges and on the beach. **Pheasant-tailed Jacana** is regular on floating vegetation, mainly at the northern end.

Accommodation: camping or a hotel in Salalah.

Little Bittern

Khawr Sawli

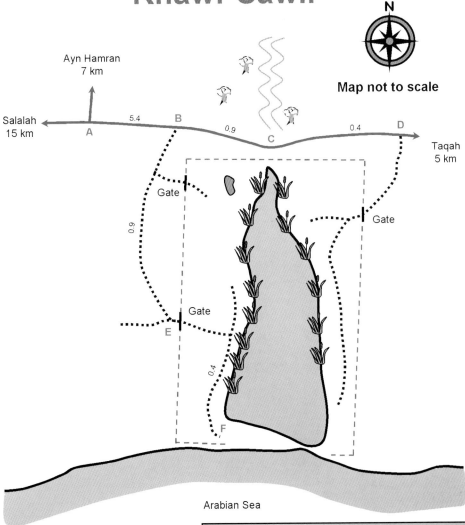

Ayn Hamran
7 km

Salalah
15 km

5.4

B

0.9

C

0.4

D

Taqah
5 km

A

Gate

0.9

Gate

Gate

E

0.4

F

Arabian Sea

Map not to scale

Waypoints and Coordinates			
A	K50	N17 02.266	E54 16.527
B	K51	N17 02.599	E54 19.500
C	K54	N17 02.693	E54 19.939
D	K55	N17 02.598	E54 20.187
E	K52	N17 02.142	E54 19.636
F	K53	N17 01.981	E54 19.713

Pintail

10.6 Khawr Taqah ***   2WD

Key species: Yellow Bittern, eagles, Pheasant-tailed Jacana, waders, gulls, terns, 'Dhofar Swift' *Apus sp.*

Despite being smaller than most khawrs along the Dhofar coast, Taqah rates as one of the best for birds. The *khawr*, adjacent to the scenic village of Taqah, 30 km east of Salalah, is viewable directly from the road, as well as a track running around the southern side, readily passable by 2WD unless rain has occurred recently. The floating vegetation at the centre of the *khawr* is one of the more reliable sites for **Pheasant-tailed Jacana**, and the extensive reed beds usually hold species of interest, such as **crakes** in winter or **Yellow Bittern** in summer. Recent records suggest **Allen's Gallinule** might occur regularly during the summer monsoon.

Pheasant-tailed Jacanas

A series of plantations and fields between the *khawr* and the village is worthy of investigation, attracting a variety of migrants, especially **pipits**, **wagtails**, **flycatchers** and **shrikes**. The resident form of **Black Kite**, rare in Oman, breeds in this area.

The trees on the western side of the *khawr* often have **eagles** such as **Imperial, Steppe**, and **Greater Spotted Eagle**, and the open marshy areas throughout hold a variety of **waders**, usually including **Pacific Golden Plover, Temminck's Stint** and, in some years, **Little Pratincole**.

Being an important fishing village, the beach front of Taqah is likely to be crammed with **gulls** and **terns**, the majority being **Siberian Gull**. **Gull-billed Tern** can often be found patrolling the beach, and **Caspian** and **Saunders's Tern** are regular.

The cliffs to the east of the village, marked with a small watchtower, make an excellent photographic vantage point, looking back over the fishing boats and **gulls** along the beach. During May to July they are also one of the breeding sites for the distinctive '**Dhofar Swift**' *Apus sp.* visiting Dhofar during the monsoon, from which it is possible to obtain excellent views as they fly past at eye-level. **Dolphins** can often be seen just offshore, as well as the occasional **Red-billed Tropicbird**. If traveling by 4WD it is possible to continue across the stony plains to Khawr Rawri (10.7).

Accommodation: camping or a hotel in Salalah.

Khawr Taqah

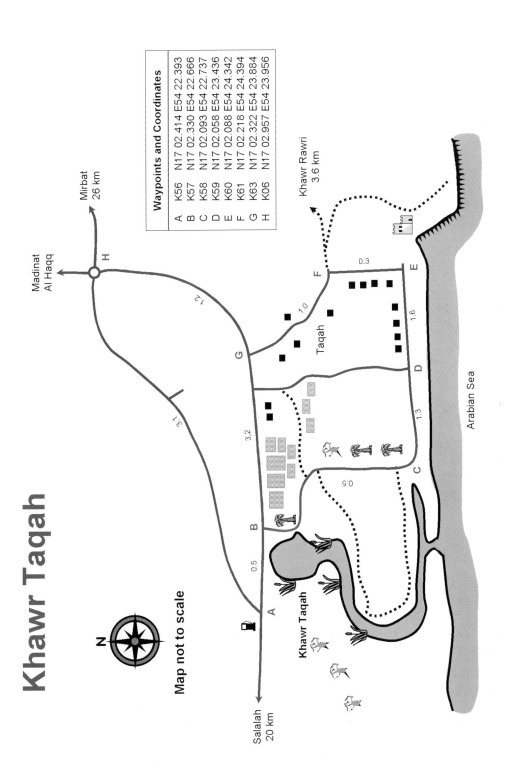

Map not to scale

Waypoints and Coordinates		
A	K56	N17 02.414 E54 22.393
B	K57	N17 02.330 E54 22.666
C	K58	N17 02.093 E54 22.737
D	K59	N17 02.058 E54 23.436
E	K60	N17 02.088 E54 24.342
F	K61	N17 02.218 E54 24.394
G	K63	N17 02.322 E54 23.884
H	K06	N17 02.957 E54 23.956

Mirbat
26 km

Madinat
Al Haqq

Salalah
20 km

Taqah

Khawr Taqah

Khawr Rawri
3.6 km

Arabian Sea

Key species: ducks, eagles, Arabian Partridge, waders, gulls, terns, 'Dhofar Swift' *Apus sp.*, Arabian Warbler, Black-crowned Tchagra.

Khawr Rawri, 33 km east of Salalah, boasts one of the most impressive species lists of any site in Dhofar, mainly on account of the surrounding hills supporting a number of the Dhofar specialities, together with limited areas of reeds. The *khawr*, situated at the outflow of Wadi Darbat (10.8), can flow strongly during the monsoon. As vegetation is rather sparse, the small patches of reeds and bushes at the northern end often hold a good selection of migrants. Several specialities are found reliably in this area. Check the bushes for **Black-crowned Tchagra** and **Arabian Warbler**. **Arabian Partridge** often calls from the cliffs on the western side from which **South Arabian Wheatear** is also known, though not common. A small trail leads up the rocks on the eastern side from which the whole northern half of the *khawr* can be scanned for ducks. During the summer monsoon the distinctive '**Dhofar Swift**' *Apus sp.* is numerous.

With the excavation of the ruins of the ancient town of Sumhuram dating back to the 4th century BC, a gate with a RO 1 admission charge has been erected along the eastern approach road. The point below the ruins is a good place to view the southern half of the *khawr*. The long shallow arms of the *khawr* are worth the short walk as, depending on the water levels, they often have migrant **crakes**, and **waders** including **Jack Snipe**, as well as **Bluethroat**.

The deeper, central parts of the *khawr*, hold the majority of **ducks** usually numbering several hundred in the peak of winter. **Cotton Teal** is regular, as is **Ferruginous Duck** and occasionally **Red-crested Pochard**. Overhead, eagles are prevalent, with **Bonelli's**, **Imperial** and **Greater Spotted Eagle** all regular.

The beach and shallows of the southern end are good for **waders**, roosting **gulls** and **terns**. The cliffs at either side of the beach provide good sea-watching points with **Masked Booby**, **Red-billed Tropicbird**, **Persian Shearwater**, **Wilson's Storm-petrel**, **Socotra Cormorant** and **Bridled Tern**.

Accommodation: camping or a hotel in Salalah.

Khawr Rawri

Khawr Rawri

Map not to scale

Madinat Al Haqq

Salalah
29 km

Taqah
2 km

Wadi Darbat,
Tawi Atayr

A

3.3

B   0.7   C   0.7   D

0.2

H

Mirbat
21 km

2.1

Entrance
Gate

Ruins

E

0.3

F

Taqah
3.6 km

1.6

G

Waypoints and Coordinates			
A	K06	N17 02.957	E54 23.956
B	K64	N17 03.305	E54 25.664
C	G08	N17 03.527	E54 25.970
D	K09	N17 03.454	E54 26.384
E	K23	N17 02.443	E54 26.144
F	K25	N17 02.269	E54 26.092
G	K27	N17 01.868	E54 26.378
H	K65	N17 03.128	E54 25.586

Key species: eagles, Pheasant-tailed Jacana, Bruce's Green Pigeon, African Scops Owl, Singing Bush Lark, Dhofar specialities.

Wadi Darbat is situated behind the massive cliff visible, on the northern side of the main highway, when passing Khawr Rawri (10.7). In years of heavy monsoon rain, several waterfalls cascade over the cliffs forming an impressive sight.

Access into the *wadi* is via the paved road signposted off the road to Tawi Atayr (10.9). Wadi Darbat, one of the most beautiful *wadis* of the Dhofar mountains, is a popular picnic area. The wide grassy base comprises a series of vegetated lakes surrounded by well-wooded mountains, which hold many of the Dhofar specialities. **African Paradise Flycatcher**, **Blackstart**, **Tristram's Grackle**, **White-breasted White-eye** and **Rüppell's Weaver** are abundant. Others, such as **Arabian Partridge**, **Arabian Warbler**, **South Arabian Wheatear**, and **Black-crowned Tchagra** are scarce but regularly recorded.

Wadi Darbat after the monsoon

During the summer monsoon **Bruce's Green Pigeon**, **Grey-headed Kingfisher** and **Didric Cuckoo** are present in good numbers. **African Scops Owl** is common by voice, and **Spotted Eagle Owl** occurs, though the extensive woodlands make it difficult to find. The grassy plains have breeding **Singing Bush Lark** from April to late-September.

Wadi Darbat is good for **raptors**, especially **eagles**; **Short-toed**, **Greater Spotted**, **Imperial**, **Steppe** and **Bonelli's Eagle** are all regular and **Verreaux's Eagle** has been seen on several occasions.

The *wadi* can be explored via a network of tracks, or on foot. Do not drive off road in the wet season as the ground will be waterlogged and very soft. Walking the edges of the lakes is recommended to search for **waders**, **crakes** and **bitterns**. This is a regular site for **Pin-tailed Snipe** and **White-breasted Waterhen**. **Pheasant-tailed Jacana** winters and has bred once. Where the drivable road and tracks end at the upper parts of the *wadi* it is possible to continue on foot for several km offering excellent birdwatching in magnificent surroundings.

Accommodation: camping or a hotel in Salalah.

Wadi Darbat

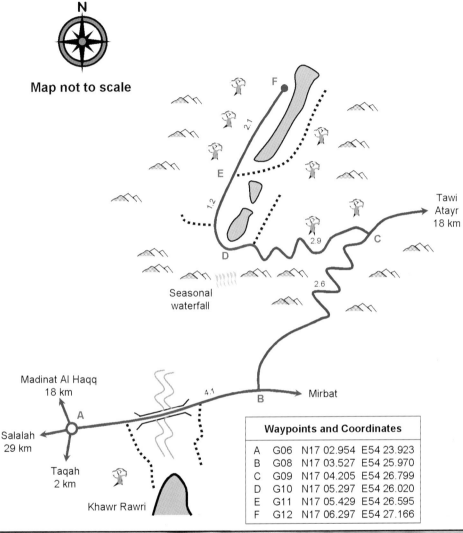

N

Map not to scale

F

E

2.1

1.2

D

C

Tawi Atayr
18 km

2.9

2.6

Seasonal
waterfall

Madinat Al Haqq
18 km

A

4.1

B

Mirbat

Salalah
29 km

Taqah
2 km

Khawr Rawri

Waypoints and Coordinates			
A	G06	N17 02.954	E54 23.923
B	G08	N17 03.527	E54 25.970
C	G09	N17 04.205	E54 26.799
D	G10	N17 05.297	E54 26.020
E	G11	N17 05.429	E54 26.595
F	G12	N17 06.297	E54 27.166

Didric Cuckoo

10.9 Tawi Atayr **   2WD

Key species: Bonelli's Eagle, Arabian Partridge, South Arabian Wheatear, Yemen Serin.

Tawi Atayr is *the* place in Oman to see **Yemen Serin**. Discovery of this isolated, breeding population in 1997, was a major surprise, representing a 1,000 km range extension from the nearest known population in Yemen. In addition to the **serin**, Tawi Atayr has the attraction of its spectacular sinkhole, plus other interesting birds. The sinkhole was formed long ago when the cave below collapsed, and is now several hundred metres deep and wide, with trees and a small lake inside. It is around here that birdwatchers should concentrate their efforts.

Yemen Serin

Climbing into the sinkhole requires specialised equipment, but the sides and trees below can be scanned from several vantage points around its perimeter. The **serins** are most often present in the shadows of the overhanging rocks on the northern side of the sinkhole, so best views are obtained by walking down from the buildings to the north. Alternatively, view with a telescope from the southern side, though the distance generally makes for poor views.

The surrounding rocky terrain with interspersed trees and bushes can be explored. **Arabian Partridge** is frequently encountered and **South Arabian Wheatear** is common. **Black-crowned Tchagra** and **Arabian Warbler** occur, but are uncommon. **Bonelli's Eagle** breeds in the sinkhole, which also supports **Bruce's Green Pigeon** and **Grey-headed Kingfisher** in small numbers.

The paved road from the highway to Tawi Atayr crosses the higher plains of the Dhofar mountains. All along this road is good for soaring **eagles**, especially **Greater Spotted** and **Imperial Eagle**. **Lappet-faced Vulture**, uncommon in south Oman, is found regularly, as well as **Barbary**, **Peregrine** and **Saker Falcon**. During migration the grassy plains should have good numbers of **European Roller** and **White Stork**.

For those with time and 4WD an interesting drive is to follow the track behind the sinkhole to Jabal Samhan that, after about 20 km, emerges at the edge of the escarpment overlooking the coastal plain above Mirbat - a spectacular view.

Accommodation: camping or a hotel in Salalah.

Tawi Atayr

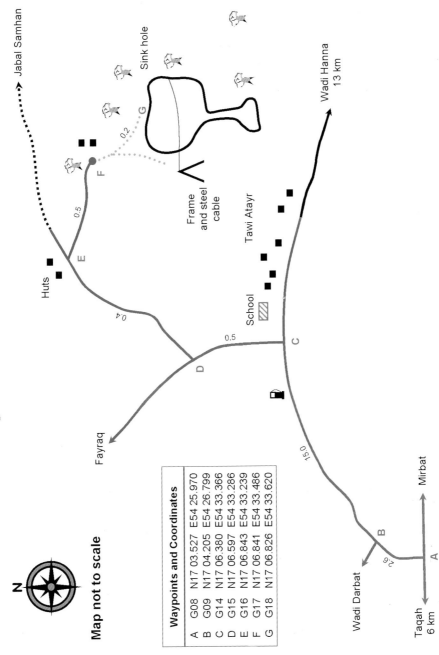

Map not to scale

Waypoints and Coordinates			
A	G08	N17 03.527	E54 25.970
B	G09	N17 04.205	E54 26.799
C	G14	N17 06.380	E54 33.366
D	G15	N17 06.597	E54 33.286
E	G16	N17 06.843	E54 33.239
F	G17	N17 06.841	E54 33.486
G	G18	N17 06.826	E54 33.620

Jabal Samhan

Sink hole

Frame and steel cable

Tawi Atayr

Wadi Hanna 13 km

Huts

Fayraq

School

Wadi Darbat

Mirbat

Taqah 6 km

10.10 Wadi Hanna **

Key species: Bonelli's Eagle, Bruce's Green Pigeon, Arabian Warbler, Black-crowned Tchagra, Golden-winged Grosbeak.

With its scattered **Baobab Trees** *Adansonia digitata*, Wadi Hanna appears reminiscent of Africa. The upper parts of the *wadi* are well wooded, and hold a collection of the Dhofar specialities including the elusive **Golden-winged Grosbeak**.

Access is either via the graded track, just off the main Salalah - Mirbat highway or over the mountain *via* Tawi Atayr (10.9). With 2WD only the first couple of km from the highway is usually passable, after which the track is steep and tyre grip difficult. In 2006 work started to pave this road, which has now been abandoned, resulting in a terribly scarred mountain face.

Consistently the best area is along the short track to the west, 2.9 km from the main highway, recognised as the area where the **Baobab Trees** first appear in the natural vegetation. **Golden-winged Grosbeak** breeds in this area, principally in April and May, but is nowhere common. Listen for the soft Goldfinch-like song, and watch for birds passing-over as they prefer to keep to treetops. Walking up or down the road is worthwhile not only for the grosbeak, but also **Arabian Partridge**, **Black-crowned Tchagra** and **Arabian Warbler**, which are as common here as anywhere.

The track ends after 0.3 km at a giant **Baobab Tree** and a footpath leads to a small permanent spring with many trees that should be checked for migrant **warblers** and **flycatchers**. **Bruce's Green Pigeon** is present throughout the summer, and the cliffs towering above hold **Bonelli's Eagle** and, in winter, **Short-toed Eagle**.

As a short side trip, the cliffs just off the highway, 5.4 km before the Wadi Hanna turn-off, if coming from Salalah, are a regular site for **Red-billed Tropicbird** from April to October.

Accommodation: camping or a hotel in Salalah.

Wadi Hanna

Wadi Hanna

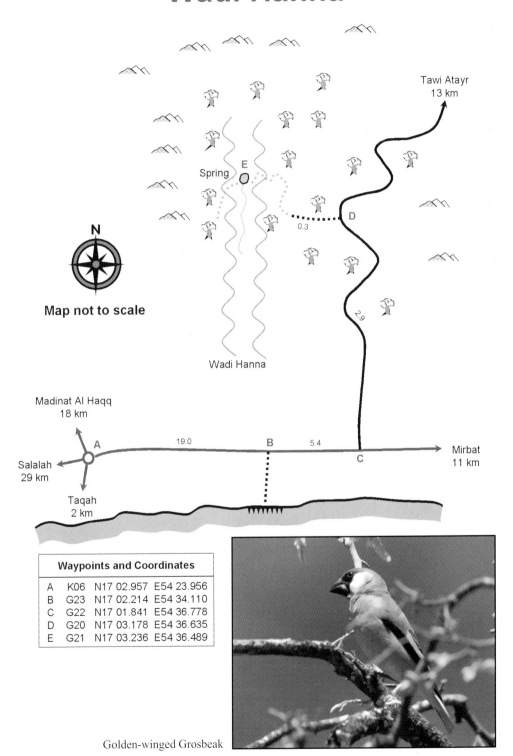

N

Map not to scale

Spring
E

Tawi Atayr
13 km

0.3

D

2.9

Wadi Hanna

Madinat Al Haqq
18 km

A   19.0   B   5.4

Salalah
29 km

C

Mirbat
11 km

Taqah
2 km

Waypoints and Coordinates			
A	K06	N17 02.957	E54 23.956
B	G23	N17 02.214	E54 34.110
C	G22	N17 01.841	E54 36.778
D	G20	N17 03.178	E54 36.635
E	G21	N17 03.236	E54 36.489

Golden-winged Grosbeak

10.11 Ras Mirbat and Ras Janjari *** 2WD/4WD

Key species: Jouanin's Petrel, Pale-footed Shearwater, Persian Shearwater, Wilson's Storm-petrel, Red-billed Tropicbird, Masked Booby.

Ras Mirbat, 60 km east of Salalah, is one of the premier sea-watching headlands in Oman. Due to its more southerly location, Ras Janjari, 12 km farther southeast is probably even better, but requires 4WD to access, and is consequently less frequently visited.

Sea-watching at either locality is best in the early morning, when the sun is still relatively low toward the east, especially at Mirbat where the passage of **seabirds** is best viewed facing southwest. Sea-watching can be good throughout the year, although April to November is best when both breeding and non-breeding visitors from the southern oceans are present. High seas, and potentially fog, during the summer monsoon mean the optimal period is between September and November. The main attractions are undoubtedly **Jouanin's Petrel** and **Persian Shearwater**, which are common from May to October. Other summer visitors include **Wilson's Storm-petrel**, **Pale-footed Shearwater**, with **Swinhoe's Storm-petrel** an overlooked possibility. **Masked Booby** is common throughout the year, and other regulars likely to be recorded are **Red-billed Tropicbird** and **Socotra Cormorant**.

Jouanin's Petrel

At Mirbat the best position to view from is the rocks to the south of the small mosque at the southern edge of town, although unfortunately the elevation is only a few metres above sea level.

Those with more time and a 4WD might be interested to take the paved road as far as Hinu, then the rough track to Ras Janjari. The headland is marked by a small stone pile, visible to the south of the track, 12 km from Mirbat. It is necessary to walk the last hundred metres to the headland for the best view, which is at least ten metres above sea-level although has a small island just offshore. The white sandy beaches in the area are very picturesque and a frequent weekend camping spot.

During the summer monsoon the seas are far too rough, but from October local fishing boats may be arranged from Mirbat harbour, or from the occasional fishermen at Ras Janjari, to take birdwatchers out to sea. The price will have to be negotiated. Such trips can be very rewarding and offer much closer views of the **seabirds** than is possible from land.

Accommodation: camping or a hotel in Salalah.

Ras Mirbat and Ras Janjari

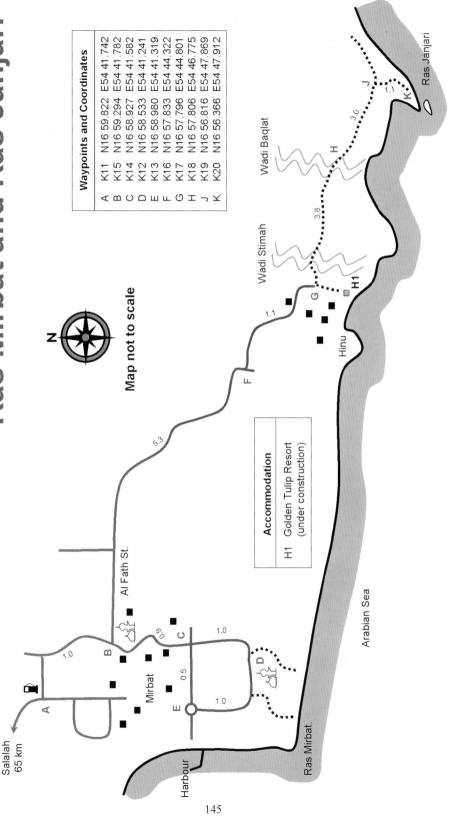

Map not to scale

N

Waypoints and Coordinates		
A	K11	N16 59.822 E54 41.742
B	K15	N16 59.294 E54 41.782
C	K14	N16 58.927 E54 41.582
D	K12	N16 58.533 E54 41.241
E	K13	N16 58.980 E54 41.319
F	K16	N16 57.833 E54 44.322
G	K17	N16 57.796 E54 44.801
H	K18	N16 57.806 E54 46.775
J	K19	N16 56.816 E54 47.869
K	K20	N16 56.366 E54 47.912

Ras Janjari

Wadi Baqlat

Wadi Stimah

Hinu

H1

Accommodation

H1 Golden Tulip Resort
(under construction)

Arabian Sea

Ras Mirbat.

Al Fath St.

Mirbat

Harbour

Salalah
65 km

145

10.12 Salalah Nature Reserve **

Key species: Red-crested Pochard, Ferruginous Duck, herons, ducks, waders.

In the southeastern part of Salalah city, the Salalah Nature Reserve (or Khawr Salalah Bird Sanctuary) is passed when travelling the coastal route toward Raysut (10.14) and Al Mughsayl (10.15). As the *khawr* is fenced and access restricted, it is most easily viewed from the road. Being adjacent to the Royal Palace, the area is slightly sensitive and photography is not permitted. The best access to the site is to drive to the guard post at the southwestern corner and seek permission from the guard to walk to the hide from which a good view can be obtained.

The open water of the eastern end is very attractive to **ducks** and is a good locality for **Ferruginous Duck**, **Cotton Teal**, and **Red-crested Pochard**. The open grassy banks always hold **Squacco Heron** and the shallows of the southern edge attract a few **waders** that can include **Avocet**. The highest counts of **Glossy Ibis** in Oman are from here. **Caspian**, **Gull-billed** and **Saunders's Tern** regularly patrol the *khawr*.

Slightly farther west, the narrower parts of the *khawr* have dense reeds and sedges. During migration these are good for **Little Bittern**, and no doubt **crakes** as well. **Greater Spotted** and **Imperial Eagle** can often be seen on the bank behind the *khawr*.

Habitat to the north of the road consists of agricultural fields and date palms, which are worth a look during migration for **pipits**, **wagtails** and **shrikes**. The local, resident form of **Black Kite** can sometimes be seen flying over.

Accommodation: camping or a hotel in Salalah.

Caspian Tern

Salalah Nature Reserve

Map not to scale

Waypoints and Coordinates

A	K39	N17 00.343	E54 02.457
B	K43	N17 00.252	E54 03.487
C	X06	N17 00.158	E54 03.947
D	K44	N16 59.895	E54 04.448
E	K45	N17 00.097	E54 05.805
F	K47	N17 01.519	E54 10.349
G	X07	N16 59.709	E54 03.937

Accommodation

H1   Crowne Plaza Salalah
H2   Salalah Beach Villas

Raysut

Al Awqdayn roundabout

Salalah Ring Road, Airport

Salalah City

Salalah Ring Road

As Saadah

Taqah 29 km

Palace Area

Salalah Nature reserve

Hide

Guard Post

Arabian Sea

1.8

0.7

0.8

1.3

2.3

8.7

10.13 Ayn Sahnawt *

Key species: Arabian Partridge, African Scops Owl, Spotted Eagle Owl, South Arabian Wheatear, Arabian Warbler, Black-crowned Tchagra, migrants.

Tucked into the foothills of the Dhofar mountains, Ayn Sahnawt, 10 km north of Salalah off the Thumrayt road, comprises a small pool fed by a natural spring, surrounded by low cliffs, scattered trees and small shrubs. Although the area holds birds similar to Ayn Hamran (10.4) or Ayn Razat (10.3), seasonal variance can result in certain species being found more easily here.

Access is now paved from the road to Shir, terminating at a parking area near the spring. The spring has been walled to produce a deep natural pool and is frequently used as a swimming and picnic spot. The cliffs around the pool were formerly a regular site for **Spotted Eagle Owl**, which still occur in the area, though are now less frequently seen.

The surrounding areas can be explored on foot, and any of the Dhofar specialities are likely to be encountered, such as **Arabian Partridge**, **Bruce's Green Pigeon**, **Arabian Warbler**, **South Arabian Wheatear** and **Black-crowned Tchagra**. Watch the mountains above for soaring **raptors** that might include **Verreaux's Eagle** on the lookout for its main prey item, the **Rock Hyrax** *Procavia capensis*, which is common in this area.

Arabian Partridge

The road to Shir winds through a beautiful, well-wooded *wadi*, the first few km of which are excellent for **African Scops Owl**, and is probably the best place in Oman to see this bird. A good spot is the stretch from two to five km past the Ayn Sahnawt turning, where after dusk the hills echo to the call of numerous individuals for most of the year. Take care to park off the road as this stretch is narrow with frequent speeding vehicles.

Accommodation: camping or a hotel in Salalah.

Ayn Sahnawt

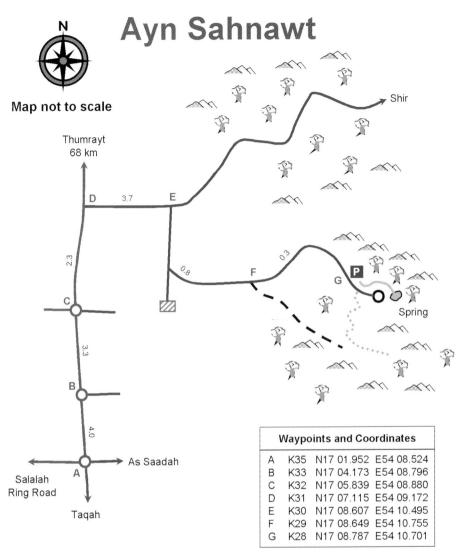

N

Map not to scale

Thumrayt
68 km

D   3.7   E

Shir

2.3

0.8

0.3

C

F   G **P**

Spring

3.3

B

4.0

Salalah
Ring Road

A   As Saadah

Taqah

Waypoints and Coordinates			
A	K35	N17 01.952	E54 08.524
B	K33	N17 04.173	E54 08.796
C	K32	N17 05.839	E54 08.880
D	K31	N17 07.115	E54 09.172
E	K30	N17 08.607	E54 10.495
F	K29	N17 08.649	E54 10.755
G	K28	N17 08.787	E54 10.701

Black-crowned Tchagra

10.14 Raysut and West Khawr *

Key species: Red-billed Tropicbird, Crab Plover, waders, gulls, terns.

The main highway west of Salalah has a few birdwatching stops en route to Al Mughsayl (10.15). Starting from Al Awqdayn roundabout at the western end of the Salalah ring-road, the first site passed, after 1.4 km, is West Khawr (Khawr Awqdayn) which can only be reached on the return direction, due to the dual carriageway. Although fairly disturbed, **ducks** and **herons** are normally present, and a drive along the western side can be good for **waders** including **Pacific Golden Plover**.

Either side of the Salalah Hilton Hotel are two small *khawrs*, known collectively as Khawr Muhit, the larger of which has a few remnant mangroves. The gardens of the hotel, in an otherwise largely barren strip of coastline, are likely to attract migrants.

From the roundabout marked **E** on the map a road leads up the hill through an industrial area. After about 1 km this road ends in a T-junction. Turn left and continue to the waste disposal site on the left. In winter this is a major site for **eagles**, mainly **Steppe Eagle**, and for **White Stork** and **Black Kite**. Further along, the road ends at a sewage treatment plant which can be worth exploring as can the steep *wadi* behind the plant.

At Al Mughsayl roundabout continue straight over toward Raysut village. After a further 2.0 km a road leads to the new Salalah port, before which the remaining mudflats can be scanned and hold a collection of the usual **waders**, including **Terek Sandpiper** and sometimes **Crab Plover**. In winter, the area will have thousands of **Siberian**, **Caspian**, **Sooty** and **Slender-billed Gull**. Close attention of **Sooty Gulls** might be rewarded, as several records of the vagrant **White-eyed Gull** are from here, especially in late September.

Continue toward Raysut village, taking the track just before the village. The high cliffs here, as well as being a good sea-watching lookout, hold breeding **Red-billed Tropicbird**.

Red-billed Tropicbird

In recent years a **House Crow** expansion has started from Raysut, which could unfortunately mark the start of a massive expansion into south Oman.

Accommodation: camping or a hotel in Salalah.

Raysut and West Khawr

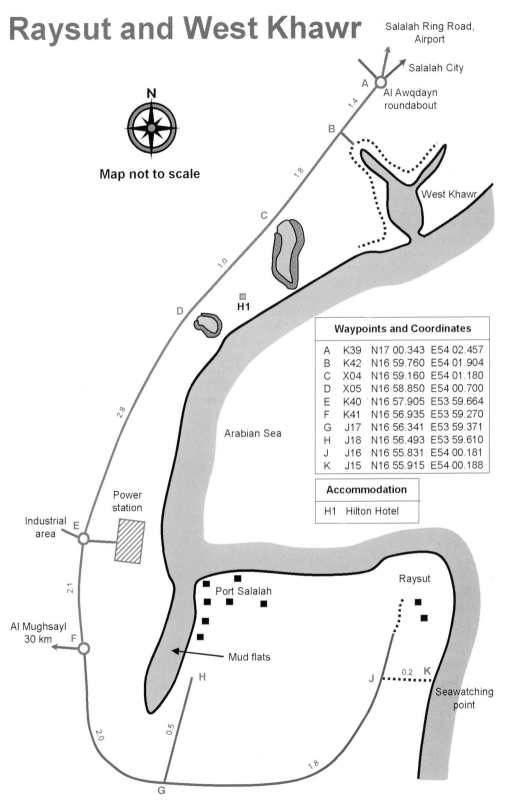

N

Map not to scale

Salalah Ring Road, Airport

Salalah City

A — Al Awqdayn roundabout

1.4

B

1.8

West Khawr

C

1.0

D

H1

Arabian Sea

Waypoints and Coordinates

A	K39	N17 00.343	E54 02.457
B	K42	N16 59.760	E54 01.904
C	X04	N16 59.160	E54 01.180
D	X05	N16 58.850	E54 00.700
E	K40	N16 57.905	E53 59.664
F	K41	N16 56.935	E53 59.270
G	J17	N16 56.341	E53 59.371
H	J18	N16 56.493	E53 59.610
J	J16	N16 55.831	E54 00.181
K	J15	N16 55.915	E54 00.188

Accommodation

H1	Hilton Hotel

2.8

Power station

Industrial area — E

2.1

Al Mughsayl 30 km — F

Raysut

Port Salalah

Mud flats

H

J — 0.2 — K

Seawatching point

2.0

0.5

G

1.8

10.15 Al Mughsayl ***   4WD/2WD

Key species: Brown Booby, Socotra Cormorant, herons, ducks, Verreaux's Eagle, crakes, Pheasant-tailed Jacana, waders, gulls, terns, Hume's Tawny Owl, South Arabian Wheatear.

Al Mughsayl is the most important birdwatching site west of Salalah, with over 270 species recorded. It consists of three distinct areas: the seabird watching site at the famous blowholes, the *khawr*, and the *wadi* farther inland. The blowholes and the *khawr* are reached on paved roads, but the *wadi* requires a 4WD.

To reach Al Mughsayl take the main highway west out of Salalah and turn right at the roundabout at Raysut. The road passes through a barren plateau with few birds. After 6.3 km from the roundabout a small *wadi* holds a few **Frankincense Trees** *Boswellia sacra*. The coast is reached again after a further 17.7 km and the road follows the beach for another 5.5 km. Look here for **South Arabian Wheatear** and the occasional **Long-legged Buzzard** and **Barbary Falcon** on the cliffs and wires along the road. Just beyond the *khawr* a road leads off to the left, where it ends after a kilometre at a parking area for the blowholes; these are formed when the waves press seawater through rock crevices, especially at high tide. Walk under the rock overhang for an excellent view of the sea, especially in the afternoon with the sun behind. Scan the sea through a telescope for interesting **seabirds**. With patience a **Brown Booby** or two can usually be found along with **Persian Shearwater**, **Masked Booby** and **Socotra Cormorant**. The best time is autumn from September to November.

The *khawr* itself is best watched from the road across the dam, but be sure to park well off the road. Khawr Al Mughsayl used to be one of the best of the Dhofar lagoons with a large variety of **herons**, **ducks** and **waders** including **Purple Heron**, **Cotton Teal**, **Ferruginous Duck**, **Pheasant-tailed Jacana**, **Black-winged Stilt**, **Pacific Golden Plover**, **Long-toed Stint**, **Black-tailed Godwit** and **Marsh** and **Terek Sandpiper**. **Glossy Ibis**, **Spoonbill** and **Greater Flamingo** are usually present in good numbers. More unusual species have included **Yellow Bittern**, **Ruddy Shelduck**, **Red-crested Pochard**, **Spotted Thick-knee** and **White-tailed Plover**. A massive cyclone a few years ago changed the area and the *khawr* is now smaller and quite a distance from the road with fewer birds being observed. New pools, however, formed on the seaside of the road and are worth checking. A **Malachite Kingfisher** was seen on the rocks here recently.

Coastal cliffs at Al Mughsayl

Across the road towards the blowholes, a track leads north, passing close to the *khawr* before heading into the *wadi*. The initial 3-4 kilometres can usually be driven by 2WD, and passes a small pool which can be good for **crakes**. Thereafter, it becomes rough and a 4WD is definitely needed to reach the interesting parts of the *wadi*. This *wadi*, known as Wadi Ashawq, is the most accessible location in Oman for **Hume's Tawny Owl** and many birdwatchers have both seen and heard this much sought after species here. The best site is a small plateau 7.0 km from the main highway, reached on a track which can be very rough. The track is steep in places and goes through the *wadi* at one stretch. Another key species in Dhofar which sometimes put in an appearance is **Verreaux's Eagle**. **Frankincense Trees** are found on the hillsides along the *wadi*.

Accommodation: camping or a hotel in Salalah.

Al Mughsayl

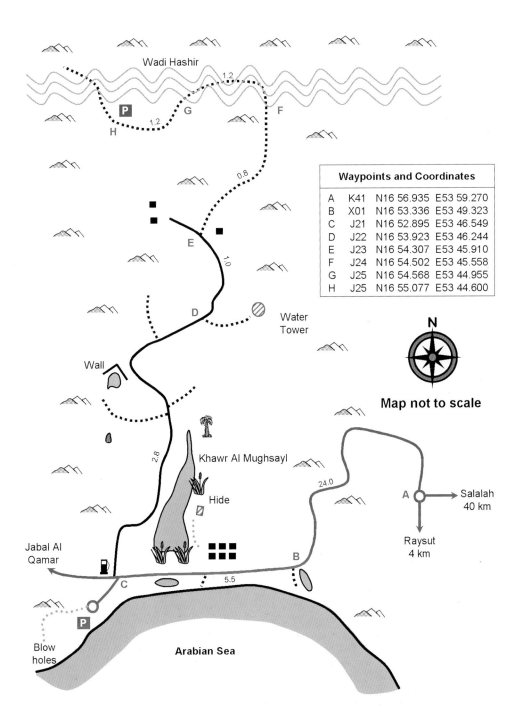

Wadi Hashir

P

1.2

G

F

H

1.2

0.8

E

1.0

Waypoints and Coordinates			
A	K41	N16 56.935	E53 59.270
B	X01	N16 53.336	E53 49.323
C	J21	N16 52.895	E53 46.549
D	J22	N16 53.923	E53 46.244
E	J23	N16 54.307	E53 45.910
F	J24	N16 54.502	E53 45.558
G	J25	N16 54.568	E53 44.955
H	J25	N16 55.077	E53 44.600

D

Water
Tower

N

Map not to scale

Wall

2.8

Khawr Al Mughsayl

24.0

Hide

A

Salalah
40 km

Jabal Al
Qamar

B

Raysut
4 km

C

5.5

P

Blow
holes

Arabian Sea

10.16 Jabal Al Qamar *   2WD/4WD

Key species: Verreaux's Eagle, Arabian Partridge, South Arabian Wheatear, Yemen Serin.

West of Al Mughsayl (10.15) the main highway enters the mountains and it does so in spectacular fashion. Soon after Al Mughsayl the road rises steeply but descends through several hairpin turns into a *wadi* filled with **Frankincense Trees** *Boswellia sacra* only to rise again through even more hairpin turns cut straight out of the mountain side. The views are magnificent along the way. The road eventually levels out on top of the ridge at 1,200m. The hillsides are rather barren, though the **Dragon Blood Trees** *Dracaena serrulata* add interest. As birds are not plentiful few birders travel this route, but species to look out for include **South Arabian Wheatear** and, with a bit of luck, **Hooded Wheatear** and **Arabian Partridge** or, with even more luck, **Verreaux's Eagle** and **Lappet-faced Vulture**. The road continues for a considerable distance towards the Yemeni border, and is longer than it seems on a map, as it constantly twists and turns with the contours of the mountains. With plenty of time, though, the trip all the way to the border post at Sarfayt can be interesting. One graded side road leading off to Rakhyut on the coast runs through well wooded hills before descending steeply towards the village. **Arabian Partridge** is common in this area, and a few unconfirmed records of **Yemen Serin** are from here as well. The *khawr* at the end of the road supports **waterbirds** similar to those found at other Dhofar lagoons.

Accommodation: camping or a hotel in Salalah.

Dragon's Blood Trees at Jabal Al Qamar

Other Sites

Through the previous ten sections we have attempted to present the most important and more easily accessible birdwatching sites in Oman. However, the list of good sites is not thereby exhausted. For the more adventurous birders with plenty of time on their hands, further areas can be investigated.

Daymaniyat Islands

This chain of nine islands lies off the north coast at Barka. Boat trips to the islands can be arranged through the As Sawadi Beach Resort (2.1), but these trips are mainly for divers and, since the islands form a protected nature reserve, landing on the islands requires a permit from the Ministry of Regional Municipalities, Environment and Water Resources in Muscat. During the summer breeding season landing is strictly forbidden and rigorously enforced. During autumn, however, the boat trip can be rewarding for **seabirds** and **Persian Shearwater**, **Red-billed Tropicbird**, **Red-necked Phalarope**, **Bridled Tern** as well as **Sooty Falcon** should be seen.

Al Hallaniyyat Islands

Off the southeast coast lie five rocky islands of which only the main island is inhabited. The seas in this area can be very rough at the best of times and during the summer monsoon, no boats can reach here for months. Outside the monsoon season, a *dhow* runs infrequently from Mirbat (10.11) to the main island, a voyage taking about eight hours. There is no telling when the *dhow* will return. Camping equipment and all supplies must be brought along. In autumn the **seabirds** along the way should be interesting, but in midwinter most birds seem to have departed. The *dhow* will only pull in at the main island whereas the outer two islands, Al Qibliyah in the east supporting a huge colony of **Masked Booby** and **Al Hasikiyah** in the west with breeding **Masked Boobies** and **Socotra Cormorants** would be difficult to reach. From Hasik or from the north shore of the bay at Ash Shuwaymiyyah (9.4), it may be possible to hire a fishermen to go to one of the islands which in clear weather are visible from shore. This should only be attempted during periods with calm weather.

The Empty Quarter

West of the Muscat - Salalah highway lies the vast area called the Empty Quarter, or Ar Rub Al Khali, stretching well into Saudi Arabia and the United Arab Emirates. It is an area of huge sand dunes and few tracks provide access. A visit would be an expedition and should be well prepared. At least two 4WDs stocked with extra fuel tanks, plenty of water, a GPS, good maps and local knowledge are essential before attempting a visit. Common resident birds include **Hoopoe Lark** and **Brown-necked Raven**. During migrations surprising discoveries could be made. If sand dunes are a goal in themselves, the dunes along the Muscat - Salalah highway 70 km south of Al Ghabah Hotel (about 400 km south of Muscat) are much more accessible.

The Wahibah Sands

South of the Bid Bid - Sur highway lies an isolated sand sea known at Ramlat Al Wahibah. With a 4WD one can drive into the sands from Al Mintirib. With several vehicles and a local guide one can actually drive all the way to the coast where the dunes are enormous. Experience with driving conditions in sand is essential. Few birds can be expected, but have included **Lappet-faced Vulture** and **Desert Eagle Owl**. Travel agents in Muscat arrange overnight tours on camels to tented tourist camps in the Wahibah Sands. Though not many birds could be expected, such trips would offer a real Arabian adventure.

SITE SPECIES LISTS

The following tables provide a complete list of all species recorded to date from each of the sites covered in the **Site Guide** section. These have been compiled from many years of personal observations as well as from hundreds of thousands of records from visiting and resident birdwatchers.

Rather than providing a simple list of species recorded at a site, an indication has been given as to the likelihood of finding each species at the appropriate time of year, details of which are covered in the **Bird Finder** section. For example, Teal is listed as abundant at Al Ansab Lagoons, where it occurs as a winter visitor, during which time it will likely be recorded on all visits.

Key:

a - abundant   A species difficult to miss. Not necessarily numerically abundant, but generally very obvious and should be recorded on all visits. Often refers to large conspicuous birds such as Grey Heron or Spoonbill.

c - common   A species that would be expected to be recorded on the majority of visits. Might refer to less conspicuous, but vocal, species readily found by voice, such as Didric Cuckoo.

f - fairly common   A species that would be recorded on about half the visits made to a site.

u - uncommon   A species that would not generally be expected to be encountered, but that does occur regularly or maybe irregularly in good numbers. Might include scarce migrants, or resident species which are difficult to find due to low densities.

r - rare   A species that has occurred generally less than ten times at the site, and could not be expected. Might refer to a particularly elusive resident such as Dunn's Lark, or an erratic migrant.

v - vagrant   A species occurring only as a vagrant in Oman.

Spoonbill

156

It should be noted that these lists reflect our current knowledge of the distribution and status of Oman's bird. With increased observer activity, many seemingly scarce species will no doubt be found to be more common than previous thought. Lists for some of the less frequently visited sites are likely to reflect observer bias to the time of year when they are visited.

The tables cover the ten regions, and each of their sites as numbered in the **Site Guide** section. For convenience, the site numbers are shown below. Numbers after the site give the total number of species recorded at that site. Low species number may indicate a site with a limited variety of habitat, but can also indicate a site less frequently visited. Records from these sites are particularly welcome.

1 The Capital Area
1.1	Al Ansab Lagoons	273
1.2	Al Qurm Natural Park	283
1.3	Al Amrat Waste Disposal Site	48
1.4	Yiti	139
1.5	Hotel gardens	151

2 Al Batinah
2.1	Ras As Sawadi	198
2.2	Sun Farms, Sohar	260
2.3	Majis	127
2.4	Liwa	140
2.5	Shinas	187
2.6	Khatmat Milahah	121

3 The Northeast Coast
3.1	Qurayyat	250
3.2	Sur Lagoon and Sewage Plant	229
3.3	Khawr Jirama	116
3.4	Ras Al Hadd and Ras Al Jinz	194
3.5	Ras Al Khabbah and Ar Ruways	137

4 Al Hajar Mountains
4.1	Al Ghubrah Bowl	52
4.2	Jabal Shams	65
4.3	Sayq Plateau	111

5 Musandam
5.1	Khasab	206
5.2	Sall Ala	121
5.3	As Sayh Plateau	133
5.4	Ar Rawdah	107
5.5	Strait of Hormuz	92

6 Al Buraymi Area
6.1	Fossil Valley	68
6.2	Jabal Qatar	70
6.3	Al Buraymi Sewage Plant	118

7 The Central Desert
7.1	Jaluni	192
7.2	Al Ghaftayn Hotel	141
7.3	Muntasar	216
7.4	Qatbit	214
7.5	Al Balid Farm	167
7.6	Shisr and Haylat Ar Rakah	104
7.7	Wadi Rabkut	66
7.8	Thumrayt Waste Disposal Site	45

8 Barr Al Hikman and Masirah
8.1	Barr Al Hikman	188
8.2	Hilf	325
8.3	Sur Masirah	140
8.4	Ras Abu Rasas	67

9 The Southeast Coast
9.1	Ad Duqm	115
9.2	Khawr Dhurf	178
9.3	Khawr Ghawi	109
9.4	Ash Shuwaymiyyah	155

10 Dhofar
10.1	Salalah Farms	245
10.2	East Khawr	262
10.3	Ayn Razat	152
10.4	Ayn Hamran	180
10.5	Khawr Sawli	225
10.6	Khawr Taqah	257
10.7	Khawr Rawri	271
10.8	Wadi Darbat	187
10.9	Tawi Atayr	113
10.10	Wadi Hanna	105
10.11	Ras Mirbat and Ras Janjari	153
10.12	Salalah Nature Reserve	204
10.13	Ayn Sahnawt	141
10.14	Raysut and West Khawr	243
10.15	Al Mughsayl	271
10.16	Jabal Al Qamar	215

Common Name	Capital Area					Al Batinah						Northeast					Hajar		
	1	2	3	4	5	1	2	3	4	5	6	1	2	3	4	5	1	2	3
Little Grebe	a	u				r	u			r		r	r						
Great Crested Grebe		v																	
Black-necked Grebe	c	u				r	r		r	r		u	u		r				
Albatross sp.															v				
Jouanin's Petrel										r	r	r	r		f	f			
Cory's Shearwater															v	v			
Streaked Shearwater															v				
Pale-footed Shearwater								r				r	r		f	f			
Wedge-tailed Shearwater					r			r							r				
Sooty Shearwater															v	v			
Persian Shearwater		r		r	r	u				u	r	u	r		a	a			
Wilson's Storm-petrel					r							r	r		u	r			
White-faced Storm-petrel																v			
Swinhoe's Storm-petrel																v			
Red-billed Tropicbird		r		r	r	u						r			u	u			
Red-footed Booby															v				
Masked Booby		r				r			r	r		r	r		u	u			
Brown Booby						r						r			r	r			
Cormorant	a	f		r	r	c	r	f	f	c	r	f	f	r	f	f			
Socotra Cormorant		r				u			r	r		r	r		r	r			
White Pelican	v	v								v									
Dalmatian Pelican	v									v		v							
Lesser Frigatebird							v									v			
Bittern	r	r								r									
Little Bittern	f	u			r				r			r		r	r				
Yellow Bittern		r							v										
Night Heron	a	u	r			r	r		r	r		u	r	r	r	r			
Striated Heron	u	c	r	r		u		r	a	f		f	u	u	r	r			
Squacco Heron	f	f	r	r			u		u	f		u		u					
Indian Pond Heron	f	f					r		u	c		f	r	r		r			
Cattle Egret	c	f			r	r	a	u				u	r						
Western Reef Heron	c	a	a	u		a	r	f	a	a	r	a	a	f	a	f			
Little Egret	a	c	u	r		u	u	u	f	a		f	f	r	r	r			
Intermediate Egret	r	r	r				u	r	r	r		r	r	r					
Great White Egret	f	a	a	r		u	u	r	u	a		c	a	f	r	r			
Grey Heron	a	a	a	r		a	f	c	a	a	r	a	a	c	a	u			
Purple Heron	f	u	r			r	u		r	u		r	r	r	r	r			
Goliath Heron		v										v							
Black Stork	v																		
Abdim's Stork													r						
White Stork	r	r	r			r	f	r		r	r	f	r	r	r				
Glossy Ibis	u	f		r		r	u					f	r		r	r			
Sacred Ibis																			
Spoonbill	u	u		c		r	r		r	c		c	c	r	r	r			
Greater Flamingo	f	u		u	r	u	r	u	r	f		a	a	a	f	r			
Lesser Flamingo														v					
Whooper Swan	v											v							
White-fronted Goose		r					r					r	r						
Greylag Goose	r	r					r					r	r						
Ruddy Shelduck	u									r		r							
Shelduck	r						r					u							
Cotton Teal	r																		
Wigeon	f	u		r		r	u	r	r	r		f	u	r	r				
Gadwall	f	u		r			u			r		f	r						

158

Common Name	Capital Area					Al Batinah						Northeast					Hajar		
	1	2	3	4	5	1	2	3	4	5	6	1	2	3	4	5	1	2	3
Teal	a	c		r		r	f	u	r	u		c	f			r			r
Mallard	c	c		r	r	r	f	u		r	r	f	u		r				r
Pintail	f	u		r		r	u	r		r		f	f	r	r	r			
Garganey	c	c		r		r	f		r	r		f	f	r	r	r			
Shoveler	c	f		r		r	f			r		f	f		r				
Red-crested Pochard	r	r					r			r		r							
Pochard	f	u					r	r		r		u	r						
Ferruginous Duck	u	r					r					r	r		r				
Tufted Duck	f	r					r	r	r	r		r	r						
Red-breasted Merganser		v				v													
Honey Buzzard		r					r			r	r								
Crested Honey Buzzard							v		v										
Black-winged Kite	v	v				v													
Black Kite	r	r	r				r	r			r	r	r	r					
Pallas's Fish Eagle	v																		
Egyptian Vulture	c	u	a	a	u	f	u	u	r	r	r	a	a	r	r	r	r	a	a
Griffon Vulture	r			r				r				r	r					r	
Lappet-faced Vulture	u		f	r		r	r	r	r		r	u	r	r		r	r	c	f
Black Vulture																			
Short-toed Eagle	u	r		r		r	u		r	r	r	r	r	r		r		r	r
Marsh Harrier	a	c		r	r	u	a	u	r	u	r	r	c	r	r	r			
Hen Harrier	r	r					u					r							
Pallid Harrier	u	u					c		r			r	r		r				
Montagu's Harrier	f	r				r	c					r	r		r	r			
Sparrowhawk	f	u		r	r	r	u			r	u	r	r		r	r		r	r
Shikra							v												
Common Buzzard	r	r					r					r							
Long-legged Buzzard	u	u					r			r		r	r		r		r		
Lesser Spotted Eagle	v											v							
Greater Spotted Eagle	a	u	a		r	r	c		r	r	r	c	u	r					r
Steppe Eagle	c	r	a	r		r	u			r	r	f	r	r	r			r	r
Tawny Eagle																			
Imperial Eagle	f	r	f	r		r	f			r		f	r		r				r
Golden Eagle	r	r				r	r					r			r	r		r	
Booted Eagle	u	r					u			r		r	r		r				
Bonelli's Eagle	f	u		r		r	u		r	r	r	u	r	r	r	r		r	r
Osprey	f	u		c	u	a	r		u	c		a	a	c	c	u			
Lesser Kestrel	r	r				r	u	r			r	r				r			
Kestrel	f	u	u	r	f	u	a			r	r	u	r	r	u	u	u	f	u
Amur Falcon	r	r				r	r					r	r		r				
Merlin							v												
Hobby	u	u			r	r	u	r		r		r	r	r	r	r			
Sooty Falcon	f	f		r	r	c	r					r	r		r	r			r
Lanner Falcon	r					r	r							r					r
Saker Falcon	r	r				r	u				r	r	r		r				
Peregrine Falcon	u	r		r		u	u			r	r	r	r	r	u	r		r	r
Barbary Falcon	u	r		r	r	r	u				r	u	r	r	r	r	r		
Arabian Partridge	r				r							r			r			r	r
Sand Partridge	u	r		r	r		r					u	r		r		f	u	r
Grey Francolin	f	a	r	u	f	u	c	f	r	u	f	c	u		r	r	c	r	u
Quail	u	f		r	r	r	f	r	r	r	r		r	r					
Water Rail	r	r							r	r		r							
Spotted Crake	f	u					r					r	r		r				
Little Crake	r	r										r	r						

Common Name	Capital Area					Al Batinah						Northeast					Hajar		
	1	2	3	4	5	1	2	3	4	5	6	1	2	3	4	5	1	2	3
Baillon's Crake	f	u											r						
Corncrake		r					r												
White-breasted Waterhen	r																		
Moorhen	a	c		r	r		r					u	c		r				r
Purple Gallinule		v																	
Coot	f	u		r			r	r				u	r						
Common Crane	r						u			r									
Demoiselle Crane	r														r				
Houbara Bustard										r			r						
Pheasant-tailed Jacana	r	r										r							
Painted Snipe	v																		
Oystercatcher		u			r	a	r	u	r	f		f	a	c	c	f			
Black-winged Stilt	a	c					r	a		u	r	c	a	r	r	r			
Avocet	r	r				r				r		f	r		r				
Crab Plover	r	u			r	u			r	u	r	u	r	a	f	r			
Stone Curlew	r	r			r		r		r		r	r							r
Great Stone Plover		r								r		r							
Cream-coloured Courser	r	r					u					r			r	r			
Collared Pratincole	u	r					c					r	r		r				
Black-winged Pratincole		v																	
Little Pratincole	r						r												
Little Ringed Plover	u	c		r	r	r	a		r	r	r	f	u	r	r				
Ringed Plover	u	c		r	r	f	c	u	r	f		f	u	r	f				
Kentish Plover	u	c	f	r		a	u	u	a	a		c	c	f	c	r			
Lesser Sand Plover	u	c	a	r		a	u	c	f	a		a	a	c	a	r			
Greater Sand Plover	r	c	c	r		a	u	u	c	c		a	a	f	c	r			
Caspian Plover	r	r					u					r	r						
Dotterel							v												
American Golden Plover													v						
Pacific Golden Plover	u	c		r	r	f	f		r	r	r	f	u	r	r	r			
European Golden Plover		v					v					v							
Grey Plover	r	f		c	r	c	u	c	r	c	r	f	a	c	c	r			
Spur-winged Plover	r						r												
Red-wattled Plover	a	a	r	r	r	f	a	a	r	f	f	a	c			r			
Sociable Plover	r						u						r		r				
White-tailed Plover	f	u				r	c					r	f						
Lapwing	r	r					u						r						
Great Knot		r				r	r					r							
Knot						v													
Sanderling	r	f		r	r	c	r	f	c	c	r	f	r	r	f	u			
Little Stint	c	a		r		a	a	u	r	c		a	a	f	f	r			r
Temminck's Stint	c	c				r	c			r		f	u	r					r
Long-toed Stint	r	r					r					r	r						
Baird's Sandpiper															v				
Pectoral Sandpiper							v												
Curlew Sandpiper	u	f		r	r	u	f	r	r	u		f	u	u	u	r			
Dunlin	f	c		r	r	c	f	c	u	c	r	c	f	f	f				
Broad-billed Sandpiper	u	u					r	u		u		u	r	r	r	r			
Ruff	c	a		r	r	r	a	u	r	r	r	c	c	r	r				
Jack Snipe	u	u					r					r	r	r					
Common Snipe	a	c			r	r	c			r		c	f						r
Great Snipe	r	r					r												r
Pintail Snipe	u	u			r		u					r	r						
Long-billed Dowitcher		v					v												

Common Name	Capital Area					Al Batinah						Northeast					Hajar		
	1	2	3	4	5	1	2	3	4	5	6	1	2	3	4	5	1	2	3
Black-tailed Godwit	u	u		r	r	r	f			r	r	f	u	r	r				
Bar-tailed Godwit	r	c		a	r	c	r	u	u	c		c	c	c	c	r			
Whimbrel	r	a		c	u	f	u	f	f	c		f	a	c	c	u			
Slender-billed Curlew				v															
Curlew	u	a		a	r	a	c	c	f	a		a	a	a	f	u			
Spotted Redshank	u	u		r			u		r			r	r	r					
Redshank	c	a		a	r	c	c	f	a	a		a	a	a	c	u			
Marsh Sandpiper	u	u		r		r	u		r	r		u	u	r	r	r			
Greenshank	f	a		a	r	c	u	c	c	a	r	a	a	f	f	r			r
Lesser Yellowlegs		v																	
Green Sandpiper	c	c	r	r		r	c	u	r	r		f	f	r	r				r
Wood Sandpiper	a	c		r	r	r	a			r	r	c	c	r					r
Terek Sandpiper	u	f		r		c	u	u	f	c		f	f	a	f	r			
Common Sandpiper	a	a	u	a	a	f	a	c	c	a		a	a	r	f	r			r
Turnstone	u	u		r	r	u	u	u	u	r	u	f	u	u	f	r			
Red-necked Phalarope	u	u		r	r	r	r	u		r	r	u	u	r	f	c			
Grey Phalarope		r																	
Pomarine Skua	r	u		r	r	u	r	r	r	r		r	r	r	f	f			
Arctic Skua		u		r	r	f		u	r	f		u	r		c	f			
Long-tailed Skua		v																	
Antarctic Skua												v							
South Polar Skua												v							
Sooty Gull	r	c		a	r	a	r	a	a	c	r	a	a	r	a	a			
Great Black-headed Gull	u	u		a	r	c	r	u	u	c	r	c	f	r	c	c			
Black-headed Gull	f	f	u	f	r	c	f	c	u	c	r	f	a	r	u	u			
Slender-billed Gull	u	c		a	r	a	r	c	c	a		a	a	u	a	c			
Common Gull		r						r		r		r	r		r				
Baltic Gull		r		r		r				r		r	r	r	r	r			
Siberian Gull	r	f	r	r	r	f	r	a	r	f		f	u	r	c	c			
Caspian Gull	f	u	r	r	r	c	r	a	a	a	r	a	a	r	c	a			
Kittiwake																r			
Gull-billed Tern	r	u				u	r	r	r	u		f	u	f	u	r			
Caspian Tern	r	u		r		c		u	f	c		f	a	f	a	c			
Swift Tern	r	c		a	c	a		c	f	c	r	a	a	r	a	a			
Lesser Crested Tern	r	u		r		a	r	f	f	c	r	c	c	r	f	f			
Sandwich Tern	r	c		u	r	a		c	f	c	r	a	a	u	a	a			
Roseate Tern	r	r			r	r						u			r	r			
Common Tern	r	u				f		c	u	f		f	r	r	f	c			
White-cheeked Tern	r	u		r	r	c	r	c	r	f	r	f	r	r	u	f			
Bridled Tern		r		r	r	u		u	r	r		f	r		f	c			
Sooty Tern												v		r					
Little Tern	r	r				r			r	r		r	r	r	r	r			
Saunders's Tern	u	u				u		u	u	f		f	r	r	f	f			
Whiskered Tern	a	u		r		r	c		r	r		f	u	r	r				
White-winged Black Tern	f	u					a	r	r	r		u	r			r			
Lesser Noddy												r				r			
Common Noddy						r						r		r	r				
Indian Skimmer		v																	
Lichtenstein's Sandgrouse	f	u			r		r				r	u	r	r	r	r	r	r	r
Crowned Sandgrouse							r												
Spotted Sandgrouse							r												
Chestnut-bellied Sandgrouse	f	r				u	c	u	r	f	r	f	u	r	r	r			
Pin-tailed Sandgrouse							v												
Rock Dove	f	u	u	r	r	r	u	r	r	r	r	f	r		r		u	u	u

Common Name	Capital Area					Al Batinah						Northeast					Hajar		
	1	2	3	4	5	1	2	3	4	5	6	1	2	3	4	5	1	2	3
Stock Dove							v												
Woodpigeon	r						r										f	f	f
Collared Dove	a	u			r	u	a	c	r	f	f	u	r	r	r		r		
Red Turtle Dove							v												
Turtle Dove	r	r					u		r	r	r	r			r				
Rufous Turtle Dove	r	v					v					v							
Laughing Dove	a	a	a	f	a	f	a	a	f	c	c	a	a	r	f	r	c	f	a
Namaqua Dove		r					u		r	u		r	r		r				
Ring-necked Parakeet	u	a		r	a	u	f	a	u	f	c	f	r						r
Jacobin Cuckoo	r																		
Common Cuckoo	r	r					r					r			r			r	
Koel					r		r							r					
Barn Owl					r	r	r	r			r								
Striated Scops Owl									r	u		r					u	r	r
European Scops Owl	r						r					r							r
Spotted Eagle Owl	r											r							
Little Owl	r	r		r	r		r				r	r	r		r	r	r	r	r
Short-eared Owl		r				r	r						r						
European Nightjar	u	r			r	r	r	u	r			r	r		u	r			r
Egyptian Nightjar	u	r					r			r		r	r		r	r			
Common Swift	u	u			r	r	r	r		r		r	r		r	r		r	r
Pallid Swift	f	c	f	r	u	c	u	c	r	u	r	u	r		r	r	r	f	r
Alpine Swift	r				r														r
Little Swift	r				r	r	r				r								
White-collared Kingfisher		r							a	f									
Common Kingfisher	f	a		r	r	r			a	a		f	r	r	r	r			r
Little Green Bee-eater	c	a	r	c	f	f	a	c	r	u	f	a	f		r	r	r		r
Blue-cheeked Bee-eater	u	u			r	r	a	c	u	f	r	u	r		u	r	r	r	r
European Bee-eater	u	u				r	u	u	r	r			r		r			r	r
European Roller	u	u				r	f	u	r	r	r	u	r	u	u	r			
Indian Roller	f	a	u	c	r	f	a	c	f	c	f	a	a		r		r		
Hoopoe	r	u		r	f	u	c	f	r	u	f	u	r		r			r	r
Wryneck	r	u			r	r	r	r	r	r		r						r	r
Black-crowned Finch Lark	u	u		r		u	a	u	u	f	u	f	u		f	u	r		
Bar-tailed Desert Lark															r				
Desert Lark	f	r	c	c	r	r	r		r	r	u	f	u	r	u	r	a	c	f
Hoopoe Lark		r				u	r		r			r	r	r	f	r			
Bimaculated Lark	r						u				r		r		r				
Short-toed Lark	r	u				r	c				r	u	u		r	r			
Lesser Short-toed Lark	r	r				r	u	r			r	r	r		r				
Crested Lark	f	a	u	r	r	c	a	c	c	c	f	a	c	r	f	u			r
Small Skylark	v						r							v					
Skylark	r	u			r	r	f	r		r		r	r						
Brown-throated Sand Martin	v	v					v												
Sand Martin	f	f		r	r	r	c	u	r	r	r	u	u	r	u	r		r	r
Pale Martin							v												
African Rock Martin	f	c	c	u	a	u	u		r	u	r	c	u	r	r	r	a	c	a
Crag Martin	r	r				r	r						r			r			
Barn Swallow	c	c	r	r	u	u	c	u	r	f	r	f	f		f	f	r	r	r
Wire-tailed Swallow	v						v												
Red-rumped Swallow	u	r				r	u		r	r		r	r		r	r			
Streak-throated Swallow	v																		
House Martin	u	u			r		u	u	r				r			r			r
Richard's Pipit		r			r	r	f			r		r	r		r				

Common Name	Capital Area					Al Batinah						Northeast					Hajar		
	1	2	3	4	5	1	2	3	4	5	6	1	2	3	4	5	1	2	3
Blyth's Pipit							v												
Tawny Pipit	u	u		r	r	u	c	f	r	u	u	f	u		r	r	r	r	r
Long-billed Pipit	u	r	r	r	u		u			r	r	u			r		u	f	f
Tree Pipit	u	u			r	r	u					r	r		r				r
Meadow Pipit							v												v
Red-throated Pipit	f	u			r	r	c	u		r	r	u	u	r	r	r			
Water Pipit	f	u				r	c		r	r		f	r						
Buff-bellied Pipit							v						v						
Yellow Wagtail	c	f			r	r	a	f		r		f	f	r	u	r			
Citrine Wagtail	c	c				r	c		r	r		f	f	r	r				
Grey Wagtail	u	r			r	r	u	r			r			r	r			r	r
White Wagtail	c	c	c	r	a	u	a	c	r	u		c	a		u	r			r
White-cheeked Bulbul	u	a			r	r	r		f	f	r								
Red-vented Bulbul	r	f			f	a													r
Yellow-vented Bulbul	c	a	u	c	a	u	f	a	r	f	c	a	u	r			a	c	a
Grey Hypocolius	v																		
Rufous Bush Robin	f	u		r	r	r	u	r		r	r	u	r	r	r	r		r	
Nightingale	r	r				r		r					r						r
Bluethroat	f	f				r	u					r	u		r				r
White-throated Robin															r			r	
Eversmann's Redstart						r													r
Black Redstart	u	u	u	r	u	r	u	f		r	c	f	r				u	u	f
Common Redstart		r		r		r	r			r	r						r	r	r
Whinchat	r	r		r		u		r											
Stonechat	r	u		r		u							r						r
Pied Stonechat		v																	
Isabelline Wheatear	u	u	r	r	r	r	a	u	r	u	r	u	r	r	r	r		r	r
Northern Wheatear	r	r		r		r	f		r	r	r	u	r		r		r		r
Pied Wheatear	r	r		r	r	r	u			r	r	r	r					r	r
Black-eared Wheatear							v												v
Desert Wheatear	f	u	r	r	f	u	c	c	u	f	r	f	f	r	c	f	r	u	u
Finsch's Wheatear							v				v								
Red-tailed Wheatear	f	u	f	c	r	u	u			r	u	f	u	r	f	r	u	f	u
Eastern Pied Wheatear							r				f		r						
Hooded Wheatear	r			r		r							r		r			r	r
Hume's Wheatear	f	r	f	a	u	r	r				r	u	r	r	u		u	c	c
White-crowned Black Wheatear							v												
Rock Thrush	r	r		r	r	r	r	r				r		r	r			r	u
Blue Rock Thrush	r	r	u	r	f	r		r				r		r	r		r	r	u
Ring Ouzel																			v
Black-throated Thrush	r	r		r							r								r
Song Thrush	r	r		r		r						r	r				r		r
Mistle Thrush																			v
Graceful Prinia	a	a	r	r	f	u	c	a	u	f	r	c	f				r		u
Scrub Warbler		r	r			r					r	r					r	u	f
Grasshopper Warbler		r																	
Savi's Warbler	v	v																	
Moustached Warbler	v																		
Sedge Warbler	r	r		r							r								
Paddyfield Warbler	v	v																	
Blyth's Reed Warbler	v																		
Marsh Warbler	r	r			r	r				r		r	r						
European Reed Warbler	f	u					r	r	r	r		r	r				r		
Clamorous Reed Warbler	c	c			r	r			f	c		u	f	r					

163

Common Name	Capital Area					Al Batinah						Northeast					Hajar		
	1	2	3	4	5	1	2	3	4	5	6	1	2	3	4	5	1	2	3
Great Reed Warbler	r	r										r							
Olivaceous Warbler	u	u	r	r	r	r	u			r	r	r	r	r	r				r
Booted Warbler	r	r							r	r									
Sykes's Warbler									c	f									
Upcher's Warbler	u	r		r		r	r				r	r	r				r	r	r
Icterine Warbler											v								
Ménétries's Warbler	u	u			r	r	u	u	u	r	r	u	r		r		r	r	
Desert Warbler	u	u		r	r	r	r	r	r	u	u	f	r		r		r		
Orphean Warbler	u	r		r	r	r	r	r		r	u	r	r						r
Barred Warbler	r	r																	r
Lesser Whitethroat	u	r		r	r	r	r	r	u		r	u	r	r	r				r
Hume's Lesser Whitethroat													v						
Desert Lesser Whitethroat	c	u	f	u	r	r	u	a	r	r	a	f	u	r	r		f	f	f
Whitethroat	f	u		r	r	r	r	r		r	r	u	r		u	r		r	r
Garden Warbler		v				v													
Blackcap	r					r				r									r
Green Warbler		r				r													r
Inornate Warbler		v																	
Hume's Warbler		v																	
Bonelli's Warbler	v																		
Wood Warbler		r						r							r	r			
Plain Leaf Warbler	r	r			r	r					c	r	r				r	r	u
Chiffchaff	c	c		r	r	r	u	f	u	f	u	u	r	r	r		r	r	u
Willow Warbler	r	r					r					r	r		r				r
Spotted Flycatcher	f	u	r	r	u	r	u	u		r		u	r		u	r		r	u
Red-breasted Flycatcher		r			r							r			r				r
Arabian Babbler	f	c	r	r	r	f	f	f	r	u	a	c	r		r		f	f	c
Nile Valley Sunbird																			r
Purple Sunbird	c	a	f	u	a	f	c	a	u	c	c	a	f		r		c	u	f
Golden Oriole	r	r		r	r	r	r	r		r	r	r	r		r	r			r
Isabelline Shrike	c	c	r	r	f	u	c		f	f	f	f	f	r	f	r	r	u	u
Red-backed Shrike	r	r							r	r		r	r		r	r			
Long-tailed Shrike		r										r							
Lesser Grey Shrike							r						r						
Southern Grey Shrike	f	u	r	r	r	u	c	f	u	c	f	f	f	r	f	u	c	r	r
Steppe Grey Shrike	r	r				r	u		r	r		r	r			r			
Woodchat Shrike	r	r				r	r				r	r					r	r	r
Masked Shrike	r										r								
Black Drongo	v																		
Magpie		v																	
House Crow	f	a	u	r	a	a	a	a	f	a	f	a	r		r				
Brown-necked Raven	f	u	a	f	u	u	u	u		r	r	f	c	r	c	f	u	c	c
Brahminy Starling		v																	
Starling	r	u		r	r		f	r			r	r	u						
Rose-coloured Starling	r	u						u				r	r		r				
Common Mynah	c	a	u		a	u	c	a	u	f	u	u	r						
Bank Mynah				v						v									
House Sparrow	a	a	f	u	a	f	a	a	f	f	c	a	a	r	u	r	u	r	c
Spanish Sparrow	r	u			r	r	r			r	r	r	r						
Pale Rock Sparrow							u			r					r	r	r	r	
Yellow-throated Sparrow	r	u		r	r	r	r	u	r	r	u	u	r	r	r		r	r	
Indian Silverbill	c	a	u	r	r	r	a	c	r	u	u	f	r		r		r		r
African Silverbill						r													
Brambling		r																	

164

Common Name	Capital Area					Al Batinah						Northeast					Hajar		
	1	2	3	4	5	1	2	3	4	5	6	1	2	3	4	5	1	2	3
Siskin																			v
Trumpeter Finch							r					r							
Common Rosefinch		r																	r
House Bunting	f	u	f	r	u	r	u	u			r	u	r	r			u	u	u
African Rock Bunting							r												
Ortolan Bunting	r	r				r	r												r
Little Bunting																			v
Yellow-breasted Bunting							r												
Red-headed Bunting							v												
Black-headed Bunting		r					r								r				
Corn Bunting	r	r					u	r				r	r						

European Bee-eaters

Common Name	Musandam					Buraymi			Central Desert								BaH & M			
	1	2	3	4	5	1	2	3	1	2	3	4	5	6	7	8	1	2	3	4
Little Grebe								r										r		
Great Crested Grebe																	v			
Black-necked Grebe																	r	u		
Jouanin's Petrel																			r	r
Cory's Shearwater																				v
Pale-footed Shearwater																				f
Wedge-tailed Shearwater					r															
Persian Shearwater	r							u										r		c
Wilson's Storm-petrel	r							u										r	r	f
Red-billed Tropicbird	r							f									r			u
Masked Booby																	r	r	r	c
Brown Booby																	r			r
Cormorant	u				r					r	r						c	u	f	
Socotra Cormorant	c	r			f												u	r	r	
Lesser Frigatebird																		v		
Bittern											r							r	r	
Little Bittern									r		r		r					u		
Night Heron	r								r	r	r	r	r				r	f		
Striated Heron	f				r				r		r	r					u	u		r
Squacco Heron	r								r		r						r	f		
Indian Pond Heron	r								r		r	r					r	u		
Cattle Egret	r							r	r	r	u	u	r	r				f		
Western Reef Heron	a				r				r	r	r	r	r				a	f	f	c
Little Egret	f							r	r	r	r		u				u	u	r	
Intermediate Egret	r																r	r		
Great White Egret	u											r					c	u	u	
Grey Heron	a				r			r	u	r	u	r	f	r			a	a	c	f
Purple Heron	r								r		r	r		r			r	u		
Goliath Heron																	v			
Abdim's Stork									r											
White Stork									u	r	r	r	c	r		r		u	r	
Glossy Ibis								r	r		r	r						u		
Spoonbill	r								r								c	u	r	
Greater Flamingo	f		r					r	r		r						a	c	c	r
Lesser Flamingo										v										
White-fronted Goose											r							r		
Greylag Goose											r		r					u	r	
Egyptian Goose								v												
Ruddy Shelduck																		r		
Shelduck								r									r			
Cotton Teal																		r		
Wigeon	r							r			r						r	u	r	
Gadwall								r			r	r						u		
Teal	f							c			u	r					r	f	r	
Mallard	f							f	r		u	r	r				r	f		
Pintail	r							f	r		r	r	r				r	c	r	
Garganey	r					r		u	r		u	r					r	f	r	
Shoveler	r							f	r		r	r						f		
Red-crested Pochard								r										r		
Pochard								r			r							u		
Ferruginous Duck								r										u		
Tufted Duck								r			r							u		
Honey Buzzard							r					r	r				r	r		
Crested Honey Buzzard	v																			

Common Name	Musandam 1	2	3	4	5	Buraymi 1	2	3	Central Desert 1	2	3	4	5	6	7	8	BaH & M 1	2	3	4
Black Kite	r				r			r			r		r	r			r	u	r	
Egyptian Vulture	r				r	r	r	r	c	u	r	r		r	r	r	r	c	f	r
Griffon Vulture						r	r	r		r								r		
Lappet-faced Vulture						r	u							r	r					
Black Vulture																		v		
Short-toed Eagle	r	r	r	r		r	r		u	r	r				r		r	u	r	
Marsh Harrier	r							r	r	r	u	u	f	r			c	a	f	
Hen Harrier									r		r		r				r	r		
Pallid Harrier			r	r					r	r	u	u	f		r		u	u	r	
'Ringtail' Harrier																	r			
Montagu's Harrier				r						r	r	r	f	r	r	r	r	u	r	
Goshawk																		v		
Sparrowhawk	r	u	u	r			r		u		u	u	r	r	r			f		
Shikra												v						v		
Common Buzzard										r		r	r					r		
Long-legged Buzzard	r					r			f	r	f	r	u	r	r		r	u		
Lesser Spotted Eagle																		v		
Greater Spotted Eagle						r			r		r	r	r			a	r	u		
Steppe Eagle	r		r				r	r	r	r	r			r	r	a		r	r	
Imperial Eagle							r		r		r			r	r	f	r	u		
Golden Eagle									f	r	f	r	r	r			r	r		
Booted Eagle													r				r	r		
Bonelli's Eagle	r	r	r				u	r			r						r	u		
Osprey	f			c					r		r	r					c	c	f	f
Lesser Kestrel	r	r	u	r		r				r		r	r			r	r	r		
Kestrel	u	u	c	f	r	r	r		f	r	u	r	c	f	r	r	r	f	r	r
Amur Falcon										r		r	r					u	r	
Hobby						r			u		r	r	r	r	r		r	f		
Sooty Falcon					u												r	r		
Lanner Falcon			r						r		r		r					r		
Saker Falcon			r						r	r	r		r				r	r		
Peregrine Falcon	r		r	r	r				r	r	r			r	r		u	f	r	
Barbary Falcon	r	r	r	r	r	r	c		r								r	u		
Chukar	u	f	c	c	r		r													
Arabian Partridge						r			r					r						
Sand Partridge	r	r	u	r	r	r	c		u					r	u	r	r			
Grey Francolin	r	r	r	c				r												
Quail	r		r	r					r	r	u	u	r	r			r	f		
Little Button Quail		v																		
Water Rail																	r			
Spotted Crake									r		r	r	r					f		
Little Crake											r						r			
Baillon's Crake									r		r							f		
Corncrake												r	r					u		
White-breasted Waterhen												r	r					u		
Moorhen								r	r		r	r						u		
Lesser Moorhen																		v		
Allen's Gallinule																		v		
Purple Gallinule																		v		
Coot									r		r	r					r	f		
Common Crane													r					r		
Demoiselle Crane																		r		
Houbara Bustard									u			r		u			r	r		
Pheasant-tailed Jacana																		r		

Common Name	Musandam					Buraymi			Central Desert								BaH & M			
	1	2	3	4	5	1	2	3	1	2	3	4	5	6	7	8	1	2	3	4
Painted Snipe																	v			
Oystercatcher	f																a	u	f	f
Black-winged Stilt	r			r				a			r		r				u	c		
Avocet								r									r	u		
Crab Plover	r																c	r	c	
Stone Curlew	r	r				r			u		r	r	r	r	r			r		
Spotted Thick-knee									f								r			
Cream-coloured Courser							r	r	f	r	r	r	u	r	r		r	u	r	
Collared Pratincole									r		r	r	r					u		
Black-winged Pratincole										v										
Little Pratincole																		u		
Little Ringed Plover	r							u	r	r	r	r	r				r	c	r	
Ringed Plover	c				r			r	r	r	r	u	r				f	c	r	
Kentish Plover	u				r			f	r		u	r	r				c	f	c	
Lesser Sand Plover	f				r				r		u	r					c	f	f	r
Greater Sand Plover	u				r			r			r	r	r				c	u	f	
Caspian Plover											r	r	r				r	r	r	
Pacific Golden Plover	r									r		r		r			r	f	r	r
Grey Plover	c									r		r	r				c	f	c	r
Spur-winged Plover								r												
Red-wattled Plover	f	r						a	r	r		r		r				u		
Sociable Plover												r						r	r	
White-tailed Plover									r		r	r	r				r	u		
Lapwing											r							r		
Great Knot																	f		r	
Knot																	v	v		
Sanderling	r							r		r	r						c	u	f	r
Little Stint	f				r			a		r	f	u	r				c	c	f	r
Temminck's Stint	r							r	r	r	u	r	r				r	f	r	
Long-toed Stint																	r	r		
Curlew Sandpiper	r							r		r	r						c	f	f	
Dunlin	f							r	r		u	r					c	f	f	
Broad-billed Sandpiper	r										r	r					c	u	r	r
Ruff	r							c	r	r	f	r	r				r	c	r	r
Jack Snipe	r							r	r	r	r	r					r	u		
Common Snipe	u							c	r	r	f	u	r				r	c	r	
Great Snipe											r	r	r				r			
Pintail Snipe								r	r		u	u					c			
Woodcock																	v			
Black-tailed Godwit	r								r								r	u	r	
Bar-tailed Godwit	f																a	u	c	
Whimbrel	c				r				r		r	r					c	f	c	r
Slender-billed Curlew																	v			
Curlew	c				r						r	r	r				a	f	f	r
Far Eastern Curlew																	v			
Spotted Redshank	r							r	r		r						r	u		
Redshank	c							r			u	r					a	f	f	r
Marsh Sandpiper	r										r	r					u	u	r	
Greenshank	c							r	r		r	r	r				c	f	f	r
Green Sandpiper	r	r		r				c	u	u	f	u	r	r			r	f		
Wood Sandpiper	r							f	r	r	f	r	r					f		
Terek Sandpiper	r							r	r	r	r	r					c	u	c	
Common Sandpiper	a				r			c	r	r	u	r	r	r			f	c	u	u
Turnstone	r								r		r	r					c	f	f	c

168

Common Name	Musandam 1	2	3	4	5	Buraymi 1	2	3	Central Desert 1	2	3	4	5	6	7	8	BaH & M 1	2	3	4
Red-necked Phalarope	r				r			r	r	r	u	r					r	f	r	f
Grey Phalarope				r							r							r		
Pomarine Skua				r													r	r	r	r
Arctic Skua	r			r													r	u	f	r
Long-tailed Skua																				v
Antarctic Skua																				v
Sooty Gull	r				f				r			r					c	f	f	a
White-eyed Gull																	v			
Great Black-headed Gull	f				r				r								f	u	r	r
Black-headed Gull	a				f		r		r		r	r		r			u	u	r	
Slender-billed Gull	c				u		r			r		r					c	f	f	r
Common Gull																		r		r
Baltic Gull	r											r					r			
Siberian Gull	r									r	r		r				u	u	r	c
Caspian Gull	u			r				r		r		r	r				f	u	r	c
'large white-headed gull'																	u			
Gull-billed Tern																	c	u	f	r
Caspian Tern	r																c	u	c	r
Swift Tern	u																c	u	f	a
Lesser Crested Tern	r			r													f	u	f	f
Sandwich Tern	c			r					r								c	u	f	f
Roseate Tern																	r		r	r
Common Tern	f	r		r										r			u	r	r	f
White-cheeked Tern	u			u													u	r	r	f
Bridled Tern	r			c													r	r	r	c
Sooty Tern	r			r																
Little Tern																	r		r	
Saunders's Tern	r								r		r						c	u	f	u
Whiskered Tern				r				r									u	u	r	
Black Tern																	v			
White-winged Black Tern																	r	u		
Lesser Noddy									r										r	u
Common Noddy	r				r				r								r	r		c
Lichtenstein's Sandgrouse	r	u	r	f	r	r	f		f						f					
Crowned Sandgrouse									c	r	f	u	r	u	r		r	r		
Spotted Sandgrouse									r	r	a	f	c	r	r	r				
Chestnut-bellied Sandgrouse						r	r	r	c	r	u	r	r	r	f		r	c	r	
Rock Dove	c	f	c	c	r		r	u	f	r	f	f	u	a	r	c	r	r		
Collared Dove	r	r	r	r		r	r	c	f	u	f	c	c	a	r		r	f	r	
Red Turtle Dove																	v			
Turtle Dove	r	u	r	r				r	f	r	f	u	r	r			r	u	r	
Rufous Turtle Dove										v		r	r				u			
Laughing Dove	a	a	a	a	r	c	u	c	c	a	f	a	c	a	r	r	f	a	r	
Namaqua Dove			r					r	r	r	r	u	r	r	r		r			
Ring-necked Parakeet	f	r		r	r	r		r									u	r		
Jacobin Cuckoo			r						r	r			r				r			
Great Spotted Cuckoo																	v			
Indian Hawk Cuckoo																	v			
Plaintive Cuckoo																	v			
Common Cuckoo	r	r	r	r					u	r	r	u	r	r	r		r	c	r	
Koel									r		u	u	r					c		
Barn Owl									r		r			r			r			
African Scops Owl																	r			
Striated Scops Owl	r	u	r	r																

Common Name	Musandam					Buraymi			Central Desert								BaH & M			
	1	2	3	4	5	1	2	3	1	2	3	4	5	6	7	8	1	2	3	4
European Scops Owl	r								r	r	r	r	r				r	u		
Desert Eagle Owl	r		r			r	r		r	r	r	r					r	r		
Spotted Eagle Owl														r	r					
Little Owl	r	u	u	u		f	r	r	f		r						r	r		
Long-eared Owl																		v		
Short-eared Owl									r		r	r					r	u	r	
European Nightjar									f	r	r	u	u	r			r	u		r
Egyptian Nightjar						r			r	r	r	r	r					r		
Common Swift	r	r	r		r		r		r		r	r	r				r	r		
Pallid Swift	u	u	f	r	u		r	r	r		r	r					r			
'Dhofar Swift'																	r			
Common/Pallid/Dhofar Swift																	r			
Little Swift												r					r			
Grey-headed Kingfisher									r								r			
White-collared Kingfisher																	r			
Common Kingfisher	f			r		r											u	c		
White-throated Bee-eater										v										
Little Green Bee-eater	r	u	r	c		r	f	f	r		r	r			r	r	r			
Blue-cheeked Bee-eater	r	r	r	r				r	f	r	f	u	u	r	r		r	f	r	
European Bee-eater	r	r	u	r			r		u	r	r	r	r	r				u	r	
European Roller	r	r	r	r				r	f	f	f	f	f	f	u		r	c		
Indian Roller	a	f	r	r				r	r	r	r	r	r					f		
Hoopoe	f	u	u	r	r	r			f	c	u	f	u	r		r	r	f		
Wryneck	r	r	r						r	r		u	r					f	r	
Black-crowned Finch Lark				r	r	f	r	f	a	c	c	f	a	c	f	u	u	f	r	r
Dunn's Lark									r	r		r	r	r	u					
Bar-tailed Desert Lark									u			r	r	r	u					
Desert Lark	f	c	a	a	r	r	c	f	u	r	r	r	r	r	a	u	r	r		
Hoopoe Lark						r			c	c	f	c	a	f	c	f	f	u	r	r
Bimaculated Lark		r		r					r		r	r					r	r		
Red-capped Lark																		v		
Short-toed Lark	r	r	u	r		r		r	u	f	f	f	c	r	r	r	r	u	r	r
Lesser Short-toed Lark		r							r		r	r	r					u	r	
Crested Lark	r	c	u	f		r		c	f	f	a	u	r	r	r	r	f	f	u	
Skylark	r		r	r		r			r		r		r					u		
Sand Martin	r	r	r		r			f	r	u	f	f	u	r		r	u	f	r	
African Rock Martin	c	f	a	c	r	r	c	c	r	r		r	r	r	r	a		r		
Crag Martin	r		u	r	r	r	r					r	r							
Barn Swallow	f	u	f	u	r	r		c	a	c	c	c	c	f	r	u	f	c	r	r
Lesser Striped Swallow																		v		
Red-rumped Swallow	r		r						r		r	r	r				r	u	r	
Streak-throated Swallow												v								
House Martin	r	r	u	r	r	r		r	r	r	r	r	r	r			r	u		r
Richard's Pipit	r	r	r			r				r	u	r	r				r	u		
Blyth's Pipit																		v		
Tawny Pipit	r	u	f	r	r	u	r	r	u	u	c	f	c	r		r	u	f	r	
Long-billed Pipit		r	c	r				r	r	r	r	r	r	r	r				r	
Olive-backed Pipit																		v		
Tree Pipit	r	r	f						r	u	f	f	u				r	c	r	
Meadow Pipit	v		v									v	v							
Red-throated Pipit	u	u	f	r				r	u	r	f	u	u	r			r	f		
Water Pipit	r		r					r	r	r	f	r	r				r	u		
Forest Wagtail												v						v		
Yellow Wagtail	u	r	u	r	r			f	f	f	f	f	f	f	r		u	c	r	r

170

Common Name	Musandam					Buraymi			Central Desert								BaH & M			
	1	2	3	4	5	1	2	3	1	2	3	4	5	6	7	8	1	2	3	4
Citrine Wagtail	r				r			c	r	r	f	u	r	r		r	r	u		
Grey Wagtail	u						r	r	u	r	u	u	r	r	r		r	f	r	r
White Wagtail	f	r	r	r	r			c	c	c	a	c	c	f	r	a	f	c	r	r
White-cheeked Bulbul	f		f	r			r	r												
Yellow-vented Bulbul	c	a	a	a	r	r	c	r				r			f	r		r		
Grey Hypocolius	v	v	v	v						r	u	u								r
Radde's Accentor			v																	
Black-throated Accentor																		v		
Rufous Bush Robin	u	f	u	r	r		r	r	f	c	u	f	u	r			r	u	r	
Robin	v		v									v								
Thrush Nightingale		v										v						v		
Nightingale	r	u	u	r					r	r	r	u	r	r			r	u		
Bluethroat	r	r	r	r				u	u	u	u	f	r	r			r	c	r	
White-throated Robin	r	u	u	r	r							r					r			
Eversmann's Redstart		r	f	r													r			
Black Redstart	f	f	c	f	r		r	r	f	c	f	c	f	f	r		r	c	r	
Common Redstart	u	f	c	u	r		r		u	u	u	u	r	r	r		r	u	r	
Blackstart											r	r		r	c	r				
Whinchat	r	r	u						r		r	r	r					u		
Stonechat	u	r	u	r	r				r	r	u	r		r			r	r		
Pied Stonechat	v	v	v																	
Isabelline Wheatear	u	c	c	u	r	c	r	f	u	c	f	c	c	u	f	u	r	u	r	r
Northern Wheatear	u	f	c	u		r	r	r	u	u	u	f	u	r	r		r	u		
Pied Wheatear	f	f	c	f	r	u	r		r	u	u	f	f		r	r	r	u		r
Cyprus Pied Wheatear												v								
Black-eared Wheatear	v		v									v						v		
Desert Wheatear	r	f	f	f		c	u	f	c	c	c	a	a	a	c	c	c	f	f	u
Finsch's Wheatear			v			v														
Red-tailed Wheatear	r	f	f	f	r	c	c	r	r	r	r	r	r			u	r	u	r	
Eastern Pied Wheatear	r	f	f	u							r	r						r	r	
Mourning Wheatear	v	v	v	v								v								
South Arabian Wheatear									r						r	r				r
Hooded Wheatear		r	r	r		r			r		r					r	r			
White-crowned Black Wheatear														v				v		
Rock Thrush	r	u	c	r	r	r	r		r	u	r	u	u	r	r	r		u	r	
Blue Rock Thrush	u	r	f	r	r	r	r		u	r	r	u	r	r				u		
White's Thrush																		v		
Ring Ouzel			v															v		
Eyebrowed Thrush																		v		
Dusky Thrush											v		v					v		
Black-throated Thrush	r	r	r	r					r			r		r				u		
Song Thrush	r	r	u	r					r	r	u	f	r	r			r	f		
Mistle Thrush		v	v	v														v		
Graceful Prinia	f	r		r			r	c			r	r								
Scrub Warbler	r	r	u	r			f	r												
Grasshopper Warbler		r	r									r						r		
Savi's Warbler											v		v							
Sedge Warbler			r					r			r	r						u		
Paddyfield Warbler												v								
Marsh Warbler		r	r	r					u	f	r	u	r	r				r		
European Reed Warbler	r							r	r	r	r	r	r				r	u		
Clamorous Reed Warbler	r							r	r	r	r	r	r				u	u		
Great Reed Warbler			r	r						r	r	r	r					u		

171

Common Name	Musandam					Buraymi			Central Desert								BaH & M			
	1	2	3	4	5	1	2	3	1	2	3	4	5	6	7	8	1	2	3	4
Olivaceous Warbler	r	u	r	r	r		r		f	c	u	f	f	r	r		r	f	r	
Booted Warbler		r	r	r						r	r	r	r				r	u		
Sykes's Warbler																		r		
Upcher's Warbler	r	u	r	r	r	r	u	r	r	u	r	u	r	r	r		r	u		
Icterine Warbler	v																	v		
Ménétries's Warbler	r	u	u	r			r	r	r	r	c	u	c	f	u	r		r	f	r
Desert Warbler	r	u	r	u	r	c	f	r	u	r	f	u	r	r	c	r	f	u	r	
Orphean Warbler		r	r	r		r	u		u	r	r	u	r	r	r			u		
Barred Warbler	r	u	r	r			r		r			u	r					u		
Lesser Whitethroat	r	f	r	u		r	f		r	c	u	c	f	r	r		r	f	r
Hume's Lesser Whitethroat							r													
Desert Lesser Whitethroat	r	c	f	f	r	r	f	r	c	c	f	c	f	c	f		r	f	r
Whitethroat	r	u	u	r	r	r		r	u	c	u	f	c	u	r		r	f	r
Garden Warbler										v	v	v	v					v		
Blackcap	r	r	r	r	r				r	r	r	u	r	r	r			r		
Green Warbler		r							r		r	r	r					u		
Greenish Warbler																		v		
Inornate Warbler										v		v						v		
Hume's Warbler	v											v	v					v		
'Yellow-browed' Warbler																		u		
Bonelli's Warbler																		v		
Wood Warbler		r								r	r	r	r				r	f	r	
Plain Leaf Warbler	r	f	f	f			c	r		r		r	r					r		
Chiffchaff	u	r	u	r	r		r		u	c	f	c	f	c	u		r	c	r	
Willow Warbler	u	u	f	r	r				r	u	r	u	u				r	u	r	
Blue-and-white Flycatcher																		v		
Asian Brown Flycatcher																		v		
Spotted Flycatcher	r	u	f	r					f	c	f	c	c	u	u	r	r	f	r	
Red-breasted Flycatcher	r		r						r	f	u	f	r				r	c	r	
Semi-collared Flycatcher	r		r															r	r	
Pied Flycatcher													v							
Arabian Babbler	r	a	r	a	r	r	r		f		r			f	r		r			
Nile Valley Sunbird											r			r						
Purple Sunbird	c	f	f	c		r	f	u										u		
Shining Sunbird														r	r					
Palestine Sunbird															r					
Oriental White-eye																	u			
White-breasted White-eye											r	u	r	r	r					
Golden Oriole	r	r	r						u	u	u	u	r	r				f		
Isabelline Shrike	c	f	c	f	r	r	r	r	f	c	c	c	c	f	f		u	c	r	
Red-backed Shrike	r	u	r	r					u	r	u	u	r	r			r	u	r	
Bay-backed Shrike		v	v	v					v									r		
Long-tailed Shrike																		r		
Lesser Grey Shrike	r	r	u						r		r	r						r		
Southern Grey Shrike	f	c	u	a	r	c	u	c	a	f	c	u	c	u	a	r	u	u	r	
Steppe Grey Shrike		r	r				r	r	r	r	r	r	r	r				r	r	
Woodchat Shrike	u	u	f	u		r					r							r		
Masked Shrike	r	u	u	r		r			r	r	r	u	r	r				r		
Black Drongo													v					v		
House Crow	f	r				r		r										r		
Brown-necked Raven	f	u	f	r	u	c	r	r	a	c	c	a	f	a	f	r	f	f	f	c
Fan-tailed Raven											r		r	r		r				
Tristram's Grackle													r	r		u				
Amethyst Starling													v							

Common Name	Musandam					Buraymi			Central Desert								BaH & M			
	1	2	3	4	5	1	2	3	1	2	3	4	5	6	7	8	1	2	3	4
Brahminy Starling											v	v						v		
Starling	r								u		r						r	f	r	
Rose-coloured Starling									f	u	u	u	f	r		r		f	r	
Wattled Starling									r		r	r						r		
Common Mynah	u			r	r			r												
House Sparrow	a	c	c	c		r	r	c	r	a	r	r	r					r		
Spanish Sparrow	r	r	r	r				r	r	r	r			r			r	r		
Pale Rock Sparrow	r	r	r	r	r	r	r		r	r	r	r	r	r				u		
Yellow-throated Sparrow		r	r	r		r	r		u	r	r	u	r					f	r	
Rüppell's Weaver												r								
Indian Silverbill	u	u		r			r	r		r								u	r	
African Silverbill												r	r							
Brambling			r						r									r		
Siskin											v	v								
Trumpeter Finch	r	r	r	u		r	u		r	r	r							r		
Common Rosefinch							r		r	u	u	u	r					f		
House Bunting	r	u	c	f	r	r	c	f	r	r		r	r				r	r		
Cinereous Bunting	v	v	v									v								
Ortolan Bunting	u	u	f	r						r	u	r	f	r	r			u		
Grey-necked Bunting			v															v		
Cretzschmar's Bunting											v	v		v				v		
Rustic Bunting												v								
Little Bunting																		v		
Yellow-breasted Bunting	r								r		r		r					r		
Reed Bunting																		v		
Red-headed Bunting			v									v								
Black-headed Bunting	u	u	u	r	r				r	r	r	u						u		
Corn Bunting		r	r						r	r	r	r	r					r		

Grey-necked Bunting

Common Name	Southeast				Dhofar															
	1	2	3	4	1	2	3	4	5	6	7	8	9	10	11	12	13	14	15	16
Little Grebe		u				f			f	u	c	a				c	r	u	f	r
Great Crested Grebe						v					v									
Black-necked Grebe		r				f			u	r	f	r				u		u	u	
Jouanin's Petrel	r	r				r			r	r	u				c			r	r	
Cory's Shearwater															v					
Pale-footed Shearwater	r	r		r		r			r	r	r				c			r	r	r
Wedge-tailed Shearwater	r					r			r	r	r				u					
Persian Shearwater	r	r		r		u			r	u	u				a			u	f	u
Wilson's Storm-petrel	r	r				r			r	r	r				c	r		u	r	r
Black-bellied Storm-petrel															v					
Swinhoe's Storm-petrel															v			v	v	
Red-billed Tropicbird	r	r		r						r	f				f		c	r	r	r
Masked Booby	u	r	r	c		f			u	f	f				a	r		u	f	r
Brown Booby	r			r		r			r	u	r				f	r		u	f	
Cormorant	u	u	u	r	r	f			u	u	f	r			u	f		f	f	f
Socotra Cormorant	f	r	r	c		u			r	u	u				f	r		f	c	r
White Pelican						v										v				
Pink-backed Pelican					v	v										v		v		
Lesser Frigatebird				v											v					
Bittern		r				r			r	r	r					r		r	r	
Little Bittern						f	u	r	u	f	f	u				u	r	r	f	r
Yellow Bittern						u			r	r	r					r		v	r	
Night Heron		r	r		r	f	r	r	u	f	f	u			u	u	u	u	f	r
Striated Heron		r		r	r	r			r	f	f				u	r		f	u	
Squacco Heron		r			r	f	r		f	c	c	f				a	r	f	f	u
Indian Pond Heron		r			r	u	r		r	f	u	r			u	u	r	r	u	r
Cattle Egret	r	r	r	r	a	f			u	f	c	r			u	f	r	f	f	r
Western Reef Heron	a	a	a	f	r	a			f	a	c	r			f	c		a	a	f
Little Egret	r	f	f	r	f	a	r	r	a	a	a	c			u	a	r	a	a	f
Black Egret										v										
Intermediate Egret	r	r	r			f			u	u	f					r		u	r	
Great White Egret	f	c	f	r	r	f			f	f	c	r				f		c	f	r
Grey Heron	a	a	a	f	a	a	f	u	a	a	a	c	r		f	a	u	a	a	c
Purple Heron		r		r	u	c	r	r	c	c	f	u				c		c	c	r
Goliath Heron																v				
Black-headed Heron					v	v				v						v			v	
Black Stork						v				v	v									
Abdim's Stork					u	r			r	r	r		r			r		u	r	
White Stork					a	r	r		r	r	r	u	u	r	u	u	r	u	u	r
Glossy Ibis					u	c			c	c	c	r		r	u	a	r	f	c	r
Sacred Ibis					v	v												v		v
Spoonbill	f	a	c	r	r	f			f	c	c				u	c		c	c	r
African Spoonbill						v			v	v	v					v		v	v	
Greater Flamingo	a	a	a	u	r	a			c	c	a	r			u	a		c	a	r
Lesser Flamingo		v				v			v	v	v					v	v	v	v	
Fulvous Whistling Duck						v			v							v				
Lesser Whistling-Duck						v			v	v		v								
Bewick's Swan											v					v		v		
White-fronted Goose		r		r		r			r	r	u					r		r	u	
Lesser White-fronted Goose						v				v										
Greylag Goose		r									u					r			r	
Ruddy Shelduck		r	r	r		r			r	r	u					r		r	u	
Shelduck	r	r	r			r			r	r	r		r		u	r		r	u	r
Comb Duck						v										v				

174

Common Name	Southeast 1	2	3	4	Dhofar 1	2	3	4	5	6	7	8	9	10	11	12	13	14	15	16
Cotton Teal					f				u	u	u	r				f		r	f	r
Wigeon		c	r	r	u			f		u	c	r				c		u	f	r
Gadwall		u			u				u	r	f	r				f		r	f	
Teal		c	r	r	r	f		r	f	f	c	f		u		c		f	c	r
Mallard		f	r	r		f	r	r	u	u	c	f				u		r	f	r
Pintail	r	a	r	r	r	f		r	c	f	c	f				c		f	c	r
Garganey		f		r	r	c		r	a	c	c	f			u	a	r	f	c	r
Shoveler		a	r	r		c		r	c	f	c	u			u	a		f	c	r
Marbled Teal										v										
Red-crested Pochard		r				r			r	r	r					r		r	u	
Pochard		u	r			f			u	r	f	r				f		r	f	r
Ferruginous Duck		r			r	u			u	r	f	u				u		r	f	r
Tufted Duck		f				f	r		f	r	f	r				f		r	f	
Red-breasted Merganser										v										
Honey Buzzard					r		r			r		r							r	
Crested Honey Buzzard					v													v		
Black-winged Kite					v															
Black Kite					f	f		r	r	u	r		r			r	r	f		r
Pallas's Fish Eagle											v					v				
Egyptian Vulture	r		r	u	f	r	r	r	r	r	r	r	r	r	f	r	r	u	u	r
Griffon Vulture					r			r					r					r	r	r
Lappet-faced Vulture					r			r			r	r	u	r			r		r	r
Short-toed Eagle	r	r		r	u	r	u	f	r	r	u	f	u	f	u		u	r	u	u
Marsh Harrier	f	c	c		a	c		r	c	c	c	u	r		u	c		f	f	r
Hen Harrier		r	r		u	r		r	r	r	r	r				r	r			
Pallid Harrier		r	r		c	r	r	r	r	u	u		r	r		r	r	r	r	r
Montagu's Harrier		r	r		c	r	r	r	r	f	u	r	r		u	r	r	r	r	r
Sparrowhawk		r	r		f	r	u	u	r	r	r	u	u	f		r	u	r	r	u
Shikra						v								v						
Common Buzzard					u	r	r	r		r	r	r			u	r		r	r	r
Long-legged Buzzard	r	r	r		u	r	r	r	r	r	u	u	r	r		r	r	r	u	r
Lesser Spotted Eagle					v			v	v	v								v	v	
Greater Spotted Eagle	r	r		r	a	f	r	u	f	c	c	f	r	u	u	f	r	f	f	r
Steppe Eagle		r			c	r	u	u	u	u	f	f	u	r	u	r	r	u	u	u
Imperial Eagle		r	r	r	c	r	u	f	u	f	f	f	f	u	u	r	u	u	f	f
Golden Eagle		r	r	r	r	r		r			r	r	r	r		r	r	r	r	r
Verreaux's Eagle				r			u	f		r		u		r		r	r	u	r	r
Booted Eagle					f	r	r	u		r	u	u	r	r	u	r	r	r	r	r
Bonelli's Eagle		r		r	f	r	u	f	r	u	f	f	f	f	u	r	f	r	f	u
Osprey	c	c	a	c	f	c		r	c	c	c	u		f		c		a	c	u
Lesser Kestrel				r	u		r	r		r	r	r	r	r		r	r		r	r
Kestrel	r	r		u	a	u	f	f	r	u	c	f	f	f	f	r	c	f	c	a
Amur Falcon					f	r		r		r	r	r	r						r	r
Merlin		v																	v	
Hobby	r				f	r	r	r	r	r	r	u	r	r	u	r	r	r	r	r
Sooty Falcon				r	r						r	r						r		
Lanner Falcon				r	r		r	r	r	r						r		r	r	r
Saker Falcon			r	r			r	r		r			r					r	r	
Peregrine Falcon	r	r	r	r	f	u	r	r	u	u	f	r	r	r	u	u	r	u	u	r
Barbary Falcon	r	r	r	r	u	r	r	r	r	u	r	r	r	r	u		r	r	u	r
Arabian Partridge				u	r		f	f			u	f	u	f			c		f	c
Sand Partridge	r			u		r	r				r			r				r	r	r
Grey Francolin	r	r																		
Quail		r			f		r	r	r	r	r	r		r	u				r	r

175

Common Name	Southeast				Dhofar															
	1	2	3	4	1	2	3	4	5	6	7	8	9	10	11	12	13	14	15	16
Harlequin Quail					v															
Little Button Quail					v															
Water Rail										r	r							r	r	
Spotted Crake						r				r	r					r			r	
Little Crake						r	r		r	u	r	r				r		r	r	r
Baillon's Crake					r	r		r	u	f	u	r				r		r	u	r
Corncrake							r				r					r				r
White-breasted Waterhen				r			r	r	r	r	r	r				r			r	
Moorhen		r		r		a	r	r	a	a	a	a				a	r	c	a	f
Allen's Gallinule					v	v				v	v								v	
Purple Gallinule						v														
Watercock												v								
Coot		c		r		a			a	f	c	u				c	r	f	c	r
Red-knobbed Coot						v						v				v				
Common Crane				r	u	r				r	r	r					r		r	
Demoiselle Crane					r	r										r		r		
Houbara Bustard		r													u		r			
Pheasant-tailed Jacana					r	f			u	f	c	u				u		u	f	r
Painted Snipe									v							v			v	
Oystercatcher	a	u	c	u	r	c			u	f	f	r			f	f	r	c	f	r
Black-winged Stilt	u	r	r		r	c			f	f	c	u			u	a		f	c	r
Avocet	f	f	f			r			r	u	r					u		f	r	
Crab Plover	c		f		r	r			r	u	r				u			u	r	r
Stone Curlew					r						r				u	r		r	r	
Spotted Thick-knee	r	r			r	r		r			r			r			r	r	r	
Cream-coloured Courser	r	r	r	r	f	r	r	r	r	r	r		r		u			r	r	r
Collared Pratincole	r				f	u			r	u	r					r		r	u	r
Black-winged Pratincole					v															
Little Pratincole		r			u	r			r	r	r							r	r	
Little Ringed Plover	r	r		r	c	f			u	f	f	r			u	f	r	c	f	r
Ringed Plover	f	f	f	r	f	c			u	c	f	r			u	f		c	c	r
Kentish Plover	f	c	c	u	r	c			c	c	f	r			u	f		c	c	r
Lesser Sand Plover	f	f	c	u	r	c			u	f	f				u	u		c	f	r
Greater Sand Plover	f	f	c	u	r	f	r		u	f	u					u		c	f	r
Caspian Plover		r			r	r				r	r					r		r	r	
Pacific Golden Plover	r	f	r	r	f	f			r	f	f	r			u	f		f	f	r
European Golden Plover						v					v									
Grey Plover	c	f	c	r	r	f			u	f	f				u	u		c	c	
Spur-winged Plover						r				r									r	
Red-wattled Plover					u	r		r	r	r	r	r								
Sociable Plover					u															
White-tailed Plover		r			r	r			r	f	r	r				u		r	r	r
Lapwing		r			r	r				r						r				r
Great Knot						r												r		
Knot						v														
Sanderling	f	f	f	f		f			u	f	f				u	u		f	f	
Little Stint	f	c	c	u	f	c			c	c	c	u			u	f	r	c	c	u
Temminck's Stint	r	r	r		f	f	r	r	f	c	f	u			u	f	r	f	f	r
Long-toed Stint		r	r		r	r			r	u	r					r		r	r	
Pectoral Sandpiper					v	v					v									
Sharp-tailed Sandpiper										v										
Curlew Sandpiper	f	f	f	r	u	f	r		u	f	f	r			u	u		f	f	r
Dunlin	f	f	c	r	r	f			f	f	f				u	f		c	f	r
Broad-billed Sandpiper	r	r	f	r	r	u			r	u	u					r		f	u	

Common Name	Southeast 1	2	3	4	Dhofar 1	2	3	4	5	6	7	8	9	10	11	12	13	14	15	16
Buff-breasted Sandpiper					v															
Ruff	r	r		r	c	c			f	c	c	u			u	c		f	c	r
Jack Snipe		r			r	r		r	r	u	r					r		r	r	
Common Snipe		u		r	f	f	r	u	f	c	c	f	r		u	f	r	f	c	r
Pintail Snipe		r		r	r	r	r	u	r	u	f	r	r		u	r	r	r	u	
Long-billed Dowitcher			v		v					v									v	
Woodcock			v																	
Black-tailed Godwit	r	f	f		r	f			f	c	c				u	f		f	c	r
Bar-tailed Godwit	c	f	c	r	r	f			u	f	f	r			u	f		f	f	r
Whimbrel	f	r	f	r	u	f		r	u	f	f				f	u		c	f	r
Slender-billed Curlew		v																		
Curlew	c	f	c	u	f	f	r	r	f	f	c				u	c	r	c	c	r
Spotted Redshank		r			r	u			u	u	u	r			u	u		u	f	
Redshank	f	f	c	r	u	c	r	r	f	c	f	u			f	c		a	c	u
Marsh Sandpiper	r	r	r	r	r	u			u	f	f	r				f		f	f	r
Greenshank	f	f	f	r	f	c	r	u	c	c	c	f			f	a	r	a	a	u
Green Sandpiper	r	r	r		f	f	u	f	f	f	f	f	r	r	u	u	u	f	f	u
Wood Sandpiper		r			c	f	r	r	f	c	c	f			u	f	r	f	c	r
Terek Sandpiper	u	r	f	r	r	f	r		u	f	f				u	f		c	f	r
Common Sandpiper	f	u	u	r	c	c	c	c	c	c	c	f	r	u	f	c	f	a	c	c
Turnstone	f	u	f	r	r	f			u	f	f				f	u		f	f	r
Wilson's Phalarope					v					v										
Red-necked Phalarope	r	r	r		r	r			r	u	r				f	r		r	r	
Grey Phalarope										r										
Pomarine Skua	r	r			r	r			r	r	r			r	f			r	r	
Arctic Skua	r	r	r	r	r				r	r	r				f	r			r	r
Sooty Gull	a	f	f	a	r	a		r	f	a	a				c	f	r	a	a	f
White-eyed Gull										v								v		
Great Black-headed Gull	f	u	u	r		u			r	u	u				u	r		f	f	r
Black-headed Gull	f	r	u	u		f			u	f	f				u	u		f	f	r
Slender-billed Gull	c	f	c	u	r	f			u	c	f				f	f	r	c	c	r
Common Gull										r										
Baltic Gull		r			r										u			r	r	
Siberian Gull	c	f	u	f	r	c			f	f	f				f	f		f	c	
Caspian Gull	c	f	u	f		f			f	f	f	r			f	f		f	c	r
Kittiwake										v										
Gull-billed Tern	f	u	u	r		f			u	f	f	r			u	f		f	u	
Caspian Tern	c	c	c		r	f			u	f	u				u	u		f	u	r
Swift Tern	a	f	c	f	r	c			f	c	c				c	f		c	a	u
Lesser Crested Tern	f	u	u	r	r	f			u	f	u				f	u		f	f	r
Sandwich Tern	c	f	f	f	r	c			f	c	f				f	f		c	c	r
Roseate Tern		r				r			r	r					u			r	r	
Common Tern	r	r	r		r	f			u	f	f	r			f	f		f	f	r
White-cheeked Tern	u	r	r	r	r	f			u	f	f				u	u		f	f	r
Bridled Tern	r	r		r		r			r	u	u				c	r		u	u	r
Little Tern						r			r	r	r					r		r	r	
Saunders's Tern	f	f	f	r	r	f			u	f	f				f	u		f	u	r
Whiskered Tern	r	u			c	c			f	f	c	u				f		f	f	r
Black Tern					v					v										
White-winged Black Tern	r	r	r	r	c	f			r	u	f	r			u	f		u	u	r
Lesser Noddy															u					
Common Noddy		r							r	r					f			r	r	r
Lichtenstein's Sandgrouse	r	r		r			r			r			r	u		r			r	r
Crowned Sandgrouse		f	r	r	r					r										

177

Common Name	Southeast				Dhofar															
	1	2	3	4	1	2	3	4	5	6	7	8	9	10	11	12	13	14	15	16
Spotted Sandgrouse	r	r		r	r			r	r	r	r									
Chestnut-bellied Sandgrouse	r	f	r	r	f	r	r	r	u	r	u			r	u	r	r	r	r	
Rock Dove				r	u	r	f	f	r	u	f	c	a	f	f	r	c	c	c	c
Collared Dove		r			a	c	r	u	u	c	u	r	r	r	u	f	r	c	r	
Turtle Dove		r			u	r	r	r	r	r	r						r		r	r
Rufous Turtle Dove					r	r				r		r					r			
Laughing Dove	r	r	r	f	a	f	a	a	u	f	c	c	c	c	u	u	a	f	c	a
Namaqua Dove					u	r	u	r	u	u	u	r			u			r	r	r
Bruce's Green Pigeon				r	r	r	c	c			r	f	r	f		r	u		r	u
Ring-necked Parakeet					f	f		r	r	r	r					u	r	r	r	
Jacobin Cuckoo					r			r	r		r									
Didric Cuckoo					r	r	f	f	r	r	r	u	r	f			f	r	r	u
Common Cuckoo		r		r	u	r	r	u	r	r	r	r		r	u		r	r	r	r
Koel					r			r		r	r	r								
Barn Owl	r				u					r	r					r				
African Scops Owl					r		r	u			r		r			r		u		r
European Scops Owl					r			r		r						r	r			r
Spotted Eagle Owl					r	r	r	u			r	r	r	r			r		r	
Little Owl	r	r		r				r											r	
Hume's Tawny Owl				u															u	
Short-eared Owl			r		r					r	r				u	r			r	
Nubian Nightjar							v				v									
European Nightjar	r			r	r	r	r	u	r	r	r	r	r		u	r	u	r	r	r
Egyptian Nightjar						r	r		r	r	r		r		u		r			
Common Swift	r				r	r		r		r	r	r	r	r				r		r
Pallid Swift	r			r	r	r		r	r	r	r	r	r	r	u		r	r	r	
'Dhofar Swift'					c	u	r	u	r	f	f	u	f	u	u	r	r	f	r	r
Alpine Swift					u	r	r	u		r	r	r		r						
Little Swift					r		r		r	r	r	r	r	r					r	r
Grey-headed Kingfisher					c	r	f	c	r	u	f	f	u	f		r	c	u	r	c
Common Kingfisher		r				r	r	r	r	u	r	r				r	r	r	r	r
Malachite Kingfisher										v									v	v
Pied Kingfisher											v									
Little Green Bee-eater				r	u	u	u	f	u	u	f	r	r	r	u	r	u	u	f	r
Blue-cheeked Bee-eater		r		r	f	u	r	u	u	f	f	u	r	r	u	u	r	u	u	r
European Bee-eater		r			r	r	r	r	r	r	r	r		r			r	r	r	
European Roller		r		r	a	r	r	u	r	f	u	u	r	r	u	r	r	u	u	u
Lilac-breasted Roller																		v		
Indian Roller					r													v		r
Hoopoe	r	r			f	r	u	f	r	r	u	u	r	u	u		u	r	u	f
Wryneck		r			r		r	u	r	r	r	r	r				r	r	r	r
Singing Bush Lark					a	r	r	r	r	u		f	r	r		r	r	u	r	r
Black-crowned Finch Lark	r	u	r	r	c	r	r	u	r	r	f	r		r	u	r	u	u	r	r
Dunn's Lark																		r		
Bar-tailed Desert Lark					r															▸
Desert Lark	r	r	r	f		r	r	r		r	r				u			r	f	r
Hoopoe Lark	r	r	r	r				r					r			r			r	
Bimaculated Lark					u														r	
Short-toed Lark		r	r		f	r	r		r	r	r				u			r	r	▸
Lesser Short-toed Lark		r					r				r					r			r	
Crested Lark	r	c	f	r	a	c	r	f	c	c	f	r	r	r	u	c	r	a	u	▸
Skylark					r															
Sand Martin	r	r	r		c	u	r	r	u	f	f	r	r		u	r	r	r	u	▸
African Rock Martin		r		f	c	f	c	c	u	u	c	c	a	c	u	r	a	f	c	c

178

Common Name	Southeast				Dhofar															
	1	2	3	4	1	2	3	4	5	6	7	8	9	10	11	12	13	14	15	16
rag Martin					r		r	r			r		r	r			r	r	r	
arn Swallow	r	u	u	r	a	f	r	u	f	f	f	u	r	r	f	u	r	u	f	f
Wire-tailed Swallow					v															
ed-rumped Swallow				r	r	r		r			r	r				r				
ouse Martin		r			r	r				r	r	r	r				r	r		
ichard's Pipit		r			f	r	r			r	r						r		r	r
awny Pipit	r	f	u	r	c	u	r	u	u	u	f	r	r		u	r	r	f	f	r
ong-billed Pipit				r	u	r	u	u	u	r	u	r	u		u	r	u	r	f	f
ree Pipit	r	r		r	f	r	r	u		r	r	u	r	u		r	r	r	r	r
ed-throated Pipit		r	r	r	c	r	r	r		u	f	r	r			r	r	f	f	r
ater Pipit		r			r	r				r	r						r		r	r
olden Pipit					v															
orest Wagtail							v			v		v								
ellow Wagtail		u	r	r	a	f	r	u	f	f	c	u	r		u	u	r	u	f	f
itrine Wagtail		r			f	f	r	r	f	c	c	f	r			r	r	u	c	r
rey Wagtail		r		r	r	r	f	c	r	r	r	u	f	u		r	f	r	r	r
hite Wagtail	f	f	r	r	a	f	u	u	u	f	f	u	r		u	u	r	f	f	f
ellow-vented Bulbul				a	a	f	a	a	f	f	c	c	c	c	u	u	a	f	c	a
ufous Bush Robin	r	r		r	f	r	u	f	r	r	f	r	r	u	u	r	u	u	u	r
hrush Nightingale								v												
ightingale					u	r	f	r			u	r	u			r	r	r	r	r
uethroat		r	r		f	u	r	r	u	u	u	u	r			r	r	r	r	r
ack Redstart			r	r		r	r	r			r	r	r	r			r		r	r
ommon Redstart	r				r		r	r		r										
ackstart				r	r	r	a	a	r	r	c	a	f	a	u	r	a	u	c	a
hinchat					r	r										r		r		r
onechat					f	r		r	r		r		r				r	r		r
abelline Wheatear	r	u	r	r	c	u	r	u	u	u	f	r	u	r	u	r	r	f	f	r
orthern Wheatear		r		r	u	r		r		r	r		r	r	u	r		r	u	r
ed Wheatear	r	r		r	r		r	r		r		r				r	r	r	r	
esert Wheatear	f	f	f	f	a	f	r	u	f	f	c	u	u	r	f	u	u	c	c	f
ed-tailed Wheatear		r	r		r			r			r		r	u		r		r	r	r
ourning Wheatear								v				v							v	v
outh Arabian Wheatear				c	r	r	u	r	r		r	u	a	r	u		c	r	c	f
ooded Wheatear	r			r								r							r	r
hite-crowned Black Wheatear												v								
ck Thrush				r			r	r		r	r	r				r			r	r
ue Rock Thrush				r	r			u	u		f	r	r	r	u		u		f	r
ng Ouzel																				v
ebrowed Thrush								v												
ng Thrush						r	r					r								
stle Thrush								v												
aceful Prinia		r	r		a	c	u	f	c	c	f	u	r	r		c	f	f	u	f
rub Warbler							r	r					r						r	
asshopper Warbler							r					r								
vi's Warbler							v													
oustached Warbler					v				v											
dge Warbler					r	r				r										r
arsh Warbler					u	r	r	u	r	u	u	r		r	u		r	u	r	r
ropean Reed Warbler				r	r	u	r	r	u	u	r	r				r	r	r	r	r
amorous Reed Warbler	r				u	f	u	r	f	f	f	r				u		r	f	r
eat Reed Warbler		r			u	r	r	r	r	r	u	r						r	r	
vaceous Warbler		r		r	u	r	u	f	r	r	u	u	r	r		r	u	u	r	r
oted Warbler						r											r		r	

179

Common Name	Southeast				Dhofar														
	1	2	3	4	1	2	3	4	5	6	7	8	9	10	11	12	13	14	15
Upcher's Warbler					r	r	r	u		r	r	r	r						r
Ménétries's Warbler				u	r	r		r		r	r		r				r	r	r
Desert Warbler	r	r	r				r	r		r						r	r	r	r
Arabian Warbler				r	r	r	u	f	r	u	u	r	f	u		r	f		u
Orphean Warbler							u	r		r	r		r						
Barred Warbler								r			r		r				r		r
Lesser Whitethroat		r		r	r	r	u	f	r	r	r	u	r	r			r	r	r
Hume's Lesser Whitethroat								v											
Desert Lesser Whitethroat				r	r		r	u	r	r	r	r	r	r				r	r
Whitethroat		r		r	f	r	u	f	r	r	u	u	r	u	u	r	u	u	r
Garden Warbler				v				v											
Blackcap					r		r	r											r
Wood Warbler					r		r	u		r	r	r	r		r		r	r	
Plain Leaf Warbler					r														
Chiffchaff		r	r		r	r	u	f	r	r	r	u		r		r	r	r	r
Willow Warbler			r		r		r	r	r	r	r	r	r	r		r	r	r	
Spotted Flycatcher		r		r	f	r	f	f	u	u	f	f	u	u	u	r	f	u	f
Blue-and-white Flycatcher					v														
Red-breasted Flycatcher				r		r	r	r		r		r					r	r	
African Paradise Flycatcher				r	u	r	c	a	r	r	r	c	f	a			a	r	r
Arabian Babbler	r		r		r		r	r				r							
Nile Valley Sunbird							r			r								r	
Purple Sunbird					r	r	r					r						r	
Shining Sunbird				r	f	f	a	c	u	u	f	f	f	f	u	u	c	u	u
Palestine Sunbird				r	u	u	f	c	u	u	f	u	f	u		r	c	r	u
White-breasted White-eye				r	f	r	a	a	r	u	u	c	f	a			a	u	u
Golden Oriole				r	r	r	r	u		r	r	r	r	r		r	r	r	r
Black-crowned Tchagra					r	r	u	f	r		u	r	r	u			f		r
Isabelline Shrike	r	u	r	r	a	f	f	f	f	c	c	f	u	f	u	f	f	f	c
Red-backed Shrike		r		r	u	r	r	r	r	r	r	r	r	r		r	r	r	r
Long-tailed Shrike					r		r	r			r	r							
Lesser Grey Shrike					r														
Southern Grey Shrike	r	r	r	r	f	r	r	f	u	u	u	r	r	r	u	r	r	r	u
Steppe Grey Shrike					u	r	r	r	r	u	r		r		u				r
Masked Shrike							r	u				r		r					
House Crow					r	r				r					u	r		f	
Brown-necked Raven	f	r	r	u								r		u					r
Fan-tailed Raven					f	r	f	a	u	f	c	c	a	c	f	r	a	u	c
Tristram's Grackle				c	u	r	a	a	r	u	c	c	a	c	f	r	a	c	a
Brahminy Starling											v								
Starling		r	r	r	f	r			r	u	r								
Rose-coloured Starling		r		r	c	r			r	u	r		r				r	r	r	r
Wattled Starling				r	r			r		r	r								
Common Mynah							r												
House Sparrow							r									r			
Spanish Sparrow					r														
Pale Rock Sparrow					r		r	r	r	r	u						r	r	r
Yellow-throated Sparrow					r					r	r								r
Rüppell's Weaver					a	f	a	a	u	f	c	c	c	c	u	f	c	c	r
African Silverbill					a	f	f	c	u	f	f	c	c	f		f	c	f	r
Yemen Serin													f	r					
Golden-winged Grosbeak							r	u						u				r	r
Trumpeter Finch					r														
Common Rosefinch					r		r	r											

180

Common Name	Southeast				Dhofar																
	1	2	3	4	1	2	3	4	5	6	7	8	9	10	11	12	13	14	15	16
House Bunting				r		r	u	u	r		r	r	r	r			r		u	r
African Rock Bunting				r	f	u	a	a	r	u	c	a	a	a	u	r	a	f	f	a
Cinereous Bunting																	v			
Ortolan Bunting					r		r						r					r		
Black-headed Bunting							r			r	r		r							
Corn Bunting					r															

African Rock Bunting

BIRD FINDER

As well as providing an overview of distribution and status, this detailed checklist provide notes on how, where, and when to best find the resident and migrant species of birds in Oman. For quic reference, each site mentioned is shown with its corresponding number in the **Site Guide** section. Thus, A Ansab Lagoons is site (1.1). Where relevant to finding that species, suggestions are also given on habita preferences and habits. For more detail on status and distribution of each species, please refer to the *Oma Bird List, Edition 6* (Eriksen, Sargeant and Victor, 2003). Vagrants, marked with an *, are generally n discussed below, but are listed in the **Oman Bird List** (p 230). The number in front of each species is th species number derived from the Euring list in Voous (1977).

7 Little Grebe *Tachybaptus ruficollis*
A common breeding resident at Al Ansab Lagoons (1.1), Wadi Darbat (10.8), *khawrs* of coastal Dhofa and occasionally elsewhere. Also an uncommon passage migrant and winter visitor to north and sou Oman from September to April.

12 Black-necked Grebe *Podiceps nigricollis*
An uncommon winter visitor to Al Ansab Lagoons (1.1) where a few birds can be present from Octobe to April. Elsewhere an irregular passage migrant and winter visitor in very small numbers from earl September to late-April. Small numbers can be found on the *khawrs* of south Oman throughout the wint months.

35 Jouanin's Petrel *Bulweria fallax*
Oman is an excellent country to find this poorly known and much sought after species, the nest of which has only recently been described from Socotra (Teleb, 2002). Although the exact status in Oman in uncertain, it is common off southeast coasts and Masirah from late May to October. As this species tends to stay well offshore, good sites are prominent headlands such as Ras Mirbat and Ras Janjari (10.11), where it is almost guaranteed from May to November, with often in excess of 50 individuals in a morning. In north Oman the prime spots are the cliffs at Ras Al Khabbah (3.5), and Ras Al Hadd (3.4) between June and November. It is scarce in Oman wa-ters between December and April, and is unrecorded from Musandam. A few individuals have been found in the deserts of south Oman indicating pos-sible breeding in the interior moun-tains. Nesting on islands or coastal cliffs is also a possibility.

Jouanin's Petrel

*36 Cory's Shearwater *Calonectris diomedea*
Recorded as a vagrant from south and east Oman between May and November. This species is almc certainly overlooked, and more thorough sea-watches during spring and autumn could be rewarding.

38 Pale-footed Shearwater *Puffinus carneipes*
A fairly common summer visitor off south Oman from late-April to mid-November, becoming less common farther north. The best places to observe this bird are from the southern and eastern headlands of Ras Mirbat and Ras Janjari (10.11), Ras Madrakah (9.2), Ras Al Khabbah (3.5), and Ras Al Ya on Masirah, where it is regular between late-May and October.

Pale-footed Shearwater

41 Wedge-tailed Shearwater *Puffinus pacificus*
A rare summer visitor mostly reported well offshore from August to November. May occur at other times, but often confused with Jouanin's Petrel. The most reliable land based sites for this bird are Ras Mirbat (10.11), Ras Madrakah (9.2) and Ras Al Hadd (3.4). Although never recorded from Masirah, sea-watches from the headlands at Ras Abu Rasas (8.3) and Ras Al Ya are likely to record it.

*43 Sooty Shearwater *Puffinus griseus*
A vagrant chiefly recorded in April and May, when it is almost certainly overlooked and is probably a regular passage migrant.

49 Persian Shearwater *Puffinus (lherminieri) persicus*
Another Oman speciality. Widespread, and frequently common off all coasts, mostly from May to November. It is present, but can be difficult to find outside this period. Concentrations, sometimes of several thousands, occur off south Oman from May to November during which time it breeds on Al Hallaniyyat Islands. Any sea-watch off south Oman, such as at Ras Mirbat (10.11) or Al Mughsayl (10.14) from end-April to early-December should produce this bird, often quite close to shore. In north Oman, it is regularly seen from east coast promontories, particularly from September to November, when post-breeding dispersal increases numbers. Good sites include Ras Al Hadd (3.4), Ras Al Khabbah (3.5), Ras As Sawadi (2.1), Qurayyat (3.1) and Shinas (2.5). Most Musandam records are from October, but good numbers have been seen also in April.

Persian Shearwater

50 Wilson's Storm-petrel *Oceanites oceanicus*
A fairly common summer visitor to Oman waters from early-May to late-November, rarely in other months. Most common and easily found off south Oman from June to November, such as at Ras Mirbat (10.11) and Al Mugsayl (10.14). Similarly, can be observed from east coast headlands including Ras Al Khabbah (3.5) and Ras Al Hadd (3.4), or from fishing or dolphin watching trips at this time of year.

*56 Swinhoe's Storm-petrel *Oceanodroma monorhis*
This species was first recorded in 1997, but has been seen annually in recent years. Undoubtedly overlooked, and probably a regular, though scarce visitor. It should be looked for during any sea-watch off south or east Oman between June and December, especially between Ras Mirbat (10.11) and Ras Al Khabbah (3.5). The bird has also been recorded on summer pelagic trips from Muscat.

64 Red-billed Tropicbird *Phaethon aethereus*
A fairly common, but localised breeding visitor to offshore islands and coastal cliffs, principally from late-March to late-September. Less common in other months when they tend to stay far out at sea. They are frequent off the south coast during the summer monsoon. The most reliable sites are the cliffs at Raysut (10.14), or sea-watching from Ras Mirbat (10.11). Birdwatching at any headland with cliffs along the east coast should eventually find this species. Visitors to Muscat might consider taking a fishing boat out to Fahl island (1.2) where it breeds in small numbers from June to early-October.

68 Masked Booby *Sula dactylatra*
A common visitor off south Oman, occasionally along other coasts, but rare north of Muscat. As the main breeding colonies are on Al Hallaniyyat Islands, this species is easily observed from southern coasts, often close to shore, throughout the year.

70 Brown Booby *Sula leucogaster*
An uncommon visitor off south Oman in small numbers throughout the year. Rarely seen along other coasts. Most frequent off Al Mughsayl (10.15) and Ras Mirbat (10.11).

72 Cormorant *Phalacrocorax carbo*
A common winter visitor from early-November to late-March, rarely in other months.

81 Socotra Cormorant *Phalacrocorax nigrogularis*
A locally common visitor to Musandam, central and south Oman coasts and Masirah, sometimes in massive flocks. Uncommon elsewhere. Present throughout the year, but commonest over the winter months, when any sea-watch from south Oman headlands, such as at Ras Mirbat (10.11), should record it. Another reliable area, during winter, is along the western coastal road of Musandam. The island of Hamr Nafun near Ad Duqm (9.1) is a major roosting site, and large numbers are often seen feeding offshore there.

95 Bittern *Botaurus stellaris*
A rare passage migrant and winter visitor from mid-September to late-April. The majority of records are from the *khawrs* of coastal Dhofar.

98 Little Bittern *Ixobrychus minutus*
A fairly common summer visitor to south Oman, where a small number breeds on coastal *khawrs*. A few are suspected, though not proven, to also breed in north Oman at Al Ansab Lagoons (1.1) and Al Qurm Natural Park (1.2). Elsewhere, an uncommon migrant and rare in winter. Good sites to look for this species are the reed beds of East Khawr (10.2) and Khawr Taqah (10.6).

99 Yellow Bittern *Ixobrychus sinensis*
Previously overlooked in Oman, this species is now considered to be a regular summer visitor from April to August to the coastal *khawrs* of Dhofar, where it almost certainly breeds. Undoubtedly the easiest site to observe this bird is East Khawr (10.2), by scanning the reed beds at the northern end in early morning. It is also regular at Khawr Taqah (10.6) and Khawr Al Mughsayl (10.15).

104 Night Heron *Nycticorax nycticorax*
A common passage migrant and winter visitor, mainly from mid-August to late-April. Usually seen singly but large parties occur. Around Muscat a few birds usually winter in the thick foliage of Al Ansab Lagoons (1.1) from which they emerge just before dusk. In south Oman it is found regularly at Khawr Rawri (10.7) and Khawr Taqah (10.6).

107 Striated Heron *Butorides striatus*
A common breeding resident and passage migrant on mainland coasts and offshore islands. As this species has a preference for mangroves, around Muscat it can be found readily behind Al Qurm Natural Park (1.2). Other areas where the bird is common include Liwa (2.4), Shinas (2.5), Sur Lagoon (3.2), Raysut (10.14) and Khawr Rawri (10.7).

108 Squacco Heron *Ardeola ralloides*
A common passage migrant and winter visitor, with a few remaining over the summer especially in south Oman. The exact status is confused, as birds in non-breeding plumage are difficult to separate from the similarly-plumaged Indian Pond Heron. In south Oman it is easily observed at any of the *khawrs* of coastal Dhofar.

109 Indian Pond Heron *Ardeola grayii*
A fairly common passage migrant and winter visitor from early-September to late-June, rarely in July and August. Possibly confused with immature and non-breeding plumaged Squacco Heron. Records suggest that the species has a preference for mangroves, and has a bias toward north Oman, with Shinas (2.5) and Qurayyat (3.1) being particularly good sites. Of the south Oman *khawrs*, Khawr Taqah (10.6) and Khawr Rawri (10.7) are the most reliable sites.

111 Cattle Egret *Bubulcus ibis*
A common winter visitor from mid-October to early-May, with a few remaining throughout the summer, especially in the south. A hard species to miss, even around Muscat, where it frequents the grassy verges of the main highways. A few records from both north and south Oman refer to the eastern form *coromandus*. In recent years the species tried, unsuccessfully, to nest at Sun Farms, Sohar (2.2).

118 Western Reef Heron *Egretta gularis*
A localised breeding resident and abundant passage migrant and winter visitor, with a few non-breeding birds throughout the year. Found in small numbers along all coasts. Particularly numerous at Barr Al Hikman (8.1). Both dark and white phase individuals occur.

119 Little Egret *Egretta garzetta*
An abundant passage migrant and winter visitor. Many remain over the summer.

120 Intermediate Egret *Egretta intermedia*
An uncommon winter visitor, mainly from early-August to late-April, but recorded in all months. Most records are from the *khawrs* of south Oman. Beware the small eastern *modesta* form of Great White Egret which strongly resembles Intermediate Egret.

121 Great White Egret *Egretta alba*
An abundant passage migrant and winter visitor from early-September to early-May, rarely in other months. Most numerous at Barr Al Hikman (8.1).

122 Grey Heron *Ardea cinerea*
An abundant passage migrant and winter visitor from early-September to mid-March. Many non-breeding birds remain over the summer.

124 Purple Heron *Ardea purpurea*
An abundant passage migrant and winter visitor from mid-August to late-April with some staying over summer. In south Oman easily found at any reedy *khawr* such as East Khawr (10.2), Khawr Sawli (10.5), Khawr Taqah (10.6) or Khawr Rawri (10.7). In north Oman most regular at Al Ansab Lagoons (1.1) or Al Qurm Natural Park (1.2).

132 Abdim's Stork *Ciconia abdimii*
A rare and irregular visitor from Africa, chiefly to farmlands near Salalah (10.1) from October to May. Absent in some years, but quite common in others. Vagrant to northern Oman.

134 White Stork *Ciconia ciconia*
A common passage migrant and winter visitor from mid-August to mid-April, rarely in summer. Most wintering birds are on farmlands around Salalah (10.1). Sometimes present on farmlands along Al Batinah, particularly near Sohar (2.2).

Glossy Ibis

136 Glossy Ibis *Plegadis falcinellus*
An abundant passage migrant and winter visitor to *khawrs* of coastal Dhofar where some stay over summer. Uncommon elsewhere, and no records from Musandam. Easily found at East Khawr (10.2), Khawr Al Mughsayl (10.15) and Khawr Rawri (10.7). Most records in north Oman are from Al Ansab Lagoons (1.1), Al Qurm Natural Park (1.2) and Qurayyat (3.1).

*142 Sacred Ibis *Threskiornis aethiopicus*
Wild birds only occur as vagrants. However, feral birds, presumed to originate from UAE, are frequent in northern Oman.

144 Spoonbill *Platalea leucorodia*
In south Oman an abundant passage migrant and winter visitor to the *khawrs* of coastal Dhofar, where many birds remain over summer. Also occurs as a locally common winter visitor to central Oman, where most readily found at Barr Al Hikman (8.1). In north Oman the best localities are Qurayyat (3.1) and Shinas (2.5).

147 Greater Flamingo *Phoenicopterus ruber*
A locally abundant passage migrant and winter visitor to the east coast and Masirah from early-October to early-June, with large numbers present at Barr Al Hikman (8.1) at this time. A common year-round, non-breeding visitor to the *khawrs* of coastal Dhofar. Uncommon and irregular elsewhere. In north Oman most regularly seen along the eastern coast between Khawr Jirama (3.3) and Sur 3.2), as well as at Qurayyat (3.1) and occasionally as far north as Shinas (2.5).

*148 Lesser Flamingo *Phoenicopterus minor*
A vagrant with irregular, local eruptions into south Oman. As small groups have frequently remained lengthy periods around the *khawrs* of coastal Dhofar, this species should be checked for carefully among any flocks of Greater Flamingo in such places as Khawr Al Mughsayl (10.15), Khawr Rawri (10.7), or Salalah Nature Reserve (10.12).

159 White-fronted Goose *Anser albifrons*
A rare winter visitor from early-November to late-February, occasionally in other months. Surprisingly, most records are from south Oman with Khawr Rawri (10.7), Salalah Nature Reserve (10.12) and Khawr Sawli (10.5) the most regular sites.

161 Greylag Goose *Anser anser*
A rare winter visitor from early-November to early-April. This species could turn up at any coastal location.

*170 Egyptian Goose *Alopochen aegyptaicus*
Vagrant. However, this species breeds ferally in good numbers in UAE, and is possibly on the verge of spreading into Oman. The most likely site for this bird to occur in Oman would be Al Buraymi Sewage Plant (6.3), followed by the most northerly *khawrs* such as Shinas (2.5).

171 Ruddy Shelduck *Tadorna ferruginea*
An uncommon and irregular passage migrant and winter visitor from early-November to mid-March, rarely in other months. Seen mostly at *khawrs* of coastal Dhofar, in very small numbers, with Khawr Rawri (10.7) and Khawr Al Mughsayl (10.15) the favoured localities.

173 Shelduck *Tadorna tadorna*
For visitors from more northerly climes, this bird often seems well out of place, surrounded by barren mountains and desert landscapes. A fairly common but irregular passage migrant and winter visitor from early-November to mid-April, rarely in summer, and usually in very small numbers. Most frequently encountered around the *khawrs* of coastal Dhofar. In north Oman the most likely site is Qurayyat (3.1).

Cotton Teal

176 Cotton Teal *Nettapus coromandelianus*
A fairly common winter visitor to *khawrs* in Dhofar from late-October to late-May, rarely staying over summer. Rare in north Oman. The best sites to search for this bird are Khawr Rawri (10.7), Salalah Nature Reserve (10.12) and Wadi Darbat (10.8).

179 Wigeon *Anas penelope*
A common winter visitor from late-September to late-May to *khawrs* of coastal Dhofar and Khawr Dhurf (9.2) and less common elsewhere. In north Oman this bird is most regularly found at Al Ansab Lagoons (1.1) and Qurayyat (3.1) in small numbers, mostly in late winter.

182 Gadwall *Anas strepera*
A widespread and fairly common winter visitor from mid-October to early-April, rarely in other months. Careful scanning of any concentrations of ducks in winter will usually find a few individuals, with the most consistent sites being Al Ansab Lagoons (1.1) and Khawr Rawri (10.7).

184 Teal *Anas crecca*
An abundant passage migrant and winter visitor from early-September to late-March, rarely in other months. By far the most abundant duck wintering in Oman.

186 Mallard *Anas platyrhynchos*
A common winter visitor from mid-September to late-March, occasionally in other months. Mainly found at Al Ansab Lagoons (1.1), Khawr Dhurf (9.2) and the *khawrs* of coastal Dhofar. Rare elsewhere.

189 Pintail *Anas acuta*
An abundant passage migrant and winter visitor from late-September to late-April, occasionally in other months. The main wintering sites include Al Ansab Lagoons (1.1), Khawr Dhurf (9.2) and the *khawrs* of coastal Dhofar.

191 Garganey *Anas querquedula*
A widespread and abundant passage migrant and common winter visitor from early-August to early-May, occasionally in summer.

194 Shoveler *Anas clypeata*
An abundant passage migrant and winter visitor from late-August to early-May, rarely in summer. Most common at Khawr Dhurf (9.2) and *khawrs* of coastal Dhofar.

196 Red-crested Pochard *Netta rufina*
An uncommon passage migrant and winter visitor from mid-August to late-May, usually in very small numbers. In south Oman, where the species occurs most regularly, sites include Khawr Rawri (10.7), Khawr Al Mughsayl (10.15), and Salalah Nature Reserve (10.12). In north Oman, the only site where the species is seen with any regularity is Al Ansab Lagoons (1.1).

198 Pochard *Aythya ferina*
A fairly common winter visitor from late-September to early-March, rarely in other months. Most records are from Al Ansab Lagoons (1.1) and the *khawrs* of coastal Dhofar.

202 Ferruginous Duck *Aythya nyroca*
A fairly common winter visitor from mid-August to mid-May, rarely in summer. In south Oman most regularly seen at Salalah Nature Reserve (10.12), Khawr Rawri (10.7) and Khawr Al Mughsayl (10.15). In north Oman only seen with regularity at Al Ansab Lagoons (1.1).

203 Tufted Duck *Aythya fuligula*
A fairly common winter visitor from mid-October to late-March. Most common in south Oman, where small numbers can be found at East Khawr (10.2) and Khawr Rawri (10.7). In north Oman only regularly recorded from Al Ansab Lagoons (1.1), mainly in late winter.

231 Honey Buzzard *Pernis apivorus*
A rare passage migrant and winter visitor from early-August to early-April. Records very scattered.

*232 Crested Honey Buzzard *Pernis ptilorhynchus*
Although considered a vagrant, the exact status is confused due to identification difficulties of female and immature birds. With more experienced observers now in the field, an increasing number of records might lead to this species being shown to be more common than Honey Buzzard.

238 Black Kite *Milvus migrans*
As a regular but uncommon passage migrant and winter visitor from September to May, this species can occur almost anywhere. Additionally it is an uncommon and localised breeding resident in farmland around Salalah (10.1) where it is sometimes recorded near Taqah (10.6) or Salalah Nature Reserve (10.12). These southern birds are yellow-billed and are sometimes treated taxonomically as part of the African yellow-billed forms of the *Milvus migrans* complex.

Black Kite

247 Egyptian Vulture *Neophron percnopterus*
An abundant passage migrant and winter visitor, especially to north Oman, as well as a widespread, but uncommon, breeding resident. Large numbers gather at rubbish tips such as at Al Amrat (1.3) and Qurayyat (3.1). This is a familiar bird around Muscat and is often seen drifting over adjacent hills.

251 Griffon Vulture *Gyps fulvus*
An uncommon passage migrant and winter visitor from early-August to early-May. With records well scattered throughout the country, this species is seemingly difficult to get to grips with, and has no regular sites.

254 Lappet-faced Vulture *Torgos tracheliotos*
A fairly common winter visitor to north Oman where it also breeds in small numbers in the mountains. Regularly found along the road from Muscat to Qurayyat (1.3), and can often be observed from the lookouts high in the mountains at Jabal Shams (4.2) and the Sayq Plateau (4.3). Another good site to find the bird throughout the year, as it breeds in the vicinity, is Jabal Madar, near Sinaw. In south Oman it occurs as an uncommon visitor, that is best looked for along higher points of the road east of Al Mughsayl toward Rakhyut, and along the paved road between Tawi Atayr (10.9) and Wadi Darbat (10.8).

256 Short-toed Eagle *Circaetus gallicus*
A common and widespread passage migrant and winter visitor from late-August to late-April, rarely in summer. In south Oman in winter it can often be found soaring over Ayn Razat (10.3), Ayn Hamran (10.4), Wadi Darbat (10.8) or Wadi Hanna (10.10).

260 Marsh Harrier *Circus aeruginosus*
An abundant passage migrant and winter visitor from mid-August to late-May, rarely in summer. Very common at the *khawrs* of coastal Dhofar, and in north Oman found easily at Al Ansab Lagoons (1.1) or on farmlands along Al Batinah throughout the winter.

261 Hen Harrier *Circus cyaneus*
An uncommon passage migrant and winter visitor from late-August to mid-May. Probably overlooked, as immatures and females can be difficult to separate from those of Pallid and Montagu's Harrier. By far the most records are from farms and grassland around Salalah (10.1).

262 Pallid Harrier *Circus macrourus*
A fairly common passage migrant and winter visitor in small numbers, from late-August to early-May. This species predominantly prefers farmlands and grass cultivations, and in south Oman can most easily be seen over farms around Salalah (10.1), while in north Oman similar habitats around Sohar (2.2) are good places to look. The bird also turns up regularly in the central desert at places such as Al Balid Farm (7.5) or other watered areas.

Pallid Harrier

263 Montagu's Harrier *Circus pygargus*
A fairly common passage migrant and winter visitor from late-August to late-March, rarely in other months. Commoner than Pallid Harrier, although immatures of the two are frequently confused. Occurs in much the same areas as Pallid Harrier.

269 Sparrowhawk *Accipiter nisus*
A widespread and common passage migrant and winter visitor from late-September to late-April.

287 Common Buzzard *Buteo buteo*
An uncommon passage migrant and winter visitor from early-September to late-April, rarely in other months. Most likely to be encountered in south Oman where most frequently reported over farmlands around Salalah. (10.1). Sub-specifically identified birds refer to the form *vulpinus*.

288 Long-legged Buzzard *Buteo rufinus*
An uncommon breeding resident, mainly in central Oman. Also a regular passage migrant and winter visitor in small numbers from September to April. Although widespread in the interior deserts, lack of roads into more remote sites make finding this bird less than straightforward. The most consistent area is Muntasar (7.3) and Al Balid Farm (7.5), where the bird can often be found perched on rocky outcrops or soaring over the plains and fields. Those visiting Jaluni (7.1) should encounter this species regularly.

Greater Spotted Eagle, *fulvescens*

293 Greater Spotted Eagle *Aquila clanga*
A common passage migrant and winter visitor from early-October to late-April to north and south Oman. Has a distinct preference for the vicinity of water. In north Oman easily found at Al Amrat (1.3), Qurayyat (3.1), and usually present at Al Ansab Lagoons (1.1), as well as farmlands near Sohar (2.2). In south Oman most regularly found at Khawr Rawri (10.7) and Khawr Taqah (10.6), and occasionally at Thumrayt Waste Disposal Site (7.8). Most records refer to immature birds. About 1-2% of individuals refer to the pale *fulvescens* form. This eagle is rather vocal on its wintering grounds and its presence if often revealed by its high-pitched yelping call.

294 Steppe Eagle *Aquila nipalensis*
A common passage migrant and winter visitor from late-September to early-April, rarely in other months. This is the most numerous eagle wintering in Oman. Usually seen singly or in small numbers, but concentrations occur at rubbish tips near Al Amrat (1.3), Qurayyat (3.1), Thumrayt (7.8) and Raysut (10.14).

295 Imperial Eagle *Aquila heliaca*
A common passage migrant and winter visitor from early-September to mid-April. In south Oman it can be found along the road between Wadi Darbat (10.8) and Tawi Atayr (10.9), over farmland around Salalah (10.1), or near Khawr Rawri (10.7) or Khawr Taqah (10.6). In north Oman, most regularly found at the rubbish tips at Al Amrat (1.3) and Qurayyat (3.1).

296 Golden Eagle *Aquila chrysaetos*
A fairly common, but localised, breeding resident in the central desert. Birds are usually seen singly or in pairs, and rarely wander far from their nesting areas. The most reliable site to find this bird is Muntasar (7.3), especially in the hot season when they are dependent on the water source. Similarly, in south Oman, birds can sometimes be seen near Al Balid Farm (7.5), Dawkah or Thumrayt. It is worth checking any large eagles seen in the Dhofar mountains, such as along the road between Wadi Darbat (10.8) and Tawi Atayr (10.9) or west of Al Mughsayl (10.15). In north Oman the bird is a rare straggler, occasionally reported from a few scattered interior localities.

297 Verreaux's Eagle *Aquila verreauxii*
A rare and localised breeding resident in the mountains of Dhofar. The only readily accessible and reliable site for this species is Ayn Hamran (10.4) where they are sometimes seen patrolling the cliffs towering above the *wadi*. Birds are occasionally found in the mountains near Khawr Al Mughsayl (10.15).

Verreaux's Eagle

298 Booted Eagle *Hieraaetus pennatus*
A fairly common passage migrant and winter visitor to north and south Oman from late-September to early-May. The species is more regular in south Oman, where the best places to look are Ayn Hamran (10.4), Khawr Rawri (10.7) and farmlands surrounding Salalah (10.1). Occurrence in north Oman is erratic and irregular, with no preferred sites. Birds of both pale and dark forms are seen.

299 Bonelli's Eagle *Hieraaetus fasciatus*
An uncommon and localised breeding resident in the mountains of north and south Oman. Also a fairly common passage migrant and winter visitor. In north Oman regular sites where it is observed include Al Ansab Lagoons (1.1), Qurayyat (3.1), Jabal Qatar (6.2) and farmlands near Sohar (2.2).

301 Osprey *Pandion haliaetus*
A local breeding resident on coastal cliffs and offshore islands, and an abundant and widespread passage migrant and winter visitor. Usually seen in small numbers, but regular winter gatherings found at several sites such as at Barr Al Hikman (8.1), Ad Duqm (9.1) and Khawr Dhurf (9.2). This species is easily found along any coast of Oman and one that is very familiar to local people.

303 Lesser Kestrel *Falco naumanni*
A fairly common spring migrant from late-February to early-June and a rare autumn migrant from late-September to late-November. Observations are concentrated around mid-April when the species is easiest to find. Particularly good areas to look are grassy farmlands along Al Batinah, especially near Sohar (2.2), as well as around Salalah and As Sayh Plateau (5.3) in Musandam.

304 Kestrel *Falco tinnunculus*
An uncommon, but widespread breeding resident, as well as an abundant passage migrant and winter visitor from September to March. This bird is commonest in Dhofar in summer, but easily found throughout the country during winter.

308 Amur Falcon *Falco amurensis*
An uncommon spring migrant to south Oman from mid-March to late-May and a rare autumn migrant from mid-October to late-December, occasionally in winter. A vagrant to north Oman. The best chance of finding this bird is over the grassy farmlands of Salalah (10.1), especially from late-April to mid-May, coinciding with the species' main migration.

310 Hobby *Falco subbuteo*
A fairly common and widespread passage migrant from mid-March to early-June and early-September to late-November. Rare in other months. A notable number of records are from Masirah.

312 Sooty Falcon *Falco concolor*
A fairly common, but localised, summer breeding migrant to offshore islands in north Oman and Musandam from early-May to early-November, rarely in other months. Regularly seen hawking insects over Muscat and Ruwi urban areas on summer evenings. It can be seen over Al Qurm Natural Park (1.2) most evenings, as well as at Al Ansab Lagoons (1.1) where it hunts for dragonflies. Another excellent site to find it is the rocky islands just offshore from Ras As Sawadi (2.1). Individuals have recently been recorded from the high mountains of Sayq (4.3) in mid-summer and may well be breeding.

314 Lanner Falcon *Falco biarmicus*
Status uncertain, but apparently an uncommon visitor with records from every month, scattered throughout north and south Oman and Masirah. Some observations may refer to escaped birds from neighbouring countries, and birds with jesses are sometimes seen.

Peregrine Falcon

316 Saker Falcon *Falco cherrug*
A fairly common, though decreasing, passage migrant and winter visitor, mainly from September to April, but records from every month. As with Lanner, some records may refer to ex-captive birds as individuals with jesses have been observed. Records show no pattern and the species may be expected anywhere.

320 Peregrine Falcon *Falco peregrinus*
A regular passage migrant and winter visitor in small numbers, but does occur in all months. Also a rare breeder. Most common around Salalah and the *khawrs* of coastal Dhofar. In north Oman it is regular at Al Ansab Lagoons (1.1), and along Al Batinah coast.

321 Barbary Falcon *Falco pelegrinoides*
A fairly common, though often elusive, passage migrant and winter visitor, mainly from August to March. Also an uncommon, local breeder in mountains. In south Oman it can most often be found near coastal *khawrs* such as Khawr Rawri (10.7) and Khawr Taqah (10.6). In north Oman, it is most regular at Jabal Qatar (6.2) where it probably breeds. Otherwise erratic and could turn up anywhere.

355 Chukar *Alectoris chukar*

A fairly common breeding resident of the mountains of Musandam, where it is often found in sizable coveys. Sites to find this bird are the hilly slopes of As Sayh Plateau (5.3) and Sall Ala (5.2), as well as in Wadi Khabb Shamsi when driving the route from Bayah across the Musandam mountains.

361 Arabian Partridge *Alectoris melanocephala*

In Oman, this southeast Arabian speciality occurs as two disjunct populations in the mountains of north and south Oman. In north Oman it is an uncommon, and difficult to find resident of Al Hajar Mountains, though it is occasionally recorded from the slopes around Jabal Shams (4.2) and Sayq (4.3). This bird is

Arabian Partridge

much easier to locate in south Oman. The easiest way to find it is to walk quietly, early morning, along the *wadi* bottom in the upper parts of Ayn Hamran (10.4), particularly if the fig trees have been fruiting. They tend to run off quickly when disturbed. Other sites include the rocky slopes on the western side of the northern end of Khawr Rawri (10.7), the *wadi* behind Khawr Al Mughsayl (10.15), areas around Rakhyut, Wadi Darbat (10.8), the sinkhole at Tawi Atayr (10.9) and in Wadi Ash Shuwaymiyyah (9.4). Listening for calling birds is a good tactic, as they can be hard to see on the slopes.

363 Sand Partridge *Ammoperdix heyi*

A common resident over much of Oman, but avoiding the Empty Quarter and Masirah island. Despite its name, the species has a distinct preference for rocky mountain slopes. In north Oman, where the bird is most easily found, reliable sites include Jabal Qatar (6.2), the *wadis* behind Bawshar, Jabal Shams (4.2) and any of the *wadis* of Al Hajar Mountains. In south Oman it can be found in most *wadis* of the Dhofar mountains, particularly Wadi Andhur and Wadi Uyun. In Musandam the bird is fairly common along the road between Sall Ala (5.2) and As Sayh Plateau (5.3).

365 Grey Francolin *Francolinus pondicerianus*

A common and noisy resident of north Oman, where its range is expanding southward along the east coast, reaching *wadis* near Khawr Dhurf (9.2). Particularly common on farmlands and parks along Al Batinah. Frequently occurs in gardens - one species impossible to miss.

370 Quail *Coturnix coturnix*

A fairly common and widespread passage migrant, mainly from late-March to early-April and mid-August to early-November; less common in winter and rare in summer. Birds can, and do, turn up anywhere on migration. Only reliably found in grasslands near Sohar (2.2), where birds are present in small numbers all year and may breed.

407 Water Rail *Rallus aquaticus*
A rare passage migrant and winter visitor from mid-September to early-April. Only recorded with any regularity at Hilf (8.2) and Al Ansab Lagoons (1.1).

408 Spotted Crake *Porzana porzana*
A fairly common passage migrant and winter visitor from late-August to early-May. Most common in autumn, especially on Masirah. In north Oman it is regular at Al Ansab Lagoons (1.1). Decidedly uncommon in south Oman, where Khawr Taqah (10.6) is the most likely site.

410 Little Crake *Porzana parva*
An uncommon passage migrant and winter visitor from mid-August to late-May. The least common of the *Porzana* crakes found in Oman, and commoner in south Oman than the north. Occurs alongside both Baillon's and Spotted Crake, and can be searched for in the more reed-covered *khawrs* of Khawr Rawr (10.7), Khawr Taqah (10.6) and East Khawr (10.2). Occasionally recorded in the central desert on migration, such as at Muntasar (7.3).

411 Baillon's Crake *Porzana pusilla*
A fairly common passage migrant and winter visitor from mid-August to late-April. The commonest crake occurring in Oman. In north Oman it can be most easily found toward dusk at Al Ansab Lagoons (1.1). In south Oman it can usually be seen early morning, feeding along the reed edges of the shallower ends of East Khawr (10.2) or Khawr Rawri (10.7). During migration it can sometimes be found in the small patches of reeds at Muntasar (7.3).

Baillon's Crake

421 Corncrake *Crex crex*
A rare passage migrant and winter visitor from mid-September to early-March. Most regularly recorded from Masirah and various *wadis* of south Oman.

423 White-breasted Waterhen *Amaurornis phoenicurus*
A rare passage migrant and winter visitor from late-October to mid-June. Almost all records are from Masirah and south Oman.

424 Moorhen *Gallinula chloropus*
A locally abundant breeding resident. The main concentrations are at Al Ansab Lagoons (1.1), Wadi Darbat (10.8) and *khawrs* of coastal Dhofar, where it is impossible to miss. Elsewhere an opportunist breeder where freshwater is available.

*425 Allen's Gallinule *Porphyrula alleni*
Although considered a vagrant, this species is almost certainly overlooked owing to its secretive habit and probably occurs as a regular, though uncommon summer visitor to the Dhofar *khawrs* during the rains in July and August. The best areas to search are the reed beds of East Khawr (10.2), Khawr Rawri (10.7) and Khawr Taqah (10.6).

429 Coot *Fulica atra*
A locally common breeding resident on *khawrs* in south Oman and occasionally elsewhere. Also an abundant winter visitor, mainly to Al Ansab Lagoons (1.1), Khawr Dhurf (9.2) and *khawrs* in south Oman.

433 Common Crane *Grus grus*
A rare to uncommon passage migrant and winter visitor from early-November to late-March. Most observations are from farmlands near Sohar (2.2) and Salalah (10.1), and occasionally from the central desert
such as Al Balid Farm (7.5).

441 Demoiselle Crane *Anthropoides virgo*
A very rare passage migrant and winter visitor from early-September to mid-April. Most likely to appear
in grasslands near Salalah (10.1).

444 Houbara Bustard *Chlamydotis undulata*
One of Oman's most sought after species, but alas also one of the more elusive. An uncommon breeding
resident in the central desert and a rare passage migrant and winter visitor in small and irregular numbers.
The species is only reliably found within the boundaries of the Arabian Oryx Sanctuary, headquartered at
Jaluni (7.1) and much less frequently in Wadi Rabkut (7.7). The form *C. (u.) macqueenii* occurs.

447 Pheasant-tailed Jacana *Hydrophasianus chirurgus*
A locally common winter visitor from early-November to late-May to *khawrs* of south Oman, occasionally elsewhere. In some years a few birds stay over summer. This species is found where floating vegeta-
ion occurs, such as at Khawr Taqah (10.6) and Wadi Darbat (10.8)

450 Oystercatcher *Haematopus ostralegus*
A widespread and abundant passage migrant and winter visitor from August to April with a few birds usually staying over summer. Most numerous on Masirah and at Barr Al Hikman (8.1).

455 Black-winged Stilt *Himantopus himantopus*
A common but localised breeding resident and a widespread passage migrant and winter visitor. Rare in
Musandam. In winter it is present all along the coast, though less numerous in central Oman.

456 Avocet *Recurvirostra avosetta*
A fairly common passage migrant and winter visitor from early-September to late-April. Most common
along the central east coast from
Barr Al Hikman (8.1) to Khawr
Ghurf (9.2). In north Oman occurs
with some regularity on the saline
Khawr Al Milh at Qurayyat (3.1).
In south Oman most frequently re-
orded from Salalah Nature Reserve
(10.12).

Crab Plover
juvenile and adult

458 Crab Plover *Dromas ardeola*
This species, high on many visitors
wish-to-see list, is a fairly common, but highly localised, breeding
resident on Masirah, and a common
passage migrant and winter visitor
Khawr Jirama (3.3), Barr Al Hikman (8.1), Masirah and Ad Duqm
(8.1) only. Visitors wishing to guar-
antee finding this bird, should plan a
visit to one of these sites, as the bird
is uncommon and irregular elsewhere, occurring only as wandering
individuals. A number of records
from Ras As Sawadi (2.1).

459 Stone Curlew *Burhinus oedicnemus*
An uncommon passage migrant and winter visitor from mid-September to late-May. The bird can appear anywhere on migration, though many records are scattered in the interior and central desert. A few mid-winter records from Khatmat Milahah (2.6) might indicate wintering in small numbers.

Spotted Thick-knee

461 Spotted Thick-knee *Burhinus capensis*
A fairly common breeding resident or migrant breeder to central and south Oman, rare and irregular elsewhere. Owing to its nocturnal habits this bird can be elusive. One good way to find it is to simply drive quieter roads and desert tracks at night. Open areas east of Salalah toward Taqah (10.6) are good spots to try. Those camping out will hear the voice from time to time, especially in the Jaluni area (7.1).

462 Great Stone Plover *Esacus recurvirostris*
A rare winter visitor to north Oman from late-October to mid-February. Most records are from Shinas (2.5) where the bird should be looked for on the drier sand above the high-tide line where the *khawr* opens into the sea. Despite its size, it can be difficult to spot as it crouches, well camouflaged, on the sand. The few older records are from the Qurayyat (3.1) and Muscat areas.

464 Cream-coloured Courser *Cursorius cursor*
An uncommon but widespread breeding resident, and a fairly common passage migrant and winter visitor. Not recorded from Musandam. Erratic in appearance, often staying lengthy periods if feeding conditions are right. Probably most common in the central desert where it occurs widely but is largely nomadic. In north Oman most reliably found at Sun Farms, Sohar (2.2) in winter. In south Oman farmlands and grass lands around Salalah (10.1) are worth checking.

Cream-coloured Courser

465 Collared Pratincole *Glareola pratincola*

A fairly common passage migrant from late-March to mid-May and late-August to late-December. Also an uncommon summer breeder and an irregular winter visitor. The only consistently reliable place to observe this bird is farmlands near Sohar (2.2) between April and August where it breeds very locally.

Little Pratincole

468 Little Pratincole *Glareola lactea*

An uncommon passage migrant and winter visitor, mainly from early-November to late February to south Oman and Masirah. Rare in north Oman, and unrecorded in Musandam. The most likely localities to find this species are around the *khawrs* and farmlands near Salalah.

469 Little Ringed Plover *Charadrius dubius*

A casual breeder in north Oman and Masirah. Also an abundant passage migrant and winter visitor, mainly from August through to March. Breeding has been confirmed from widely scattered localities, chiefly in response to favourable local conditions. During migration it occurs regularly at Sun Farms, Sohar (2.2).

470 Ringed Plover *Charadrius hiaticula*

An abundant passage migrant and winter visitor from late-August to early-May, with some birds staying over summer.

477 Kentish Plover *Charadrius alexandrinus*

A common breeding resident on sandy beaches and an opportunistic breeder on temporary inland rain-water pools. Also an abundant passage migrant and winter visitor, especially at Barr Al Hikman (8.1) and Khawr Ghawi (9.3).

Kentish Plover

478 Lesser Sand Plover *Charadrius mongolus*
An abundant and widespread passage migrant and winter visitor, mainly from late-July to mid-May with some birds staying over summer. Huge wintering concentrations at Barr Al Hikman (8.1).

479 Greater Sand Plover *Charadrius lechenaultii*
A common passage migrant and winter visitor, mainly from early-August to late-May, with some staying over summer. Generally less numerous than Lesser Sand Plover, though often associated with it. Locally abundant in winter at Barr Al Hikman (8.1) and Masirah. In north Oman easily found at Ras As Sawadi (2.1), Shinas (2.5) and Qurayyat (3.1). In south Oman common around coastal *khawrs*.

480 Caspian Plover *Charadrius asiaticus*
A rare passage migrant from mid-July to late-November, and an even rarer winter visitor and spring migrant, principally to north Oman. Never present for more than a few days at any locality. The most reliable area is Sun Farms, Sohar (2.2) where the bird occurs almost annually, and should be looked for on bare or newly planted vegetable fields.

484 Pacific Golden Plover *Pluvialis fulva*
A common passage migrant and winter visitor from mid-August to mid-May, rarely in summer, and commoner in south Oman. In north Oman one favoured locality is the small area of permanent water at the rear of Al Qurm Natural Park (1.2), adjacent to the mangroves, where they winter. In south Oman the bird is usually present at one or more of the coastal *khawrs*.

485 European Golden Plover *Pluvialis apricaria*
Scarce passage migrant and winter visitor, recorded from scattered localities. Probably overlooked due to difficulties of separation from Pacific Golden Plover.

486 Grey Plover *Pluvialis squatarola*
A widespread and abundant passage migrant and winter visitor, mainly from late-August to mid-May with a few remaining over the summer. Usually in small numbers, but large wintering concentrations at Barr Al Hikman (8.1) and Masirah.

487 Spur-winged Plover *Hoplopterus spinosus*
A rare passage migrant and winter visitor from mid-October to mid-February. Most records are from north Oman in grasslands near Sohar (2.2).

490 Red-wattled Plover *Hoplopterus indicus*
A common breeding resident in north Oman, and a casual visitor elsewhere. During winter, large numbers congregate on farmlands on Al Batinah. Common in the Muscat area where it can be found throughout the year at Al Ansab Lagoons (1.1) and Al Qurm Natural Park (1.2).

491 Sociable Plover *Chettusia gregaria*
A rare passage migrant and winter visitor from early-November to early-March. Most often occurs on farmlands near Sohar (2.2) and Salalah (10.1).

Sociable Plover

492 White-tailed Plover *Chettusia leucura*
A fairly common but localised passage migrant and winter visitor from late-July to late-March. In north Oman it is best found at Al Ansab Lagoons (1.1) and Sun Farms, Sohar (2.2) where a few individuals always winter. In south Oman most often found at Khawr Taqah (10.6).

493 Lapwing *Vanellus vanellus*
A widespread but uncommon and irregular passage migrant and winter visitor from early-November to mid-March, occurring almost anywhere, especially on farmlands near Sohar (2.2) and Salalah (10.1).

495 Great Knot *Calidris tenuirostris*
A rare, but regular, winter visitor to Barr Al Hikman (8.1) from mid-August to late-May. Vagrant elsewhere. The best place to search for this bird is just inland of the beach south of the Masirah ferry at Shannah, where access requires a 4WD or some walking across the flats. As this species usually associates with Bar-tailed Godwit carefully scanning through any large flocks is the best way to find them.

Great Knot

497 Sanderling *Calidris alba*
An abundant passage migrant and winter visitor from mid-August to late-May with some birds staying over summer. The largest concentrations are at Barr Al Hikman (8.1). This species can be found in small numbers on any sandy beach.

501 Little Stint *Calidris minuta*
An abundant passage migrant and winter visitor from early-August to late-May with some birds staying over summer. Huge numbers winter at Barr Al Hikman (8.1). One of the most common and widespread waders in Oman.

502 Temminck's Stint *Calidris temminckii*
An abundant passage migrant and winter visitor from mid-August to mid-May, occasionally in summer. Much less numerous than the previous species and mostly only present in small numbers. However, very widespread, and usually present at any of the coastal *khawrs*. Rare in Musandam, which has little suitable habitat.

503 Long-toed Stint *Calidris subminuta*
An uncommon passage migrant and winter visitor from mid-August to early-June, primarily to south Oman. Oddly, most records are from Thumrayt. Otherwise most frequent around East Khawr (10.2) or Khawr Taqah (10.6).

509 Curlew Sandpiper *Calidris ferruginea*
An abundant and widespread passage migrant and winter visitor from late-July to early-May with a few birds staying over summer.

512 Dunlin *Calidris alpina*
An abundant passage migrant and winter visitor from early-September to early-May with a few birds in summer.

514 Broad-billed Sandpiper *Limicola falcinellus*
A common passage migrant and winter visitor from late-July to late-March.

517 Ruff *Philomachus pugnax*
An abundant and widespread passage migrant and winter visitor from late-July to early-April with a few birds staying over summer.

518 Jack Snipe *Lymnocryptes minimus*
A fairly common passage migrant and winter visitor from mid-September to early-April, occurring widely across Oman. Certainly under-recorded due to its somewhat secretive habits. The most reliable site for this bird is Al Ansab Lagoons (1.1). In south Oman it can sometimes be found in the shallower parts of Khawr Rawri (10.7), East Khawr (10.2) or Khawr Taqah (10.6). Frequently found around Thumrayt.

519 Common Snipe *Gallinago gallinago*
An abundant and widespread passage migrant and winter visitor from mid-August to mid-May, rarely in summer.

520 Great Snipe *Gallinago media*
Rare passage migrant from August to April. Most records refer to passage birds in October on Masirah.

521 Pintail Snipe *Gallinago stenura*
A fairly common passage migrant and winter visitor from early-August to early-June, chiefly to Dhofar *khawrs* and Hilf (8.2) on Masirah. Uncommon in north Oman and unrecorded in Musandam. Probably overlooked due to similarity with Common Snipe. Many records from Thumrayt, Muntasar (7.3) and Wadi Darbat (10.8). Of the Dhofar *khawrs*, Khawr Rawri (10.7), Khawr Taqah (10.6) and Khawr A Mughsayl (10.15) are the better sites.

532 Black-tailed Godwit *Limosa limosa*
A common passage migrant and winter visitor, mainly from August to April. Most common in south Oman where it can usually be found at any of the *khawrs* of coastal Dhofar. In north Oman most often recorded from Al Ansab Lagoons (1.1), Sun Farms, Sohar (2.2) or Qurayyat (3.1), but small numbers can turn up anywhere along the coast.

534 Bar-tailed Godwit *Limosa lapponica*
An abundant passage migrant and winter visitor from late-August to mid-May, with some birds staying over summer. Huge concentrations winter at Barr Al Hikman (8.1).

538 Whimbrel *Numenius phaeopus*
An abundant passage migrant and winter visitor from mid-July to end-April. Large wintering populations winter at Barr Al Hikman (8.1) and Masirah.

541 Curlew *Numenius arquata*
An abundant passage migrant and winter visitor, mainly from late-July to mid-April. A few in summer. Particularly numerous at Barr Al Hikman (8.1). Some sub-specifically identified refer to form *orientalis*.

Spotted Redshank

545 Spotted Redshank *Tringa erythropus*
A common, though never numerous, and widespread passage migrant and winter visitor from early-July to late-May. More records are from north Oman. In south Oman regularly found at any of the Dhofar *khawrs*.

546 Redshank *Tringa totanus*
An abundant passage migrant and winter visitor from early-July to early-May with some birds staying over summer. Huge numbers winter at Barr Al Hikman (8.1). One of the most widespread and common waders in Oman.

547 Marsh Sandpiper *Tringa stagnatilis*
A common passage migrant and winter visitor from early-August to mid-April, rarely in other months.
Usually quite easy to find at the Dhofar *khawrs*.

548 Greenshank *Tringa nebularia*
An abundant passage migrant and winter visitor, mainly from end-July to end-April, less common in summer. Usually in small numbers, but numerous at Barr Al Hikman (8.1).

553 Green Sandpiper *Tringa ochropus*
An abundant and widespread passage migrant and winter visitor from late-July to early-May, rarely at other times. Often occurs inland and at creeks and temporary pools in the mountains.

Terek Sandpiper

554 Wood Sandpiper *Tringa glareola*
An abundant passage migrant and winter visitor from early-August to early-May, less common in summer.

555 Terek Sandpiper *Xenus cinereus*
An abundant and widespread passage migrant and winter visitor. Usually in small numbers but very common at Barr Al Hikman (8.1). More common during migration than in mid winter, when it can usually be found at coastal creeks and *khawrs*. Rarely recorded inland. In north Oman reliable sites for this bird are Ras As Sawadi (2.1), Shinas (2.5), and adjacent to the mangroves behind Al Qurm Natural Park (1.2). Commoner in south Oman and easily found near the beach at Dhofar *khawrs*.

556 Common Sandpiper *Actitis hypoleucos*
An abundant and widespread passage migrant and winter visitor, mainly from late-July to early-May, but recorded in every month. Often seen in grassy areas along the highways around Muscat.

561 Turnstone *Arenaria interpres*
An abundant passage migrant and winter visitor from early-August to mid-May, some staying over summer. Particularly common at Barr Al Hikman (8.1).

564 Red-necked Phalarope *Phalaropus lobatus*
A common passage migrant and winter visitor from early-August to late-May, rarely in summer. Although small numbers are sometimes seen at coastal *khawrs* and inland pools, this bird is maritime in habits. Huge rafts are often found at sea, and can usually be seen from any sea-watching point. Good areas include Ras Mirbat (10.11), Al Mughsayl (10.15), Ras Madrakah (9.2), Ras Al Khabbah (3.5), Ras Abu Rasas (8.4) and Qurayyat (3.1). This species should also be encountered on fishing or dolphin-watching trips off Muscat.

565 Grey Phalarope *Phalaropus fulicarius*
Rare passage migrant and winter visitor. Almost certainly under-recorded due to the abundance of Red-necked Phalarope.

566 Pomarine Skua *Stercorarius pomarinus*
A fairly common passage migrant mainly from July to November, but with records from every month. Less frequent and numerous than Arctic Skua. Most likely to be found while sea-watching from any good promontory such as Ras Al Khabbah (3.5) or Ras Mirbat (10.11), but can be found occasionally harassing gulls or terns wherever they occur in concentrations.

567 Arctic Skua *Stercorarius parasiticus*
A fairly common passage migrant, mainly from July to November, but records from every month. Much the commonest skua in Oman.

*569A Antarctic Skua *Catharacta antarctica* and ***570 South Polar Skua** *Catharacta maccormicki*
These two southern skuas probably occur as regular migrants in Oman waters, but identification difficulties of the *Catharacta* complex make specific identification difficult in most cases, and many records refer to *Catharacta sp.* The most likely sea-watching points for these birds to be observed would be Ras Mirbat (10.11), Ras Janjari (10.11), Ras Al Khabbah (3.5), and Ras Al Ya and Ras Abu Rasas (8.4) on Masirah.

571 Sooty Gull *Larus hemprichii*
An abundant breeding resident on offshore islands, and a visitor to all coasts throughout the year. The largest concentrations, sometimes in tens of thousands, are along the east and south coasts and Masirah. Generally the only gull present in the summer months.

Great Black-headed Gull

*572 White-eyed Gull *Larus leucophthalmus*
Vagrant. Probably occurs as a regular visitor as post-breeding dispersal from colonies in Yemen, but overlooked due to superficial similarities with Sooty Gull. Most records are from September to November, when close inspection of gulls along the south Dhofar coast might pay off.

573 Great Black-headed Gull *Larus ichthyaetus*
A common winter visitor from late-November to late-March, rarely in other months. Less common in south Oman. This bird arrives 'late' in Oman, and is very difficult to find before December, but then easily found at most localities along the east coast. Very common around Ras Al Hadd (3.4) and farther south. Also regular wintering birds at Qurayyat (3.1) and Ras As Sawadi (2.1). From January to March it spreads further north along the coast when found at sites such as Shinas (2.5) and beyond. Many obtain full breeding plumage in February and March before moving north to breed.

582 Black-headed Gull *Larus ridibundus*
A common and widespread winter visitor from December to March, with some birds staying over summer. Easily found along all coasts, and abundant in some years in north Oman.

585 Slender-billed Gull *Larus genei*
An abundant passage migrant and winter visitor, mostly from early-October to early-April, but a few birds in all months. Often, massive flocks at Barr Al Hikman (8.1), and common along all coasts of Oman.

590 Common Gull *Larus canus*
Scarce winter visitor. Probably widely overlooked within the huge flocks of wintering gulls in Oman.

592.9 Large white-headed gull sp. *Larus fuscus / cachinnans / heuglini*
Due to taxonomic uncertainties and identification difficulties presented by large, white-headed gulls in Arabia, no clear understanding currently exists as to the exact status and distribution of the various forms in Oman. Large, white-headed gulls are an abundant and widespread passage migrant and winter visitor from late-August to mid-April. Huge numbers winter along all coasts particularly the east coast from Ras Al Hadd (3.4) to Khawr Dhurf (9.2) and on Masirah. The largest count is over 100,000 from Barr Al Hikman (8.1).

Siberian Gull

591.1 Baltic Gull *Larus (fuscus) fuscus*
Usually considered a race of Lesser Black-backed Gull, but here treated as a separable form, distinct from *graellsii* and *intermedius*, neither of which have to date been recorded in Oman. Occurs as a rare passage migrant and winter visitor.

591.2 Siberian Gull *Larus heuglini*
An abundant passage migrant and winter visitor, mainly from late-September to late-March with a few records at other times.

Caspian Gull

592.2 Caspian Gull *Larus (cachinnans) cachinnans*
A common passage migrant and winter visitor, mainly from late-August to late-March with a few records at other times. The form *barabensis* "Baraba Gull" also occurs, though its relative status is unclear due to identification difficulties.

605 Gull-billed Tern *Gelochelidon nilotica*
A common passage migrant and winter visitor with records in every month, though never numerous. Much commoner in south Oman. Reliable sites include Qurayyat (3.1), Khawr Jirama (3.3), East Khawr (10.2) and Khawr Taqah (10.6).

606 Caspian Tern *Sterna caspia*
A common passage migrant and winter visitor with records in every months. Seen along all coasts, but large numbers only from Barr Al Hikman (8.1) to Khawr Ghawi (9.3) in winter. Reliable sites in north Oman are Ras As Sawadi (2.1) and Ras Al Hadd (3.4). In south Oman it is regular at all Dhofar *khawrs*.

608 Swift Tern *Sterna bergii*
An abundant breeding resident, passage migrant and winter visitor. Large concentrations seen along all coasts, especially around Masirah.

609 Lesser Crested Tern *Sterna bengalensis*
A common and widespread passage migrant, and summer and winter visitor. Less numerous than Swift Tern. Good sites, where this bird is usually present, include Ras As Sawadi (2.1), Shinas (2.5), Qurayyat (3.1), and the *khawrs* of coastal Dhofar.

611 Sandwich Tern *Sterna sandvicensis*
An abundant passage migrant, and summer and winter visitor. Seen along all coasts, often in mixed flocks with the previous two species.

614 Roseate Tern *Sterna dougallii*
A fairly common breeding summer visitor to offshore islands from late-April to early-October, uncommon elsewhere and rarely in other months. However, as most nesting sites are remote and off-limits, this can be a difficult species to find near the mainland. Probably the most reliable and easiest place to see it is at Qurayyat (3.1) between June and August, when it is present in small numbers, especially around Khawr Al Milh and Daghmar, and further down the coast at Dibab. Otherwise this bird turns up only irregularly along the entire coastline.

615 Common Tern *Sterna hirundo*
A common passage migrant, and an uncommon summer and winter visitor along all coasts. May be confused in autumn with White-cheeked Tern as juveniles of the two species are not easily separated.

620 White-cheeked Tern *Sterna repressa*
A common summer breeding visitor to offshore islands, and a common and widespread passage migrant from April to October. Uncommon at other times. Widespread and can be found within any tern concentrations at such sites as Qurayyat (3.1) or Ras As Sawadi (2.1).

Bridled Tern

622 Bridled Tern *Sterna anaethetus*
A common summer breeding visitor to offshore islands from mid-April to mid-November, rarely in other months. As the largest colonies are on the Daymaniyat Islands, it is easy to see off adjacent coastal areas such as Ras As Sawadi (2.1). Also very likely to be seen offshore from headlands of the east coast and Masirah such as at Ras Al Khabbah (3.5) Ras Al Ya and Ras Madrakah.

623 Sooty Tern *Sterna fuscata*
A rare breeding summer visitor to offshore islands where it breeds amongst Bridled Terns. As strictly pelagic, this species is very rarely seen from the mainland. Probably the best way to attempt to find this species is to join one of the dive trips out toward the Daymaniyat islands from Ras As Sawadi (2.1) where it might be viewable from the boat. [As a protected area, no landings are permitted on Daymaniyat islands]. A number of records relate to Musandam where the species breeds on remote islands.

624 Little Tern *Sterna albifrons*
A rare passage migrant and summer visitor from mid-April to early-November. Most readily found on its spring migration when numbers along the east coast sites are elevated. Likely under-recorded due to the difficulty in separation from the much commoner Saunders's Tern.

625 Saunders's Tern *Sterna saundersi*
A fairly common, but localised breeding resident or migrant breeder to beaches. Also a common passage migrant and winter visitor. Common in south Oman where easily found along all coastlines. In north Oman most easily found at Shinas (2.5), Ras As Sawadi (2.1) and sometimes Qurayyat (3.1).

626 Whiskered Tern *Chlidonias hybridus*
A common and widespread passage migrant and winter visitor, less common in summer. In north Oman, occurs with regularity at Al Ansab Lagoons (1.1) and near Sohar (2.2). In south Oman, easily found at any of the Dhofar *khawrs*. Rare in Musandam and on Masirah.

628 White-winged Black Tern *Chlidonias leucopterus*
A common passage migrant from late-March to late-May and early-September to mid-December, less common in summer and winter. In north Oman the only regular sites are Al Ansab Lagoons (1.1) and grasslands near Sohar (2.2). In south Oman regular at farmlands (10.1) and all the Dhofar *khawrs*. Rare on Masirah and unrecorded in Musandam.

629 Lesser Noddy *Anous tenuirostris*
A rare summer visitor to Masirah from early-June to early-August, rarely to mid-October, vagrant elsewhere. The most reliable, and only regular, site to find this species is at Ras Abu Rasas (8.4) from June to July, where they congregate in small numbers with Common Noddy.

630 Common Noddy *Anous stolidus*
A fairly common migrant breeder to offshore islands from late-March to mid-November, rarely in other months. Occasionally seen from the mainland at such places as Ras Al Khabbah (3.5), Ras Mirbat (10.11) and Qurayyat (3.1). Regular at Ras Abu Rasas (8.4) in mid-summer.

Common Noddy

657 Lichtenstein's Sandgrouse *Pterocles lichtensteinii*
A fairly common breeding resident over much of the country, but avoids the Empty Quarter and Masirah. Difficult to observe during the day except when accidentally flushed. Best found at dusk when they come to drink. This species is much commoner in north Oman. The best site to try to see it is Al Ansab Lagoons (1.1) where just before dark a few birds may fly over calling. In south Oman, records are spread in a number of *wadis* of the Dhofar mountains, but nowhere is it common.

Lichtenstein's Sandgrouse

658 Crowned Sandgrouse *Pterocles coronatus*
A common breeding resident in the deserts of central and southern Oman, where it inhabits flat stony plains. Comes to water in early to mid morning. Most frequently recorded from the Arabian Oryx Sanctuary where they come to drink daily at the water hole at the headquarters at Jaluni (7.1). Other reliable sites are Muntasar (7.3) and Qatbit (7.4) where small numbers are usually mixed in with the more numerous Spotted Sandgrouse that come to drink daily.

659 Spotted Sandgrouse *Pterocles senegallus*
A fairly common breeding resident in the deserts of central and southern Oman where it mainly inhabits sandy deserts. Occurs as a vagrant in northern Oman. Comes to water in the early to mid morning, often in huge flocks, especially at Muntasar (7.3) where the species visits daily in varying, but usually large, numbers. Also regular, but in smaller numbers, at the oasis at Qatbit (7.4) and at Al Balid Farm (7.5).

660 Chestnut-bellied Sandgrouse *Pterocles exustus*
A common and widespread breeding resident over most of the country. Comes to water early to mid morning and late afternoon, often in great numbers. By far the most widespread and easily seen sandgrouse in Oman, and often present on Al Batinah coast over farmland and scrubland. Frequent at Al Ansab Lagoons (1.1) where they often drink in the afternoon. In south Oman common over farmland near Salalah (10.1).

665 Rock Dove *Columba livia*
An abundant and widespread breeding resident in the mountains of north and south Oman and at inland desert locations, though mostly absent from central Oman, except near permanent water. Genuine wild populations predominate, though feral birds are often present near main towns and villages.

670 Wood Pigeon *Columba palumbus*
A rare and localised breeding resident in the mountains of north Oman. This isolated form resembles ssp. *iranica*. Found at high elevations, mainly in juniper woodlands above 2,000 m during the summer breeding season, but descends to lower elevations in winter. By far the best site to observe this bird is on the Sayq Plateau (4.3) where it is common throughout the year, along the highest section of the paved road in the most heavily wooded areas. It is recorded from Jabal Shams (4.2) from April to November where it undoubtedly breeds and in Wadi Sahtan from December to May. An interesting record of more than 100 individuals from Wadi Tayin in late-December might indicate a regular wintering locality. Any well-wooded area, high in Al Jabal Al Akhdar is likely to hold small numbers, but most are difficult to access.

Wood Pigeon

684 Collared Dove *Streptopelia decaocto*
A common breeding resident and abundant passage migrant and winter visitor, particularly to farmlands in north and south Oman. Widespread and easily found.

687 Turtle Dove *Streptopelia turtur*
An uncommon summer breeding visitor and common passage migrant from early-April to late-November, rarely in winter. Occurs almost anywhere on migration.

689 Rufous Turtle Dove *Streptopelia orientalis*
A rare autumn passage migrant to Masirah, mainly from early-September to early-December, rarely in other months. Vagrant elsewhere. Most likely to be found in the few wooded *wadis* around Hilf (8.2).

690 Laughing Dove *Streptopelia senegalensis*
An abundant and widespread breeding resident over most of the country. One of the most familiar birds, found in a variety of habitats often near human habitation, such as parks, gardens, farms and cultivation, but also in remote mountains and *wadis*. Ssp. *senegalensis* in south Oman, *cabayensis* elsewhere.

692 Namaqua Dove *Oena capensis*
An uncommon breeding resident in south Oman and rare visitor elsewhere. However, recorded in every month, and records are becoming more frequent. Regular in the scrub and near date palms behind Shinas (2.5), as well as around Sohar (2.2) where it probably breeds. In south Oman most often seen in farmland around Salalah (10.1), in Ayn Hamran (10.4) and around Thumrayt.

703 Bruce's Green Pigeon *Treron waalia*
A fairly common summer breeding visitor to mountain valleys and foothills of south Oman. A few birds over winter. Usually associated with fig trees where it blends in remarkably well with the foliage. Best located by listening for its distinctive whistling call regularly uttered when feeding. Good places to search for it are the largest trees near the stream at Ayn Razat (10.3) and along the *wadi* bottom at Ayn Hamran (10.4) where it should be present even in mid-winter. Also try Wadi Darbat (10.8) and Wadi Hanna (10.10).

Bruce's Green Pigeon

712 Ring-necked Parakeet *Psittacula krameri*
A common breeding resident in Musandam and northern Oman. First recorded in south Oman in December 1988 and has since established a small population in Salalah and Taqah. Recently recorded on Masirah. In north Oman large communal roosts at the InterContinental Hotel gardens (1.5) in Muscat.

715 Jacobin Cuckoo *Clamator jacobinus*
A rare passage migrant, mainly on Masirah, with records from early-June to early-December.

720 Didric Cuckoo *Chrysococcyx caprius*
A fairly common summer breeding visitor to south Oman from mid-April to mid-October, where it parasitises Rüppell's Weaver (**1612**). Present in well wooded *wadis* of coastal Dhofar such as Ayn Hamran (10.4), Wadi Hanna (10.10) and Wadi Darbat (10.8). Most easily located by voice.

724 Common Cuckoo *Cuculus canorus*
A fairly common and widespread passage migrant from mid-February to late-May and early-August to late-December. The majority of records are from south Oman, where it is frequently recorded from inland oases. This species may breed in the mountains of Musandam, where calling birds and agitated behaviour have been recorded in April and May.

Koel

734B Koel *Eudynamys scolopacea*
A rare and irregular visitor, to scattered localities along the east and south coast, recorded in every month except July and September. In recent years small numbers have been wintering around Hilf (8.2) on Masirah.

735 Barn Owl *Tyto alba*
A fairly common, but infrequently seen, breeding resident over much of the country, although unrecorded from Musandam. Present all along Al Batinah coast where occasionally seen crossing the highway at night. Occurs in parks and larger gardens around Muscat and Salalah. Occasionally heard at Khatmat Milahah (2.6). In Central Oman occurs, and breeds, around Jaluni (7.1).

737A African Scops Owl *Otus senegalensis*
Status uncertain, although presumed to be a breeding resident on the well wooded slopes, and in the *wadis*, of the mountains of south Oman such as at Ayn Hamran (10.4), Ayn Sahnawt (10.13) and Wadi Darbat (10.8). This species is readily located by voice, and calls throughout the year, principally between September and April.

738 Striated Scops Owl *Otus brucei*
A speciality, and an uncommon breeding resident of north Oman, with perhaps some local movement. Although chiefly a montane species, it can be found down to sea level in suitably wooded habitat, especially Ghaf *Prosopis cineraria* woodland. The species is most common in the foothill *wadis* and higher parts of Al Jabal Al Akhdar such as on the Sayq Plateau (4.3), or in the mountains of Musandam in Sall Ala (5.2) or at Ar Rawdah (5.4). One site, accessible by 2WD, is Khatmat Milahah (2.6). It has also been found around Shinas (2.5) and Sohar. The bird is most readily detected by voice, but the limited calling period from January to April makes determining the true status difficult, and the bird is apparently absent from many suitable areas of habitat.

739 European Scops Owl *Otus scops*
An uncommon passage migrant from mid-March to early-May and mid-August to mid-December, rarely recorded in other months. Migration through Oman is very widespread, and this bird is most frequently recorded at inland desert locations.

744 Desert Eagle Owl *Bubo (bubo) ascalaphus*
A rare, but widespread, breeding resident, that can be considered the most difficult of the resident owls in Oman to find. Most often seen by chance while driving in the interior. Sites where this bird is probably resident include Jaluni (7.1), Jabal Qatar (6.2) and As Sayh Plateau (5.3).

745 Spotted Eagle Owl *Bubo africanus*
A rare breeding resident of well-wooded habitat in *wadis* and on mountain slopes of both north and south Oman. Recent records from Ayn Hamran (10.4), Ayn Sahnawt (10.13), and Ayn Razat (10.3). Unfortunately this bird is a frequent road casualty, with a significant proportion of records concerning dead individuals, especially along the Salalah to Thumrayt road.

757 Little Owl *Athene noctua*
A fairly common and widespread breeding resident, although less common in Dhofar. Often seen perched on rocky outcrops by the roadside when driving in the interior. Common on the hillsides at As Sayh Plateau (5.3), Fossil Valley (6.1) and Ras Al Jinz (3.4).

762 Hume's Tawny Owl *Strix butleri*
Only discovered in Oman since 1977, where it is presumably a rare breeding resident, in several remote wadis in the mountains of southern Oman, especially on Jabal Samhan, where very difficult to access. Regularly found in Wadi Shuwaymiyyah (9.4) and the *wadi* behind Khawr Al Mughsayl (10.15).

768 Short-eared Owl *Asio flammeus*
A rare to uncommon passage migrant and winter visitor from early-October to late-April, chiefly to coastal locations.

778 European Nightjar *Caprimulgus europaeus*
A fairly common and widespread passage migrant from early-April to late-May and early-September to early-December, rarely recorded at other times.

781 Egyptian Nightjar *Caprimulgus aegyptius*
A rare passage migrant and winter visitor from mid-September to mid-May. In recent winters this bird has been present at Al Ansab Lagoons (1.1), especially from mid-February to mid-March, which might indicate this as a regular wintering site.

795 Common Swift *Apus apus*
A fairly common passage migrant from February to March, though recorded in every month. In south Oman the status is less clear due to confusion with 'Dhofar Swift' (see below). Sub-specifically identified birds refer to *pekinensis*.

796 Pallid Swift *Apus pallidus*
A common migrant breeder to north Oman and Musandam, and a common passage migrant over much of the country. The breeding range of Pallid Swift is usually shown to include south Oman (e.g. Chantler and Dreisens, 1995), but the status is unclear due to confusion with 'Dhofar Swift'. In north Oman, migration of Pallid Swift is a common sight with hundreds of individuals passing over each evening between January and late-April.

"Dhofar Swift" *Apus sp.*
Status unclear. During the summer monsoon a distinctive *Apus sp.* swift is a common breeding visitor to the coastal cliffs of Dhofar. The taxonomic position of these birds is confused. Superficially the appearance is intermediate between Common Swift (**795**) and Pallid Swift (**796**) especially in colouration. However the underparts have notably pale fringes and the pale throat patch is large. Many observers have noted the close similarity to Forbes-Watson's Swift *A. berliozi* (Tibbutt, 2006). In May 1993 three birds were collected and sent to museums in Europe and USA. Unfortunately, identification was not unanimous, nor conclusive. To our knowledge no DNA analysis has been performed. This confusing situation has led to these swifts being variously reported as either Common Swift or Pallid Swift. Often recorded in large flocks, these swifts are common at Taqah (10.6), Khawr Rawri (10.7) and near Salalah from April until at least September.

'Dhofar Swift'

798 Alpine Swift *Apus melba*
A rare and irregular passage migrant from early-January to early-April and mid-August to late-November, rarely at other times. Most frequently recorded from Dhofar, where the cliffs above Ayn Hamran (10.4) are the only regular site.

800 Little Swift *Apus affinis*
A rare but widespread autumn passage migrant from mid-October to mid-December.

829 Grey-headed Kingfisher *Halcyon leucocephala*
A common summer breeding visitor to south Oman from late-April to late-November where it primarily inhabits well-wooded *wadis* and parkland. This species is common at Ayn Razat (10.3), Ayn Hamra (10.4), Ayn Sahnawt (10.13), Wadi Darbat (10.8) and Wadi Hanna (10.10).

830A White-collared Kingfisher *Halcyon chloris*
The globally threatened and genetically isolated *kalbaensis* form of the White-collared Kingfisher is highly localised resident of mangroves in extreme north Oman. The breeding stronghold is at Khawr Kal ba just north of the border in the UAE. In Oman the only sites where it occurs, and possibly breeds, a

White-collared Kingfisher

Liwa (2.4) and Shinas (2.5). To have the best chance of seeing this species it is advisable to visit at lo tide when mud is exposed and the birds venture out of the mangroves to feed. Recently this species h been recorded from the mangroves of Mahawt island off Filim (8.1) where it is assumed to be resider Whether the form here is *kalbaensis* has yet to be ascertained.

831 Common Kingfisher *Alcedo atthis*
A common and widespread passage migrant and winter visitor from early-August to late-April. In nor Oman most common at Al Qurm Natural Park (1.2), Shinas (2.5) and Qurayyat (3.1). In south Oman le common, but regular at any of the *khawrs* of coastal Dhofar.

38 Little Green Bee-eater *Merops orientalis*

common breeding resident in north and south Oman, but avoids the central desert. A widespread and familiar species. Forms *cyanophrys* and *muscatensis* occur.

Blue-cheeked Bee-eater

9 Blue-cheeked Bee-eater *Merops superciliosus*

common summer breeding visitor to Al Batinah north, and a widespread and common passage migrant roughout the country from early-March to early-January. In summer can easily be found perched on res along the main highway near Sohar and further north. Breeding numbers have declined in recent ars due to loss of breeding habitat and increased human disturbance.

0 European Bee-eater *Merops apiaster*

fairly common, though declining summer breeding visitor to Al Batinah north occasionally in mixed onies with Blue-cheeked Bee-eater. Elsewhere it occurs widely as a fairly common passage migrant th records from early-March to early-December.

1 European Roller *Coracias garrulus*

common and widespread passage migrant, chiefly from late-March to early-June and mid-August to d-December.

3 Indian Roller *Coracias benghalensis*

common breeding resident in north Oman and Musandam. A rare visitor to Masirah and south Oman. e of the most familiar and conspicuous birds in north Oman.

5 Hoopoe *Upupa epops*

uncommon breeding resident in north Oman, and a common and widespread passage migrant and nter visitor from early-August to mid-May. In the Muscat area can be found throughout the year in Al rm Natural Park (1.2).

3 Wryneck *Jynx torquilla*

fairly common passage migrant and winter visitor from late-August to mid-April. Most frequently orded at Hilf (8.2), and Qurayyat (3.1).

952 Singing Bush Lark *Mirafra cantillans*
A common migrant breeder to farmlands and grassy plains in south Oman, where it breeds in seemingl
incredible densities. Most records are from early-April to late-September, but singing birds may be hear
from mid-January. Difficult to find from October to December. Easily found on dairy farms in Salala
(10.1), Wadi Darbat (10.8), and around Taqah (10.6).

953 Black-crowned Finch Lark *Eremopterix nigriceps*
An abundant breeding resident over much of the country, although it wanders greatly outside the summe
breeding season. Sometimes gathers in huge post-breeding flocks of more than 1,000 birds. This speci
inhabits a range of dry open habitats. Reliable sites close to Muscat in summer include Qurayyat (3.1) an
Ras As Sawadi (2.1). In winter can be found all along Al Batinah.

954 Dunn's Lark *Eremalauda dunni*
A rare and nomadic breeding resident of the interior parts of south Oman with irregular post-breedir
movements. This species probably rates as the most difficult of all Oman's resident birds to find whic
relies mostly on luck. One possibility is to drive the graded road from Thumrayt to Shisr (7.6), stoppir
and exploring en route. The *wadi* 10 km after the turnoff from the main road has been a regular site in th
past. Birds are sometimes seen coming to drink at sites in the central desert such as Jaluni (7.1). Similarl
birds are occasionally seen at water near Thumrayt. Wadi Rabkut (7.7) is another site where it has bee
seen irregularly.

955 Bar-tailed Desert Lark *Ammomanes cincturus*
An uncommon breeding resident of the interior parts of central and south Oman with irregular post-bree
ing movements. Occurrence and sites to look for this species are the same as for Dunn's Lark. As it
much more common than Dunn's Lark it should be encountered given a reasonable amount of time spe
driving in the interior. The best habitats in which to search are those most sandy and devoid of veget
tion.

957 Desert Lark *Ammomanes deserti*
A common and widespread breeding resident over much of the country, although few records from M
sirah. Some post-breeding dispersal occurs. Easily encountered in any rocky desert area, both in t
lowlands and mountains.

958 Hoopoe Lark *Alaemon alaudipes*
An common breeding resident across much of the interior, with some post-breeding dispersal. One of t
most conspicuous birds in the interior, seen en route if driving from Muscat to Salalah. In north Omar
is most easily found near Ras Al Hadd (3.4), Ras Al Khabbah (3.5) and further south. North of Musc
and along Al Batinah this bird can be scarce, but is regularly found in dunes behind Ras As Sawadi (2.
In south Oman it is largely absent from the coast, but can be found along the Salalah to Thumrayt ro
around the Thumrayt Waste Disposal Site (7.8) and especially farther north at Al Balid Farm (7.5).

962 Bimaculated Lark *Melanocorypha bimaculata*
An uncommon winter visitor chiefly from early-November to late-February. Usually seen in sizea
flocks on farmlands around Sohar (2.2) and Salalah (10.1), where they have a distinct preference for d
up or newly planted vegetable fields, rather than grass.

968 Short-toed Lark *Calandrella brachydactyla*
A common and widespread passage migrant and winter visitor, sometimes in flocks of thousands, mai
from mid-September to mid-March. Migration occurs on a wide front with birds common at both coas
and interior locations. Breeding has been confirmed at Sun Farms, Sohar (2.2).

970 Lesser Short-toed Lark *Calandrella rufescens*
An uncommon, but widespread, passage migrant and winter visitor on farmlands from early-Septem
to late-April. No regular wintering sites are known.

72 Crested Lark *Galerida cristata*
An abundant breeding resident over most of Oman. Large post-breeding flocks occur. A species impossible to miss.

75 Small Skylark *Alauda gulgula*
Given the difficulties of identification, this species is almost certainly over-looked and probably occurs as a scarce, but regular, winter visitor to grasslands of Al Batinah coast, especially around Sohar (2.2) where any flocks of larks should be closely scrutinised.

76 Skylark *Alauda arvensis*
An uncommon passage migrant and winter visitor from mid-September to mid-April, primarily to north Oman and Masirah. The species is only regu-larly recorded from grasslands near Sohar (2.2).

Small Skylark

81 Sand Martin *Riparia riparia*
A common passage migrant and winter visitor from early-August to early-June, more numerous in autumn than spring.

90 African Rock Martin *Ptyonoprogne fuligula*
An abundant breeding resident in north and south Oman, occasionally elsewhere.

91 Crag Martin *Ptyonoprogne rupestris*
A rare and irregular, but widespread, passage migrant and winter visitor, mainly from April to June and August to November, but with records in every month. This bird is probably overlooked, due to its simi-larity to the much commoner African Rock Martin.

92 Barn Swallow *Hirundo rustica*
An abundant and widespread passage migrant and winter visitor mainly from early-August to mid-May, less common in summer.

95 Red-rumped Swallow *Hirundo daurica*
An uncommon, but widespread passage migrant, mainly from mid-February to mid-April and late-July to late-October, although records in every month except June.

101 House Martin *Delichon urbica*
A fairly common and widespread passage migrant, mainly from late-January to mid-May and mid-July to late-October, rarely in summer and winter.

102 Richard's Pipit *Anthus richardi*
A fairly common and widespread passage migrant and winter visitor, mainly from mid-September to mid-April, rarely at other times.

104 Blyth's Pipit * *Anthus godlewskii*
A vagrant which is almost certainly overlooked due to its similarity to Richard's Pipit. Probably occurs as a scarce winter visitor to grasslands along Al Batinah. Best looked for at Sun Farms, Sohar (2.2).

1005 Tawny Pipit *Anthus campestris*
A common and widespread passage migrant and winter visitor from early-August to mid-May, often oc
curring in large numbers on farmlands around Sohar (2.2), Salalah (10.1) and Al Balid Farm (7.5).

1007 Long-billed Pipit *Anthus similis*
A fairly common breeding resident of the mountains of north and south Oman. Disperses after breeding
when it often occurs as low as sea level in winter. In north Oman in summer occurs in the high Al Jabal A
Akhdar on the Sayq Plateau (4.3) and Jabal Shams (4.2). Common in the Musandam mountains betwee
Khasab (5.1) and As Sayh Plateau (5.3). In south Oman this species is widespread in the Dhofar mour
tains, including Tawi Atayr (10.9), and occurs widely in the *wadis* of the coast in winter such as at Ay
Hamran (10.4), Khawr Al Mughsayl (10.15) and Ayn Razat (10.3).

1008 Olive-backed Pipit *Anthus hodgsoni*
A rare passage migrant on Masirah from mid to late-March and early-September to late-December. Th
favoured location is Hilf (8.2).

1009 Tree Pipit *Anthus trivialis*
A fairly common and widespread passage migrant and winter visitor from early-August to late-May.

1012 Red-throated Pipit *Anthus cervinus*
A common and widespread passage migrant and winter visitor from late-August to mid-May easily foun
on farmlands in north and south Oman and in wet areas near the coast.

1014 Water Pipit *Anthus spinoletta*
A fairly common winter visitor from early-September to mid-April. Commoner in north Oman than th
south. Easily found at Sun Farms, Sohar (2.2).

1017 Yellow Wagtail *Motacilla flava*
An abundant and widespread passage migrant and winter visitor, mainly from mid-August to mid-Ma
rarely in summer. The following forms occur - *beema* (common), *thunbergi* (fairly common), *feldeg*
(fairy common), *flava* (fairly common), *lutea*, *taivana* and *leucocephala* (rare).

beema / feldegg / lutea / leucocephal

018 Citrine Wagtail *Motacilla citreola*
A common passage migrant and winter visitor from mid-August to late-April. The form *citreola* is common with *calcarata* and *werae* occasionally recorded.

019 Grey Wagtail *Motacilla cinerea*
A common passage migrant and winter visitor from early-August to late-April. In south Oman regular at Ayn Hamran (10.4) and Ayn Razat (10.3).

020 White Wagtail *Motacilla alba*
An abundant and widespread passage migrant and winter visitor from mid-August to early-May. The form *alba* predominates, while *personata* 'Masked Wagtail' is uncommon, though recorded regularly from farmland near Sohar (2.2). The race *leucopsis* is a vagrant recorded once at Al Ansab Lagoons (1.1).

035 White-cheeked Bulbul *Pycnonotus leucogenys*
A fairly common breeding resident in Musandam and lately spreading into northern Oman and the capital area, presumably originating from escapes. Readily found at Liwa (2.4) and Shinas (2.5). In the capital area most easily found at Al Qurm Natural Park (1.2) and the gardens of Al Bustan Palace Hotel (1.5).

035B Red-vented Bulbul *Pycnonotus cafer*
An uncommon, but slowly increasing, breeding resident, presumably originating from escapes. The most reliable site to find this bird is the gardens of As Sawadi Beach Resort (2.1), or the gardens of Al Bustan Palace Hotel (1.5). Other areas where it is regularly seen include Al Qurm Natural Park (1.2), Sultan Qaboos University botanical garden and Riyam Park in Mutrah (1.5).

036 Yellow-vented Bulbul *Pycnonotus xanthopygos*
An abundant breeding resident in Musandam, north and south Oman, although not recorded on Masirah. A very familiar bird of parks, gardens and *wadis*, most abundant in the foothills of the Dhofar Mountains.

049 Grey Hypocolius *Hypocolius ampelinus*
A scarce winter visitor from mid November to early April, but has become more regular in recent years with a few birds regularly wintering in the Muntasar (7.3) and Qatbit (7.4) areas.

Grey Hypocolius

1095 Rufous Bush Robin *Cercotrichas galactotes*
A common and widespread passage migrant, mainly from mid-March to mid-May and early-August to mid-November.

1104 Nightingale *Luscinia megarhynchos*
A fairly common and widespread passage migrant from early-March to mid-May and early-August to mid-November, rarely in winter. Most common in south Oman where often heard singing in autumn. Site where this species occurs in good numbers include Ayn Hamran (10.4) and Ayn Razat (10.3).

1106 Bluethroat *Luscinia svecica*
A fairly common passage migrant and winter visitor from early-September to mid-April. In north Oman winters at Al Ansab Lagoons (1.1) and at Al Qurm Natural Park (1.2). In south Oman most regular in reed edges of Khawr Rawri (10.7) and East Khawr (10.2).

White-throated Robin

1117 White-throated Robin *Irania gutturalis*
A rare passage migrant with records in April, July, August, October and December. Only regular in Musandam, where the passage occurs in a narrow window of the last three weeks of April. At this time can be readily found at Sall Ala (5.2) and on As Sayh Plateau (5.3).

1118 Eversmann's Redstart *Phoenicurus erythronotus*
A rare winter visitor from early-November to late-February. Previously considered a vagrant, but recent observations indicate a small wintering population in Musandam. Most easily found on As Sayh Plateau (5.3) or Sall Ala (5.2).

1121 Black Redstart *Phoenicurus ochruros*
A common and widespread passage migrant and winter visitor from late-September to early-May. More common in north Oman, where readily found on any wooded gravel plain such as Khatmat Milahah (2.6) and Qurayyat (3.1). Also common at Sayq Plateau (4.3) and Jabal Shams (4.2). In south Oman rarely recorded on the coast, but regular in winter around Thumrayt. The form *semirufus* that occurs is reminiscent of Common Redstart, and a pitfall for the unwary observer.

Black Redstart

1122 Common Redstart *Phoenicurus phoenicurus*
A fairly common and widespread passage migrant from early-March to late-May and early-September to mid-December. The main spring passage, in April, follows the departure of most of the wintering Black Redstart population. Very common on As Sayh Plateau (5.3) in mid April. The forms *phoenicurus* and *samamisicus* 'Ehrenberg's Redstart' occur.

1135 Blackstart *Cercomela melanura*
A common resident in the mountains and foothills of south Oman. Vagrant elsewhere. Abundant in Ayn Hamran (10.4), Wadi Darbat (10.8) and Ayn Razat (10.3).

1137 Whinchat *Saxicola rubetra*
An uncommon but widespread passage migrant and winter visitor from late-August to late-May.

1139 Stonechat *Saxicola torquata*
A fairly common passage migrant and winter visitor from mid-September to mid-May. No regular wintering sites are know, though it occurs most frequently on farmland near Sohar (2.2) and Salalah (10.1) and at Al Qurm Natural Park (1.2). The form *maura* 'Siberian Stonechat' predominates.

1144 Isabelline Wheatear *Oenanthe isabellina*
An abundant and widespread passage migrant and winter visitor, mainly from mid-September to late-April.

1146 Northern Wheatear *Oenanthe oenanthe*
A fairly common and widespread passage migrant from early-February to late-May and early-September to late-November, with a distinct peak in April.

1147 Pied Wheatear *Oenanthe pleschanka*
A fairly common passage migrant and winter visitor from early-September to early-May. The heaviest passage is in March, when this species is often numerous in Musandam such as on As Sayh Plateau (5.3). Five records refer to the rare *vittata* form.

1149 Desert Wheatear *Oenanthe deserti*
An abundant and widespread passage migrant and winter visitor from early-August to early-May. One of the most numerous species in the arid interior in winter.

1152 Red-tailed Wheatear *Oenanthe xanthoprymna*
A common passage migrant and winter visitor from early-September to late-March. This species prefers rocky habitats. Sites where it is regularly found include hillsides near Al Ansab Lagoons (1.1), Qurayyat (3.1), Fossil Valley (6.1), Jabal Qatar (6.2), the coastal road from Qurayyat to Sur, and all sites in Al Hajar Mountains (4). Three records refer to the western form *xanthoprymna*.

Eastern Pied Wheatear

1153 Eastern Pied Wheatear *Oenanthe picata*
An uncommon passage migrant and winter visitor from mid-September to late-March to Musandam and Khatmat Milahah (2.6), rarely in other locations. The form *picata*, the only form found in Oman, is strikingly similar to Hume's Wheatear, and another pitfall for the unwary birdwatcher.

1154A South Arabian Wheatear *Oenanthe lugentoides*
A common breeding resident in south Oman and along the Huqf Escarpment in the south-east. Most easily found in the *wadi* behind Khawr Al Mughsayl (10.15). Other good sites to find this bird include Ayn Sahnawt (10.13), Wadi Darbat (10.8), Tawi Atayr (10.9), Wadi Shuwaymiyyah (9.4) and higher elevations in the Dhofar mountains.

1155 Hooded Wheatear *Oenanthe monacha*
An uncommon breeding resident and a fairly common passage migrant and winter visitor mainly from mid-September to mid-May. Records are widely scattered with no specific pattern of occurrence. The best areas to search for it are the mountains of Musandam, particularly around As Sayh Plateau (5.3), the Fahud area of north Oman, and higher sites in the Dhofar mountains such as Jabal Al Qamar (10.16). In some years it has wintered at Al Bustan Palace Hotel gardens (1.5).

1156 Hume's Wheatear *Oenanthe alboniger*
A common breeding resident in the mountains of Musandam and northern Oman, though occurs down to sea level where rocky hills and *wadis* reach the coast. Easily found at all sites in Al Hajar Mountains (4) and Musandam (5). Near Muscat can be seen in any *wadi* in the mountains such as the road to Yiti (1.4) or Qurayyat (3.1).

1162 Rock Thrush *Monticola saxatilis*
A fairly common and widespread passage migrant from late-February to early-May and early-September to late-November, uncommon in winter. Most easily found on passage in the higher mountains such as on As Sayh Plateau (5.3) or Sayq Plateau (4.3).

1166 Blue Rock Thrush *Monticola solitarius*
A common and widespread passage migrant and winter visitor from early-September to late-March. In winter can be found at most mountain sites in both north and south Oman.

Black-throated Thrush

1197 Black-throated Thrush *Turdus ruficollis*
An uncommon and irregular winter visitor from late-October to mid-March. The most regular sites are north Masirah near Hilf (8.2) and As Sayh Plateau (5.3), but not recorded annually.

1200 Song Thrush *Turdus philomelos*
An uncommon but widespread passage migrant and winter visitor from late-October to mid-April.

1227 Graceful Prinia *Prinia gracilis*
An abundant breeding resident in Musandam, north and south Oman, absent from the central desert. A familiar bird of parks and gardens.

Scrub Warbler

1231 Scrub Warbler *Scotocerca inquieta*
A fairly common, but local, breeding resident in the mountains of north and south Oman from which it descends to lower elevations in winter. In summer easily found at higher elevations such as on the Sayq Plateau (4.3), Jabal Shams (4.2), As Sayh Plateau (5.3), Jabal Qatar (6.2), and the Dhofar mountains at Wadi Uyun. In winter occurs in similar areas but also moves into the lower *wadis*.

1236 Grasshopper Warbler *Locustella naevia*
A rare passage migrant from late-March to early-May and mid-August to late-November. Its skulking habits mean it is certainly recorded far less than it should be.

1243 Sedge Warbler *Acrocephalus schoenobaenus*
A rare passage migrant from mid-March to early-June and early-September to late-November. Most records are from Hilf (8.2).

1250 Marsh Warbler *Acrocephalus palustris*
A fairly common spring passage migrant from late April to late-May, rarely in other months. Very large numbers are recorded in most years during early to mid-May, when large falls often occur inland such as at Jaluni (7.1) and in the gardens of the resthouses along the Salalah road.

1251 European Reed Warbler *Acrocephalus scirpaceus*
A fairly common passage migrant from late-February to mid-April and early-August to mid-November, and an uncommon winter visitor. Some later records in May show confusion with much more common Marsh Warbler during this period.

1252 Clamorous Reed Warbler *Acrocephalus stentoreus*
A common passage migrant and winter visitor, mainly from early-August to mid-April. Also a migrant breeder or breeding resident in reed beds and mangroves. Easily found around the *khawrs* of coastal Dhofar, Al Ansab Lagoons (1.1), Liwa (2.4), Shinas (2.5) and Al Qurm Natural Park (1.2).

1253 Great Reed Warbler *Acrocephalus arundinaceus*
An uncommon passage migrant and winter visitor from mid-August to mid-May. Exact status uncertain due to possible confusion with much more common Clamorous Reed Warbler.

1255 Olivaceous Warbler *Hippolais pallida*
A common and widespread passage migrant from early-March to late-May and early-August to mid-November.

1256 Booted Warbler *Hippolais caligata*
An uncommon passage migrant from mid-March to mid-June and early-August to mid-November.

1256 Sykes's Warbler *Hippolais (caligata) rama*
An uncommon local migrant or possibly resident breeder in mangroves on Al Batinah north, chiefly at Liwa (2.4) and Shinas (2.5).

1257 Upcher's Warbler *Hippolais languida*
A fairly common passage migrant, mainly from mid-March to mid-May and mid-July to late-October. The period of heaviest passage is usually around the last week of April and first week of May when good sites to look are any woodlands along Al Batinah, Ras As Sawadi (2.1), Hilf (8.2), Ayn Hamran (10.4), *wadis* around Thumrayt, and especially the gardens of the guesthouses along the Salalah road at Al Ghaftayn (7.2) and Qatbit (7.4).

1266 Ménétries's Warbler *Sylvia mystacea*
A fairly common and widespread passage migrant and winter visitor from mid-September to mid-May. Although never numerous, regular sites where this species winters in small numbers include Al Ansab Lagoons (1.1), Khatmat Milahah (2.6), and along the coastal road from Qurayyat to Sur in north Oman. In south Oman likely localities are any *wadis* in the foothills of the Dhofar mountains such as Ayn Hamran (10.4), Ayn Sahnawt (10.13) or Al Mughsayl (10.15). It also winters in reasonable numbers on Masirah.

1270 Desert Warbler *Sylvia nana*
A common passage migrant and winter visitor from late-September to early-April, rarely in other months. Often associates with wheatears, especially Desert Wheatear (**1149**). Occurs commonly in winter in low scrub along the coast such as at Shinas (2.5), Liwa (2.4), Ras As Sawadi (2.1), Qurayyat (3.1) and Barr Al Hikman (8.1). Also in the interior such as at Muntasar (7.3) and Wadi Rabkut (7.7).

1271 Arabian Warbler *Sylvia leucomelaena*
A fairly common breeding resident in the foot-hills and mountains of south Oman. Most eas-ily found at Ayn Hamran (10.4), Ayn Sahnawt (10.13), Khawr Rawri (10.7) or Wadi Hanna (10.10).

1272 Orphean Warbler *Sylvia hortensis*
A fairly common and widespread passage mi-grant and winter visitor from late-August to late-May. Small numbers winter at Khatmat Milahah (2.6). Also regular in Musandam and around Jaluni (7.1).

Arabian Warbler

1273 Barred Warbler *Sylvia nisoria*
A rare passage migrant from mid-April to early-May and early-September to late-October. This species could occur anywhere on passage, but regular sites are Musandam (5), Masirah (8) and Al Hajar Moun-tains (4).

1274 Lesser Whitethroat *Sylvia curruca*
A fairly common passage migrant and winter visitor from early-September to late-May.

1274A Hume's Lesser Whitethroat * *Sylvia curruca althaea*
Considered a vagrant, this species is almost certainly overlooked due to taxonomic confusion and identi-fication difficulties of the *S. curruca* complex.

1274B Desert Lesser Whitethroat *Sylvia curruca minula*
A common and widespread passage migrant and winter visitor from early-September to late-May. By far the most numerous form of the *curruca* complex. Winters in large numbers across much of Oman, and readily found in most habitats with bushes.

1275 Whitethroat *Sylvia communis*
A common passage migrant from late-April to late-May and mid-August to mid-November, but uncom-mon in winter.

1276 Garden Warbler *Sylvia borin*
A rare passage migrant from mid-April to mid-May and early-September to mid-November.

1277 Blackcap *Sylvia atricapilla*
A rare to uncommon passage migrant from mid-March to mid-May and early-September to early-December.

1291 Green Warbler *Phylloscopus nitidus*
A rare passage migrant mid-August to mid-November. Most records are from Masirah (8).

1308 Wood Warbler *Phylloscopus sibilatrix*
A fairly common passage migrant from late-March to mid-May and early-August to late-December. More common in south Oman and on Masirah, where most regular at Hilf (8.2).

1309 Plain Leaf Warbler *Phylloscopus neglectus*
A fairly common passage migrant and winter visitor from mid-October to late-March to extreme north Oman and Musandam (5). Elsewhere rare. Can be found in woodlands at Khatmat Milahah (2.6) or around Jabal Qatar (6.2) and Sayq (4.3). Most easily located by its sparrow-like call-note, most unlike a *Phylloscopus* warbler.

Plain Leaf Warbler

1311 Chiffchaff *Phylloscopus collybita*
A common and widespread passage migrant and winter visitor from mid-August to late-May. Forms *abietinus* and *tristis* occur.

1312 Willow Warbler *Phylloscopus trochilus*
A fairly common passage migrant from early-March to early-June and late-August to late-November. Most common in south Oman.

1335 Spotted Flycatcher *Muscicapa striata*
An abundant and widespread passage migrant from mid-April to late-May and late-August to mid-November, occasionally at other times with records in every month.

1343 Red-breasted Flycatcher *Ficedula parva*
A fairly common passage migrant and winter visitor from mid-August to late-April. Most frequent in south Oman and on Masirah (8).

1347 Semi-collared Flycatcher *Ficedula semitorquata*
A rare passage migrant from early-March to mid-April and late-September to late-October. Few records in recent years. This species occurs nowhere with regularity – best sites to look are Musandam (5) and on Masirah (8).

1353 African Paradise Flycatcher *Terpsiphone viridis*
A common breeding resident in wooded areas in south Oman. Easily found in well-wooded *wadis* with water such as Ayn Hamran (10.4), Wadi Hanna (10.10), Ayn Razat (10.3) and Wadi Darbat (10.8). The form *harterti* occurs.

1379 Arabian Babbler *Turdoides squamiceps*
A common breeding resident over much of the country, but less common in south Oman and absent from Masirah. A common and well-known species of gardens and parks.

1492 Nile Valley Sunbird *Anthreptes metallicus*
An uncommon and irregular winter visitor to south Oman, chiefly to areas around Salalah and Thumrayt. Also a rare breeding visitor to remote inland *wadis* in south Oman. This is an extremely difficult bird to pin down, erratic in both its occurrence and localities. It probably occurs almost annually in the Thumrayt area, so checking areas with acacias is worthwhile. Most occurrences in Salalah have been from the town gardens and parks, rather than outlying *wadis.*

1493 Purple Sunbird *Nectarinia asiatica*
A common breeding resident in northern Oman, where it is a well-known garden species. A few vagrant individuals have reached Masirah (8) and south Oman. Form *brevirostris* occurs.

1494 Shining Sunbird *Nectarinia habessinica*
A common breeding resident in south Oman. Particularly common in parks and gardens such at Ayn Razat (10.3), Ayn Hamran (10.4), Wadi Darbat (10.8), and Wadi Hanna (10.10).

1495 Palestine Sunbird *Nectarinia osea*
A common breeding resident in south Oman. Less numerous than Shining Sunbird and occasionally hard to find. Most common in parks and gardens and in the mountains. The most reliable sites to find this bird are at Ayn Razat (10.3), Ayn Hamran (10.4) and Tawi Atayr (10.9).

1501 Oriental White-eye *Zosterops palpebrosa*
A recent discovery in Oman and Arabia, and a presumed breeding resident. Highly localised, and only known from the mangroves of Mahawt island near Barr Al Hikman (8.1). This bird inhabits the taller mangroves around the southern end of the island, which can be visited, at high tide only, by hiring a local boat from Filim for the two kilometres to the island. Although landing on the island is possible, the recommended method to see the white-eye is to simply drift close to the mangrove and listen for their calls and watch for movement. The total population must be very small. A total of 14 were counted during a short survey in 1999.

Oriental White-eye

1504 White-breasted White-eye *Zosterops abyssinica*
A common breeding resident in wooded areas in south Oman. Easily found at sites such as Ayn Hamran (10.4), Ayn Razat (10.3), Wadi Hanna (10.10), and Ayn Sahnawt (10.13).

1508 Golden Oriole *Oriolus oriolus*
A fairly common and widespread autumn passage migrant from mid-August to late-October and a rare spring migrant from early-April to late-May, occasionally in summer and winter.

1509 Black-crowned Tchagra *Tchagra senegala*
A fairly common breeding resident in foothills and mountains of south Oman. Can be skulking and elusive, but this is a fairly vocal bird. Most easily found in Ayn Hamran (10.4) and Ayn Sahnawt (10.13), but other good sites include Khawr Rawri (10.7) and Wadi Hanna (10.10). Form *percivali* occurs.

1514 Isabelline Shrike *Lanius isabellinus*
An abundant passage migrant and winter visitor from mid-August to late-May, rarely in summer.

1515 Red-backed Shrike *Lanius collurio*
A fairly common autumn passage migrant from late-August to late-November and a rare spring migrant from mid-April to mid-May. Occasional in summer and winter. Most common on Masirah, central and south Oman.

1517 Long-tailed Shrike *Lanius schach*
Rare winter visitor from late-October to early-April often recorded as long-staying individuals.

1519 Lesser Grey Shrike *Lanius minor*
A rare but widespread passage migrant and winter visitor with records from early-January to mid-June and late-July to early-November.

1520 Southern Grey Shrike *Lanius (excubitor) meridionalis*
An abundant breeding resident over most of the country, and a common passage migrant and winter visitor. Resident, and some migrant birds, *aucheri*, form part of the *meridionalis* complex, now usually considered distinct from the *excubitor* Great Grey Shrike complex.

Steppe Grey Shrike

1520 Steppe Grey Shrike *Lanius (excubitor/meridionalis) pallidirostris*
An uncommon, but widespread passage migrant from February to May and September to December.

1523 Woodchat Shrike *Lanius senator*
An uncommon passage migrant from early-February to late-April and, occasionally, late-August to late-October. Reliably found from late-March to early-April on As Sayh Plateau (5.3) in Musandam.

1524 Masked Shrike *Lanius nubicus*
A rare, but widespread, passage migrant from late-February to late-May, rarely in winter or autumn. No regular sites are known for this bird, though early-April in Musandam (5) and Jaluni (7.1) are likely possibilities.

1562 House Crow *Corvus splendens*
A common breeding resident in Musandam and along Al Batinah to at least Dibab, south of Qurayyat 3.1). This species is spreading, and has now established a small population in south Oman, where regularly recorded around Raysut (10.14), Salalah and Ras Mirbat (10.11). Vagrant to Masirah (8).

571 Brown-necked Raven *Corvus ruficollis*
An abundant breeding resident over most of the country except the Dhofar mountains where Fan-tailed Raven (**1574**) replaces it. Generally shies away from towns, but common at rubbish tips. Frequently seen in the arid interior.

1574 Fan-tailed Raven *Corvus rhipidurus*
An abundant breeding resident in the Dhofar mountains where it replaces Brown-necked Raven (**1571**). Occasionally wanders into the desert as far north as Dawkah. Easily found at sites such as Ayn Hamran (10.4), Wadi Hanna (10.10) and around Salalah and Taqah (10.6).

1575 Tristram's Grackle *Onychognathus tristramii*
An abundant breeding resident in the Dhofar mountains. Vagrant elsewhere. Easily found at sites such as Ayn Hamran (10.4), Wadi Hanna (10.10), Wadi Darbat (10.8) and around villages along the south coast.

1582 Starling *Sturnus vulgaris*
A fairly common and widespread winter visitor from late-October to early-March.

1584 Rose-coloured Starling *Sturnus roseus*
A fairly common and widespread passage migrant and winter visitor from early-August to early-May, rarely in summer. Slightly less common than Starling, with more records from south Oman, especially in farmland around Salalah (10.1).

1586 Wattled Starling *Creatophora cineracea*
An uncommon and irregular passage migrant and winter visitor with records from early-June to late-February. Rare in north Oman.

1587 Common Mynah *Acridotheres tristis*
A common and spreading breeding resident in north Oman. First reported in November 1982, but now very common over much of Al Batinah, around Al Buraymi (6) and Musandam (5).

1588 Bank Mynah *Acridotheres ginginianus*
A rare, but spreading resident, presumably originating from UAE where it is locally common. Expected to spread further into Oman in future. This species is fairly common in the border area near Bayah en route to Musandam, and at Al Ayn adjacent to Al Buraymi (6). A few recent records around Muscat could have originated from escaped individuals, although there is at least one record of proven breeding near Seeb.

1591 House Sparrow *Passer domesticus*
A common breeding resident in the northern half of the country. A small colony has settled in Thumrayt, but otherwise it remains absent from south, and most of central, Oman. Form *hufufae* occurs.

1592 Spanish Sparrow *Passer hispaniolensis*
A rare and irregular passage migrant and winter visitor from early-November to mid-April.

Spanish Sparrow

1601 Pale Rock Sparrow *Petronia brachydactyla*

Pale Rock Sparrow

A fairly common and widespread passage migrant and winter visitor from early-September to mid-May, rarely in other months, and has bred erratically. This species is usually found in small flocks and is most often located by its soft, but distinctive call, reminiscent of distant bee-eaters as they fly over. Although it occurs widely, it is nowhere regular. The best sites are Hilf (8.2) and farmland around Sohar (2.2) from September to October.

1602 Yellow-throated Sparrow *Petronia xanthocollis*

A fairly common passage migrant, and an uncommon winter visitor. Also a migrant breeder to the northern half of the country. On passage it often occurs in large, noticeable flocks. This species breeds from April to June, when it can be found in areas of arid scrub, such as at Ras As Sawadi (2.1), Khatmat Milahah (2.6), and Jabal Qatar (6.2). Form *transfuga* occurs.

1612 Rüppell's Weaver *Ploceus galbula*

A common breeding resident in south Oman. The main breeding season is during the summer monsoon when it is parasitised by Didric Cuckoo (**720**). Common in most habitats, including woodland and scrub around the *khawrs* of coastal Dhofar as well as in towns and villages.

1618 Indian Silverbill *Euodice malabarica*

A common breeding resident in Musandam (8) and north Oman. Vagrant elsewhere. Occurs in a wide range of habitats including parks and gardens.

1619 African Silverbill *Euodice cantans*

A common breeding resident in south Oman.

1638 Brambling *Fringilla montifringilla*

A rare late autumn passage migrant from mid-November to mid-December, once in early February. Erratic in occurrence and not recorded from south Oman.

1646 Yemen Serin *Serinus menachensis*

A highly localised breeding resident of the sinkhole at Tawi Atayr (10.9), and possibly other localities in the Dhofar mountains where similar habitat occurs.

1647 Golden-winged Grosbeak *Rynchostruthus socotranus*

An uncommon breeding resident in the Dhofar mountains. This is the most elusive of the southern Oman specialities. Probably the best site to find this species is Wadi Hanna (10.10) where, during March and April, males are more evident when they sing from exposed treetops. Immature birds can also be found with some regularity at Ayn Hamran (10.4) during the summer monsoon, especially during July and August. The song and call notes are reminiscent of Goldfinch *Carduelis carduelis*.

1676 Trumpeter Finch *Bucanetes githagineus*

An uncommon but presumed breeding resident, and an irregular passage migrant and winter visitor. The only regular site for this bird is Jabal Qatar (6.2) where good habitat exists as well as a permanent spring which the birds are attracted. Elsewhere it occurs only as an irregular and nomadic visitor.

1679 Common Rosefinch *Carpodacus erythrinus*

An uncommon passage migrant from mid to late-March and late-August to late-December. Occurs with most regularity at Hilf (8.2), Dawkah, Jaluni (7.1) and Thumrayt.

1863 House Bunting *Emberiza striolata*
A common breeding resident in northern Oman, less common in Dhofar (10) and occasionally elsewhere. Possibly also a passage migrant and winter visitor. Good sites to find this bird in north Oman include Qurayyat (3.1), As Sayh Plateau (5.3), and Jabal Qatar (6.2). In south Oman most likely at Ayn Hamran (10.4) and Ayn Razat (10.3).

1864 African Rock Bunting *Emberiza tahapisi*
An abundant breeding resident in the mountains and foothills of Dhofar.

1865 Cinereous Bunting * *Emberiza cineracea*
Although considered a vagrant, the distribution of records suggests this species is probably a regular but scarce passage migrant during April to Musandam (5) where it should be looked for among Ortolan Buntings in fields around Khasab (5.1) and As Sayh plateau (5.3).

Ortolan Bunting

1866 Ortolan Bunting *Emberiza hortulana*
An uncommon to fairly common passage migrant from early-April to late-May and mid-August to late November, rarely in summer or winter. Regularly seen in good numbers in Musandam in April. Elsewhere it occurs regularly inland at sites such as Qatbit (7.4) and Jaluni (7.1), as well as at Hilf (8.2).

1876 Yellow-breasted Bunting *Emberiza aureola*
A rare passage migrant from early-August to mid-December, once in mid-April. Most likely to occur on Masirah (8).

1881 Black-headed Bunting *Emberiza melanocephala*
An uncommon but widespread passage migrant from early-April to early-May and early-August to mid-November, rarely in winter. Most regular on As Sayh Plateau (5.3) in April and on Masirah in autumn.

1882 Corn Bunting *Miliaria calandra*
A rare passage migrant and winter visitor mid-September to mid-March. The only regular site is Sur Farms, Sohar (2.2), where small numbers winter annually.

Escapes

The following species and records, not included on the main Oman list, are considered to be escapes. Only the regularly occurring escapes are included.

129 Yellow-billed Stork *Mycteria ibis*
Two birds flying into Oman at Khawr Kalba in December 1998. A single bird at Khawr Al Mughsayl (10.15) in September 2005.

Sacred Ibis

142 Sacred Ibis *Threskiornis aethiopicus*
Four at Al Qurm Natural Park (1.2) first reported in March 1996, with one still present in May 2001. Subsequent records of a single from Sohar in January 2000, and four at Al Ansab Lagoons (1.1) in March 2005, that may have originated from UAE feral populations.

288 Spot-billed Duck *Anas poecilorhyncha*
Up to four at East Khawr (10.2) from June 1995 to at least April 2000, known to have gone missing from nearby Robat Palace. Some breeding suspected.

295 Marbled Teal *Marmaronetta angustirostris*
Up to four birds at *khawrs* near Salalah from June 1992 to at least April 2000.

314 Lanner Falcon *Falco biarmicus*
Occasionally birds are seen with jesses.

316 Saker Falcon *Falco cherrug*
Occasionally birds are seen with jesses.

320 Peregrine Falcon *Falco peregrinus*
Occasionally birds are seen with jesses.

428 Helmeted Guineafowl *Numida meleagris*
One at Ayn Sahnawt (10.13) in March 1990 known to have escaped. Ten at Barka in January 1998.

714A Alexandrine Parakeet *Psittacula eupatria*
Three at Salalah in April 1977. Two in Al Bustan Palace Hotel gardens in January 1994.

714B Budgerigar *Melopsittacus undulatus*
Two at Salalah in March 1967, bred ferally. Another 13 near Salalah in July 1989. One at West Khawr (10.14) in June 1992. One at Madinat as Sultan Qaboos in September 1998. One at Al Ansab Lagoons (1.1) in March 2001.

1612A Jackson's Golden-backed Weaver *Ploceus jacksoni*
An adult male at Al Ansab Lagoons (1.1) from July 1997 to at least August 2004. One at Al Qurm Natural Park (1.2) from April 2003 to September 2004.

1612C Streaked Weaver *Ploceus manyar*
A pair at Al Qurm Natural Park (1.2) from March to September 2004, nested and attempted to breed but not thought to be successful.

1612D Baya Weaver *Ploceus philippinus*
Up to four at Al Qurm Natural Park (1.2) from May to November 2004.

1612E Red-billed Quelea *Quelea quelea*
Records from Al Qurm Natural Park (1.2) in April 2004, October 2006 and December 2007.

1615 Common Waxbill *Estrilda astrild*
One at Al Qurm Natural Park (1.2) in May 1988. Up to 30 birds there from August 1999 to June 2006.

1615A Crimson-rumped Waxbill *Estrilda rhodopyga*
Up to six at Al Qurm Natural Park from January 2004 to July 2006.

1616A Red Avadavat *Amandava amandava*
At least four at Rusail in July 1982 and three again in October 1987. One at Al Ansab Lagoons (1.1) in November 2001. Three at Al Qurm Natural Park in April 2002, and a single there in January 2004.

1620B Scaly-breasted Munia *Lonchura punctulata*
One reported from north Oman in November 1974. One at Al Ansab Lagoons (1.1) in April 1998. Up to 23 at Al Qurm Natural Park (1.2) from September 1999 to December 2005.

Scaly-breasted Munia

1620C Black-headed Munia *Lonchura malacca*
One at Al Ansab Lagoons (1.1) in February 1989. One at Al Qurm Natural Park (1.2) in May 2004 and again in November 2006.

1620E Yellow-crowned Bishop *Euplectes afer*
One at Al Ansab Lagoons (1.1) in March 1998. Up to four at Al Qurm Natural Park (1.2) from March 1998 to March 2006. Three at Ras Al Hamra in September 2003.

1620G Southern Red Bishop *Euplectes orix*
Up to two at Al Qurm Natural Park (1.2) from November 2001 to December 2007.

THE OMAN BIRD LIST

The 495 species of birds accepted at present by the Oman Bird Records Committee (OBRC) are listed below with their common and scientific names as well as an indication of their status. Lower case letters refer to rare or uncommon species, upper case letters to common or abundant species. The following key is used:

mb	migrant breeder
pm	passage migrant
rb	resident breeder
sb	summer visitor (breeding)
sv	summer visitor (non-breeding)
v(n)	vagrant with n accepted records
wv	winter visitor

Species listed with an asterix (*) are vagrants with less than 10 accepted records. OBRC would be grateful for detailed descriptions and/or photographs if such species are encountered. For more details, please refer to **Bird recording in Oman**, p 8. For details on where to find individual species, the reader is referred to the **Bird Finder** section, p 182. Tick boxes are provided and can be used as a quick summary for a trip list or even a life long country list! For more information on status and distribution as well as details of all vagrant records, see the *Oman Bird List, Edition 6* (Eriksen, Sargeant and Victor, 2003).

	Common name	Scientific name	Status
☐☐☐	Little Grebe	*Tachybaptus ruficollis*	RB/pm/wv
☐☐☐	Great Crested Grebe *	*Podiceps cristatus*	v(6)
☐☐☐	Black-necked Grebe	*Podiceps nigricollis*	pm/wv
☐☐☐	Albatross sp. *	*Diomedea sp.*	v(1)
☐☐☐	Jouanin's Petrel	*Bulweria fallax*	mb
☐☐☐	Cory's Shearwater *	*Calonectris diomedea*	v(9)
☐☐☐	Streaked Shearwater *	*Calonectris leucomelas*	v(1)
☐☐☐	Pale-footed Shearwater *	*Puffinus carneipes*	sv
☐☐☐	Wedge-tailed Shearwater *	*Puffinus pacificus*	sv
☐☐☐	Sooty Shearwater *	*Puffinus griseus*	v(7)
☐☐	Persian Shearwater	*Puffinus (lherminieri) persicus*	SV
☐☐	Wilson's Storm-petrel	*Oceanites oceanicus*	SV
☐☐	White-faced Storm-petrel *	*Pelagodroma marina*	v(2)
☐☐	Black-bellied Storm-petrel *	*Fregetta tropica*	v(2)
☐☐	Swinhoe's Storm-petrel	*Oceanodroma monorhis*	sv
☐☐	Red-billed Tropicbird	*Phaethon aethereus*	sb
☐☐	Red-footed Booby *	*Sula sula*	v(2)
☐☐	Masked Booby	*Sula dactylatra*	SB
☐☐	Brown Booby	*Sula leucogaster*	pm/sv/wv
☐☐	Cape Gannet *	*Morus capensis*	v(1)
☐☐	Cormorant	*Phalacrocorax carbo*	pm/WV
☐☐	Socotra Cormorant	*Phalacrocorax nigrogularis*	pm/wv
☐☐	White Pelican *	*Pelecanus onocrotalus*	v(6)
☐☐	Dalmatian Pelican *	*Pelecanus crispus*	v(3)
☐☐	Pink-backed Pelican *	*Pelecanus rufescens*	v(1)
☐☐	Great Frigatebird *	*Fregata minor*	v(1)
☐☐	Lesser Frigatebird *	*Fregata ariel*	v(5)
☐☐	Bittern	*Botaurus stellaris*	pm/wv
☐☐	Little Bittern	*Ixobrychus minutus*	sb/pm/wv
☐☐	Yellow Bittern	*Ixobrychus sinensis*	sv/sb?
☐☐	Night Heron	*Nycticorax nycticorax*	PM/WV
☐☐	Striated Heron	*Butorides striatus*	RB/PM
☐☐	Squacco Heron	*Ardeola ralloides*	PM/WV
☐☐	Indian Pond Heron	*Ardeola grayii*	pm/wv

			Common Name	Scientific Name	Status
☐ ☐ ☐	Cattle Egret	*Bubulcus ibis*	WV
☐ ☐ ☐	Western Reef Heron	*Egretta gularis*	PM/WV/rb
☐ ☐ ☐	Little Egret	*Egretta garzetta*	PM/WV
☐ ☐ ☐	Black Egret *	*Egretta ardesiaca*	v(1)
☐ ☐ ☐	Intermediate Egret	*Egretta intermedia*	wv
☐ ☐ ☐	Great White Egret	*Egretta alba*	PM/WV
☐ ☐ ☐	Grey Heron	*Ardea cinerea*	PM/WV
☐ ☐ ☐	Purple Heron	*Ardea purpurea*	PM/WV
☐ ☐ ☐	Goliath Heron *	*Ardea goliath*	v(5)
☐ ☐ ☐	Black-headed Heron *	*Ardea melanocephala*	v(4)
☐ ☐ ☐	Black Stork *	*Ciconia nigra*	v(5)
☐ ☐ ☐	Abdim's Stork	*Ciconia abdimii*	wv
☐ ☐ ☐	White Stork	*Ciconia ciconia*	PM/WV
☐ ☐ ☐	Glossy Ibis	*Plegadis falcinellus*	PM/WV
☐ ☐ ☐	Sacred Ibis *	*Threskiornis aethiopicus*	v(5)
☐ ☐ ☐	Spoonbill	*Platalea leucorodia*	PM/WV
☐ ☐ ☐	African Spoonbill *	*Platalea alba*	v(4)
☐ ☐ ☐	Greater Flamingo	*Phoenicopterus ruber*	PM/WV
☐ ☐ ☐	Lesser Flamingo *	*Phoenicopterus minor*	v(5)
☐ ☐ ☐	Fulvous Whistling Duck *	*Dendrocygna bicolor*	v(2)
☐ ☐ ☐	Lesser Whistling-Duck *	*Dendrocygna javanica*	v(1)
☐ ☐ ☐	Mute Swan *	*Cygnus olor*	v(2)
☐ ☐ ☐	Bewick's Swan *	*Cygnus columbianus*	v(3)
☐ ☐ ☐	Whooper Swan *	*Cygnus cygnus*	v(2)
☐ ☐ ☐	White-fronted Goose	*Anser albifrons*	wv
☐ ☐ ☐	Lesser White-fronted Goose *	*Anser erythropus*	v(3)
☐ ☐ ☐	Greylag Goose	*Anser anser*	wv
☐ ☐ ☐	Egyptian Goose *	*Alopochen aegyptiacus*	v(3)
☐ ☐ ☐	Ruddy Shelduck	*Tadorna ferruginea*	pm/wv
☐ ☐ ☐	Shelduck	*Tadorna tadorna*	pm/wv
☐ ☐ ☐	Comb Duck *	*Sarkidiornis melanotos*	v(1)
☐ ☐ ☐	Cotton Teal	*Nettapus coromandelianus*	wv
☐ ☐ ☐	Wigeon	*Anas penelope*	WV
☐ ☐ ☐	Gadwall	*Anas strepera*	wv
☐ ☐ ☐	Teal	*Anas crecca*	PM/WV
☐ ☐ ☐	Mallard	*Anas platyrhynchos*	WV
☐ ☐ ☐	Pintail	*Anas acuta*	PM/WV
☐ ☐ ☐	Garganey	*Anas querquedula*	PM/WV
☐ ☐ ☐	Shoveler	*Anas clypeata*	PM/WV
☐ ☐ ☐	Marbled Teal *	*Marmaronetta angustirostris*	v(1)
☐ ☐ ☐	Red-crested Pochard	*Netta rufina*	pm/wv
☐ ☐ ☐	Pochard	*Aythya ferina*	wv
☐ ☐ ☐	Ferruginous Duck	*Aythya nyroca*	wv
☐ ☐ ☐	Tufted Duck	*Aythya fuligula*	wv
☐ ☐ ☐	Red-breasted Merganser *	*Mergus serrator*	v(3)
☐ ☐ ☐	Honey Buzzard	*Pernis apivorus*	pm/wv
☐ ☐ ☐	Crested Honey Buzzard *	*Pernis ptilorhynchus*	v(7)
☐ ☐ ☐	Black-winged Kite *	*Elanus caeruleus*	v(7)
☐ ☐ ☐	Black Kite	*Milvus migrans*	pm/wv
☐ ☐ ☐	Pallas's Fish Eagle *	*Haliaeetus leucoryphus*	v(4)
☐ ☐ ☐	Egyptian Vulture	*Neophron percnopterus*	PM/WV/rb
☐ ☐ ☐	Griffon Vulture	*Gyps fulvus*	pm/wv
☐ ☐ ☐	Lappet-faced Vulture	*Torgos tracheliotos*	pm/wv/rb
☐ ☐ ☐	Black Vulture *	*Aegypius monachus*	v(2)
☐ ☐ ☐	Short-toed Eagle	*Circaetus gallicus*	PM/WV
☐ ☐ ☐	Marsh Harrier	*Circus aeruginosus*	PM/WV
☐ ☐ ☐	Hen Harrier	*Circus cyaneus*	pm/wv
☐ ☐ ☐	Pallid Harrier	*Circus macrourus*	pm/wv

	Common Name	Scientific Name	Status
☐☐☐	Montagu's Harrier	*Circus pygargus*	PM/WV
☐☐☐	Goshawk *	*Accipiter gentilis*	v(1)
☐☐☐	Sparrowhawk	*Accipiter nisus*	PM/WV
☐☐☐	Shikra *	*Accipiter badius*	v(9)
☐☐☐	White-eyed Buzzard *	*Butastur teesa*	v(1)
☐☐☐	Common Buzzard	*Buteo buteo*	pm/wv
☐☐☐	Long-legged Buzzard	*Buteo rufinus*	rb/pm/wv
☐☐☐	Lesser Spotted Eagle *	*Aquila pomarina*	v(8)
☐☐☐	Greater Spotted Eagle	*Aquila clanga*	PM/WV
☐☐☐	Steppe Eagle	*Aquila nipalensis*	PM/WV
☐☐☐	Tawny Eagle *	*Aquila rapax*	v(5)
☐☐☐	Imperial Eagle	*Aquila heliaca*	PM/WV
☐☐☐	Golden Eagle	*Aquila chrysaetos*	rb
☐☐☐	Verreaux's Eagle	*Aquila verreauxii*	rb
☐☐☐	Booted Eagle	*Hieraaetus pennatus*	pm/wv
☐☐☐	Bonelli's Eagle	*Hieraaetus fasciatus*	rb/pm/wv
☐☐☐	Osprey	*Pandion haliaetus*	PM/WV/rb
☐☐☐	Lesser Kestrel	*Falco naumanni*	pm
☐☐☐	Kestrel	*Falco tinnunculus*	PM/WV/rb
☐☐☐	Amur Falcon	*Falco amurensis*	pm
☐☐☐	Merlin *	*Falco columbarius*	v(4)
☐☐☐	Hobby	*Falco subbuteo*	pm
☐☐☐	Sooty Falcon	*Falco concolor*	sb
☐☐☐	Lanner Falcon	*Falco biarmicus*	pm?/wv?
☐☐☐	Saker Falcon	*Falco cherrug*	pm/wv
☐☐☐	Peregrine Falcon	*Falco peregrinus*	pm/wv/rb
☐☐☐	Barbary Falcon	*Falco pelegrinoides*	pm/wv/rb
☐☐☐	Chukar	*Alectoris chukar*	rb
☐☐☐	Arabian Partridge	*Alectoris melanocephala*	rb
☐☐☐	Sand Partridge	*Ammoperdix heyi*	RB
☐☐☐	Grey Francolin	*Francolinus pondicerianus*	RB
☐☐☐	Quail	*Coturnix coturnix*	PM/WV/rb?
☐☐☐	Harlequin Quail *	*Coturnix delegorguei*	v(1)
☐☐☐	Little Button Quail *	*Turnix sylvatica*	v(2)
☐☐☐	Water Rail	*Rallus aquaticus*	pm/wv
☐☐☐	Spotted Crake	*Porzana porzana*	pm/wv
☐☐☐	Little Crake	*Porzana parva*	pm/wv
☐☐☐	Baillon's Crake	*Porzana pusilla*	pm/wv
☐☐☐	Corncrake	*Crex crex*	pm/wv
☐☐☐	White-breasted Waterhen	*Amaurornis phoenicurus*	pm/wv
☐☐☐	Moorhen	*Gallinula chloropus*	RB
☐☐☐	Lesser Moorhen *	*Gallinula angulata*	v(1)
☐☐☐	Allen's Gallinule *	*Porphyrula alleni*	v(8)
☐☐☐	Purple Gallinule *	*Porphyrio porphyrio*	v(4)
☐☐☐	Watercock *	*Gallicrex cinerea*	v(1)
☐☐☐	Coot	*Fulica atra*	PM/WV/rb
☐☐☐	Red-knobbed Coot *	*Fulica cristata*	v(5)
☐☐☐	Common Crane	*Grus grus*	pm/wv
☐☐☐	Demoiselle Crane	*Anthropoides virgo*	pm/wv
☐☐☐	Little Bustard *	*Tetrax tetrax*	v(1)
☐☐☐	Houbara Bustard	*Chlamydotis undulata*	pm/wv/rb
☐☐☐	Pheasant-tailed Jacana	*Hydrophasianus chirurgus*	WV
☐☐☐	Painted Snipe *	*Rostratula benghalensis*	v(6)
☐☐☐	Oystercatcher	*Haematopus ostralegus*	PM/WV
☐☐☐	Black-winged Stilt	*Himantopus himantopus*	RB/PM/WV
☐☐☐	Avocet	*Recurvirostra avosetta*	pm/wv
☐☐☐	Crab Plover	*Dromas ardeola*	PM/WV/rb
☐☐☐	Stone Curlew	*Burhinus oedicnemus*	pm/wv

☐☐☐	Spotted Thick-knee	*Burhinus capensis*	rb
☐☐☐	Great Stone Plover	*Esacus recurvirostris*	wv
☐☐☐	Cream-coloured Courser	*Cursorius cursor*	pm/wv/rb
☐☐☐	Collared Pratincole	*Glareola pratincola*	pm/wv/sb
☐☐☐	Black-winged Pratincole *	*Glareola nordmanni*	v(9)
☐☐☐	Little Pratincole	*Glareola lactea*	pm/wv
☐☐☐	Little Ringed Plover	*Charadrius dubius*	PM/WV/rb
☐☐☐	Ringed Plover	*Charadrius hiaticula*	PM/WV
☐☐☐	Kentish Plover	*Charadrius alexandrinus*	RB/PM/WV
☐☐☐	Lesser Sand Plover	*Charadrius mongolus*	PM/WV
☐☐☐	Greater Sand Plover	*Charadrius leschenaultii*	PM/WV
☐☐☐	Caspian Plover	*Charadrius asiaticus*	pm/wv
☐☐☐	Dotterel *	*Charadrius morinellus*	v(7)
☐☐☐	American Golden Plover *	*Pluvialis dominica*	v(1)
☐☐☐	Pacific Golden Plover	*Pluvialis fulva*	PM/WV
☐☐☐	European Golden Plover	*Pluvialis apricaria*	pm/wv
☐☐☐	Grey Plover	*Pluvialis squatarola*	PM/WV
☐☐☐	Spur-winged Plover	*Hoplopterus spinosus*	pm/wv
☐☐☐	Red-wattled Plover	*Hoplopterus indicus*	RB
☐☐☐	Sociable Plover	*Chettusia gregaria*	pm/wv
☐☐☐	White-tailed Plover	*Chettusia leucura*	pm/wv
☐☐☐	Lapwing	*Vanellus vanellus*	pm/wv
☐☐☐	Great Knot	*Calidris tenuirostris*	wv
☐☐☐	Knot *	*Calidris canutus*	v(5)
☐☐☐	Sanderling	*Calidris alba*	PM/WV
☐☐☐	Little Stint	*Calidris minuta*	PM/WV
☐☐☐	Temminck's Stint	*Calidris temminckii*	PM/WV
☐☐☐	Long-toed Stint	*Calidris subminuta*	pm/wv
☐☐☐	Baird's Sandpiper *	*Calidris bairdii*	v(1)
☐☐☐	Pectoral Sandpiper *	*Calidris melanotos*	v(8)
☐☐☐	Sharp-tailed Sandpiper *	*Calidris acuminata*	v(1)
☐☐☐	Curlew Sandpiper	*Calidris ferruginea*	PM/WV
☐☐☐	Dunlin	*Calidris alpina*	PM/WV
☐☐☐	Broad-billed Sandpiper	*Limicola falcinellus*	PM/WV
☐☐☐	Buff-breasted Sandpiper *	*Tryngites subruficollis*	v(1)
☐☐☐	Ruff	*Philomachus pugnax*	PM/WV
☐☐☐	Jack Snipe	*Lymnocryptes minimus*	pm/wv
☐☐☐	Common Snipe	*Gallinago gallinago*	PM/WV
☐☐☐	Great Snipe	*Gallinago media*	pm
☐☐☐	Pintail Snipe	*Gallinago stenura*	pm/wv
☐☐☐	Long-billed Dowitcher *	*Limnodromus scolopaceus*	v(9)
☐☐☐	Woodcock *	*Scolopax rusticola*	v(2)
☐☐☐	Black-tailed Godwit	*Limosa limosa*	pm/wv
☐☐☐	Bar-tailed Godwit	*Limosa lapponica*	PM/WV
☐☐☐	Whimbrel	*Numenius phaeopus*	PM/WV
☐☐☐	Slender-billed Curlew *	*Numenius tenuirostris*	v(5)
☐☐☐	Curlew	*Numenius arquata*	PM/WV
☐☐☐	Far Eastern Curlew *	*Numenius madagascariensis*	v(1)
☐☐☐	Spotted Redshank	*Tringa erythropus*	PM/WV
☐☐☐	Redshank	*Tringa totanus*	PM/WV
☐☐☐	Marsh Sandpiper	*Tringa stagnatilis*	PM/WV
☐☐☐	Greenshank	*Tringa nebularia*	PM/WV
☐☐☐	Lesser Yellowlegs *	*Tringa flavipes*	v(1)
☐☐☐	Green Sandpiper	*Tringa ochropus*	PM/WV
☐☐☐	Wood Sandpiper	*Tringa glareola*	PM/WV
☐☐☐	Terek Sandpiper	*Xenus cinereus*	PM/WV
☐☐☐	Common Sandpiper	*Actitis hypoleucos*	PM/WV
☐☐☐	Turnstone	*Arenaria interpres*	PM/WV

☐☐☐	Wilson's Phalarope *	*Phalaropus tricolor*	v(2)
☐☐☐	Red-necked Phalarope	*Phalaropus lobatus*	PM/WV
☐☐☐	Grey Phalarope	*Phalaropus fulicarius*	pm/wv
☐☐☐	Pomarine Skua	*Stercorarius pomarinus*	pm
☐☐☐	Arctic Skua	*Stercorarius parasiticus*	pm
☐☐☐	Long-tailed Skua *	*Stercorarius longicaudus*	v(5)
☐☐☐	Antarctic Skua *	*Catharacta antarctica*	v(3)
☐☐☐	South Polar Skua *	*Catharacta maccormicki*	v(3)
☐☐☐	Sooty Gull	*Larus hemprichii*	RB
☐☐☐	White-eyed Gull *	*Larus leucophthalmus*	v(9)
☐☐☐	Great Black-headed Gull	*Larus ichthyaetus*	WV
☐☐☐	Black-headed Gull	*Larus ridibundus*	WV
☐☐☐	Brown-headed Gull *	*Larus brunnicephalus*	v(1)
☐☐☐	Slender-billed Gull	*Larus genei*	PM/WV
☐☐☐	Common Gull	*Larus canus*	wv
☐☐☐	Baltic Gull	*Larus (fuscus) fuscus*	pm/wv
☐☐☐	Siberian Gull	*Larus heuglini*	PM/WV
☐☐☐	Caspian Gull	*Larus cachinnans*	PM/WV
☐☐☐	Kittiwake *	*Rissa tridactyla*	v(2)
☐☐☐	Gull-billed Tern	*Gelochelidon nilotica*	PM/WV
☐☐☐	Caspian Tern	*Sterna caspia*	PM/WV
☐☐☐	Swift Tern	*Sterna bergii*	RB/PM/WV
☐☐☐	Lesser Crested Tern	*Sterna bengalensis*	PM/SV/WV
☐☐☐	Sandwich Tern	*Sterna sandvicensis*	PM/SV/WV
☐☐☐	Roseate Tern	*Sterna dougallii*	sb
☐☐☐	Common Tern	*Sterna hirundo*	PM/sv/wv
☐☐☐	Arctic Tern *	*Sterna paradisaea*	v(3)
☐☐☐	White-cheeked Tern	*Sterna repressa*	sb/pm
☐☐☐	Bridled Tern	*Sterna anaethetus*	SB
☐☐☐	Sooty Tern	*Sterna fuscata*	sb
☐☐☐	Little Tern	*Sterna albifrons*	pm/sv
☐☐☐	Saunders's Tern	*Sterna saundersi*	PM/WV/rb
☐☐☐	Whiskered Tern	*Chlidonias hybridus*	PM/WV
☐☐☐	Black Tern *	*Chlidonias niger*	v(7)
☐☐☐	White-winged Black Tern	*Chlidonias leucopterus*	PM/wv
☐☐☐	Lesser Noddy	*Anous tenuirostris*	sv
☐☐☐	Common Noddy	*Anous stolidus*	sb
☐☐☐	Indian Skimmer *	*Rynchops albicollis*	v(1)
☐☐☐	Lichtenstein's Sandgrouse	*Pterocles lichtensteinii*	rb
☐☐☐	Crowned Sandgrouse	*Pterocles coronatus*	RB
☐☐☐	Spotted Sandgrouse	*Pterocles senegallus*	RB
☐☐☐	Chestnut-bellied Sandgrouse	*Pterocles exustus*	RB
☐☐☐	Pin-tailed Sandgrouse *	*Pterocles alchata*	v(3)
☐☐☐	Rock Dove	*Columba livia*	RB
☐☐☐	Stock Dove *	*Columba oenas*	v(2)
☐☐☐	Woodpigeon	*Columba palumbus*	rb
☐☐☐	Collared Dove	*Streptopelia decaocto*	RB/PM/WV
☐☐☐	African Collared Dove *	*Streptopelia roseogrisea*	v(3)
☐☐☐	Red Turtle Dove *	*Streptopelia tranquebarica*	v(3)
☐☐☐	Turtle Dove	*Streptopelia turtur*	PM/sb
☐☐☐	Rufous Turtle Dove	*Streptopelia orientalis*	pm
☐☐☐	Laughing Dove	*Streptopelia senegalensis*	RB
☐☐☐	Namaqua Dove	*Oena capensis*	rb
☐☐☐	Bruce's Green Pigeon	*Treron waalia*	sb
☐☐☐	Ring-necked Parakeet	*Psittacula krameri*	RB
☐☐☐	Jacobin Cuckoo	*Clamator jacobinus*	pm
☐☐☐	Great Spotted Cuckoo *	*Clamator glandarius*	v(1)
☐☐☐	Indian Hawk Cuckoo *	*Cuculus varius*	v(1)

☐☐☐	Didric Cuckoo	*Chrysococcyx caprius*	sb
☐☐☐	Plaintive Cuckoo *	*Cacomantis (merulinus) passerinus*	v(3)
☐☐☐	Common Cuckoo	*Cuculus canorus*	pm/sb?
☐☐☐	Koel	*Eudynamys scolopacea*	pm
☐☐☐	Barn Owl	*Tyto alba*	rb
☐☐☐	African Scops Owl	*Otus senegalensis*	rb
☐☐☐	Striated Scops Owl	*Otus brucei*	rb
☐☐☐	European Scops Owl	*Otus scops*	pm
☐☐☐	Desert Eagle Owl	*Bubo (bubo) ascalaphus*	rb
☐☐☐	Spotted Eagle Owl	*Bubo africanus*	rb
☐☐☐	Little Owl	*Athene noctua*	rb
☐☐☐	Hume's Tawny Owl	*Strix butleri*	rb
☐☐☐	Long-eared Owl *	*Asio otus*	v(6)
☐☐☐	Short-eared Owl	*Asio flammeus*	pm/wv
☐☐☐	Nubian Nightjar *	*Caprimulgus nubicus*	v(7)
☐☐☐	European Nightjar	*Caprimulgus europaeus*	pm
☐☐☐	Egyptian Nightjar	*Caprimulgus aegyptius*	pm/wv
☐☐☐	Common Swift	*Apus apus*	pm
☐☐☐	Pallid Swift	*Apus pallidus*	SB/PM
☐☐☐	'Dhofar Swift'	*Apus sp.*	SB
☐☐☐	Alpine Swift	*Apus melba*	pm
☐☐☐	Little Swift	*Apus affinis*	pm
☐☐☐	Grey-headed Kingfisher	*Halcyon leucocephala*	SB
☐☐☐	White-collared Kingfisher	*Halcyon chloris*	rb
☐☐☐	Common Kingfisher	*Alcedo atthis*	PM/WV
☐☐☐	Malachite Kingfisher *	*Alcedo cristata*	v(3)
☐☐☐	Pied Kingfisher *	*Ceryle rudis*	v(4)
☐☐☐	White-throated Bee-eater *	*Merops albicollis*	v(2)
☐☐☐	Little Green Bee-eater	*Merops orientalis*	RB
☐☐☐	Blue-cheeked Bee-eater	*Merops superciliosus*	SB/PM
☐☐☐	European Bee-eater	*Merops apiaster*	pm/sb
☐☐☐	European Roller	*Coracias garrulus*	PM
☐☐☐	Lilac-breasted Roller *	*Coracias caudata*	v(1)
☐☐☐	Indian Roller	*Coracias benghalensis*	RB
☐☐☐	Hoopoe	*Upupa epops*	PM/WV/rb
☐☐☐	Wryneck	*Jynx torquilla*	pm/wv
☐☐☐	Singing Bush Lark	*Mirafra cantillans*	SB
☐☐☐	Black-crowned Finch Lark	*Eremopterix nigriceps*	RB
☐☐☐	Dunn's Lark	*Eremalauda dunni*	rb
☐☐☐	Bar-tailed Desert Lark	*Ammomanes cincturus*	rb
☐☐☐	Desert Lark	*Ammomanes deserti*	RB
☐☐☐	Hoopoe Lark	*Alaemon alaudipes*	RB
☐☐☐	Thick-billed Lark *	*Ramphocoris clotbey*	v(1)
☐☐☐	Bimaculated Lark	*Melanocorypha bimaculata*	wv
☐☐☐	Red-capped Lark *	*Calandrella cinerea*	v(1)
☐☐☐	Short-toed Lark	*Calandrella brachydactyla*	PM/WV
☐☐☐	Lesser Short-toed Lark	*Calandrella rufescens*	pm/wv
☐☐☐	Crested Lark	*Galerida cristata*	RB
☐☐☐	Small Skylark	*Alauda gulgula*	wv
☐☐☐	Skylark	*Alauda arvensis*	pm/wv
☐☐☐	Brown-throated Sand Martin *	*Riparia paludicola*	v(5)
☐☐☐	Sand Martin	*Riparia riparia*	PM/WV
☐☐☐	Pale Martin *	*Riparia diluta*	v(2)
☐☐☐	African Rock Martin	*Ptyonoprogne fuligula*	RB
☐☐☐	Crag Martin	*Ptyonoprogne rupestris*	pm/wv
☐☐☐	Barn Swallow	*Hirundo rustica*	PM/WV
☐☐☐	Wire-tailed Swallow *	*Hirundo smithii*	v(3)
☐☐☐	Lesser Striped Swallow *	*Hirundo abyssinica*	v(1)

☐☐☐	Red-rumped Swallow	*Hirundo daurica*	pm
☐☐☐	Streak-throated Swallow *	*Hirundo fluvicola*	v(4)
☐☐☐	House Martin	*Delichon urbica*	pm
☐☐☐	Richard's Pipit	*Anthus richardi*	pm/wv
☐☐☐	Blyth's Pipit *	*Anthus godlewskii*	v(4)
☐☐☐	Tawny Pipit	*Anthus campestris*	PM/WV
☐☐☐	Long-billed Pipit	*Anthus similis*	rb
☐☐☐	Olive-backed Pipit	*Anthus hodgsoni*	pm
☐☐☐	Tree Pipit	*Anthus trivialis*	pm/wv
☐☐☐	Meadow Pipit *	*Anthus pratensis*	v(5)
☐☐☐	Red-throated Pipit	*Anthus cervinus*	PM/WV
☐☐☐	Water Pipit	*Anthus spinoletta*	WV
☐☐☐	Buff-bellied Pipit *	*Anthus rubescens*	v(5)
☐☐☐	Golden Pipit *	*Tmetothylacus tenellus*	v(1)
☐☐☐	Forest Wagtail *	*Dendronanthus indicus*	v(5)
☐☐☐	Yellow Wagtail	*Motacilla flava*	PM/WV
☐☐☐	Citrine Wagtail	*Motacilla citreola*	PM/WV
☐☐☐	Grey Wagtail	*Motacilla cinerea*	PM/WV
☐☐☐	White Wagtail	*Motacilla alba*	PM/WV
☐☐☐	White-cheeked Bulbul	*Pycnonotus leucogenys*	rb
☐☐☐	Red-vented Bulbul	*Pycnonotus cafer*	rb
☐☐☐	Yellow-vented Bulbul	*Pycnonotus xanthopygos*	RB
☐☐☐	Grey Hypocolius	*Hypocolius ampelinus*	wv
☐☐☐	Radde's Accentor *	*Prunella ocularis*	v(1)
☐☐☐	Black-throated Accentor *	*Prunella atrogularis*	v(1)
☐☐☐	Rufous Bush Robin	*Cercotrichas galactotes*	PM
☐☐☐	Black Bush Robin *	*Cercotrichas podobe*	v(1)
☐☐☐	Robin *	*Erithacus rubecula*	v(3)
☐☐☐	Thrush Nightingale *	*Luscinia luscinia*	v(8)
☐☐☐	Nightingale	*Luscinia megarhynchos*	pm
☐☐☐	Bluethroat	*Luscinia svecica*	pm/wv
☐☐☐	White-throated Robin	*Irania gutturalis*	pm
☐☐☐	Eversmann's Redstart	*Phoenicurus erythronotus*	wv
☐☐☐	Black Redstart	*Phoenicurus ochruros*	PM/WV
☐☐☐	Common Redstart	*Phoenicurus phoenicurus*	pm
☐☐☐	Blackstart	*Cercomela melanura*	RB
☐☐☐	Whinchat	*Saxicola rubetra*	pm/wv
☐☐☐	Stonechat	*Saxicola torquata*	pm/wv
☐☐☐	Pied Stonechat *	*Saxicola caprata*	v(5)
☐☐☐	Isabelline Wheatear	*Oenanthe isabellina*	PM/WV
☐☐☐	Northern Wheatear	*Oenanthe oenanthe*	pm
☐☐☐	Pied Wheatear	*Oenanthe pleschanka*	pm/wv
☐☐☐	Cyprus Pied Wheatear *	*Oenanthe cypriaca*	v(1)
☐☐☐	Black-eared Wheatear *	*Oenanthe hispanica*	v(9)
☐☐☐	Desert Wheatear	*Oenanthe deserti*	PM/WV
☐☐☐	Finsch's Wheatear *	*Oenanthe finschii*	v(4)
☐☐☐	Red-tailed Wheatear	*Oenanthe xanthoprymna*	PM/WV
☐☐☐	Eastern Pied Wheatear	*Oenanthe picata*	pm/wv
☐☐☐	Mourning Wheatear *	*Oenanthe lugens*	v(9)
☐☐☐	South Arabian Wheatear	*Oenanthe lugentoides*	RB
☐☐☐	Hooded Wheatear	*Oenanthe monacha*	pm/wv/rb
☐☐☐	Hume's Wheatear	*Oenanthe alboniger*	RB
☐☐☐	White-crowned Black Wheatear *	*Oenanthe leucopyga*	v(7)
☐☐☐	Rock Thrush	*Monticola saxatilis*	pm
☐☐☐	Blue Rock Thrush	*Monticola solitarius*	PM/WV
☐☐☐	White's Thrush *	*Zoothera dauma*	v(1)
☐☐☐	Ring Ouzel *	*Turdus torquatus*	v(9)
☐☐☐	Eyebrowed Thrush *	*Turdus obscurus*	v(3)

☐☐☐	Dusky Thrush *	*Turdus naumanni eunomus*	v(3)
☐☐☐	Black-throated Thrush	*Turdus ruficollis*	wv
☐☐☐	Song Thrush	*Turdus philomelos*	pm/wv
☐☐☐	Mistle Thrush *	*Turdus viscivorus*	v(7)
☐☐☐	Cetti's Warbler *	*Cettia cetti*	v(1)
☐☐☐	Fan-tailed Cisticola *	*Cisticola juncidis*	v(1)
☐☐☐	Graceful Prinia	*Prinia gracilis*	RB
☐☐☐	Scrub Warbler	*Scotocerca inquieta*	rb
☐☐☐	Grasshopper Warbler	*Locustella naevia*	pm
☐☐☐	River Warbler *	*Locustella fluviatilis*	v(1)
☐☐☐	Savi's Warbler *	*Locustella luscinioides*	v(9)
☐☐☐	Moustached Warbler *	*Acrocephalus melanopogon*	v(7)
☐☐☐	Sedge Warbler	*Acrocephalus schoenobaenus*	pm
☐☐☐	Paddyfield Warbler *	*Acrocephalus agricola*	v(9)
☐☐☐	Blyth's Reed Warbler *	*Acrocephalus dumetorum*	v(3)
☐☐☐	Marsh Warbler	*Acrocephalus palustris*	pm
☐☐☐	European Reed Warbler	*Acrocephalus scirpaceus*	pm/wv
☐☐☐	Clamorous Reed Warbler	*Acrocephalus stentoreus*	PM/WV/rb
☐☐☐	Great Reed Warbler	*Acrocephalus arundinaceus*	pm/wv
☐☐☐	Olivaceous Warbler	*Hippolais pallida*	PM
☐☐☐	Booted Warbler	*Hippolais caligata*	pm
☐☐☐	Sykes's Warbler	*Hippolais (caligata) rama*	rb
☐☐☐	Upcher's Warbler	*Hippolais languida*	PM
☐☐☐	Olive-tree Warbler *	*Hippolais olivetorum*	v(2)
☐☐☐	Icterine Warbler *	*Hippolais icterina*	v(9)
☐☐☐	Ménétries's Warbler	*Sylvia mystacea*	pm/wv
☐☐☐	Sardinian Warbler *	*Sylvia melanocephala*	v(1)
☐☐☐	Desert Warbler	*Sylvia nana*	PM/WV
☐☐☐	Arabian Warbler	*Sylvia leucomelaena*	RB
☐☐☐	Orphean Warbler	*Sylvia hortensis*	pm/wv
☐☐☐	Barred Warbler	*Sylvia nisoria*	pm
☐☐☐	Lesser Whitethroat	*Sylvia curruca*	pm/wv
☐☐☐	Hume's Lesser Whitethroat *	*Sylvia curruca althaea*	v(2)
☐☐☐	Desert Lesser Whitethroat	*Sylvia curruca minula*	PM/WV
☐☐☐	Whitethroat	*Sylvia communis*	PM/wv
☐☐☐	Garden Warbler	*Sylvia borin*	pm
☐☐☐	Blackcap	*Sylvia atricapilla*	pm
☐☐☐	Green Warbler	*Phylloscopus nitidus*	pm
☐☐☐	Greenish Warbler *	*Phylloscopus trochiloides*	v(2)
☐☐☐	Arctic Warbler *	*Phylloscopus borealis*	v(1)
☐☐☐	Yellow-browed Warbler *	*Phylloscopus inornatus*	v(7)
☐☐☐	Hume's Warbler *	*Phylloscopus humei*	v(7)
☐☐☐	Bonelli's Warbler *	*Phylloscopus bonelli*	v(2)
☐☐☐	Wood Warbler	*Phylloscopus sibilatrix*	pm
☐☐☐	Plain Leaf Warbler	*Phylloscopus neglectus*	pm/wv
☐☐☐	Chiffchaff	*Phylloscopus collybita*	PM/WV
☐☐☐	Willow Warbler	*Phylloscopus trochilus*	pm
☐☐☐	Blue-and-white Flycatcher *	*Muscicapa cyanomelana*	v(2)
☐☐☐	Asian Brown Flycatcher *	*Muscicapa dauurica*	v(1)
☐☐☐	Spotted Flycatcher	*Muscicapa striata*	PM
☐☐☐	Red-breasted Flycatcher	*Ficedula parva*	pm/wv
☐☐☐	Semi-collared Flycatcher	*Ficedula semitorquata*	pm
☐☐☐	Pied Flycatcher *	*Ficedula hypoleuca*	v(1)
☐☐☐	African Paradise Flycatcher	*Terpsiphone viridis*	RB
☐☐☐	Arabian Babbler	*Turdoides squamiceps*	RB
☐☐☐	Penduline Tit *	*Remiz pendulinus*	v(1)
☐☐☐	Nile Valley Sunbird	*Anthreptes metallicus*	wv
☐☐☐	Purple Sunbird	*Nectarinia asiatica*	RB

☐☐☐	Shining Sunbird	*Nectarinia habessinica*	RB
☐☐☐	Palestine Sunbird	*Nectarinia osea*	RB
☐☐☐	Oriental White-eye	*Zosterops palpebrosa*	rb
☐☐☐	White-breasted White-eye	*Zosterops abyssinica*	RB
☐☐☐	Golden Oriole	*Oriolus oriolus*	pm
☐☐☐	Black-crowned Tchagra	*Tchagra senegala*	rb
☐☐☐	Isabelline Shrike	*Lanius isabellinus*	PM/WV
☐☐☐	Red-backed Shrike	*Lanius collurio*	pm
☐☐☐	Bay-backed Shrike *	*Lanius vittatus*	v(9)
☐☐☐	Long-tailed Shrike	*Lanius schach*	wv
☐☐☐	Lesser Grey Shrike	*Lanius minor*	pm/wv
☐☐☐	Southern Grey Shrike	*Lanius meridionalis*	RB/PM
☐☐☐	Steppe Grey Shrike	*Lanius (meridionalis) pallidiroistris*	pm
☐☐☐	Woodchat Shrike	*Lanius senator*	pm
☐☐☐	Masked Shrike	*Lanius nubicus*	pm
☐☐☐	Black Drongo *	*Dicrurus macrocercus*	v(3)
☐☐☐	Magpie *	*Pica pica*	v(1)
☐☐☐	House Crow	*Corvus splendens*	RB
☐☐☐	Brown-necked Raven	*Corvus ruficollis*	RB
☐☐☐	Fan-tailed Raven	*Corvus rhipidurus*	RB
☐☐☐	Tristram's Grackle	*Onychognathus tristramii*	RB
☐☐☐	Amethyst Starling *	*Cinnyricinclus leucogaster*	v(1)
☐☐☐	Brahminy Starling *	*Sturnus pagodarum*	v(8)
☐☐☐	Starling	*Sturnus vulgaris*	wv
☐☐☐	Rose-coloured Starling	*Sturnus roseus*	pm/wv
☐☐☐	Wattled Starling	*Creatophora cinerea*	pm/wv
☐☐☐	Common Mynah	*Acridotheres tristis*	RB
☐☐☐	Bank Mynah	*Acridotheres ginginianus*	rb
☐☐☐	House Sparrow	*Passer domesticus*	RB
☐☐☐	Spanish Sparrow	*Passer hispaniolensis*	pm/wv
☐☐☐	Pale Rock Sparrow	*Petronia brachydactyla*	pm/wv
☐☐☐	Yellow-throated Sparrow	*Petronia xanthocollis*	pm/wv/sb
☐☐☐	Rüppell's Weaver	*Ploceus galbula*	RB
☐☐☐	Indian Silverbill	*Euodice malabarica*	RB
☐☐☐	African Silverbill	*Euodice cantans*	RB
☐☐☐	Brambling	*Fringilla montifringilla*	pm
☐☐☐	Yemen Serin	*Serinus menachensis*	rb
☐☐☐	Golden-winged Grosbeak	*Rhynchostruthus socotranus*	rb
☐☐☐	Goldfinch *	*Carduelis carduelis*	v(1)
☐☐☐	Siskin *	*Carduelis spinus*	v(6)
☐☐☐	Trumpeter Finch	*Bucanetes githagineus*	rb/pm/wv
☐☐☐	Common Rosefinch	*Carpodacus erythrinus*	pm
☐☐☐	House Bunting	*Emberiza striolata*	RB
☐☐☐	African Rock Bunting	*Emberiza tahapisi*	RB
☐☐☐	Cinereous Bunting *	*Emberiza cineracea*	v(8)
☐☐☐	Ortolan Bunting	*Emberiza hortulana*	pm
☐☐☐	Grey-necked Bunting *	*Emberiza buchanani*	v(4)
☐☐☐	Cretzschmar's Bunting *	*Emberiza caesia*	v(2)
☐☐☐	Rustic Bunting *	*Emberiza rustica*	v(4)
☐☐☐	Little Bunting *	*Emberiza pusilla*	v(5)
☐☐☐	Yellow-breasted Bunting	*Emberiza aureola*	pm
☐☐☐	Reed Bunting *	*Emberiza schoeniclus*	v(1)
☐☐☐	Red-headed Bunting *	*Emberiza bruniceps*	v(4)
☐☐☐	Black-headed Bunting	*Emberiza melanocephala*	pm
☐☐☐	Corn Bunting	*Miliaria calandra*	pm/wv

References and selected bibliography

Alström, P. (1991). 'A Radde's Accentor *Prunella ocularis* from Oman reidentified as Black-throated Accentor *P. atrogularis.' Sandgrouse* **13**(2): 106-108.

Aspinall, S. (1994). 'Spring migration of Lesser Kestrel *Falco naumanni* through the United Arab Emirates and northern Oman 1994.' *Emirates Bird Report* **18**: 96-99.

Bannon, J. and C. Richardson (1991). 'A weekend trip to Khasab and the Musandam region.' *Oman Bird News* **11**: 2-3.

Bourne, W. R. P. (1988). 'Observations on birds and other wildlife at sea around Oman in 1987-1988.' *Oman Bird News* **5**: 1-3.

Bourne, W. R. P. and G. Bundy (1990). 'Records of Brown-headed Gull *Larus brunnicephalus* and Grey-headed Gull *L. cirrocephalus* around Arabia.' *Sandgrouse* **12**: 37-42.

Bradshaw, C. (2001). 'Blyth's Reed Warbler: problems and pitfalls.' *Brit. Birds* **94**(5): 236-245.

Brown, I. J. A. (1993). 'Description of nest of Golden-winged Grosbeak.' *Bull. Orn. Soc. Middle East* **31**: 27-28.

Bundy, G. (1986). 'Blackstarts in southern Oman.' *Sandgrouse* **7**: 43-46.

Carey, G. and U. Olsson (1995). 'Identification of Common, Wilson's, Pintail and Swinhoe's Snipes.' *Birding World* **8**: 179-190.

Carter, I. (2000). 'Early spring in Oman.' *Birding World* **13**: 75-76.

Chantler, P. and G. Driessens (1995). *Swifts. A guide to swifts and treeswifts of the world*, Pica Press, Sussex, UK.

Clark, W. S., R. Frumlin and H. Shirhai (1990). 'Field identification of Sooty Falcon.' *Brit. Birds* **83**(2): 47-54.

Clark, W. S. and H. Shirihai (1995). 'Identification of Barbary Falcon.' *Birding World* **8**: 336-343.

Clark, W. S. (1997). 'Identification of perched Montagu's and Pallid Harriers.' *Birding World* **10**: 267-269.

Clark, W. S. and N. J. Schmitt (1998). 'Ageing Egyptian Vultures.' *Alula* **4**: 122-127.

Clement, P. (1987). 'Field identification of West Palearctic wheatears.' *Brit. Birds* **80**: 137-157, 187-238.

Clement, P. (1995). 'Southern and eastern Great Grey Shrikes in northwest Europe.' *Birding World* **8**: 300-309.

Collinson, M. (2001). 'Greenish Warbler, 'Two-barred Greenish Warbler,' and the speciation process.' *Brit. Birds* **94**(6): 278-283.

Colston, P. and M. D. Gallagher (1983). 'First record of Sooty Shearwater *Puffinus griseus* for Arabia.' *Bull. Brit. Orn. Club* **103**(2): 36-37.

Colston, P. R. and M. D. Gallagher (1984). 'First record of the Pied Stonechat *Saxicola caprata* for Arabia.' *Bull. Brit. Orn. Club* **104**(2): 69-71.

Corso, A. and W. S. Clark (1998). 'Identification of Amur Falcon.' *Birding World* **11**: 261-268.

Corso, A. (1999). 'Separating juvenile Imperial and Greater Spotted Eagle, in particular of pale morph 'fulvescens'.' *Dutch Birding* **21**: 150-151.

Corso, A. (2001). 'Identification of Black-winged Pratincole.' *Alula* **7**(1): 31.

De Kniff, P. (1991). 'Little-known West Palearctic birds: Cinereous Bunting.' *Birding World* **4**(11): 384-391.

Dean, A. R. (1980). 'Field characters of Desert and Bar-tailed Desert Larks.' *Brit. Birds* **73**: 476-477.

Doherty, P. (1991). 'Identification of juvenile Long-toed Stint and Least Sandpiper.' *Birding World* **4**: 279-281.

Eriksen, H. (2004). 'The first Cape Gannet *Sula capensis* in Oman and the Middle East.' *Sandgrouse* **26**(2): 146-148.

Eriksen, H., J. Eriksen, S. Al-Saadi and D. E. Sargeant (2001). Oriental White-eye - new to Oman and Arabia, *Sandgrouse* **23**(2) 130-133.

Eriksen, H. and J. (1999a). 'The first record of Yellow Bittern *Ixobrychus sinensis* in Oman and Arabia.' *Sandgrouse* **21**(2): 178-179.

Eriksen, H. and J. (1999b). *Birdlife in Oman*, Al Roya Publishing, Ruwi, Oman.

Eriksen, H. and J. (2000). 'Collared Pratincoles breeding in Oman.' *Sandgrouse* **22**(2): 101-103.

Eriksen, J. (1988). 'Identification and status of the Plain Leaf Warbler.' *Sandgrouse* **10**: 107-109.

Eriksen, J. (1996). 'The birds of Barr Al Hikman, Sultanate of Oman.' Sandgrouse **18**(2): 19-29.

Eriksen, J. (1997). 'The first Crested Honey Buzzard *Pernis ptilorhynchus* in Oman.' *Sandgrouse* 19(2): 143-144.

Eriksen, J. (1998). *Breeding bird atlas of Oman*, Oman Bird Records Committee, Muscat, Oman.

Eriksen, J. (1999a). Bird studies in Oman: 1980-1999. *In* The Natural History of Oman: A Festschrift for Michael Gallagher, Ed. M. Fisher, S. A. Ghazanfar and J. A. Spalton, Blackhuys Publishers, Leiden, The Netherlands, p99-107.

Eriksen, J. (1999b). 'New breeding birds in Oman.' *Phoenix* **16**: 22.

Eriksen, J. (2008). *The Birds of Al Jabal Al Akhdar*, Centre for Environmental Studies and Research, Sultan Qaboos University, Muscat, Oman.

Eriksen, J. and M. C. Jennings (2006). 'First breeding of Red-tailed Shrike in Arabia.' *Phoenix* **22**: 1-2.

Eriksen, J., D. E. Sargeant and R. Victor (2003). *Oman bird list, edition 6*, Centre for Environmental Studies and Research, Sultan Qaboos University, Muscat, Oman.

Fernie, R. (1991). 'Raptor migration over Musandam.' *Oman Bird News* **11**: 8-10.

Forsman, D. (1994). 'Field identification of Crested Honey Buzzard.' *Birding World* **7**: 396-403.

Foster, D. (1989). 'The Great Knot in Oman.' *Oman Bird News* **5**: 3-5.

Foster, D. J. G. and C. M. Greaves (1986). 'First record of Long-billed Dowitcher in the Sultanate of Oman.' *Sandgrouse* **8**: 113-114.

Fry, C. H. (1990). 'Foraging behaviour and identification of Upcher's Warbler.' *Brit. Birds* **83**(6): 217-221.

Fry, C. H., H. Eriksen, J. Eriksen (1993). 'The Hoopoe's spreadeagle posture: predator reaction or sunning?' *Brit. Birds* **86**(3): 121-124.

Fry, C. H. (1992). 'Nests of Golden-winged Grosbeak in Oman.' *Phoenix* **9**: 28-30.

Fry, C. H., J. Eriksen and B. Al-Arimy. (1994). 'Competitive overlap of co-breeding bee-eaters *Merops apiaster* and *M. persicus*.' *J. Ornithologie* **135**: 133.

Fry, H. and J. Eriksen (1989). 'The Eastern Pied Wheatear *Oenanthe picata* in Arabia.' *Oman Bird News* **7**: 4-7.

Gallagher, M. (1983). 'The Kuria Murias re-visited and the discovery of Persian Shearwater nesting.' *J. RAF Orn. Soc.* **14**: 148-153.

Gallagher, M. (1989a). 'The Ostrich in Oman.' *Bull. Orn. Soc. Middle East* **22**: 40.

Gallagher, M. (1989c). 'Pale Rock Sparrows in Oman.' *Oman Bird News* **5**: 7-8.

Gallagher, M. and K. Stanley Price (1990). 'The Spotted Thick-knee *Burhinus capensis* and Stone Curlew *B. oedicnemus* in Arabia.' *Sandgrouse* **12**: 8-24.

Gallagher, M. and M. W. Woodcock (1980). *The Birds of Oman*. London, UK, Quartet.

Gallagher, M. D. (1977). 'Birds of Jabal Akhdar. In The Scientific Results of the Oman Flora and Fauna Survey 1975.' *J. Oman Studies Spec. Rep.* **1**: 27-58.

Gallagher, M. D. (1982). 'Nesting of the Lappet-faced Vulture *Torgus tracheliotus* in Oman.' *Bull. Brit. Orn. Club* **102**(4): 135-139.

Gallagher, M. D. (1985). 'Seabirds of the Kuria Muria islands in the Arabian Sea.' *Sea Swallow* **34**: 5-18.

Gallagher, M. D. (1988a). 'The Ostrich in Oman.' *Sandgrouse* **10**: 99-101.

Gallagher, M. D. (1988b). 'Birds of the Wahiba Sands. *In* R. W. Dutton (ed.) The Scientific Results of the Royal geographical Society's Oman Wahiba Sands Project 1985-1987.' *J. Oman Studies Spec. Rep.* **3**: 415-436.

Gallagher, M. D. (1990). 'Does Jouanin's Petrel breed in Oman?' *Oman Bird News* **8**: 7-8.

Gallagher, M. D. (1993). 'Socotra Cormorants on Jazirat Hamar an Nafur.' *Oman Bird News* **14**: 15-17.

Gallagher, M. D. and M. R. Brown (1982a). 'The Golden Eagle breeding in Oman, Eastern Arabia.' *Sandgrouse* **4**: 100-107.

Gallagher, M. D. and T. D. Rogers (1980). 'On some birds of Dhofar and other parts of Oman. *In* The Scientific Results of the Oman Flora and Fauna Survey 1977 (Dhofar).' *J. Oman Studies Spec. Rep.* **2**: 347-385.

Gallagher, M. D., C. M. Saunders, S. A. Webb and P. R. Colston (1984). 'The Blue and White Flycatcher: first records from Arabia.' *Sandgrouse* **6**: 59-61.

Garner, M. (1997). 'Large white-headed gulls in the UAE - a contribution to their field identification.' *Emirates Bird Report* **19**: 94-103.

Green, M., M. McGrady, S. Newton and J. Uttley. (1994). 'Counts of shorebirds at Barr Al Hikman and Ghubbat Al Hashish, Oman, winter 1989-90.' *Wader Study Group Bull.* **72**: 39-43.

Grieve, A., B. J. N. Hill, P. A. Lassey and D. I. M. Wallace (2005). 'The first American Golden Plover *Pluvialis dominica* in Oman and Arabia.' *Sandgrouse* **27**(1): 75-77.

Gustad, J. R. and K. Schølberg (2002). 'The first Red-knobbed Coots *Fulica cristata* in Oman and the Middle East.' *Sandgrouse* **24**(1): 65-67.

Harris, A., H. Shirihai, et al. (1996). *The Macmillan birder's guide to European and Middle Eastern birds*. London, UK, Macmillan.

Harrison, I. (2007). 'Recent decisions by the Oman Bird Records Committee - an update on first records for the Sultanate of Oman.' *Sandgrouse* **29**(2): 216-218.

Hedley, R., S. Tibbett and R. Midgley (1986). 'Wilson's Phalarope in Oman: the first record for Arabia.' *Sandgrouse* **8**: 113-114.

Hirschfeld, E. (1991). 'Oriental Skylark in Arabia.' *Oman Bird News* **10**: 1-3.

Hirschfeld, E. (1992a). 'Identification of Rufous Turtle Dove.' *Birding World* **5**: 52-57.

Hirschfeld, E. (1992b). 'Observations of seabirds off Dhofar (Oman), 1990-2.' *Sandgrouse* **14**(2): 62-71

Jennings, M. C. (1986). 'Occurrence of White-eyed Gull *Larus leucoptalmus* on Masirah Island.' *J. RAF Orn. Soc.* **16**: 107.

Jennings, M. C. (2006). 'Wood Pigeons in the Jebel Al Akhdar, Northern Oman.' *Phoenix* **22**: 20.

Kirwan, G. M. (1998). 'Pale Rock Sparrow *Carpospiza brachydactyla*, a little-known Middle Eastern bird.' *Sandgrouse* **20**(1): 8-12.

Madge, S. and D. Parr (1981). 'The field identification of the Arabian Warbler.' *Sandgrouse* **2**: 103-106.

Nikander, P. J. (2001). 'Oman.' *Alula* **7**(3): 114-121.

Olsen, K. M. and H. Shirihai (1997). 'Field identification of White-cheeked Tern.' *Alula* **3**: 150-159.

Page, D. (2001). 'Separating *Acrocephalus* and *Hippolais* warblers.' *Brit. Birds* **94**(1): 44.

Pomeroy, C. A., Ed. (1983). 'Report of the RAFOS Masirah Island Expedition 22nd October - 26th November 1979.' *J. RAF Orn. Soc.* **13**: 92p.

Porter, R. F., S. Christensen, P. Schiermacker-Hansen (1996). *Field guide to the birds of the Middle East*, T & A D Poyser, London, UK.

Richardson, C. (1999). 'Notes on Eastern Pied Wheatear *Oenanthe picata* and Hume's Wheatear *Oenanthe alboniger*, based on observations in eastern Arabia.' *Sandgrouse* **21**(2): 124-127.

Richardson, C. and S. J. Aspinall (1998). *The Shell birdwatching guide to the United Arab Emirates*, Hobby Publication, Dubai, UAE and London, UK.

Rogers, T. D. (1988). *A new list of the birds of Masirah Island, Sultanate of Oman*, Oman Bird Record Committee, Muscat, Oman.

Round, P. D. and T. A. Walsh (1981). 'The field identification and status of Dunn's Lark.' *Sandgrouse* **3**: 78-83.

Shirihai, H., D. A. Cristie and A. Harris (1996). 'Identification of *Hippolais* warblers.' *Brit. Birds* **89**: 114-138.

Svensson, L. (2001). 'Identification of Western and Eastern Olivaceous, Booted and Sykes's Warblers.' *Birding World* **14**(5): 192-219.

Taleb, N. M. A. (2002). 'The discovery of a breeding colony of Jouanin's Petrel *Bulweria fallax* on Socotra, Yemen.' *Sandgrouse* **24**(2): 105-108.

Tibbett, S. (2006). 'Forbes-Watson's Swift nesting in Dhofar.' *Phoenix* **22**: 23.

Voous, K. H. (1977). 'List of recent Holarctic species.' *Ibis*: **119**: 223-250, 376-406.

Walker, F. J. (1981). 'Notes on the birds of northern Oman.' *Sandgrouse* **2**: 33-55.

Walker, F. J. (1981). 'Notes on the birds of Dhofar, Oman.' *Sandgrouse* **2**: 56-85.

Walter, H. (1979). 'The Sooty Falcon *Falco concolor* in Oman: results of a breeding survey, 1978.' *J. Oman Studies* **5**: 9-59.

Wilson, S. (1999). 'Summer observations of seabirds in the Gulf of Oman.' *Phoenix* **16**: 15-16.

Worfolk, T. (2000). 'Identification of Red-backed, Isabelline and Brown Shrikes.' *Dutch Birding* **22**(6): 323-362.

Gazetteer

Place	Lat.	Long.	Place	Lat.	Long.
Abb island	20°29'N	58°10'E	Empty Quarter	18°45'N	53°15'E
Ad Duqm	19°38'N	57°38'E			
Al Ansab Lagoons	23°34'N	58°20'E	Filim	20°37'N	58°11'E
Al Ashkharah	21°51'N	59°35'E	Fossil Valley	24°17'N	55°51'E
Al Balid Farm	18°20'N	54°04'E	Fuhud	22°19'N	56°29'E
Al Batinah	23°40'N	58°00'E			
Al Buraymi	24°15'N	55°47'E	Ghubbat Hashish	20°32'N	58°10'E
Al Bustan Palace Hotel	23°34'N	58°37'E	Ghubrah Bowl	23°15'N	57°42'E
Al Fahl Island	23°41'N	58°30'E			
Al Ghabah Motel	21°21'N	57°15'E	Hallaniyyat Islands	17°30'N	55°58'E
Al Ghaftayn Motel	19°38'N	55°31'E	Hamr Nafun	19°48'N	57°48'E
Al Hamra	23°07'N	57°17'E	Haql	20°21'N	58°48'E
Al Hijj	20°46'N	58°17'E	Hat	23°11'N	57°23'E
Al Jabal Al Hajar	23°10'N	57°40'E	Hayma	19°58'N	56°17'E
Al Kamil	22°14'N	59°12'E	Haylat Ar Rakah	18°18'N	53°53'E
Al Khaluf	20°28'N	58°04'E	Hilf	20°40'N	58°52'E
Al Khuwayr	23°36'N	58°26'E	Huqf Escarpment	19°50'N	57°20'E
Al Qurm Natural Park	23°36'N	58°28'E			
Al Udhaibah	23°36'N	58°22'E	Ibra	22°43'N	58°32'E
Al Wuttayyah	23°36'N	58°30'E	Ibri	23°14'N	56°31'E
Ar Rawdah	25°52'N	56°17'E	InterContinental Hotel	23°37'N	58°28'E
Ar Rub Al Khali	18°45'N	53°15'E	Izki	22°57'N	57°46'E
Ar Rustaq	23°23'N	57°26'E			
As Seeb	23°41'N	58°11'E	Jaluni	19°56'N	57°06'E
As Seeb Intern. Airport	23°35'N	58°17'E	Jabal Al Qamar	16°48'N	53°20'E
saylah	21°57'N	59°39'E	Jabal Harim	25°58'N	56°14'E
yn Hamran	17°06'N	54°17'E	Jabal Madar	22°16'N	58°20'E
yn Razat	17°08'N	54°14'E	Jabal Qatar	24°18'N	55°54'E
yn Sahnawt	17°08'N	54°11'E	Jabal Samhan	17°12'N	54°55'E
			Jabal Shams	23°14'N	57°16'E
ahla	22°58'N	57°18'E	Jarziz Farm	17°02'N	54°08'E
andar Khayran	23°32'N	58°44'E	Jiddat Al Harasis	19°45'N	56°30'E
andar Jassah	23°33'N	58°39'E	Jinawt	17°49'N	55°26'E
arka	23°43'N	57°53'E			
arr Al Hikman	20°42'N	58°42'E	Khalidiyyah	26°03'N	56°22'E
wshar	23°32'N	58°23'E	Khasab	26°12'N	56°15'E
ayah	25°38'N	56°16'E	Khatmat Milahah	24°57'N	56°22'E
mmah	22°59'N	59°08'E	Khawr Al Mughsayl	16°53'N	53°47'E
rkat Al Mawz	22°56'N	57°40'E	Khawr An Najd	26°06'N	56°20'E
akha	26°09'N	56°09'E	Khawr Barr Al Hikman	20°50'N	58°44'E
			Khawr Dhurf	18°56'N	57°21'E
ghmar	23°12'N	58°59'E	Khawr Ghawi	18°34'N	56°38'E
wkah	18°40'N	54°04'E	Khawr Jirama	22°29'N	59°44'E
aymaniyat islands	23°51'N	58°05'E	Khawr Kalba	24°59'N	56°22'E
ofar mountains	17°12'N	54°06'E	Khawr Kashmir	24°23'N	56°44'E
bab	23°05'N	59°03'E	Khawr Masirah	20°40'N	58°45'E
st Khawr	17°01'N	54°11'E	Khawr Rawri	17°02'N	54°26'E

Place	Lat.	Long.
Khawr Sallan	24°24'N	56°43'E
Khawr Sawli	17°03'N	54°20'E
Khawr Stimah	16°56'N	54°45'E
Khawr Shumayr	18°34'N	56°38'E
Khawr Taqah	17°02'N	54°23'E
Kumzar	26°20'N	56°25'E
Liwa	24°33'N	56°35'E
Madinat As Sultan Qaboos	23°36'N	58°27'E
Mahawt island	20°34'N	58°10'E
Mahdah	24°24'N	55°59'E
Majis	24°27'N	56°40'E
Marmul	18°10'N	55°15'E
Marsawdad	19°26'N	54°25'E
Masirah	20°25'N	58°50'E
Mintirib	22°26'N	58°48'E
Mirbat	16°59'N	54°42'E
Muntasar	19°27'N	54°37'E
Musandam	26°00'N	56°15'E
Muscat	23°37'N	58°35'E
Mutrah	23°37'N	58°34'E
Nakhal	23°23'N	57°50'E
Nizwa	22°56'N	57°32'E
Qantab	23°33'N	58°38'E
Qatbit	19°09'N	54°27'E
Qurayyat	23°16'N	58°55'E
Rakhyut	16°45'N	53°25'E
Raja Farm, Ar	24°20'N	56°45'E
Ramlat Al Wahibah	22°00'N	58°45'E
Ras Abu Rasas	20°10'N	58°33'E
Ras Ad Duqm	19°40'N	57°43'E
Ras Al Hadd	22°32'N	59°46'E
Ras Al Hamra	23°39'N	58°29'E
Ras Al Jinz	22°25'N	59°51'E
Ras Al Khabbah	22°14'N	59°49'E
Ras Al Ya	20°32'N	58°57'E
Ras As Sawadi	23°47'N	57°47'E
Ras Bintawt	20°21'N	57°58'E
Ras Janjari	16°56'N	54°48'E
Ras Madrakah	19°01'N	57°48'E
Ras Mirbat	16°59'N	54°42'E
Raysut	16°57'N	53°59'E
Razat farm	17°02'N	54°13'E
Riyam Park	23°37'N	58°34'E
Rima	18°55'N	56°20'E
Rusail	23°32'N	58°11'E
Ruwi	23°35'N	58°32'E
Salalah	17°00'N	54°06'E
Salalah Nature Reserve	17°00'N	54°04'E
Sall Ala	26°04'N	56°20'E
Sahnawt Farm	17°02'N	54°12'E
Sarfayt	16°41'N	53°06'E
Sawqrah	18°09'N	56°32'E
Sayh Plateau, As	25°59'N	56°13'E
Sayq	23°04'N	57°38'E
Shelim	18°06'N	55°36'E
Shinas	24°43'N	56°29'E
Shisr	18°15'N	53°39'E
Shuwaymiyyah	17°55'N	55°27'E
Sinaw	22°29'N	58°02'E
Sohar	24°22'N	56°45'E
Strait of Hormuz	26°35'N	56°30'E
Sultan Qaboos University	23°35'N	58°10'E
Sun Farms, Sohar	24°19'N	56°45'E
Sunub	23°29'N	58°21'E
Sur	22°35'N	59°31'E
Sur Masirah	20°25'N	58°44'E
Taqah	17°02'N	54°23'E
Tawi Atayr	17°06'N	54°34'E
Thumrayt	17°39'N	54°02'E
Tibat	26°04'N	56°06'E
Tiwi	22°49'N	59°16'E
Wadi Ash Shab	22°50'N	59°15'E
Wadi Ashawq	16°54'N	53°45'E
Wadi Bani Awf	23°14'N	57°25'E
Wadi Bani Khalid	22°34'N	59°06'E
Wadi Bih	25°50'N	56°13'E
Wadi Darbat	17°06'N	54°27'E
Wadi Gharm	19°01'N	57°32'E
Wadi Hanna	17°03'N	54°37'E
Wadi Khabb Ash Shamsi	25°41'N	56°15'E
Wadi Rabkut	17°40'N	54°08'E
Wadi Sahtan	23°13'N	57°18'E
Wadi Shuwaymiyyah	17°55'N	55°27'E
Wadi Tayin	23°02'N	58°45'E
Wadi Uyun	17°15'N	53°53'E
Wahibah Sands	22°00'N	58°45'E
West Khawr	16°59'N	54°02'E
Wukan	23°08'N	57°44'E
Yiti	23°33'N	58°40'E

Index of Bird Names

Greater Flamingo

Index of Sites

Legend

Park, parkland		Mountains	
Mangrove		Palm	
Scrub		Other tree	
Lagoon, lake, water		Reeds, sedges	
Farm, fields		Waterfall	
Irrigation pivot		Cliffs	
Quarry		Viewpoint	
Miscellaneous facility		Bridge	
Parking area	P	Telecom tower	
Picnic site		Petrol Station	
Roundabout		Building, town, villa	
Roundabout with Flyover		Mosque	
Paved road – dual carriageway		Hotel, guesthouse	
(under construction)		Official campsite	
Paved road – single carriageway		Desalination plant	
Unpaved road (mostly graded)		Fort	
Driveable track (mostly 4x4 only)		Wadi	
Footpath		Generally permane stream or water flo	
Fence		Airstrip	
International boundary		Dam	

256